CAT OWNER'S HOME VETERINARY HANDBOOK

CAT OWNER'S HOME VETERINARY HANDBOOK

DELBERT G. CARLSON, D.V.M.
AND JAMES M. GIFFIN, M.D.

with special contributions by Liisa Carlson, D.V.M.

Revised and Expanded

HOWELL
BOOK
HOUSE

New York

Howell Book House
Hungry Minds, Inc.
909 Third Avenue
New York, NY 10022
www.hungryminds.com

Library of Congress Cataloging-in-Publication Data

Carlson, Delbert G.
Cat owner's home veterinary handbook / Delbert G. Carlson, James Giffin— Rev. and expanded ed.
p. cm.
Includes index.
ISBN 0-87605-796-2
1. Cat—Diseases—Handbooks, manuals, etc. I. Giffin, James M. II. Carlson, Liisa. III. Title.
SF985.C29 1995
636.8'089—dc20   95-6632
                        CIP
Manufactured in the United States of America
20 19 18 17 16 15 14 13 12

Design by Amy Peppler Adams—designLab, Seattle

This book is not intended as a substitute for the medical advice of veterinarians. The reader should regularly consult a veterinarian in matters relating to his or her cat's health and particularly with respect to any symptoms that may require diagnosis or medical attention.

Beware! When least expected, a cat will sneak up and steal your heart.
—Sue Giffin and Sydney Giffin Wiley

Dedicated
with love
to our families

Delbert G. Carlson, D.V.M.

James M. Giffin, M.D.

Liisa D. Carlson, D.V.M.

THE AUTHORS

DELBERT G. CARLSON, D.V.M.

Dr. Del Carlson, coauthor of the award-winning book *Dog Owner's Home Veterinary Handbook* (Howell Book House, Inc.) received his medical degree from the University of Minnesota Veterinary School in 1954 and interned at the Rawley Memorial Hospital in Springfield, Massachusetts.

He is a member of the Missouri Veterinary Medical Association and a past president of the Greene County Humane Society.

Today, "Doc" can be found on his farm caring for his horses, cats and dogs. He continues to consult at the pet hospital, often volunteering to spend the night with a sick dog or cat.

JAMES M. GIFFIN, M.D.

Dr. Jim Giffin has had lifelong experience with cats, dogs and horses. He is coauthor of the award-winning books *The Complete Great Pyrenees* and the *Dog Owner's Home Veterinary Handbook* (newly revised) and the *Horse Owner's Veterinary Handbook* (all from Howell Book House, Inc.).

Dr. Giffin graduated from Amherst College and received his medical degree from Yale University School of Medicine. In 1969, he established a Great Pyrenees kennel and became active in breeding, showing and judging. He finished several champions, campaigned a Best in Show winner and served on the board of directors of the Great Pyrenees Club of America, Inc.

Dr. Giffin was called to active duty in Operation Desert Storm, serving as Chief of Surgery at military hospitals in Alabama, Korea and Texas. He now makes his home in western Colorado.

Dr. Giffin is a member of the Cat Writers' Association of America.

LIISA D. CARLSON, D.V.M.

Dr. Liisa Carlson received her veterinary degree from the University of Missouri College of Veterinary Medicine and was a member of the Veterinary Honor Society *Phi Zeta*. In 1988, Liisa returned to Springfield to join her father at the Carlson Pet Hospital. She is a member of the American Veterinary Medical Society.

Liisa says, "I was fortunate to work with my father and mentor before he retired in 1993. His knowledge, compassion and love of animals is truly inspiring. I hope to follow with the same dedication and commitment that he has given for over 35 years."

In 1994, Dr. Liisa Carlson was honored as Humanitarian of the Year by the Southwest Humane Society of Springfield, Missouri.

FINDING IT QUICK IN THE
CAT OWNER'S HOME VETERINARY HANDBOOK:

A special **INDEX OF SIGNS AND SYMPTOMS** begins on the inside front cover page for fast referral. Consult this index if your cat displays unexplained behavior. It will help you locate the problem.

The detailed **CONTENTS**, beginning on page xiii, outlines the organs and the systems, which are the usual sites of disease. If you know the location of the problem, consult the contents first.

The **GENERAL INDEX**, which begins on page 411, provides a comprehensive guide to the book's medical information. (Where a page number is in boldface, it indicates a more detailed coverage of the subject.)

CROSS-REFERENCES appear throughout to guide you to supplementary information. A cross-reference indicated in caps and small caps (SKIN) identifies a chapter title; a cross reference in italics (*Basic Coat Care*) identifies a subdivision of a chapter.

Each chapter starts with a section of general information. These sections provide explanations for the terms used in describing the diseases and disorders within. These sections also describe some of the characteristics that make the cat a uniquely interesting and unusual animal.

CONTENTS

Chapter 11. CIRCULATORY SYSTEM   219

Chapter 12. NERVOUS SYSTEM   229

Chapter 13. MUSCULOSKELETAL SYSTEM   243

Chapter 14. URINARY SYSTEM 257

Chapter 15. SEX AND REPRODUCTION 271

INTRODUCTION

While it appears that people and dogs have been companions for more than 50,000 years, the association of humans and cats seems to go back only about 5,000 years. The exact origins of the domestic cat remain controversial. Fossils are found in Europe, Asia and Africa—but not in America.

Early associations between cats and people are cloaked in myth and legend. The Egyptians held cats in the highest esteem and made them the objects of worship. A famous statue depicts the goddess Bast, bearing the head of a cat. Other figures cast in gold, bronze and copper as well as wall paintings showing cats hunting with their masters attest to the prominence of cats in Egyptian life.

Phoenician sailors, while trafficking with the Egyptians, may have recognized the commercial value of cats and brought them to trading ports along the Mediterranean coast. Two thousand years later the Romans, well known for their knowledge and uses of livestock, undoubtedly recognized the value of the cat and adopted it for pest control at their military granaries. This practice would account for the wide distribution of cats throughout Europe in the time of the Roman Empire.

Since the beginning of modern history, cats have charmed, baffled, delighted and intrigued. Perhaps no other animal has had such a beguiling influence on the minds of the literary. William Blake saw the cat as a symbol of the metaphysical; elusive, indefinable; yet by its very existence affirming the hand of an ultimate creator. Thomas Gray, in quite a different vein, found a parody of human nature in the lady cat Selima, who drowned in a goldfish bowl:

> Not all that tempts your wand'ring eyes
> And heedless heart is lawful prize;
> Nor all that glitters, gold.

Cats continue to enjoy a popularity explosion. There are currently over 50 million cats in the United States, a number now passing the population of dogs.

When the first edition of *Cat Owner's Home Veterinary Handbook* went to press over a decade ago, much of what was known about cat illness and treatment was inferred from canine medicine and small-animal practice. This approach has changed. The volume of information on cat ailments and research into cat diseases has led to the establishment of feline medicine as a veterinary specialty.

In this new, fully revised and expanded edition, we have incorporated these latest advances. You will find improved and safer medications—including those used for deworming, vaccinating and treating parasites and infectious diseases. More space has been devoted to infectious diseases, their modes of transmission and how you can protect yourself as well as your cat.

A number of new diseases have been recognized and described. Other diseases, known for some time, have assumed greater importance. Among these are *Feline Immunodeficiency Disease, Idiopathic Hepatic Lipidosis, Inflammatory Bowel Disease, Cat Scratch Disease and Plague*. There is a broader understanding of reproductive physiology and a more scientific approach to the management of *Feline Urologic Syndrome*. Current research on cat behavior has led to revolutionary changes in the philosophy of treating feline behavior disorders.

The Cat Owner's Home Veterinary Handbook was the second in a series that now includes the newly revised *Dog Owner's Home Veterinary Handbook* and the *Horse Owner's Veterinary Handbook* (all from Howell Book House). The experience gained in keeping abreast of veterinary progress has helped us greatly in planning and executing this revision. Over the years we have received your questions. We have learned what you want to know and what was not covered in sufficient detail, and we have used this important information to anticipate your needs.

In writing this book, we have described the signs and symptoms that will lead you to a preliminary diagnosis—so you can weigh the severity of the problem. Some health problems are not serious and can be treated at home. Knowing when to call your veterinarian is of great importance. Delays can be costly.

At the same time, we have sought to provide guidance for the acute or emergency situations that common sense dictates you should handle on your own. Life-saving procedures such as artificial breathing, heart massage, obstetrical emergencies, poisonings and the like are illustrated and explained step by step.

A veterinary handbook is not intended to be a substitute for professional care. Book advice can never be as helpful or as safe as actual medical assistance. No text can replace the interview and physical examination, during which the veterinarian elicits the information that leads to a speedy and accurate diagnosis. But the knowledge provided in this book will enable you to work in better understanding and with more effective cooperation with your veterinarian. You'll be more alert to the symptoms of diseases and better able to describe them.

In this book you will find the basics of health care and disease prevention for the young and the old. A well-cared-for cat suffers fewer illnesses and infirmities while growing older.

The combined efforts of many people make this book possible:

Liisa Carlson reviewed the entire manuscript and made many important contributions from the perspective of the recently graduated veterinary practitioner.

We are indebted to Krist Carlson for the many new photographs showing cat ailments. Sydney Giffin Wiley created many fine drawings, as did Rose Floyd.

Diane Giffin deserves our sincere thanks for her devoted service in the preparation of the manuscript.

Recognition would not be complete without mentioning the many researchers, clinicians and educators whose work served as a source for our information. Among them are *Current Veterinary Therapy*, IX, X, XI (edited by Robert W. Kirk, D.V.M.); *Textbook of Internal Veterinary Medicine*, Third Edition (Stephen J. Ettinger, D.V.M.); *The Cat: Diseases and Clinical Management* (Robert G. Sherding, D.V.M.); *Feline Infectious Diseases* (Niles C. Pedersen, D.V.M.); *Diseases of the Cat: Medicine and*

Surgery (Jean Holzworth, D.V.M.); *Practical Feline Dermatology* (Lowell J. Ashermann, D.V.M.); *Feline Husbandry,* in *Diseases and Management in the Multiple Cat Environment*; American Veterinary Publications, Inc., 1991 (Niles C. Pedersen, D.V.M.); *Small Animal Diagnosis* (Michael D. Lorenz, D.V.M.); *Handbook of Veterinary Procedures & Emergency Treatment*, Fifth Edition (Robert W. Kirk, D.V.M., and Stephen I. Bistner, D.V.M.); *Feline Medicine and Surgery in Practice, The Compendium Collection*, 1992; *Feline Practice*, 1993 (G. D. Norsworthy, D.V.M.); *Gastroenterology in Practice, The Compendium Collection*, 1993; *Veterinary Emergency and Critical Care Medicine*, 1992 (Robert J. Murtaugh, D.V.M., and Paul M. Kaplan, D.V.M.); and the Kansas Veterinary Medical Association 1993 Annual Convention (Fred W. Scott, D.V.M., Cornell Feline Health Center College of Veterinary Medicine).

DELBERT G. CARLSON, D.V.M.

JAMES M. GIFFIN, M.D.

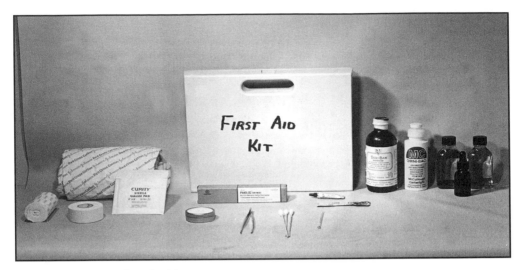

Home emergency and medical kit.

HOME EMERGENCY AND MEDICAL KIT

Adhesive tape—1-inch roll

Betadine solution (dilute 1:10)

Container (fishing tackle box)

Cotton balls

Cotton-tipped applicators

Eye dropper (plastic)

Flashlight

Gauze pads—3 x 3 inch

Gauze roll—3 inch

Hairball remedy (commercial or white petroleum jelly)

Hemostat (curved or straight)

Hydrogen peroxide (3 percent)

Linen cloth, sheet or blanket

Magazines

Masking tape

Scalpel

Scissors (blunt-tipped)

Syringe, plastic or glass, 10 cc

Teaspoon

Thermometer (preferably digital)

Triple antibiotic ointment

Tweezers (thumb forceps)

Note: Common household drugs for home veterinary use are listed in the chapter "Drugs and Medications."

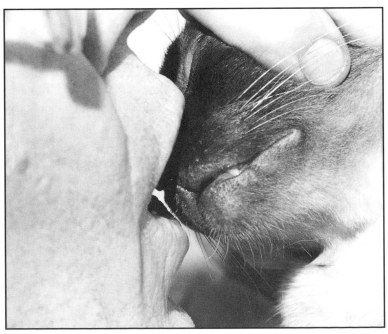

Mouth-to-nose breathing. Leaving the mouth uncovered avoids the problem of overinflation.

—J. Clawson

1

EMERGENCIES

ARTIFICIAL BREATHING AND HEART MASSAGE

Artificial breathing is an emergency procedure used to exchange air in the unconscious cat. *Heart massage* is used when no heartbeat can be heard or felt. When heart massage is combined with artificial breathing, it is called *cardiopulmonary resuscitation* (CPR). As cessation of breathing is soon followed by heart stoppage and vice versa, cardiopulmonary resuscitation is most often required in the life-threatening situation.

CPR can be performed by one person, but it is easier if two people are available. One does the breathing and the other does the heart massage.

The following emergencies may require artificial breathing or CPR:

Shock	Head Injury
Poisoning	Electric Shock
Prolonged Seizure	Obstructed Airways (Choking)
Coma	Sudden Death

Determine which basic life-support technique to employ in an unresponsive cat:

IS THE CAT BREATHING? Observe rise and fall of the chest. Feel for air against your cheek.

If YES, pull out tongue, clear airway. Observe.

If NO, feel for pulse.

DOES THE CAT HAVE A PULSE? Feel for the femoral artery located in the groin.

If YES, employ *Artificial Breathing.*

If NO, employ CPR.

ARTIFICIAL BREATHING (*MOUTH-TO-NOSE BREATHING*)

1. Lay the cat on a flat surface with its *right* side down.
2. Open the mouth and clear secretions. Check for a foreign body. If found, remove. If impossible to reach, execute the *Heimlich maneuver* (see RESPIRATORY SYSTEM: *Foreign Object in the Voice Box*).
3. Pull the tongue forward and close the mouth. Place your mouth over the cat's nose. Blow gently into the cat's nostrils. The chest will expand. Release to let the air come back out. Excess air will escape through the cat's lips, preventing overinflation of the lungs and overdistension of the stomach.
4. If the chest does not rise and fall, blow more forcefully; or if necessary, lightly seal the lips with your hand.
5. The breathing rate is one every four to five seconds (12 to 15 per minute).
6. Continue until the cat breathes on its own, or as long as the heart beats.

CPR (*ARTIFICIAL BREATHING AND HEART MASSAGE*)

1. Continue with mouth-to-nose breathing.
2. Prepare for heart massage. Place the fingers and thumb on either side of the sternum, behind the elbows.
3. Compress the chest firmly six times; administer a breath. Then repeat. Massage rate is 80 to 120 compressions per minute.
4. If possible, do not stop heart massage while administering a breath.
5. Pause every two minutes for 10 to 15 seconds to check for pulse and spontaneous breathing.
6. Continue until the heart beats and the cat breathes on its own, or until no heartbeat is felt for 30 minutes.

Heart massage. Note the placement of the fingers and thumb on either side of the sternum behind the elbow.
—J.Clawson

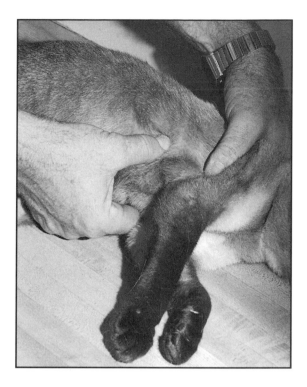

BURNS

Burns are caused by heat, chemicals, electric shocks and radiation. Sunburn is an example of a radiation burn. It occurs on the ear flaps of cats with white coats (see EARS: *Sunburn*) and on the skin of white-coated cats that are sheared in summer.

A cat may be scalded by having hot liquid spilled on it or by being involved in some other household accident. A common type of burn occurs on the foot pads after walking on a hot surface such as a tin roof, stove top or freshly tarred road.

The depth of injury depends on the length and intensity of exposure. With a superficial burn you will see redness of the skin, occasionally blistering, perhaps slight swelling; and the burn area is tender. With deep burns the skin appears white, the hair comes out easily when pulled, and pain is severe. If more than 15 percent of the body surface is deeply burned, the outlook is poor. Fluid losses are excessive. Shock can occur.

Treatment: Apply cool compresses (not ice packs) to small burns for 30 minutes to relieve pain. Replace as compress becomes warm. Clip away hair and wash gently with a surgical soap. Blot dry. Apply *Silvadene Cream* or *Triple Antibiotic Ointment*. Protect the area from rubbing by wrapping it with a loose-fitting gauze dressing.

Treat acid, alkali, gasoline, kerosene and other chemical burns by flushing with large amounts of water for five minutes. Wear gloves and bathe the cat with mild soap and water. Blot dry, and apply antibiotic ointment. Bandage loosely.

COLD TEMPERATURE EXPOSURE

HYPOTHERMIA (ABNORMALLY LOW TEMPERATURE)

Prolonged exposure to cold results in a drop in body temperature. This is most likely to occur when a cat is wet. Hypothermia also occurs with shock, after a long anesthetic and in newborn kittens. Prolonged chilling burns up the available energy and predisposes to low blood sugar.

The *signs* of hypothermia are violent shivering followed by listlessness and lethargy; a rectal temperature below 97°F (which is diagnostic); and finally, collapse and coma. Hypothermic cats can withstand extended periods of cardiac arrest because low body temperature lowers metabolic rate. CPR may be successful in such individuals.

Treatment: Wrap your cat in a blanket or coat and carry it into the house. If the cat is wet (having fallen into icy water), give a warm bath. Rub vigorously with towels to dry the skin.

Warm a chilled cat by applying warm water packs to the axilla (armpits), chest and abdomen. The temperature of the pack should be about that of a baby bottle, warm to the wrist. Take the rectal temperature every 10 minutes. Continue to change the packs until the rectal temperature reaches 100°F. *Avoid* warming with a hair dryer or air comb, which may cause burns.

As the cat begins to move about, give some honey or glucose, four teaspoons of sugar added to a pint of water.

How to warm a chilled kitten is discussed in PEDIATRICS: *Warming a Chilled Kitten*.

FROSTBITE

Frostbite often involves the toes, ears, scrotum and tail. These areas are the most exposed and only lightly protected by fur. At first the skin is pale and white. With return of circulation, it becomes red and swollen. Later it may peel. Eventually, it looks much like a burn, with a line of demarcation between live and dead tissue. The dead skin separates in one to three weeks.

Frostbite of the ear flaps is discussed in the chapter EARS.

Treatment: Warm frostbitten areas by immersing in warm (not hot) water for 20 minutes or until the tissue becomes flushed. *Never apply snow or ice*. Tissue damage is greatly increased if thawing is followed by refreezing. Do not rub or massage the affected parts. Prevent infection by applying an antibiotic ointment such as *Neomycin* or *Triple Antibiotic Ointment*. Apply a soft dry bandage for protection (see *Bandaging*).

DEHYDRATION

Dehydration is excess loss of body fluids. Usually it involves loss of both water and *electrolytes* (which are minerals such as sodium, chloride, potassium). During illness, dehydration may be due to an inadequate fluid intake. Fever increases the loss of water. This becomes significant if the cat does not drink enough to offset it. Other common causes of dehydration are prolonged vomiting and diarrhea.

One sign of dehydration is loss of skin elasticity. When the skin along the back is picked up into a fold, it should spring back into place. In dehydration, the skin stays up in a ridge. Another sign is dryness of the mouth. The gums, which should be wet and glistening, are dry and tacky to the touch. The saliva is thick and tenacious. Late signs are sunken eyeballs and circulatory collapse (shock).

Treatment: A cat that is noticeably dehydrated should receive prompt veterinary attention. Treatment is directed at replacing fluids and preventing further losses.

In mild cases without vomiting, fluids can be given by mouth. If the cat won't drink, give an electrolyte solution by bottle or syringe into the cheek pouch (see DRUGS AND MEDICATIONS). Balanced electrolyte solutions for treating dehydration in children are available at drugstores. Ringer's lactate with 5 percent Dextrose in water and a solution called *Pedialyte* are suitable for cats. They are given at the rate of two to four millileters per pound body weight per hour, depending on the severity of the dehydration (or as directed by your veterinarian).

The treatment of dehydration in infant kittens is discussed in PEDIATRICS: *Common Feeding Problems*.

DROWNING AND SUFFOCATION

Conditions that prevent oxygen from getting into the lungs and blood cause *asphyxiation*. These are carbon monoxide poisoning; inhalation of toxic fumes (smoke, gasoline, propane, refrigerants, solvents); drowning; and smothering (which can happen when a cat is left too long in an airtight space). Other causes are foreign bodies in the airways and injuries to the chest that interfere with breathing.

A cat's collar can get snagged on a fence, and the cat can strangle while struggling to get free. Be sure to provide an elastic collar that can stretch and slip over your cat's head in an emergency.

Cats are natural swimmers and can negotiate short distances well. However, they can't climb out of water over a ledge. They might drown in a swimming pool if a ramp exit is not provided.

The symptoms of oxygen lack are straining to breathe; gasping for breath (often with the head extended); extreme anxiety; and weakness progressing to loss of consciousness as the cat begins to succumb. The pupils begin to dilate. The tongue and mucous membranes turn blue, which is a reflection of insufficient oxygen in the blood. One exception to the blue color is carbon monoxide poisoning, in which the membranes are a bright red.

Treatment: The most important consideration is to provide your cat with fresh air to breathe. (Better yet, give oxygen if available.) If respiration is shallow or absent, immediately give mouth-to-nose respiration.

If the cat has a pneumothoray, an open wound into the chest (which you can determine if you hear air sucking in and out as the cat breathes), seal off the chest by pinching the skin together over the wound.

For drowning, remove as much water as possible from the lungs. Hold the cat upside down by placing your hands around the lower abdomen, and swing the cat back and forth for 30 seconds. Then position the cat on its right side with the head lower than the chest, and begin mouth to nose breathing. With heart stoppage, heart massage should be attempted. Continue efforts to resuscitate until the cat breathes without assistance or until no heartbeat is felt for 30 minutes (see CPR in this chapter).

Once the immediate crisis is over, veterinary aid should be sought. Pneumonia from inhalation is a frequent complication.

ELECTRIC SHOCKS AND BURNS

Electric shocks can be caused by chewing on electric cords and coming in contact with downed wires. A shock can cause involuntary muscle contractions of the jaw that may prevent a cat from releasing the live wire.

Cats receiveing an electric shock may be burned, or the shock may cause irregular heartbeat with signs of circulatory collapse. Electric current also damages the capillaries of the lungs and leads to the accumulation of fluid in the air sacs (*pulmonary edema*). The signs are those of difficulty in breathing.

Treatment: If your cat is found in contact with an electric cord or appliance, DO NOT TOUCH THE CAT. First, *throw the switch box and pull the plug*. If the cat is unconscious and not breathing, *administer artificial breathing*. Pulmonary edema must be treated by a veterinarian.

Mouth burns from electric cords are discussed in the chapter MOUTH AND THROAT.

HANDLING AND RESTRAINT

There are several effective methods to handle and restrain a cat. Your choice will depend on whether the individual animal is tranquil and cooperative or frightened and aggressive.

PICKING UP A CAT

As a general rule, it is advisable to reach down and pick up a cat from above. A face-to-face confrontation might provoke a cat into becoming uncooperative or aggressive.

Cooperative Cat: Place one hand around the abdomen beneath the chest and take hold of the front legs so they cross over each other, keeping your index finger between them for a secure grip. Pick up the cat and snuggle it close to your body. Cradle the chin with your other hand.

Apprehensive Cat: Reach down and lift the cat by the scruff of its neck. Most cats go limp—as they did when their mothers carried them as kittens. Support the back feet with your other hand.

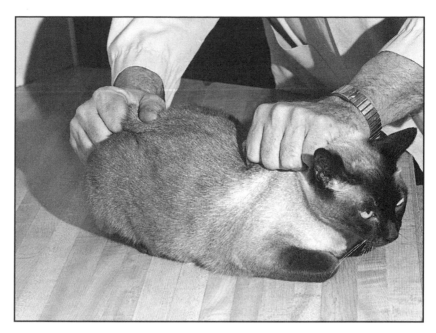

Restraining for treatment. Hold firmly for any treatment that might prove
unpleasant. —J. Clawson

Frightened Cat: Cover the animal with a towel. After a minute or two, as the
cat becomes calmer, slide the rest of the towel underneath and lift up the cat as a
bundle.

Aggressive Cat: Slip a leash or a loop of rope over the cat's head and *one front
leg.* Then lift the animal by the leash and set it down on a table or into a cat carrier
or box. This method should be used *only as a last resort* because it is certain to agitate
the cat further.

RESTRAINING FOR TREATMENT

When the cat is cooperative, routine procedures such as grooming, bathing, or even
medicating are best carried out in quiet surroundings with a minimum of physical
restraint. Approach the cat with confidence and handle it gently. Most cats can be
coaxed into accepting the procedure and do not need to be restrained.

Cooperative Cat: Lift the cat onto a smooth surface such as a tabletop. The cat
will be less secure—but still not frightened. Speak in a calm soothing voice until the
cat relaxes. Place one hand around the front of the chest to keep the cat from moving forward. Use your other hand to administer treatment.

Uncooperative Cat: Depending on the degree of agitation, several methods are
available. If cooperative enough to permit handling, then grasp the cat by the scruff
of the neck and press firmly against the top of the table so that the cat *stretches out.*
These actions will prevent you from being scratched by the cat's rear claws.

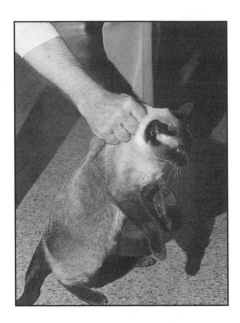

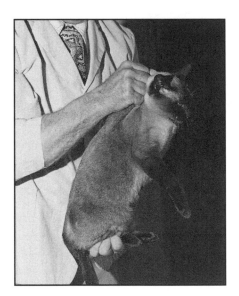

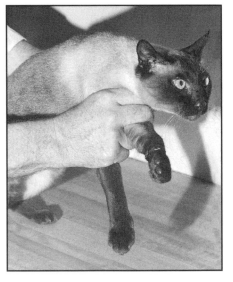

Picking up the cat. Reach down and grasp the cat by the scruff of the neck. Secure the back feet with your other hand. Note the position of the fingers, which securely immobilize the front legs. —J.Clawson

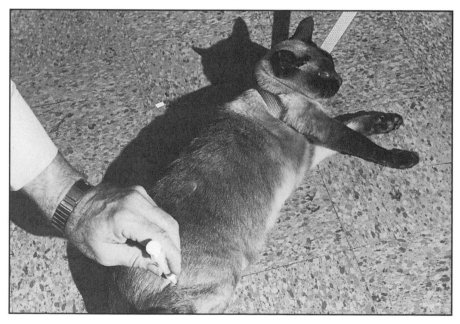

A leash and loop restraint. The cat is immobilized by drawing the leash taut. To keep the cat from being choked, the loop should include one leg. —J. Clawson

A cat bag restraint is useful for treating the head.   —J. Clawson

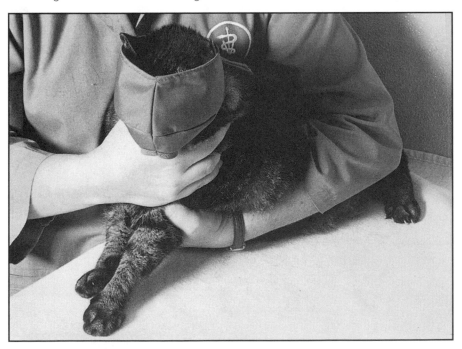

A cat muzzle that covers the eyes and ears has a calming effect.

A simple restraint can be made from a piece of cardboard. It is useful for a short procedure, such as giving a pill. —J. Clawson

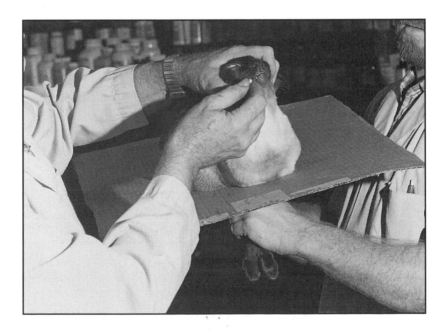

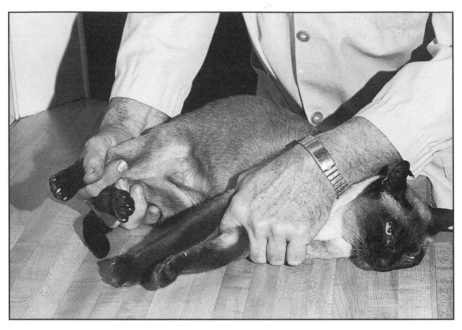

Another method of restraining for a short procedure. An assistant is required.

—J. Clawson

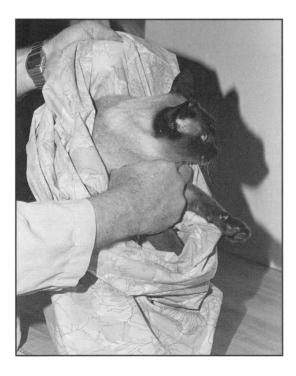

Transporting an injured or uncooperative cat. Lift the cat as described in the text and lower it into a sack or pillowcase.

—J. Clawson

When help is available, have your assistant stand behind the cat and place both hands around the cat's neck or front legs while pressing his or her arms against the cat's sides. Wrapping a towel or blanket around the cat has a calming effect and is useful for short procedures such as giving medication. An assistant is required to steady the cat and hold the wraps in place.

Note: A coat sleeve makes an excellent restraint. The cat will often scoot into it willingly. Hold the end of the sleeve securely around the cat's neck. Now you can treat the head or tail.

When procedures take longer and the cat cannot be managed by the above methods, lift the cat straight up from behind by the scruff of the neck with one hand and hold the rear paws together with the other. Press down firmly on the table so the cat is lying on its side with body extended. Now have an assistant bind the front legs together with adhesive tape, taking two or three turns below the elbows. Secure the rear legs by wrapping with tape above the hocks. Calm the cat by covering its head with a towel or cloth.

When properly restrained, cats usually settle down and accept the treatment. Once released, they soon forget the unpleasant experience.

Transporting an Injured Cat

NO MATTER HOW DOCILE BY BASIC NATURE, ANY CAT IN PAIN MAY SCRATCH OR BITE. Proper handling will prevent injuries. Furthermore,

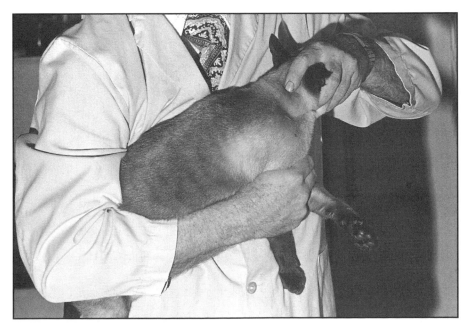

Carrying a cat. Hold the cat firmly against your body with its rear feet pressed out behind. Cover the eyes and ears with your other hand.　　　—J. Clawson

struggling can cause a weak or injured cat to tire quickly and can produce further shock and collapse.

If able to handle, pick up the cat as described for *Cooperative Cat*, then settle it over your hip so the rear claws project out behind where they can do no harm. Press the inside of your elbow and forearm against the cat's side, holding the cat firmly against your body. Cover the eyes and ears with your other hand.

If the cat is frightened or in pain, take precautions to avoid injury. Lift the cat at once from behind by the nape of the neck and lower it into a cat carrier or a cloth bag such as a pillowcase. The material must not be airtight, or the cat will smother. Once inside with no way to see out, the animal will feel secure and begin to relax. *Transport the cat to the veterinary hospital.*

If unable to handle, first throw a towel over the cat, then set a box on top. Raise the edge of the box and slide the top underneath. The cat is now enclosed and can be transported.

HEAT STROKE (OVERHEATING)

Heat stroke is an emergency that requires immediate recognition and prompt treatment. Cats do not tolerate high temperatures as well as humans. They depend on rapid breathing to exchange warm air for cool air. Heat-stressed cats drool a great deal and lick themselves to spread the saliva on their coats. The evaporation of saliva is an important additional cooling mechanism. But when air temperature is close to body temperature, cooling by evaporation is not an efficient process. Cats with airway disease also have difficulty with excess heat.

Common causes of overheating or heat stroke:

1. Increased environmental temperature such as being left in a car in hot weather or being confined to a crate without water.
2. A short-nosed breed, especially a Persian.
3. Airway disease that interferes with heat dissipation through rapid breathing.
4. Excessive heat production caused by high fever, seizures, strenuous exercise.

Heat stroke begins with rapid frantic noisy breathing. The tongue and mucous membranes are bright red; saliva is thick and tenacious; and the cat often vomits. Its rectal temperature rises, sometimes to over 106°F. The cause of the problem is usually evident by the appearance of the cat. The condition can be confirmed by taking the animal's temperature.

If the condition is allowed to go unchecked, the cat becomes unsteady and staggers; has diarrhea that is often bloody; and becomes progressively weaker. Its lips and mucous membranes become a pale blue or gray. Collapse, coma and death ensue.

Treatment: EMERGENCY MEASURES MUST BEGIN AT ONCE. Take the rectal temperature every 10 minutes. Mild cases respond by moving the cat to cooler surroundings such as an air-conditioned building or car. If the temperature is over

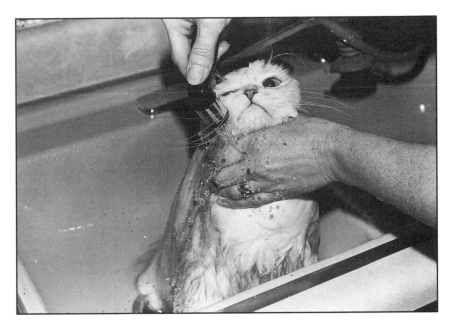

Heat stroke is an emergency. Cool the cat with a spray or immerse in a tub of cold water.

106°F or if the cat becomes unsteady, apply wet cold towels or immerse the cat in cold water until the rectal temperature reaches 103°F. As an alternative, wet the cat down with a garden hose. Ice packs can be applied to the head. Stop the cooling process and dry the cat when the temperature falls below 103°F. The thermoregulatory system is not functioning normally. Further cooling may produce hypothermia.

Heat stroke can be associated with swelling of the throat. This aggravates the problem. A cortisone injection by your veterinarian may be required to treat this.

Prevention:

1. Do not expose cats with airway disease or impaired breathing to prolonged heat.
2. Do not leave a cat in a car with the windows closed, even though the car may be parked in the shade.
3. If traveling in a car, house the cat in a well-ventilated cat carrier, or better yet an open wire cage, so the windows can be left open.
4. Provide shade and cool water to cats living outdoors in runs.

HOW TO INDUCE VOMITING

DO NOT INDUCE VOMITING IF YOUR CAT

1. Has already vomited.
2. Is unconscious or convulsing.

3. Has swallowed an acid, alkali, cleaning solution, household chemical, petroleum product.
4. Has swallowed a sharp object that could lodge in the esophagus or perforate the stomach.
5. Has swallowed the poison more than two hours before.

INDUCE VOMITING BY GIVING

1. Hydrogen peroxide 3 percent (most effective): one teaspoon per five pounds body weight (up to three teaspoons per dose) every 10 minutes or until the cat vomits. Repeat three times only.
2. Syrup of Ipecac (not *Ipecac Fluid Extract*, which is 14 times stronger): 1 teaspoon per 10 pounds body weight once only. NOTE: *Do not give a second dose unless approved by a veterinarian because of toxic effects on the heart if the cat does not vomit the syrup.*

INSECT STINGS, SPIDERS, SCORPIONS, LIZARDS

The stings of *bees, wasps, yellow jackets* and *ants* cause painful swelling at the site of the sting. If an animal is stung many times, it could go into shock as the result of absorbed toxins. Rarely, a hypersensitivity reaction (*anaphylactic shock*) can occur if the cat was exposed in the past (see page 396).

The stings of *Black widow* and *Missouri brown* spiders and *tarantulas* also are toxic to animals. The signs are sharp pain at the sting site. Later, the cat can develop chills, fever, labored breathing. Shock can occur.

The stings of *centipedes* and *scorpions* cause local reaction and at times severe illness. These bites heal slowly. Poisonous scorpions are found only in southern Arizona (two species).

Two species of poisonous lizard are found in the United States, both in southwestern states (*Gila Monster* and *Mexican Bearded Lizard*).

TREATMENT OF STINGS AND BITES

1. Identify the insect.
2. Remove an embedded stinger with tweezers, or scrape with credit card (only bees leave their stingers behind).
3. Make a paste of baking soda and apply it directly to the sting.
4. Apply ice packs to relieve swelling and pain.
5. Apply Calamine lotion and Cortaid to relieve itching.
6. If a lizard has a firm hold on the cat, pry open the lizard's jaws with pliers.

NOTE: If the cat exhibits signs of generalized toxicity or *anaphylaxis* (restlessness, agitation, face-scratching, drooling, vomiting, diarrhea, difficulty breathing, collapse or seizures), transport it immediately to the nearest veterinary facility.

PAINFUL ABDOMEN (ACUTE ABDOMEN)

An acute abdomen is an emergency that can lead to death unless treatment is started as soon as possible.

The condition is characterized by the sudden onset of abdominal pain along with vomiting; retching; extreme restlessness and inability to find a comfortable position; purring; meowing and crying; grunting; and labored breathing. The abdomen is extremely painful when pressed. A characteristic position is sometimes seen in which the cat rests its chest against the floor with its rump up in the air (prayer position). As the condition worsens, its pulse becomes weak and thready, its mucous membranes appear pale, and it goes into shock.

ONE OF THE FOLLOWING MAY BE THE CAUSE:

- Urinary obstruction caused by bladder stones
- Blunt abdominal trauma (being hit by a car) with internal bleeding
- Rupture of the bladder

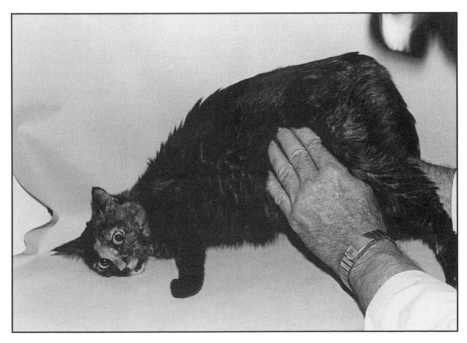

A *painful abdomen* indicates the need for *immediate* veterinary attention.

- Perforation of the stomach and intestines
- Poisoning
- Rupture of a pregnant uterus
- Acute peritonitis
- Intestinal obstruction

A cat with an acute abdomen is critically ill and should have *immediate* veterinary attention.

POISONING

GENERAL INFORMATION

A poison is any substance harmful to the body. Animal baits are palatable poisons that encourage ingestion. This makes them an obvious choice for intentional poisoning.

Cats by nature are curious and have a tendency to hunt small game or explore out-of-the-way places such as wood piles, weed thickets and storage ports. These environments put them into contact with insects, dead animals and toxic plants. It also means that in many cases of suspected poisoning the actual agent will be unknown. The great variety of potentially poisonous plants and shrubs makes identification difficult or impossible unless the owner has direct knowledge that the cat has eaten a certain plant or product. Most cases suspected of being malicious poisoning actually are not.

In some types of vegetation only certain parts of the plant are toxic. In others, all parts are poisonous. Ingestion causes a wide range of symptoms. They include: mouth irritation; drooling; vomiting; diarrhea; hallucinations; seizures; coma; and death. Other plant substances cause skin rash. Some toxic plants have specific pharmacological actions that are used in medicines.

Tables of toxic plants, shrubs and trees are included for reference. This list is a collection of common toxic plants. It is not a list of all poisonous plants.

POISONOUS HOUSEPLANTS

A. TOXIC HOUSEPLANTS may cause a rash after contact with the skin or mouth:

Chrysanthemum	Weeping fig
Creeping fig	Poinsettia

B. IRRITATING PLANTS, some of which contain *oxalic acid* that causes mouth swelling; and occasionally may cause generalized toxicity such as staggering and collapse:

Arrowhead vine	Malanga
Boston ivy	Marble queen
Caladium	Mother-in-law plant (snake plant)
Calla or Arum lily	Neththyis
Dumbcane	Parlor ivy
Elephant's ear	Pothos or Devil's lily
Emerald duke	Peace lily
Heart leaf (philodendron)	Red princess
Jack-in-the-pulpit	Saddle leaf (philodendron)
Majesty	Split leaf (philodendron)

C. TOXIC PLANTS may contain a wide variety of poisons. Most cause vomiting, abdominal pain, cramps. Some cause tremors, heart and respiratory or kidney problems, which are difficult for an owner to interpret:

Amaryllis	Ivy
Asparagus fern	Jerusalem cherry
Azalea	Needlepoint ivy
Bird of paradise	Pot mum
Creeping charlie	Ripple ivy
Crown of thorns	Spider mum
Elephant ears	Sprangeri fern
Glocal ivy	Umbrella plant
Heart ivy	

OUTDOOR PLANTS WITH TOXIC EFFECTS

A. OUTDOOR PLANTS that produce vomiting and diarrhea in some cases:

Delphinium	Skunk cabbage	Larkspur
Daffodil	Poke weed	Indian tobacco
Castor bean	Bittersweet woody	Wisteria
Indian turnip	Ground cherry	Soap berry
Fox glove		

B. TREES AND SHRUBS that are poisonous and may produce vomiting, abdominal pain and in some cases diarrhea:

Azalea (rhododendron)	Western yew	Wild cherry
	English holly	Japanese plum
Horse chestnut	Privet	Balsam pear
Buckeye	Mock orange	Black locust
Rain tree	Bird of paradise bush	English Yew
Monkey pod	Apricot, almond	
American yew	Peach cherry	

C. OUTDOOR PLANTS with varied toxic effects:

Rhubarb	Buttercup	Moonseed
Spinach	Nightshade	May apple
Sunburned potatoes	Poison hemlock	Dutchman's breeches
Loco weed	Pig weed	Angel's trumpet
Lupine	Water hemlock	Jasmine
Dologeton	Mushrooms	Matrimony vine

D. HALLUCINOGENS:

Marijuana	Nutmeg	Peyote
Morning glory	Periwinkle	Loco weed

E. CONVULSIONS:

China berry	Moonweed	Water hemlock
Coriaria	Nux vomica	

TREATING FOR CONTACT WITH TOXINS OR POISONS

If you think your cat may have been poisoned, first try to identify the poison. Most products containing chemicals are labeled for identification. Read the label. If this does not give you a clue to the plant's possible toxicity, call the emergency room of your local hospital and ask for information from the *Poison Control Center*. Alternately, call the *National Animal Poison Control Center* at (800)548-2423 or (900)680-0000. This hotline is open 24 hours a day, seven days a week. There is a credit card charge for the consultation.

The most important step in treatment is to eliminate the poison from your cat's stomach by making the cat vomit. In certain cases, induction of vomiting is contraindicated. For more information, see *How to Induce Vomiting* earlier in this chapter.

How to Delay or Prevent Absorption

Activated charcoal is used to coat the bowel and delay or prevent absorption. In most cases it is difficult to administer activated charcoal to a cat without first placing a stomach tube. Mix one part activated charcoal to six parts cold water. Give four to eight teaspoons. Follow 30 minutes later with Milk of Magnesia, $1/2$ teaspoon per five pounds body weight. Placing a stomach tube in a cat is not without risk. The best advice for a severely ill cat is to *induce vomiting and then proceed directly to the nearest veterinary facility*.

In the *less* severely ill cat, coat the bowel with milk, egg whites or vegetable oil. The dose of vegetable oil is two teaspoons for the average-sized cat. It should be added to the feed, but not force-fed by mouth because this could lead to aspiration pneumonia.

If your cat has a poisonous substance on the skin or coat, flush the area with copious amounts of water for five minutes. Wearing gloves, give the cat a complete bath in *lukewarm*, not cold, water, as described in the Skin chapter. Even if not irritating the skin, the substance should be removed. Otherwise, the cat may lick it off and swallow it. Soak gasoline and oil stains with mineral or vegetable oil (do not use paint thinner or turpentine). Work in well. Then wash with a mild soap. Rub in cornstarch or flour.

A cat beginning to show signs of nervous system involvement is in deep trouble. At this point, *get your cat to a veterinarian as quickly as possible*. Try to bring a sample of vomitus, or better yet the actual poison in the original container. Do not delay to administer first aid. If the cat is convulsing, unconscious or not breathing, see *CPR*.

Prevention: Prevent roaming, especially in grain and livestock areas where rat poisons may have been placed. Store all poisons in original containers in a safe location out of reach of cats. When using snail bait poisons, use commercial holders designed to keep bait away from pets.

The poisons discussed below are included because they are among the most frequently seen by veterinarians.

Strychnine

Strychnine is used as a rat, mouse and mole poison. It is also a common coyote bait. It is available commercially as coated pellets dyed purple, red or green. Signs of poisoning are so typical that the diagnosis can be made almost at once. Onset is sudden (less than two hours). *The first signs are agitation, excitability and apprehension.* They are followed rather quickly by intensely painful tetanic seizures that last about 60 seconds, during which the cat throws the head back, can't breathe and turns blue. The slightest stimulation such as tapping the cat or clapping the hands starts a seizure. This characteristic response is used to make the diagnosis. Other signs associated with nervous system involvement are tremors, champing, drooling, uncoordinated muscle spasms, collapse and paddling of the legs.

Seizures due to strychnine and other central nervous system toxins are sometimes misdiagnosed as epilepsy. This error would be a mistake because immediate veterinary attention is necessary. Epileptic seizures usually last a few minutes and do not recur during the same episode. Signs always appear in a certain order, and each attack is the same. They are over before the cat can get to a veterinarian. Usually, they are not considered emergencies (see Nervous System: *Seizure Disorders*).

Treatment: If your cat is showing the first signs of poisoning and hasn't vomited, induce vomiting as discussed earlier in this chapter. Do not induce vomiting if the cat exhibits signs of labored breathing.

With signs of central nervous system involvement, do not take time to induce vomiting. It is important to avoid loud noises or unnecessary handling that might trigger a seizure. *Cover your cat with a coat or blanket and go to the nearest veterinary clinic.*

Sodium Fluoroacetate (1080)

This chemical, used as a rat poison, is mixed with cereal, bran and other rat feeds. It is so potent that cats and dogs can be poisoned just by eating a dead rodent. The onset is sudden and begins with vomiting—followed by agitation, straining to urinate or defecate, a staggering gait, atypical fits or true convulsions and then collapse. Seizures are not triggered by external stimuli as are those of strychnine poisoning.

Treatment: Immediately after the cat ingests the poison, induce vomiting. Care and handling is the same as for strychnine. A specific antidote is available.

Arsenic

Arsenic is combined with metaldehyde in slug and snail baits and may appear in ant poisons, weed killers and insecticides. Arsenic is also a common impurity found in many chemicals. Death can occur quickly, before there is time to observe the symptoms. In more protracted cases the signs are thirst, drooling, vomiting, staggering, intense abdominal pain, cramps, diarrhea, paralysis and death. The breath of the cat has a strong odor of garlic.

Treatment: Induce vomiting. A specific antidote is available. See your veterinarian.

Metaldehyde

This poison, often combined with arsenic, is used commonly in rat, snail and slug baits. The signs of toxicity are excitation, drooling and slobbering, uncoordinated gait, muscle tremors and weakness that leads to inability to stand within a few hours of ingestion. The tremors are not triggered by external stimuli.

Treatment: Immediately after the cat ingests the poison, induce vomiting. The care and handling are the same as for strychnine.

Lead

Lead is found in insecticides and serves as a base for many commercial paints. Intoxication occurs mainly in kittens and young cats that chew on substances coated with a lead paint. Other sources of lead are linoleum, batteries and plumbing materials. Lead poisoning can occur in older cats following the ingestion of an insecticide containing lead. A chronic form does occur.

Acute poisoning begins with abdominal colic and vomiting. In the chronic form, a variety of central nervous system signs are possible. They include fits, uncoordinated gait, excitation, attacks of hysteria, weakness, stupor and blindness. These are signs of *encephalitis*.

Treatment: Immediately after ingestion, induce vomiting. Seek immediate medical attention. Specific antidotes are available through your veterinarian.

Phosphorus

This chemical is present in rat and roach poisons, fireworks, flares, matches and matchboxes. A poisoned cat may have a garlic odor to its breath. The first signs of intoxication are vomiting and diarrhea. They may be followed by a symptom-free interval—then by recurrent vomiting, cramps, pain in the abdomen, convulsions and coma.

There is no specific antidote. Treat as you would for strychnine.

Zinc Phosphide

This substance also is found in rat poisons. Intoxication causes central nervous system depression; labored breathing; vomiting (often of blood); weakness; convulsions; and death. There is no specific antidote. Treat as you would for strychnine.

Rodenticide Anticoagulants

Accidental ingestion of anticoagulant rodenticides placed by laymen and commercial exterminators is a common cause of bleeding in cats. These poisons exert their effect by blocking the synthesis of Vitamin K, which is required for normal blood clotting. *Vitamin K deficiency results in spontaneous bleeding.* There are no observable signs of poisoning until the cat begins to pass blood in the stool or urine, bleeds from the nose, or develops hemorrhages beneath the gums and skin. The cat may be found dead from internal hemorrhage.

The first generation coumadin anticoagulants (*warfarin, pindone*) required repeated exposure to produce lethal effects. However, newer second generation anticoagulants of the bromadiolone and brodifacoum groups, including *D-Con, Mouse Prufe II, Harvoc* and *Talan* require only a single exposure. In fact, a cat can become poisoned if it eats a rodent killed by one of these products. In addition, these poisons remain in the cat's system for a long time and can require medical treatment for up to one month.

Treatment: Identify the exact anticoagulant if possible. Induce vomiting on suspicion of ingestion. Seek veterinary attention. Spontaneous bleeding is corrected with fresh whole blood or frozen plasma. Vitamin K is a specific antidote. It is given by injection, after which the cat is placed on Vitamin K tablets for several days or weeks.

Other Rodenticides

Rampage is a popular cereal bait poison that contains Vitamin D3 (cholecalciferol). Toxic levels of Vitamin D3 cause a sudden rise in blood calcium levels, leading to vomiting and diarrhea, seizures and heart and kidney failure. Treatment is directed at lowering the serum calcium and requires veterinary management.

Bromethalin is a rodenticide found in *Assault* and *Vengeance* (Velsicol). One to two tablespoons are toxic to cats. Signs of poisoning include agitation, staggering, muscle tremors, high fever, stupor and seizures. Death is common once symptoms appear.

Induce vomiting on suspicion of ingestion and seek immediate veterinary attention.

Antifreeze (Ethylene Glycol)

Poisoning with antifreeze is one of the most common poisoning conditions found in cats because *ethylene glycol* has a sweet taste that appeals to cats and dogs. One teaspoon of antifreeze can kill an average-sized cat. Signs of toxicity, which appear suddenly, are vomiting, uncoordinated gait (seems "drunk"), weakness, stupor and coma. Death can occur in 12 to 36 hours. Convulsions are unusual. Cats that recover from the acute poisoning may have damage to their kidneys and go on to kidney failure.

Treatment: Induce vomiting on suspicion of ingestion and proceed at once to the nearest veterinary facility. Intravenous alcohol is a specific antidote. Intensive care in an animal hospital may prevent kidney complications.

Organophosphates and Carbamates

These substances are used on cats to kill fleas and other parasites. Common organophosphates are *Chloropyrifos* and *Carbaryl*, but there are others. They are also used in garden sprays and in some dewormers. Improper application of insecticides to the cat can lead to absorption of a toxic dose through the skin. These drugs affect the nervous system primarily. Insecticides are discussed in the Skin chapter.

Petroleum Products (Gasoline, Kerosene, Turpentine)

These volatile liquids can cause pneumonia if aspirated or inhaled. The signs of toxicity are vomiting, difficulty in breathing, tremors, convulsions and coma. Death is by respiratory failure.

Treatment: *Do not induce vomiting.* Administer water, fruit juice, or soda pop by mouth (one ounce per six pounds body weight). Be prepared to administer *artificial breathing*.

Chlorinated Hydrocarbons

These compounds, like the organophosphates, are incorporated into some insecticide preparations (not for use on cats). The common products in veterinary use are *Chlordane, Toxaphene, Lindane,* and *Methoxychlor*. Accidental application to cats produces muscle twitching, excitation and convulsions. Bathe the animal immediately to remove the substance from its coat. Veterinary attention is imperative.

Corrosives (Acid and Alkali)

Corrosives and caustics are found in household cleaners, drain decloggers and commercial solvents. When ingested, they cause burns of the mouth, esophagus and stomach. Severe cases are associated with acute perforation (or late stricture) of the esophagus and stomach.

Treatment: Rinse out your cat's mouth. Administer water or soda pop by mouth (one ounce per six pounds body weight), then give two teaspoons of vegetable oil once. You can add this to the cat's food. The practice of giving an acid to neutralize an alkali and vice versa is no longer recommended because it causes heat injury to the lining of the stomach.

In either situation, do not induce vomiting. Vomiting could result in rupture of the stomach and burns of the esophagus.

Garbage Poisoning (Food Poisoning)

Cats are more particular than dogs about what they eat. Nevertheless, they are also scavengers and come into contact with carrion (rotting flesh or meat), decomposing foods, animal manure and other noxious substances (some of which are listed in DIGESTIVE SYSTEM: *Diarrhea*). Cats are more sensitive than dogs to food poisoning and exhibit effects at lower levels. Signs of poisoning begin with vomiting and pain in the abdomen. In severe cases they are followed two to six hours later by a diarrhea that is often bloody. Shock may occur—particularly if the problem is complicated by bacterial infection. Mild cases recover in one to two days.

Treatment: Seek immediate veterinary attention for signs of dehydration, toxicity and shock. In mild cases, coat the bowel as described earlier in this chapter.

Toad and Salamander Poisoning

In the United States there are two species of poisonous toad (*Bufo*). The Colorado River Toad is found in the Southwest and Hawaii. The Marine Toad is found in Florida. There is one species of poisonous salamander, the California newt, found in California.

All toads have a bad taste. Cats that mouth them slobber, spit and drool. The Marine Toad is highly poisonous, causing death in as little as 15 minutes.

Symptoms in cats depend on the toxicity of the toad or salamander and the amount of poison absorbed. They vary from merely slobbering to convulsions, blindness and death.

Treatment: Flush out your cat's mouth (use a garden hose if necessary) and induce vomiting as described earlier in this chapter. Be prepared to administer CPR. Cats with salamander poisoning usually recover quickly.

People Medicines

Veterinarians frequently are called because a cat has swallowed pills intended for the owner or has eaten too many pills prescribed for the cat. (Some cat pills are flavored to encourage cats to eat them.) Drugs most commonly involved are antihistamines, pain relievers, sleeping pills, diet pills, heart preparations and vitamins.

Cats appear to be unusually sensitive to drugs and medications. The reasons for this are discussed in the chapter DRUGS AND MEDICATIONS. Common household items considered safe for humans may be toxic to cats. All episodes of drug ingestion should be taken seriously.

Treatment: Induce vomiting and coat the bowel as described earlier in this chapter. Discuss the potential toxicity of the drug with your veterinarian.

SNAKE BITES

Poisonous and nonpoisonous snakes are widely distributed throughout the United States. In general, bites of nonpoisonous snakes do not cause swelling or pain. They show teeth marks in the shape of a horseshoe (no fang marks).

Ninety percent of snake bites in cats involve the head and legs. Body bites from poisonous snakes usually are lethal.

In the United States there are four poisonous varieties: cottonmouth moccasin, rattlesnakes, copperheads and coral snakes. The diagnosis of poison snake bite is made by the appearance of the bite, the behavior of the animal and identification of the species of snake. (Kill it first if possible.)

PIT VIPERS (RATTLESNAKES, MOCCASINS, COPPERHEADS)

Identify these species by their large arrow-shaped heads, pits below and between the eyes, elliptical pupils, rough scales and the presence of fangs in the upper jaws.

The bite: There are two puncture wounds in the skin (fang marks). Signs of local reaction appear quickly and include sudden severe swelling, excruciating pain, redness and hemorrhages in the skin.

Behavior of the animal: Signs and symptoms depend on the size and species of the snake, location of the bite and amount of toxin absorbed. The first signs are extreme restlessness, panting, drooling and weakness. These are followed by diarrhea, collapse, sometimes seizures, shock and death in severe cases.

CORAL SNAKE

Identify this snake by its rather small size, small head with black nose and vivid-colored bands of red, yellow, white and black—the red and yellow bands are always next to each other. Fangs are present in the upper jaw.

The bite: There is less severe redness and swelling at the site of the bite, but the pain is excruciating. Look for the fang marks.

Behavior of the animal: Coral snake venom primarily is neurotoxic (destructive to nerve tissue). Signs include vomiting, diarrhea, urinary incontinence, paralysis, convulsions and coma.

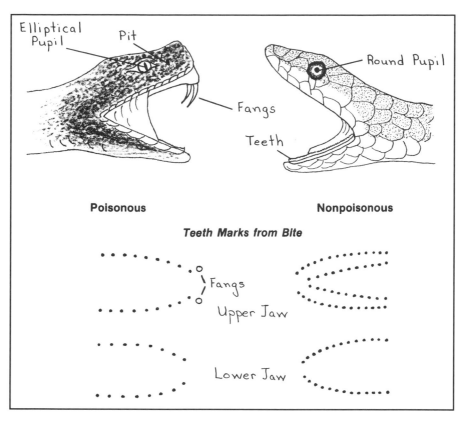

Except for the coral snake, all poisonous species in North America are pit vipers. Note the elliptical pupil, pit below the eye, large fangs and characteristic bite.

—Rose Floyd

TREATMENT OF SNAKE BITES

First identify the snake and look at the bite. If the snake is nonpoisonous, cleanse and dress the wound as described later in this chapter (see *Wounds*). If it appears that the cat has been bitten by a poisonous snake and if you are within 30 minutes of a veterinary hospital, transport at once (see *Handling and Restraint*).

If unable to get help within 30 minutes, follow these steps:

1. **KEEP THE CAT QUIET.** Venom spreads rapidly if the cat is active. Excitement, exercise, struggling—all these increase the rate of absorption.

2. If the bite is on the leg, apply a constricting bandage (handkerchief or strip of cloth) between the bite and the cat's heart. You should be able to get a finger beneath the bandage; loosen the bandage for five minutes every hour.

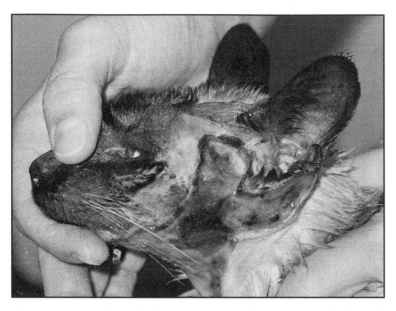

Poisonous snake bite, showing an extensive face wound after loss of devitalized tissue.

3. *Do not wash the wound* because this will increase venom absorption.
4. *Do not apply ice* because this does not slow spread and can damage tissue.
5. *Do not make cuts* over the wound or attempt to suck out venom. This usually is not successful, and you could absorb venom.

Proceed to the veterinary hospital. Further treatment involves intravenous fluids, antivenoms, antihistamines and antibiotics.

SHOCK

Shock is lack of adequate blood flow to meet the body's needs. Adequate blood flow requires effective heart pumping, open intact vessels and sufficient blood volume to maintain flow and pressure. Any condition adversely affecting the heart, vessels or blood volume can induce shock.

At first the body attempts to compensate for the inadequate circulation by speeding up the heart, constricting the skin vessels and maintaining fluid in the circulation by reducing output of urine. These activities become increasingly difficult when the vital organs aren't getting enough oxygen to carry on. After a time, shock becomes self-perpetuating. Untreated, shock causes death.

Common causes of shock are dehydration (prolonged vomiting and diarrhea); heat stroke; severe infections; poisoning; and hemorrhage. Falling from a height and being hit by a car are the most common causes of traumatic shock in the cat.

The signs of shock are a drop in body temperature, shivering, listlessness and mental depression, weakness, cold feet and legs, pale skin and mucous membranes and a weak faint pulse.

Treatment: First, evaluate. Is the cat breathing? Does it have a heartbeat? What are the extent of the injuries? Is the cat in shock? If so, proceed as follows:

1. If not breathing, proceed with *Artificial Breathing.*
2. If no heart beat or pulse, administer *CPR.*
3. If unconscious, check to be sure the airway is open. Clear secretions from the mouth with your fingers. Pull out the tongue to keep the airway clear of secretions. Keep the head lower than the body.
4. Control bleeding (as described below under *Wounds*).
5. To prevent further aggravation of shock,
   a. Calm the cat, and speak soothingly.
   b. Allow your cat to assume the most comfortable position. An animal will naturally adopt the one of least pain. Do not force the cat to lie down—this may make breathing more difficult.
   c. When possible, splint or support broken bones before moving the cat (see Musculoskeletal System: *Broken Bones*).
   d. Wrap the cat in a blanket to provide warmth and to protect injured extremities. How to handle and restrain an injured cat for transport to the veterinary hospital is discussed above (see *Handling and Restraint*). Do not attempt to muzzle a cat. This can impair breathing.

WOUNDS

In the care of wounds, the two most important considerations are (a) first *stop the bleeding,* and (b) then *prevent infection.* Be prepared to restrain before you treat the wound (see *Handling and Restraint*).

Control of Bleeding

Bleeding may be *arterial (the spurting of bright red blood)* or *venous (oozing of dark red blood)* or sometimes both. *Do not wipe* a wound that has stopped bleeding. This will dislodge the clot. *Do not pour* peroxide on a fresh wound. Bleeding then will be difficult to control.

The two methods used to control bleeding are the pressure dressing and the tourniquet.

Pressure Dressing: Take several pieces of clean or sterile gauze, place them over the wound and bandage snugly. Watch for swelling of the limb below the pressure pack. Swelling indicates impaired circulation. The bandage must be loosened or removed.

If material is not available for bandaging, place a pad on the wound and press it firmly. Hold it in place until help arrives.

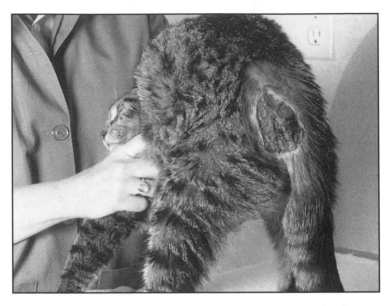

An infected cat-fight wound. It should be treated as described in the text.

A method to temporarily control arterial bleeding is to apply pressure over the artery in the groin or axilla (armpits). To locate, see CIRCULATORY SYSTEM: *Pulse.* Often this action will stop bleeding long enough to permit an assistant to apply a pressure dressing.

Tourniquet: A tourniquet may be needed to control a spurting artery. It can be applied to the leg or tail above the wound (between the wound and the heart). Take a piece of cloth or gauze roll and loop it around the limb. Then tighten it by hand or with a stick inserted into the loop, twisting the stick until bleeding is controlled. If you see the end of the artery, you might attempt to pick it up with tweezers and tie it off with a piece of cotton thread. When possible, this should be left to a trained practitioner.

A tourniquet should be loosened every 30 minutes, for two to three minutes, to let blood flow into the limb.

TREATING THE WOUND

All wounds are contaminated with dirt and bacteria. Proper care and handling will prevent some infections. Before handling a wound, make sure your hands and instruments are clean. Starting at the edges of a fresh wound, clip the hair back to enlarge the area. Cleanse the edges with a damp gauze or pad. Irrigate the wound with clean tap water. Apply antibiotic ointment. Bandage as described below.

Older wounds covered with pus and scab are cleaned with 3 percent hydrogen peroxide solution *diluted* 1 part to 5 parts water. Hydrogen peroxide can damage tissue, so use it only once. Thereafter, cleanse with a *Betadine* solution (dilute 1 part to 10 parts water). Blot dry. Apply an antibiotic ointment such as *Triple Antibiotic Ointment* or *Neomycin* and leave the wound open or bandage as described below.

Dressings over infected wounds should be changed frequently to aid in the drainage of pus and allow you to apply fresh ointment.

Fresh lacerations over ¹/₂ inch long should be sutured to prevent infection, minimize scarring and speed healing.

Wounds older than 12 hours are quite likely to be infected. Suturing is questionable.

BITES are heavily contaminated wounds. They are often puncture wounds. They are quite likely to get infected and should not be sutured. Antibiotics are indicated. Most wounds incurred in a cat fight are punctures.

With all animal bites, the possibility of rabies should be kept in mind.

BANDAGING

Bandages are more difficult to apply to cats than to dogs and, once applied, are more difficult to keep in place. Cats that do not tolerate bandages and continually remove them may be helped by tranquilization. Wounds about the head and wounds draining pus are best left open to help drainage and ease of treatment.

When a cat claws and macerates a wound or continually scratches at a skin condition, treatment can be facilitated by bandaging its back feet or clipping its nails.

Bandaging is made much easier when a cat is gently but firmly restrained as discussed earlier in this chapter. The bandaging equipment you will need is listed in the *Home Emergency and Medical Kit* at the beginning of this chapter.

Foot and Leg Bandages: *To bandage a foot*, place several sterile gauze pads over the wound. Insert cotton balls between the toes and hold in place with adhesive tape looped around the bottom of the foot and back across the top until the foot is snugly wrapped.

For leg wounds, begin by wrapping the foot as described. Then cover the wound with several sterile gauze pads and hold in place with strips of adhesive tape. Wrap the tape around the leg but do not overlap it because you want the tape to stick to the hair. This technique keeps the dressing from sliding up and down, which often happens when only a roll gauze bandage is used. Flex the knee and foot several times to assure that the bandage is not too tight and that there is good circulation and movement at the joints.

When a dressing is to be left in place for some time, check every few hours to be sure the foot is not swelling. If there is any question about the sensation or circulation to the foot, loosen the dressing. Cats will frequently attempt to lick, bite or remove dressings that are too tight and uncomfortable.

Many-Tailed Bandage: This bandage is used to protect the skin of the abdomen, flanks or back from scratching and biting and to hold dressings in place. It is made by taking a rectangular piece of linen and cutting the sides to make tails. Tie the tails together over the back to hold it in place.

A many-tailed bandage may be used to keep kittens from nursing on infected breasts.

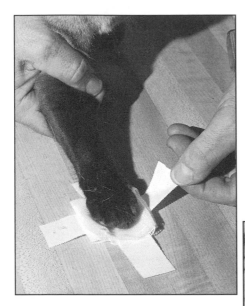

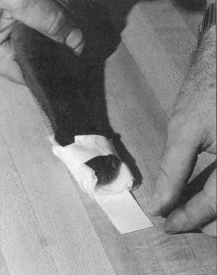

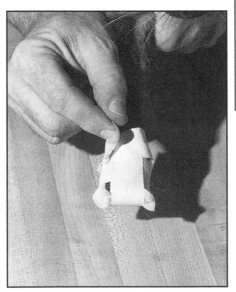

A method of applying a foot bandage. Tape loosely to allow for good circulation.

—J. Clawson

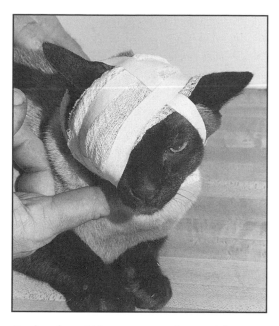

Eye bandage. Wrap a gauze roll around the eye. A pad may be placed beneath. Secure with tape to the hair. The ears should be free.

—J. Clawson

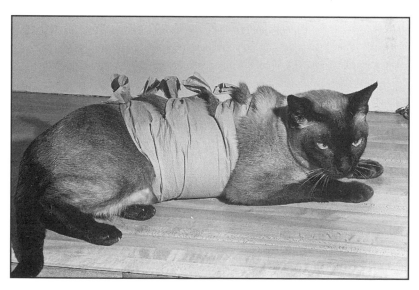

Many-tailed bandage.

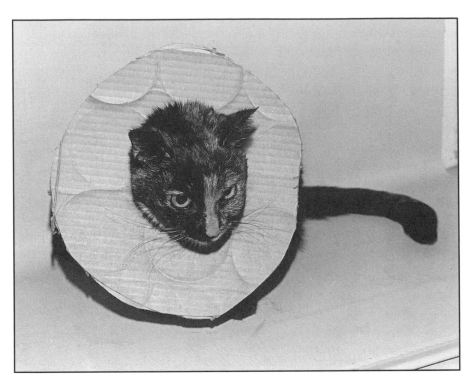

Elizabethan collar.

Eye Bandage: At times your veterinarian may prescribe an eye bandage in the treatment of an eye ailment. Place a sterile gauze square over the affected eye and hold it in place by taping around the head with one-inch adhesive. Be careful not to get the tape too tight. Apply the dressing so that the ears are free.

You may be required to change the dressing from time to time to apply medication to the eye.

Ear Bandage: These dressings are difficult to apply. Most ear injuries can be left open. To protect the ears from scratching, apply an Elizabethan collar.

Elizabethan Collar: The Elizabethan collar, named for the high neck ruff popular in the reign of Queen Elizabeth, is a useful device to keep a cat from scratching at the ears and biting at wounds and skin problems. These collars can be purchased from some veterinarians or pet stores *or* can be made from a piece of heavy flexible cardboard. Cut out a circle 12 inches in diameter. In the center, cut out a hole 4 to 5 inches in diameter. Cut out a wedge (like a piece of pie) one quarter of the circumference of the circle. Fit the collar around the cat's neck and secure the sides with adhesive tape. Make sure the collar is not too tight around the neck. Fasten the device to the cat's leather collar by strings passed through holes punched in the sides of the cardboard. Many cats cannot or will not drink while wearing an Elizabethan collar. In that case, temporarily remove the collar. Cats with Elizabethan collars must be kept indoors.

2

WORMS (INTESTINAL PARASITES)

GENERAL INFORMATION

Most owners assume that if a cat's stool is found to have parasites, then it must be suffering from disease.

This is not necessarily the case. Most cats are infested at one time or another with intestinal parasites. Some are born with them, and others acquire them later in life. When they recover, they develop a certain amount of immunity. This immunity helps to keep the worms in check.

If worms are causing a disease, there should be some change in the appearance of the stool. In turn, there is a decline in the cat's general health. You should note decreased appetite, loss of weight, sometimes protrusion of the third eyelid, diarrhea, anemia and the passage of mucus or blood.

It is probable that cats, like dogs, develop a resistance to certain intestinal parasites with larvae that migrate in the animal's tissues (e.g., roundworms, hookworms), although this has not been proven in the cat. Tapeworms have no migratory phase and thus cause little buildup of immunity.

Roundworms, tapeworms and hookworms are the most common internal worm parasites in cats. Resistance to roundworms appears age related. Kittens and young cats show less resistance and in consequence may experience a heavy infestation. This can lead to marked debility or even death. Cats over six months of age are less likely to show significant clinical signs.

Immunosuppressive drugs such as cortisone have been shown to activate large numbers of hookworm larvae laying dormant in an animal's tissues. Stressful events such as trauma, surgery, severe disease and emotional upsets (i.e., shipping), also can activate dormant larvae. This leads to the appearance of eggs in the stool.

During lactation, roundworm larvae are activated and appear in the queen's milk. Therefore, a heavy parasite problem might develop in the litter even when the mother was effectively dewormed. This can happen because none of the deworming agents are effective against larvae encysted in the tissue.

DEWORMING YOUR CAT

Although some deworming preparations are effective against more than one species of worms, there is no preparation that is effective against them all. Accordingly, for a medication to be safe and effective, a precise diagnosis is required. It is also important that the medication be given precisely as directed. Natural side effects, such as diarrhea and vomiting, must be distinguished from toxic reactions. For these reasons, it is advisable to deworm *only* under veterinary supervision.

Deworming agents effective against various species of worms are given in the accompanying table.

Kittens. Nearly all kittens are infested with roundworms. Other worms may be present, too. It is advisable to have your veterinarian check your kitten's stool before treating it for roundworms. Otherwise, other worms may go undetected.

Worm infestations are particularly harmful in kittens subjected to overfeeding, chilling, close confinement and sudden change in diet. Stressful conditions such as these should be corrected before administering a deworming agent. Do not deworm a kitten with diarrhea or other signs of illness unless your veterinarian has determined that its illness is caused by an intestinal parasite.

Kittens with roundworms should be dewormed at two to three weeks of age and again at five to six weeks (see *Roundworms*). If eggs or worms are still found in the stool, subsequent courses should be given.

Adults. Most veterinarians recommend that adult cats be dewormed only when there is specific evidence of an infestation. A stool examination is the most effective way of making an exact diagnosis and choosing the best agent.

It is not advisable to deworm a cat suffering from some unexplained illness which is assumed to be caused by worms. *All dewormers are poison*—meant to poison the worm, but not the cat. Cats debilitated by another disease may be too weak to resist the toxic effects of the deworming agent.

Cats of all ages, particularly those that hunt and roam freely, can be subject to periodic heavy worm infestations. These cats should be checked once or twice a year. If parasites are identified, they should be treated.

The Breeding Queen. Before breeding your female have her stool checked. If parasites are found, she should receive a thorough deworming. This will not protect her kittens from all worm infestation, but will decrease the frequency and severity. It will also help to put her in the best condition for a healthy pregnancy.

DEWORMING AGENTS

DRUG	TYPE OF WORM			COMMENTS
	Hook	Ascarid (round)	Tape	
Piperazine	—	★★★	—	Inexpensive. Safe. Do not overdose.
Task (*Dichlorvos*)	★★★★	★★★★	—	Do not use in sick cat. May potentiate effects of insecticides in coat preparations and flea collars.
Yomesan (*Niclosamide*)	—	—	★★★(*Taenia*) ★(*D. caninum*)	Vomiting often occurs. Fasting required.
Scoloban (*Bunamidine*)	—	★★★★(*Taenia*)	★★(*D. caninum*)	Fasting required.
DNP (*Disophenol*)	★★★★	—	—	Given by injection. Do not use in sick cat.
Nemex (*Pyrantel pamoate*)	★★★★	★★★★	—	Safe but not cleared by USDA for use in cats at this time.
Droncit (*Praziquantel*)	—	—	★★★★(*Taenia*) ★★★★(*D. caninum*) ★★★★(*Echinococcus*)	Drug of choice for tapeworms.
Vercom (*Febantel & praziquantel*)	★★★★	★★★★	★★★★	Safe. Broad spectrum. Must be given on full stomach.
Panacur (*Fenbendazole*)	★★★★	★★★★	★★★★	Safe but not cleared for use in cats at this time.

★★★★Excellent   ★★★Good   ★★Fair   ★Poor   —No effect

How to Control Worms

The life cycles of most worms are such that the possibility of reinfestation is great. To keep worms under control, you must destroy eggs or larvae *before* they reinfest the cat. This means good sanitation and maintaining clean, dry quarters for your cat.

Cats should not be crowded together on shaded earth, which provides ideal conditions for seeding eggs and larvae. A water-tight surface such as cement is the easiest to keep clean. Hose it down daily and allow it to dry in the sun. Gravel is a good substitute. Usually it provides effective drainage, and it is easy to remove stools from gravel. Concrete and gravel surfaces can be disinfected with lime, salt or borax (one ounce to 10 square feet). Remove stools from the pens daily. Lawns should be cut short and watered only when necessary. Stools in the yard should be removed at least twice a week.

The litter box should be kept clean and dry and should be washed thoroughly every three to four days with detergents and boiling water.

Fleas, lice, cockroaches, beetles, waterbugs and rodents are intermediate hosts of tapeworms or roundworms. It is necessary to get rid of these pests to control reinfestation (see SKIN: *Disinfecting the Premises*).

Many internal parasites spend the young stages of their life cycle in another animal and can only infect the cat and develop into adults when the cat preys on and eats this other animal. Accordingly, cats should not be allowed to roam and hunt. Be sure to thoroughly cook all fresh meat before feeding it to your cat.

Catteries that have continuous problems with worms often have other problems, too. They include skin, bowel and respiratory difficulties. Steps should be taken to improve the management of the cattery, especially sanitation measures.

DISEASES CAUSED BY CERTAIN WORMS

ROUNDWORMS (ASCARIDS)

Ascarids are the most common worm parasite in cats, occurring in nearly all kittens and in 25 percent to 75 percent of adults. There are three species that infest the cat. Adult roundworms live in the stomach and intestine and attain lengths up to five inches. The eggs are protected by a hard shell. They are extremely hardy and can live for months or years in the soil. They become infective in three to four weeks.

Cats acquire the disease through contact with soil containing the eggs or by eating an abnormal host, such as a beetle or rodent, which has acquired encysted larvae in its tissues. The larvae are released in the cat's digestive tract.

Larvae of the common feline roundworm *Toxocara cati* are capable of migrating in tissues. Eggs, entering via the oral route, hatch in the intestines. Larvae are carried to the lungs by the bloodstream. Here, they become mobile, crawl up the windpipe and are swallowed. This may cause bouts of coughing and gagging. They return to the intestine and develop into adults.

In the older cat, only a few larvae return to the intestine. The others encyst in tissues and remain dormant. During lactation, these dormant larvae are released, re-enter the circulation, and are transmitted to kittens via the breast milk.

Deworming the queen before or during pregnancy does not prevent all roundworm infestation of kittens after birth, but will decrease the frequency and severity. Medications do not work on encysted larvae.

Roundworms usually do not produce a heavy infestation in adult cats but may do so among those that do a lot of hunting. In kittens, a heavy infestation can result in severe illness or even death. Such kittens appear thin and have a pot-bellied look; sometimes cough or vomit; experience diarrhea; are anemic; and may come down with pneumonia as the worms migrate from the blood vessels to the air sacs of the lungs. Worms may be found in the vomitus or passed in the stool. Typically, they look like white earthworms or strands of spaghetti that are alive and moving.

Roundworms can cause a disease in humans called *visceral larvae migrans*. Most of them are caused by the dog roundworm, *Toxocara canis*, but the cat roundworm

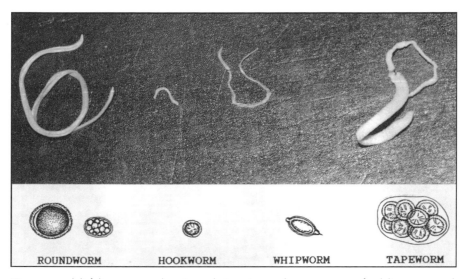

ROUNDWORM   HOOKWORM   WHIPWORM   TAPEWORM

Common adult feline worms showing relative size and appearance of adult worms and eggs. (Roundworm eggs: two species.)

also can produce this disease. Only a few cases are reported each year, usually from areas with a mild climate. There is often a history of dirt eating (of soil contaminated by the eggs). Children are most likely to be affected.

Because humans are not the normal host, the immature worms do not become adults. Instead, they migrate in the tissues and wander aimlessly, causing fever, anemia, liver enlargement, pneumonia and other ill effects. The disease runs its course in about a year. It is best prevented by controlling infestation in dogs and cats through periodic deworming and good sanitation (see Skin: *Premise Control*).

Treatment: A Piperazine compound (*Antepar*) is a safe dewormer and has been used for many years as the agent of choice. Pyrantel pamoate (*Nemex*) is also safe but has not been approved for use in cats. It is more effective than Piperazine and can be used in nursing kittens. Kittens should be dewormed by three weeks of age to prevent contamination of their quarters by roundworm eggs. A second course should be given two to three weeks later to kill any adult worms that were in the larval stage at the first deworming. Subsequent courses are indicated if eggs or worms are found in the stool.

Piperazine and Pyrantel pamoate dewormers can be obtained from your veterinarian or a pet shop. You do not have to fast your cat before using these agents. Be sure to follow the directions of the manufacturer about dosage.

HOOKWORMS (ANCYLOSTOMA)

There are four species of hookworm that afflict the cat. Hookworms are not as common in cats as they are in dogs. They are most prevalent in areas of high temperature and humidity (for example, in the southern United States), where conditions are favorable for rapid development and spread of larvae.

Hookworms are small thin worms about one-fourth to one-half inch long. They fasten to the wall of the small intestine and draw blood from the host.

The cat acquires the disease by ingesting infected larvae in soil or feces, or by direct penetration of the skin (usually the pads of the feet). The immature worms migrate through the lungs to the intestine where they become adults. In about two weeks, the cat begins to pass eggs in the feces. The eggs incubate in the soil. Depending on conditions, larvae can become infective within two to five days.

Newborn kittens do not acquire the infection *in utero* or through the milk of the queen.

The typical signs of *acute* hookworm infestation are anemia and diarrhea. With a heavy infestation stools might be bloody, wine-dark or tarry-black, but this is uncommon. A hookworm infestation can be fatal in very young kittens.

Chronic infection is a more common problem in the adult cat than it is in kittens. The signs are diarrhea, anemia, weight loss and progressive weakness. The diagnosis is made by finding the eggs in the feces.

Many cats that recover from the disease become carriers via cysts in the tissue. During periods of stress or some other illness, a new outbreak can occur as the larvae are released.

A disease in humans called *cutaneous larvae migrans* (creeping eruption) is caused by the hookworm (A. *brasiliense*). It is due to penetration of the skin by larvae present in the soil. It causes lumps, streaks beneath the skin, and itching. The condition is self-limiting.

Treatment: *Nemex* (Pyrantel pamoate) and *Vercom* (Febentel and praziquantel) have replaced *DNP* and *Task* as the agents of choice because of safety and effectiveness. Two treatments are given two weeks apart. The stool should be checked to determine the effectiveness of treatment.

To prevent reinfestation, see *How to Control Worms.*

Kittens with acute signs and symptoms require intensive veterinary management.

TAPEWORMS (CESTODES)

Tapeworms are the most common internal parasite in the adult cat. They live in the small intestine. The head (scolex) of the parasite fastens itself to the wall of the gut by hooks and suckers. The body is composed of segments containing the egg packets. Tapeworms vary in length from less than an inch to several feet. *To eliminate tapeworm infection, the head must be destroyed.* Otherwise, the worm will regenerate.

The body segments containing the eggs are passed in the feces. Fresh moist segments are capable of moving. They are about a quarter of an inch long. Occasionally, you might see them adhering to the fur about your cat's anus or in its stool. When dry, they resemble kernels of rice.

There are two common tapeworm species in the cat. Both are transmitted via an intermediate host. The worm *Diphylidium caninum* is acquired from fleas or lice that harbor immature tapeworms in their intestines. These insects acquire the parasite by eating tapeworm eggs. The cat must bite or swallow the insect.

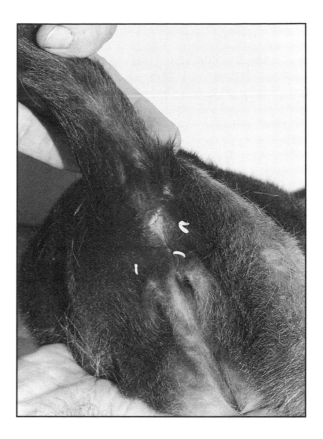

Tapeworm segments found on cat.

The tapeworm *Taenia taeniaformis* is acquired by eating uncooked meat, raw freshwater fish, or discarded animal parts.

Dibothriocephalus latus and *Spirometra mansanoides* are two uncommon tapeworms cats might acquire from eating uncooked freshwater fish or a water snake.

A child could acquire a tapeworm if it accidentally swallowed an infective flea. Except for this unusual circumstance, cat tapeworms do not present a hazard to human health.

Treatment: *Droncit* is one of the most effective preparations against both common species of cat tapeworm. Other suitable remedies are *Vercom* and *Panacur*. *Yomesan* and *Scolaban* are least effective. Use under veterinary guidance. Deworming must be combined with control of fleas and lice in the case of *D. caninum* (see *How to Control Worms*) and by preventing roaming and hunting in the case of other tapeworms.

Uncommon Worm Parasites

Pinworms are a common cause of concern to families with cats and children. Cats do not present a source of human pinworm infection as they do not acquire or spread this disease.

Eye worms occur among cats living on the West Coast of the United States. They are discussed in the chapter Eyes.

Trichinosis is a disease acquired through ingestion of uncooked pork containing the encysted larvae of *Trichina spiralis*. It is estimated that 15 percent of the people living in the United States have at some time acquired trichinosis, although only a few clinical cases are reported each year. The incidence is probably somewhat higher in cats and dogs. Prevent this disease by keeping your cat from roaming, particularly if you live in a rural area. Cook all fresh meat (your own *and* your cat's).

Whipworms are slender parasites two to three inches long that live in the cecum (first part of the large intestine). Since they are thicker at one end, they give the appearance of a whip. Whipworms are usually found incidentally and are not known to cause disease in cats. No treatment is necessary.

Flukes are flatworms ranging in size from a few millimeters up to an inch or more in length. There are several species that parasitize different parts of the cat's body, including the lung, liver and small intestine. Flukes are acquired by eating infected raw fish and small prey such as snails, frogs, crayfish.

Signs of fluke infestation are variable. Professional diagnosis is required. Drug treatment is difficult and not always successful. Infection should be prevented by cooking fish and restricting hunting.

Heartworms are common in dogs but rare in cats. They are discussed in the chapter CIRCULATORY SYSTEM.

Lungworms are slender hairlike parasites about one centimeter in length. There are several species of lungworm, but only two commonly affect cats. *Aeleurostrongylus abstrussus* has a complicated life cycle. Larvae are passed in the feces. They are taken up by snails and slugs that, in turn, are eaten by birds, rodents, frogs. When these transport hosts are eaten by the cat, eggs hatch in the intestine. Adult worms migrate to the lungs and lay eggs. Larvae migrate up the windpipe, are swallowed and pass in the feces. The second common lungworm, *Capillaria aerophila*, is acquired by the direct ingestion of infective eggs or a transport host.

Most cats do not show signs of clinical infection. Others may exhibit a persistent dry cough that is caused by a secondary bacterial infection. Occasionally a cat will experience fever, weight loss, wheezing, nasal discharge. These symptoms might suggest some other respiratory illness. A chest X ray is often normal.

Microscopic diagnosis is made by finding coiled or comma-shaped larvae in feces or sputum (*A. abstrussus*). The ova of *C. aerophila* are easily confused with the eggs of whipworms. Many cases thought to be whipworm infestation probably are due to lungworms. Lungworms are difficult to eliminate. Levamisole and fenbendazole are effective in some cases but are not currently approved for treating cats. Secondary bacterial bronchitis or pneumonia is treated with antibiotics. Veterinary management is required.

Stomach worms are most likely to affect cats living in the southwestern United States. There are three species of stomach worm that affect cats. The infection is acquired by eating beetles (cockroaches, crickets) that have ingested eggs from the soil or by contact with vomitus from an infected cat.

Recurrent vomiting is the most common symptom. Veterinary diagnosis is necessary to distinguish stomach worms from other causes of vomiting and to determine the specific species causing the infection. Piperazine derivatives are effective in some cases. Pyrantel pamoate is effective against one species. Prevent this disease by keeping your cat from roaming and hunting.

Bladder worms are common in Australia but rare in the United States. The life cycle is unknown. Worms live in the urinary bladder and pass eggs in the urine. The eggs resemble those of the whipworm. The infection causes few if any problems.

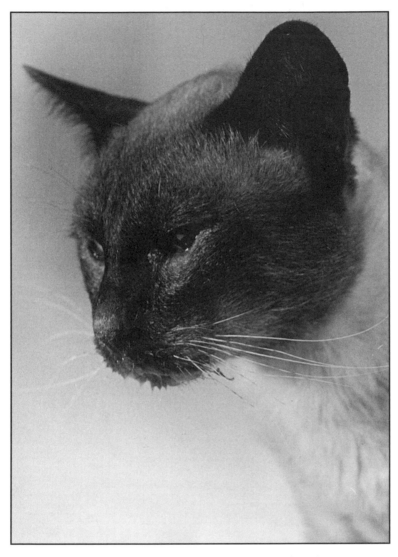

Acute upper respiratory infection, typified by discharge from the eyes, nose, and mouth.

3

INFECTIOUS DISEASES

GENERAL INFORMATION

Infectious diseases are caused by bacteria, viruses, protozoa and fungi that invade the body of a susceptible host and cause an illness.

Infectious diseases are often transmitted from one cat to another by contact with infected feces and other bodily secretions or by inhalation of germ-laden droplets in the air. A few are transmitted via the genital tract when cats mate. Others are acquired by contact with spores in the soil that get into the body through the respiratory tract or a break in the skin.

Bacteria are single-celled germs, while the virus, the tiniest germ known and even more basic than a cell, is simply a packet of molecules. Although germs exist virtually everywhere, only a few cause infection. Fewer still are contagious—i.e., able to be transmitted from one animal to another. Many infectious agents are able to survive for long periods outside the host animal. This information is especially useful in controlling the spread of infectious diseases.

ANTIBODIES AND IMMUNITY

An animal immune to a specific germ has chemical substances in its system called *antibodies*, which attack and destroy that germ before it can cause an illness.

Natural immunity exists, which is species related. A cat does not catch a disease that is specific for a horse, and vice versa. Some infectious diseases are not specific. They are capable of causing illness in several species of animals.

If an animal is susceptible to an infectious disease and is exposed, it will become ill and begin to make antibodies against that particular germ. When it recovers, these antibodies afford protection against reinfection. They continue to do so for a variable length of time. It has acquired active immunity.

Active immunity can be induced artificially by vaccination. Through vaccination the animal is exposed to heat-killed germs, live and attenuated germs rendered incapable of producing disease, or toxins and germ products. They stimulate the production of antibodies that are specific for the vaccine.

Since active immunity tends to wane with the passage of time, booster shots should be given at regular intervals to maintain a high level of antibody in the system.

Antibodies are produced by the *reticuloendothelial system*, which is made up of white blood cells, lymph nodes and special cells in the bone marrow, spleen, liver and lungs. These special cells act along with antibodies and other substances in the blood to attack and destroy germs.

Antibodies are highly specific. They destroy only the type of germ that stimulated their production. Some drugs depress or prevent antibody production. They are called immunosuppressive drugs. Cortisone is such a drug.

Run-down, malnourished, debilitated cats may not be capable of responding to a challenge by developing antibodies or building immunity to germs. Such cats can be vaccinated but should be revaccinated when in a better state of health.

Kittens under two weeks of age may not be able to develop antibodies because of physical immaturity.

Passive immunity is acquired from one animal by another. A classic example is the immunity kittens acquire from the *colostrum*, or first milk of the queen. Kittens are best able to absorb these special proteins through their intestines during the first 24 to 36 hours after birth. The length of protection is dependent on the antibody level in the blood of the queen when the kittens were born. Recently vaccinated queens have the highest antibody levels. The maximum length of protection is 16 weeks. If the queen was not vaccinated against the disease, her kittens receive no protection against it.

Passive antibodies can "tie up" vaccines given to stimulate active immunity, thus rendering them ineffective. This is one reason why vaccinations do not always work in very young kittens.

Another method of providing passive antibodies is to inject a cat with a serum from another cat that has a high level of type-specific antibody. Antitoxins and antivenoms are examples of such *immune serums*.

VACCINATIONS

Vaccines are highly effective in preventing certain infectious diseases in cats, but failures do occur. They can be due to improper handling and storage, incorrect administration or inability of the cat to respond because of a run-down condition or concurrent illness that stresses the immune system. Giving too many vaccinations at the same time can cause immune overload and a failure to produce antibodies.

Stretching out the vaccine by dividing a single dose between two cats is another reason a vaccine may not work or be effective. If a cat is already infected, vaccinating it will not alter the course of the disease.

Between six and sixteen weeks of age, a window of risk exists lasting one to two weeks during which a kitten's passive antibodies are no longer fully protective but may yet interfere with the vaccination process. For this reason, nursing kittens should not be vaccinated before six weeks of age and should not complete the vaccination series before 12 to 16 weeks of age.

Because each kitten is an individual case, proper handling and administration of the vaccine is important. Vaccinations should be given only by those familiar with the technique. When you go to your veterinarian for a booster shot, your cat will get a physical checkup and fecal exam. The veterinarian may detect worm parasites or some other condition requiring treatment.

Young kittens are highly susceptible to certain infectious diseases and should be vaccinated against them as soon as they are old enough to build an immunity. These diseases are *panleukopenia, feline viral respiratory disease complex* (FVR and FCV), *feline leukemia,* and *rabies.* Vaccines against *feline infectious peritonitis* and *feline pneumonitis* (chlamydia infection) are available and may be indicated in special situations.

To be effective, vaccinations must be kept current (see *Suggested Vaccination Schedule*).

Panleukopenia (Feline Infectious Enteritis) Vaccine

The first panleukopenia shot (FPV) should be given shortly after weaning and before a kitten is placed in a new home where it may be exposed to other cats. If a kitten is at a particular risk in an area where the disease has occurred, vaccinations can be given at six weeks of age and then at two to three week intervals until 16 weeks of age. Discuss this with your veterinarian.

Two types of vaccines are available. One contains a killed virus; the other a modified live strain.

Panleukopenia vaccine is often combined with two feline viral respiratory disease vaccines and given as a single injection.

A booster given at one to two years of age may be sufficient in cats that mix with others, as exposure to the disease boosts their immunity. However, a yearly booster is a sensible precaution.

Feline Respiratory Disease Vaccines

Your veterinarian may recommend an injectable vaccine containing weakened strains of the rhinotracheitis virus (FVR) and calicivirus (FCV). Usually, they are combined with panleukopenia vaccine and given as a single injection twice, with the last vaccination not before 12 weeks of age. Vaccines also may be given as drops into the eyes and nose. Occasionally, this is followed 7 to 10 seconds later by bouts of sneezing or an eye discharge.

Although respiratory disease vaccines are highly effective, they do not prevent all cases of illness. The cat can be exposed to individual strains of virus that are not countered by the vaccine; or the infection can be so severe that it overcomes the cat's protection against it. When this happens, the disease usually is milder.

Annual booster vaccinations are advised.

Feline Chlamydia or pneumonitis vaccine (FPN) may be advisable in areas where the disease is prevalent or where many cats are living together.

Rabies Vaccine

State and city statutes establish requirements for rabies vaccinations. Since rabies is more common in cats than in dogs, all cats should be vaccinated.

There are two general types of rabies vaccines. One is a modified live virus preparation and the other is a killed virus. The safest vaccine with the fewest side effects is the killed vaccine. *DO NOT vaccinate a feline leukemia virus positive cat with live vaccine*.

The duration of rabies vaccine protection is one to three years, depending on the specific brand of vaccine employed. *All rabies vaccinations should be administered by a veterinarian*, and in many states this is the law.

Rabies vaccines cannot be given successfully before 12 weeks of age. If a kitten is vaccinated before three months of age, it should be revaccinated at six months.

Booster vaccinations are required at one- or three-year intervals, depending on the type of vaccine initially used and the manufacturer's recommendations.

A cat being shipped across some state lines must have a current rabies vaccination.

Feline Leukemia Vaccine

The development of a vaccine against retroviral infection is a long-awaited major achievement in veterinary medicine. Currently, there are five manufacturers producing FeLV vaccines. These vaccines are not 100 percent effective. It is possible that some FeLV-vaccinated cats may still become infected.

The question of ELISA testing for FeLV before vaccinating is somewhat controversial, principally because of the increased cost associated with testing. However, testing eliminates vaccination in kittens and cats shown to be virus positive and alerts the owner and veterinarian to the possible development of FeLV-related diseases. Vaccination is not effective if the cat is positive and already infected. If the ELISA test is negative, vaccinate kittens at 12 weeks of age and again at 15 or 16 weeks. The first booster is given one year later.

Although immunity is achieved more rapidly in kittens and young cats, unprotected cats of all ages free of disease should be considered for vaccination. To be effective, a full course of vaccination must be administered. This involves two vaccinations two to three weeks apart, and an annual booster.

Feline Infectious Peritonitis Vaccine

Primucell F.I.P. is a temperature sensitive modified-live virus vaccine released in 1990. It is administered intranasally. Because the effectiveness of this vaccine is still under study, it may be advisable to restrict its use to high-risk cat populations. It is important to administer this vaccine under veterinary supervision.

VACCINATION SCHEDULE

The following suggested vaccination schedule should provide adequate protection at minimum cost. It should be modified under the following circumstances:

1. Brood females that have not been immunized within a year should be given a rhinotracheitis (FVR), calicivirus (FCV) and panleukopenia (FPV) booster shot *before* being bred.

2. Live virus vaccines should not be given to pregnant queens because of possible harmful effects on the fetus. A queen that was not vaccinated before being bred can still be immunized—provided killed virus preparations are utilized.

3. Feline pneumonitis vaccine (FPN) may be indicated in certain areas. Discuss this with your veterinarian. The first vaccination is given at 9 to 10 weeks of age and the second at 14 to 16 weeks. An annual booster is required.

4. Feline infectious peritonitis vaccine (*Primucell F.I.P.*) may be indicated in high-risk cat populations. It is given in two doses three to four weeks apart, starting at 16 weeks of age. An annual booster is required.

5. If vaccinations are due to be boosted, it is strongly recommended that these vaccines be given 7 to 10 days or more before the start of boarding.

6. If the cat is first examined when it is older than 16 weeks, veterinarians recommend that it receive a series of at least two vaccinations at a three- or four-week interval for Panleukopenia, Rhinotracheitis, Calicivirus and Feline Leukemia.

7. Fecal examinations should be performed according to the same schedule for vaccinations, and appropriate deworming for roundworms and hookworms accomplished at that time.

SUGGESTED VACCINATION SCHEDULE*

Age of Cat	Vaccine Recommended
6 to 8 Weeks	Panleukopenia (FPV), Rhinotracheitis (FVR), Calicivirus (FCV)
12 Weeks	2nd FPV, FVR, FCV; Draw ELISA test for Feline Leukemia (FeLV); If ELISA negative, give 1st FeLV
16 Weeks	1st Rabies, 2nd FeLV, 3rd FPV, FVR, FCV
15 to 16 Months & Annually	FPV, FVR, FCV, FeLV, Rabies (Rabies will be repeated according to type of vaccine initially employed.)

*Note: The age of the cat, type of vaccine and route of administration influence the effectiveness of the vaccine and the number of vaccinations required. Be sure to follow your veterinarian's recommendations.

FELINE BACTERIAL DISEASES

FELINE INFECTIOUS ANEMIA

This disease is most common in male cats one to three years of age. It is caused by a rickettsial microorganism called *Hemobartonella felis*. It attaches to the surface of red blood cells and destroys these cells, producing a hemolytic anemia.

The exact method of transmission of this disease is not known. It has been suggested that it may be transferred from one cat to another by the bite of a blood-sucking insect such as a flea or by the bite of an infected cat. Unborn kittens may be infected through the placenta if the mother harbors the microorganism. Such kittens may be stillborn; or they may die within a few hours. Experimentally, the disease can be transmitted from one cat to another by a blood transfusion. Many cats in the general population carry the infection in a latent form.

Active disease can become manifest as primary or secondary Hemobartonella infection. The primary form occurs in the absence of other disease. Untreated, the death rate is 30 percent. The more common secondary form occurs in cats whose natural immunity is suppressed by the presence of a chronic debilitating disease such as *feline infectious peritonitis* or *feline leukemia*. These cats are less likely to recover.

A cat with an acute infection exhibits fever (103°F to 106°F), suffers rapid loss of appetite and condition, appears weak and lethargic and may show signs of anemia (pale gums and mucous membranes). Jaundice can occur due to rapid destruction of red blood cells. Cats that recover may become carriers and can suffer recurrent bouts of infection or chronic anemia for years.

Any cat with anemia can be suspected of having feline infectious anemia. Your veterinarian can make the diagnosis by finding hemobartonella organisms under a microscope on a smear of blood taken from the cat. At times the organisms disappear from the circulation and may not be seen. Accordingly, more than one blood smear might be required to make the diagnosis.

Treatment: Oral tetracycline is given for two to three weeks. The cat's general condition should improve with appropriate nutritional support. Blood transfusions are indicated if the anemia is severe. Associated illnesses should be treated. Steroids are sometimes prescribed if there is believed to be an autoimmune component to the anemia.

SALMONELLA

This disease is caused by a type of salmonella bacteria that produces gastrointestinal infection in susceptible animals. It tends to afflict kittens housed in crowded, unsanitary surrounding and cats whose natural resistance has been weakened by a virus infection, malnutrition or other stress.

Signs of infection are high fever, vomiting and diarrhea (90 percent of cases), dehydration and weakness. Death will occur in about half the cases. Abortions have been reported.

Cats (and dogs) often are asymptomatic carriers. Bacteria shed in their feces can, under appropriate conditions, produce active infection in domestic animals and humans.

Diagnosis is made by identifying salmonella bacteria in stool cultures (carrier state) or in the blood, feces and infected tissues of cats suffering acute infection.

Treatment: Mild uncomplicated cases respond to correction of dehydration, vomiting and diarrhea. Antibiotics (*Chloromycetin*, Sulfa drugs) are reserved for severely ill cats. Antibiotics can *favor* the growth of resistant salmonella species and prolong fecal shedding of bacteria!

Prevent the disease by housing cats under sanitary conditions where they can be well cared for and fed.

TETANUS (LOCKJAW)

This disease is caused by a bacteria called *Clostridium tetani*. It occurs in all warm-blooded animals. It is rare in cats because they possess a high natural immunity.

Bacteria enter the skin via an open wound such as a bite or puncture. A rusty nail is a classic example. But any cut or injury to the full thickness of the skin can act as a point of entry.

The tetanus bacteria is found in soil contaminated by horse and cow manure. It is present in the intestinal tract of most animals, where it does not cause a disease.

Symptoms appear 2 to 14 days after initial injury. Tetanus bacteria grow best in tissues where the oxygen level is low (anaerobic conditions). The ideal environment is a deep wound that has sealed over, or one in which there is devitalized tissue heavily contaminated with filth. The bacteria make a toxin that affects the nervous system.

Signs of disease are due to the neurotoxin. They include: spastic contractions and rigid extension of the legs; difficulty opening the mouth and swallowing; retraction of the lips and eyeballs. The tail sometimes stands straight out. Muscle spasms are triggered by almost anything that stimulates the cat. Death is caused by dehydration, exhaustion and difficulty breathing.

Treatment: Tetanus cannot be treated at home. Fatalities may at times be avoided by prompt, early veterinary care. Tetanus antitoxins, antibiotics, sedatives, intravenous fluids and care of the wound alter the course for the better. Recovery can take four to six weeks. The disease can be prevented by prompt attention to skin wounds (see EMERGENCIES: *Wounds*).

TULAREMIA

Tularemia is an uncommon disease in cats caused by the bacteria *Francisella tularensis*. It occurs naturally in wild animals, especially rodents and rabbits. Cats (and dogs) usually acquire the disease from the bite of a blood-sucking tick or flea that has fed on an infected host. Direct contact with an infected wild animal or carcass is another route of infection.

Cats with tularemia exhibit weight loss, fever, apathy and depression, lymph node enlargement and signs of pneumonia. There may be an ulcerated skin sore at the sight of inoculation (insect bite).

Treatment: Antibiotics are the treatment of choice. Tetracycline, chloramphenicol, streptomycin and gentamicin are effective.

Public Health Considerations: Infected cats can transmit the disease to humans through bites and scratches or by contact with draining skin ulcers. Tularemia is an occupational hazard for those who handle rabbit meat and pelts.

The elimination of fleas and other insect parasites reduces the likelihood of infection, as does a policy of preventing roaming and hunting. Wear rubber gloves and use strict hygienic precautions when handling cats with draining wounds.

PLAGUE

Plague (*bubonic plague*) is a devastating disease caused by the bacteria *Yersinia pestis*. About 40 cases occur in the United States each year, with some evidence that the disease is on the increase. Ninety percent of human cases occur in New Mexico, Arizona and California. New Mexico accounts for 50 percent of annually reported cases. This disease is of concern because of potential cat-to-human transmission.

In nature, plague is perpetuated through circulation of fleas from one rodent to another. Squirrels and prairie dogs are frequently infected. Cats, dogs, wild carnivores and humans are accidental hosts. Cats and other carnivores acquire the disease by mouth contact with infected rodents. Dogs are resistant to disease and rarely develop symptoms. Cats are highly susceptible, although in 50 percent of cases, the infection is mild or inapparent.

Signs of severe illness in cats appear shortly after exposure. They include high fever, loss of appetite, apathy and depression, dehydration, cough and difficulty breathing. Large swellings (*bubos*) involve the lymph nodes, especially those beneath the jaw. These swellings form abscesses that drain infective material. The death rate in severe illness is 30 percent to 50 percent.

Diagnosis is established by chest X ray, blood and tissue cultures, gram stains and serial antibody titers to *Y. pestis*.

Treatment: Great care must be taken by all people involved in the care of a plague-infected cat. Strict hygienic and isolation precautions under professional guidance are required. Hospitalization and veterinary management are imperative. Because the disease can be rapidly fatal, treatment is started before the diagnosis is confirmed by a laboratory. *Y. pestis* is susceptible to a number of antibiotics, including streptomycin and chloramphenicol (but not penicillins). Fleas and external parasites are a danger to personnel and should be rapidly extinguished by appropriate insecticide treatment.

Public Health Considerations: The most common mode of transmission to humans is the bite of an infected flea. Cats (and dogs) may transport the flea from plague-infected wildlife. Sick cats may transmit the bacteria through bites or scratches; cats with pneumonia may transmit through droplet formation from sneezing and coughing. Handling an infected cat may result in transmission through breaks in the skin or contact with mucous membranes. All individuals who have handled, contacted or participated in the care of a plague-infected animal should contact a physician immediately for consideration of prophylactic antibiotics.

Control of fleas is of prime importance (see *Fleas* in the SKIN chapter). Exposure to plague can be minimized by preventing cats from roaming and hunting. This restriction is especially important in plague-endemic areas.

TUBERCULOSIS

This rare disease in cats is caused by the *tubercle bacillus*. There are three strains of bacilli that produce disease in humans, but only the *bovine* type infects the cat. Unlike the dog, the cat is resistant to infection by the *human* tubercle bacillus; but cats are considerably more sensitive than dogs to the bovine type.

Tuberculosis in cats usually is acquired by ingesting infected cow's milk or by eating contaminated uncooked beef. Even though there has been a steady decline in tuberculosis with pasteurization of milk and elimination of this disease from dairy herds, it has not been completely wiped out.

Bovine (cattle) tuberculosis is primarily a gastrointestinal problem. Low-grade fever with chronic wasting and loss of condition despite good care and feeding is common. Abscesses form in the intestinal lymph nodes and liver. However, lung infection does occur. Occasionally, an open wound becomes infected, leading to skin involvement with draining sinuses and a discharge containing bacteria.

Respiratory tuberculosis causes rapid labored breathing, shortness of breath and production of bloody sputum.

Treatment: The finding of tubercle bacilli in the feces, in sputum or in drainage from a wound makes the diagnosis. A chest X ray may be suggestive. Treatment, which involves antituberculus drugs, is difficult and prolonged. The hazard to human health makes euthanasia the wisest choice.

FELINE VIRUS DISEASES

FELINE VIRAL RESPIRATORY DISEASE COMPLEX

Feline viral respiratory diseases are highly contagious, often serious illnesses of cats that spread rapidly through a cattery. They are one of the most common infectious disease problems a cat owner is likely to encounter. Although few adult cats die of FVR, the death rate among young kittens approaches 50 percent.

Recently, it has been recognized that two major viral groups are responsible for the majority of clinical upper respiratory infections in cats (80 percent to 90 percent). The first is the *herpes* virus group, which produces *Feline Viral Rhinotracheitis* (FVR). The second is the *Calicivirus* group, which produces *Feline Calici Viral Disease* (FCV).

At one time *Chlamydia* was considered to be a major cause of feline respiratory disease. Current research has shown that this bacteria-like organism can cause conjunctivitis and a relatively mild persistent upper respiratory disease called *Feline Pneumonitis*.

Other viral agents, especially those of the *Reovirus* group, cause feline viral respiratory illness. They account for a minority of cases.

There are two distinct stages in the feline viral respiratory disease complex. They are the *acute* stage followed by the *chronic carrier* state.

Acute Respiratory Infection

There is considerable variation in the severity of illness. Some cats have mild symptoms, while in others the disease is rapidly progressive and sometimes fatal.

Upper respiratory infection with a severely inflamed eye, characteristic of the *herpes* virus.

The disease is transmitted from cat to cat by direct contact with infected discharge from the eyes, nose, mouth; by contaminated litter pans, water bowls, and human hands; and rarely by airborne droplets. The virus is stable outside the host for as short as 24 hours or as long as 10 days.

Regardless of which virus is responsible for the infection, the initial signs are similar. The infected organism can be identified only by viral or serologic tests. These tests are not always available in time to be of use in planning treatment.

Clinical signs appear 2 to 17 days after exposure and reach maximum 10 days later. Illness begins with severe bouts of sneezing lasting 1 to 2 days. This is followed by conjunctivitis and watery discharge from the eyes and nose, which may suggest a cold or flu. However, cats do not catch human colds. By the 3rd to the 5th day a cat exhibits fever, apathy, loss of appetite. The eye/nasal discharge becomes sticky (mucoid) or puslike (purulent). Open-mouth breathing occurs in cats with obstructed nasal passages.

Further signs depend on the particular respiratory virus in question:

With *herpes* virus, the cat develops a spastic cough. If the surface of the eye is severely inflamed, the cat may develop keratitis or corneal ulcerations. These conditions are discussed in the EYES chapter.

With a *Calicivirus*, you may see ulceration of the mucous membranes of the mouth (*Stomatitis*). This is particularly disabling as the cat loses the taste for food and refuses to eat and drink. Drooling is common. Shortness of breath and viral

Ulcers on the roof of the mouth caused by the *calicivirus*.

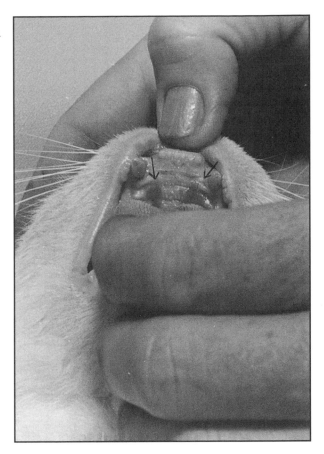

pneumonia can occur. Secondary bacterial infection, dehydration, starvation and weight loss are all complications that can lead to death.

A diagnosis can be suspected from the clinical signs. It can be confirmed by isolating the virus from the throat or by specific serologic blood tests. These tests are most important when the disease involves a cattery or a multiple-cat household.

Treatment: Cats suspected of having the disease should be strictly isolated for three to four weeks so as not to infect others.

Rest and proper humidification of the atmosphere are important. Confine your cat in a warm room and use a home vaporizer. A cold steam vaporizer offers some advantage over a heat vaporizer because it is less likely to cause additional breathing problems.

Because dehydration and loss of caloric intake seriously weaken a cat, it is important to encourage eating and drinking. Feed highly palatable food or strained baby food, diluted with water. Supplemental fluids can be given in the cheek pouch (see *How to Give Medications* in the chapter Drugs and Medications). Once the cat begins to eat and drink again, the worst of the danger is past.

Feline upper respiratory infection is a common cause of *conjunctivitis* in kittens. Typically, these eyelids are pasted shut.

Wipe secretions from the eyes, nose and mouth with moist cotton balls.

Shrink swollen nasal membranes by administering *Afrin Children's Strength Nose Drops* (.025 percent). The medicine is absorbed and works on both passages. Administer cautiously to prevent rebound congestion and excessive drying out of the mucous membranes. Administer just one drop to one nostril the first day. The next day, use the other nostril. Continue to alternate between nostrils. Use the decongestant for five to seven days.

If the cat becomes dehydrated, refuses to eat, loses weight or does not respond to home care, *seek prompt veterinary help.*

Antibiotics are important in the management of moderate to severe viral respiratory infections. They are used to prevent secondary bacterial invaders rather than to treat the respiratory virus that is insensitive to antibiotics. Ampicillin is a good choice. Antibiotics should be prescribed by a veterinarian.

Chronic Carrier State

The majority of cats that recover from the acute illness become carriers.

The herpes virus (FVR) lives and multiplies in the lining cells of the throat. During periods of stress (such as illness, anesthesia, surgery, lactation, administration of steroids) the cat's immunity breaks down and the virus is shed in mouth secretions. The cat may exhibit signs of a mild upper respiratory illness.

Calici virus can be shed continuously. Cats infected with FCV therefore present an especially serious hazard to others living on the premise. Periodic outbreaks are likely to occur.

Prevention: Separating virus-positive cats from a breeding colony or household is difficult. Several months of segregation and testing, at considerable cost and inconvenience, are required. Cats newly entering a household or cattery present a further source of potential contamination and infection. Such cats should be placed in strict isolation for 10 to 14 days and observed for signs of infection. A cat admitted as a boarder should be housed in separate quarters and handled and fed separately from the other cats. *All cats should be routinely tested for feline leukemia.* Well-ventilated surroundings and ample living space to avoid crowding are important in good cattery management.

The most effective step by far is to *vaccinate* all cats. Vaccination against FVR and FCV can be given by intramuscular or subcutaneous injection and by nose or eye drops. This oculonasal route produces solid immunity in five to six days. It also appears to increase local immunity in the eyes and nose. Vaccinate all healthy kittens using the intramuscular or subcutaneous injection in accordance with the *vaccination schedule* described earlier in this chapter.

When the queen, tom or other cats in the household are known carriers, the likelihood of causing neonatal infection in kittens is high. Inoculate the tom and queen before mating using the oculonasal route. The queen is given a second oculonasal vaccination on the day of delivery. Newborn kittens are given oculonasal vaccinations at 8 to 10 days, nine weeks, and then annually.

A *feline pneumonitis vaccine* is available but provides limited protection. Vaccinated cats can still come down with pneumonitis but usually have a shorter, milder illness. It may be advisable to use this vaccine in catteries and multiple cat households. Give according to the *vaccination schedule*.

Feline Panleukopenia (Feline Distemper)

Feline panleukopenia, also called *feline infectious enteritis*, is one of the most serious and widespread diseases. It is a leading cause of death in kittens. It has been called feline "distemper" but bears no relation to the virus that causes distemper in dogs.

Panleukopenia virus is present wherever there are susceptible animals. Mink, ferrets, raccoons and wild cats serve as a reservoir. The virus is highly contagious. It is spread by direct contact with an infected animal or its secretions. Contaminated food pans, litter boxes and the clothes or hands of personnel who have treated an infected cat are other routes of exposure.

The FPV virus is hardy. It can survive in carpets, cracks and furnishings for more than a year. It is resistant to ordinary household disinfectants but can be destroyed by a 1:32 dilution of sodium hypochlorite (bleach) in water.

Signs of acute illness appear 2 to 10 days after exposure. Early signs are loss of appetite, severe apathy and fever up to 105°F. The cat often vomits repeatedly and brings up frothy yellow-stained bile. The cat may be seen crouching in pain, the head hanging a few inches over the surface of the water bowl. If able to drink it immediately vomits. With pain in the abdomen, the cat cries plaintively.

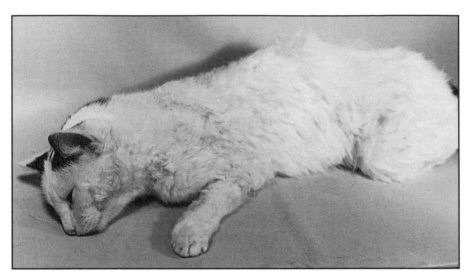

An extremely ill cat with *panleukopenia.*

Diarrhea may appear early in the disease but frequently comes on later. The stools are yellow or blood streaked. In young kittens (and some older cats) the onset can be so sudden that death occurs before the owner realizes the cat is ill. It may seem as though the cat was poisoned.

The FPV virus has a special affinity for attacking white blood cells. The reduction of circulating white cells (leukopenia) gives the disease its name.

Panleukopenia can be transmitted to kittens both before and shortly after birth. In such cases the mortality is 90 percent. Kittens recovering from neonatal infection may have cerebellar brain damage and exhibit a wobbly, jerky, uncoordinated gait that is noted when they first begin to walk. Secondary bacterial infections are common. The bacterial infection, rather than the virus itself, may be the cause of death.

Cats that survive are solidly immune to reinfection but can shed the virus for several weeks. Along with asymptomatic carriers, this leads to repeated exposure in a population of cats. It helps to boost immunity among cats that have already acquired protective antibodies.

Treatment: Detection of panleukopenia *early* in the course of the illness is of prime importance. Intensive treatment must be started at once to save the cat's life. It is better to consult your veterinarian on a "false alarm" than to wait until the cat is desperately ill. A white blood cell count serves to confirm the diagnosis. Supportive measures include fluid replacement, antibiotics, maintenance of nutrition and, occasionally, blood transfusions.

Prevention: Most cats are exposed to panleukopenia sometime during their life. Vaccination is the most effective method of preventing serious infection. Kittens should be vaccinated at 6 to 8 weeks of age and again at 10 to 12 weeks. Annual booster vaccinations are required. When a kitten is at high risk, begin vaccinating at 6 weeks and follow with vaccinations every 2 weeks until 16 weeks of age.

After vaccinating a kitten, keep it away from other cats that might carry the virus until the kitten is four months old. Wait at least three to six months before introducing a new cat into a household in which infection has occurred.

A brood queen should be vaccinated before she is bred. This can be done later if a killed vaccine is used. This builds passive antibodies that provide temporary protection for her newborn kittens.

Control measures in a household or cattery involve sanitation and good house-cleaning practices. Contaminated utensils and equipment can be disinfected by soaking them in a 1:32 dilution of sodium hypochlorite (bleach) in water.

Feline Infectious Peritonitis (FIP)

This common disease of wild and domestic cats is caused by a member of the Coronavirus group. The disease is spread from cat to cat, but requires close and continuous contact with infective secretions. The incubation period is two to three weeks or longer, but 75 percent of cats exposed experience no apparent infection. Among those that do, a mild respiratory infection, with a runny nose or eye discharge, is the most common sign. Cats that recover from mild infection can become asymptomatic carriers.

Less than 5 percent develop the secondary fatal disease known as FIP. Why some cats develop FIP and others do not is not entirely known. It is known that FIP tends to affect kittens, cats between six months and 5 years of age, and cats older than 11 years of age. There is a higher rate of infection in catteries, where conditions are apt to be crowded and greater opportunity exists for continuous and prolonged exposure. Cats that are poorly nourished, run-down or suffering from other illnesses such as *feline leukemia* are most susceptible. These factors may lower the cat's natural resistance to FIP. The strength of the particular disease, the amount of bacteria in the vaccine and the genetic predisposition of the cat may also play a role.

Feline infectious peritonitis, despite its name, is not strictly a disease of the abdominal cavity. The virus acts on capillary blood vessels throughout the body—especially those of the abdomen, chest cavity, eyes, brain, internal organs and lymph nodes. Damage to these minute blood vessels results in loss of fluid into tissues and body spaces. FIP tends to run a prolonged course. It may go on for weeks before signs are evident.

FIP OCCURS IN TWO FORMS—BOTH OF WHICH ARE INVARIABLY FATAL:

WET FORM. Early signs are nonspecific and mimic other feline disorders. They include loss of appetite, weight loss, listlessness and depression. The cat appears chronically ill. As fluid begins to accumulate in the body spaces, you may notice labored breathing from fluid in the chest or abdominal enlargement from fluid in the abdomen. Sudden death may occur from fluid in the heart sac. Other signs that accompany the wet form are fever up to 106°F, dehydration, anemia, vomiting and diarrhea. Jaundice and dark urine are caused by liver failure.

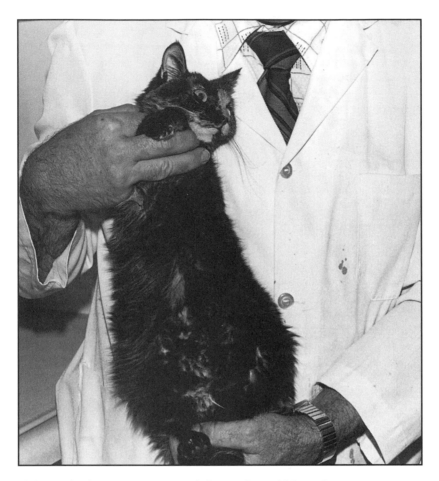

Abdominal enlargement in a cat with the wet form of feline infectious peritonitis.

DRY OR DISSEMINATED FORM. Early signs are like those of the wet form, except fluid is not produced. The disseminated form is even more difficult to diagnose. It affects a variety of organs, including the eyes (25 percent of cases), brain, liver, kidney, pancreas. At surgical exploration, which may be necessary to make the diagnosis, sticky mucus or strands of fibrous protein may be found on the surface of the liver, spleen or intestines. Ten percent to 20 percent of cats with the dry form are also infected with the feline leukemia virus.

The diagnosis of FIP can be suspected on the basis of typical clinical signs along with an abnormal blood count, liver function tests and an abnormal serum protein pattern. Analysis of peritoneal or chest fluid, if present, is helpful. Serologic blood tests to detect coronavirus antibody are not always conclusive and can lead to false positive interpretations. The only certain way to confirm the diagnosis is by organ biopsy.

Note the extreme depression, muscular wasting and prominence of the backbone.

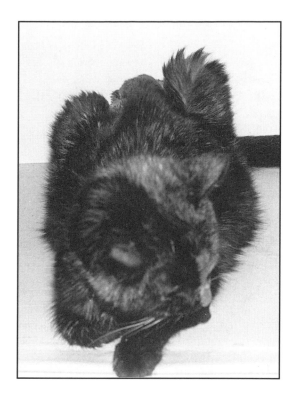

Treatment: Unfortunately, once a cat develops signs of secondary disease (either the wet or dry form), it will die within a few weeks. The cat can be made more comfortable by medications; life may be prolonged by chemotherapy or cortisone.

Prevention: An intranasal modified live vaccine (*Primucell F.I.P.*) is now available (see *Feline Infectious Peritonitis Vaccine*). Because the effectiveness of this vaccine is still under investigation, it currently is not recommended as part of the routine vaccination schedule.

As physical and environmental stresses lower a cat's immunity and increase susceptibility to the virus, it is important to maintain good nutrition, control parasites, treat health problems and groom regularly.

FIP presents its greatest hazard in multiple cat families, boarding establishments and catteries. Fortunately, the virus is easily killed by household disinfectants. Ammonia or bleach (1:32) is a good disinfectant. Disinfect cat quarters regularly. Provide a spacious enclosure for each cat and allow ample opportunity for exercise.

Routine FIP testing of all cats in a multiple cat household or cattery is advisable. However, due to the poor specificity of serologic tests used to detect coronavirus antibody, removal of healthy antibody-positive cats is justified only if there is evidence that the cat is a source of infection for other cats (for example, the queen that repeatedly produces litters of FIP-infected kittens). Kittens can be tested for coronavirus antibody at 12 to 16 weeks.

A new cat arriving in the household should be isolated for two weeks and tested for FIP. Neonatal FIP has been implicated as a cause of fading kittens. It is discussed in the PEDIATRICS chapter.

FELINE LEUKEMIA VIRUS DISEASE COMPLEX (FELV)

The feline leukemia virus is responsible for more cat diseases than any other infectious agent and is secondary only to trauma as the leading cause of death in household cats. It is the most important cause of feline cancer and significantly contributes to the severity of other cat diseases. The virus is transmitted from one cat to another by infected saliva. Sharing of water bowls, feed dishes, cat-to-cat grooming and cat bites can lead to the spread of the disease. Kittens can acquire the virus in utero and through infected milk.

The incidence of active infection is variable. Free-roaming cats have a 1 percent to 2 percent incidence. In multiple cat households and in catteries the incidence is far higher, with 20 percent to 30 percent of cats showing active viremia as determined by the presence of FeLV virus in the blood. About 50 percent show neutralizing antibodies indicating prior infection from which the cat has recovered. Repeated or continuous exposure is necessary for transmission of the disease. Virus does not appear in the blood until a cat has been exposed for at least four weeks. After 20 weeks of exposure, 80 percent of cats are infected. In others, it may take up to a year. Environmental stresses, including illness, overcrowding and poor sanitation play a role in weakening a cat's resistance to the virus and make infection more likely.

Signs of Illness. The initial illness lasts 2 to 16 weeks. Signs are nonspecific. They include fever, apathy, loss of appetite and weight. Other signs are vomiting, constipation or diarrhea. Some cats develop enlarged lymph nodes, anemia and pale mucous membranes. Death at this stage is uncommon. Having been exposed and infected, the cat has three possible outcomes. Each occurs about one-third of the time:

1. The cat develops a *transient viremia*, a free infectious virus present in blood and saliva for less than 12 weeks. This stage is followed by production of neutralizing antibodies that extinguish the disease. These cats are cured, cannot transmit the disease, have a normal life expectancy and are at no increased risk of developing FeLV-related diseases.

2. The cat develops a *persistent viremia*, a virus present in blood and saliva for over 12 weeks. Persistently viremic cats do not mount an effective antiviral immune response and are susceptible to a number of diseases that are invariably fatal. About 50 percent die within six months and 80 percent succumb within three and a half years.

3. The cat develops a *latent infection*. These cats are able to produce virus-neutralizing antibodies that eliminate virus from the blood and saliva but do not extinguish the virus completely. The virus persists in the bone marrow and in T-cell lymphocytes. Over many months, the majority of latent infected cats overcome and extinguish the virus, so the incidence of latent infection after three years is quite low. In

latent-infected cats, the disease can become activated during periods of stress or concurrent illness, leading to recurrence of viremia. Cats that remain *persistently latent* are at increased risk for developing FeLV-associated diseases.

In cats with persistent viremia the FeLV virus suppresses the cat's immunity, thereby allowing other diseases to develop. Diseases potentiated by the FeLV virus include *feline infectious peritonitis, feline infectious anemia, feline viral respiratory disease complex, toxoplasmosis*, chronic cystitis, periodontal disease, and opportunistic bacterial infections. The virus can also cause bone marrow suppression with anemia and spontaneous bleeding. Maternally transmitted infection is responsible for some cases of reproductive failure, including repeated abortion, stillbirth, fetal resorption and fading kitten syndrome. A small percentage of cats with persistent viremia develop a virus-related cancer months to years after exposure. *Lymphosarcoma* is the most common variety. One or more painless masses may be felt in the abdomen. There may be enlargement of lymph nodes in the groin, armpit, neck or chest. The cancer may spread to the eye, brain, skin, kidney and other organs, producing a variety of symptoms.

Leukemia is another malignant transformation. It is defined as rapid and uncontrolled growth of white blood cells. It may be accompanied by anemia and other changes in the blood-cell picture. It is much less common than lymphosarcoma.

Diagnosis. Presently two tests are available to detect FeLV infection:

1. The IFA test, performed by a reference laboratory, detects virus antigen in infected white blood cells. This indicates that the bone marrow is infected and there is a high probability the cat is viremic and shedding the virus in its saliva, therefore infective to other cats. About 97 percent of IFA-positive cats remain viremic for life and never extinguish the virus.

2. The ELISA test detects virus antigen in whole blood, serum, saliva and tears. A rapid screening leukemia test kit is available for home and clinic use. The ELISA test is more likely to detect weak, early or transient infections.

The common practice is to screen for FeLV using the ELISA test. If positive, the cat may have a transient viremia from which it will recover completely, or it may be in the early stages of a progressive infection. A positive ELISA test should be confirmed with an IFA. A positive IFA indicates that the cat is shedding virus and is capable of infecting others.

The ELISA test should be repeated in 8 to 12 weeks to see if the virus has been eliminated. The IFA should also be repeated at this time because if the cat was in an early stage of infection, the IFA initially may not have been positive but may become so after 12 weeks.

Cats with *latent infection* test negative on both the ELISA and IFA tests. This is because the virus is absent in both serum and white cells. The only way to make a diagnosis of latent infection is to remove a sample of the cat's bone marrow containing the dormant virus and grow the cells in culture.

Treatment: Despite research, there is no effective treatment for FeLV now. Cancers produced by the FeLV virus are not curable. Early diagnosis may allow successful relief, but not cure, in some individuals. Treatment includes the administration of antibiotics, vitamin-mineral supplements, transfusions and anticancer drugs. Cats that respond to the medications may be made more comfortable, and their lives may be prolonged. Unfortunately, there is no way to tell which cats are likely to respond. Such cats will continue to shed virus and thus present a hazard to the health of others with whom they come in contact. Many veterinarians advise putting a cat to sleep as soon as the diagnosis of cancer is confirmed.

Prevention: Control of FeLV depends on vaccination and accurate identification and removal of all virus-positive cats from multiple cat households and catteries. FeLV vaccines are not as effective as some vaccines such as the rabies vaccine but do provide important protection (see *Feline Leukemia Vaccine*).

Kittens born to immune queens acquire protective antibodies in the *colostrum* (or first milk) of the queen. This protection begins to disappear at 6 to 12 weeks of age, after which kittens are susceptible to infection and should be vaccinated.

Before giving the first vaccination, all kittens should be ELISA tested. If the test is negative, give the first vaccination at 12 weeks of age and the second vaccination 2 to 3 weeks later (see *vaccination schedule*). An annual booster is required.

The following steps may prevent spread of infection in a cattery or isolated cat colony:

1. Do not introduce new cats into the group.
2. IFA test all cats on the premises and repeat the test in three months. Remove all cats testing positive after each test.
3. All cats with two negative tests are considered free of active disease and not likely to transmit disease to other cats. Retest annually.
4. Do not allow new cats into the colony until they have been quarantined, tested twice (three months apart) and found negative.
5. Toms and queens should be certified free of virus before being used for breeding.
6. Clean and disinfect the house and cat quarters with ordinary household detergents or bleach solution. The FeLV virus is not hardy and is easily killed. Be sure to disinfect spots the cat might have soiled with urine, saliva or feces.

There is no evidence that FeLV has ever caused an illness in humans. However, the virus does replicate in human tissue cells in the laboratory. In theory, children and patients with immune deficiency diseases could be at risk. As a sensible precaution, such individuals and women of child-bearing age are advised to avoid contact with virus-positive cats.

FELINE IMMUNODEFICIENCY VIRUS INFECTION (FIV)

The feline immunodeficiency virus, first discovered in a northern California cattery in 1986, is a major cause of chronic immunodeficiency in cats. FIV is a retrovirus

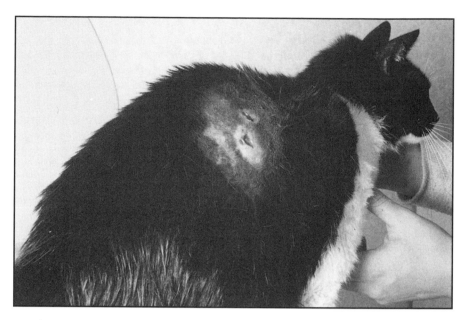

FIV infection is believed to be transmitted by cat bites such as the one causing this infected wound.

belonging to the *lentivirus* family. It is related to the AIDS virus in humans (HIV). However, these two viruses are species specific. *HIV does not produce disease in cats, and FIV does not produce disease in humans.*

Although its exact incidence has yet to be determined, FIV has been found in cats throughout the United States and is believed to affect 1 percent to 3 percent of cats in the general population. The incidence is highest in outdoor cats and in males 5 to 10 years of age. This suggests that cat bites, occurring during fights among toms, are a source of virus inoculation. *Close or casual contact alone is not a major mode of transmission.* There is no evidence that the disease is transmitted by mating.

Signs of Illness. Four to six weeks after FIV exposure, there is acute illness characterized by fever and swelling of lymph nodes. The white count is below normal. Diarrhea, skin infections and anemia can occur. After the acute infection, there is a latent period from several months up to three years, after which signs of a chronic immunodeficiency syndrome appear gradually and progress slowly (again, over a period of months or years).

Cats with chronic FIV infection present with a variety of unexplained signs of ill health, including severe mouth and gum disease; long-standing diarrhea; loss of appetite and weight with emaciation; fever; recurrent upper respiratory infections with eye and nasal discharge; ear canal infections; and recurrent urinary tract infections. These signs are similar to those associated with other immunodeficiency disorders such as *feline leukemia*, severe malnutrition, immunosuppressive drug therapy and widespread cancer.

Diagnosis. If *antibody* to FIV is found in the cat's serum using an ELISA test, it can be assumed that the cat is persistently viremic and a source of infection to other cats. However, all ELISA positive tests should be confirmed with another test such as an IFA or Western Blot Immunoassay, performed at a reference laboratory.

There are two occasions in which these tests may prove false negative. One is during the terminal stages of FIV when the cat is unable to produce detectable antibodies. The other is during the early stages when virus is present in the serum but antibodies have not yet been produced. In the latter case, the cat can be retested in two to three months.

False positive tests can occur in kittens that receive antibodies in the milk of an infected queen. Retest kittens 12 to 14 weeks later to determine if they are infected.

Treatment: There is no effective treatment for FIV virus infection now. However, the current massive effort to develop drugs to cure AIDS in humans involves FIV infection in cats as an animal research model. As this research evolves, it can be anticipated that effective treatment for cats may become available in the future. Drugs used in the treatment of AIDS may provide benefit in selected individuals. However, these drugs, especially AZT, are more toxic to cats than to humans.

Prevention: Currently, there is no vaccine available for FIV. *The most effective method of preventing the disease is to keep cats from roaming and fighting with infected strays.* This will dramatically lower the likelihood of infection. Neutering males may reduce the incidence of fighting. All cats in a multicat household should be tested. FIV-positive cats should be removed or isolated from contact with others.

CAT SCRATCH DISEASE

Cat scratch fever is included in this discussion because of its relationship to cats and the considerable cost and concern in its diagnosis and treatment. Cat scratch disease affects about 22,000 people each year, with the majority occurring in the months September through January. Patients, especially children and young adults, commonly present with enlarged tender lymph nodes of unknown cause of several weeks duration. These patients often undergo lymph node biopsy to rule out lymphoma, a condition unrelated to cat scratch disease. Once thought to be caused by a virus, the majority of cases are now believed to be caused by a newly described rickettsial organism called *Rochalimaea henselae*. A smaller number of cases may be caused by a gram negative bacteria named *Afipia felis*. Both have been found in infected tissue of patients with cat scratch disease.

The cat, an asymptomatic carrier of the infection, is able to transmit the disease to humans only during a two to three week period. In 90 percent of cases there is a history of a bite, lick or scratch (usually from a kitten). This suggests the infective organism is carried in the cat's mouth and may be transferred to its claws during self-grooming. Three to 10 days after exposure, a raised red sore develops at the site of transmittal. This occurs in about 50 percent of cases. There may be a red streak up the arm or leg. In all cases there is tender enlargement of lymph nodes in the armpit, neck or groin. The lymphadenopathy may persist for two to five months.

Less than 5 percent of those infected develop generalized signs such as low grade fever, fatigue, headache and loss of appetite. In rare cases there is involvement of the spleen, brain, joints, eyes, lungs and other organs. In immunosuppressed individuals the disease can be life threatening.

Treatment: Consult your physician and follow his or her recommendations for diagnostic tests and treatment.

Prevention: Wash all bites and cat scratches promptly. Do not allow cats to lick open wounds.

There is no way to tell when a particular cat harbors the infection. If one family member becomes ill, quarantine the cat for two to three weeks to prevent it from infecting others. As a precaution, sick children and immunodeficient individuals should avoid contact with cats under one year of age. Because of the dual potential for transmission (bites, scratches) and the brief period during which cats are infective, routine declawing of cats to prevent human illness is not recommended.

RABIES

Rabies is a fatal disease occurring in nearly all warm-blooded animals, although rarely among rodents. The main source of infection to humans is a bite from an infected animal. The effectiveness of rabies control programs in dogs makes cats more likely to transmit rabies. Other wild carnivores, especially skunks, raccoons, bats and foxes, serve as a reservoir, accounting for the occasional case. Ninety percent of cats with rabies are under three years old, and the majority are male. Rural cats are at the highest risk for rabies because of the potential for wildlife exposure.

The virus, which is present in an infected animal's saliva, usually enters at the site of a bite. Saliva on an open wound or mucous membrane also constitutes exposure to rabies. The incubation period can be 9 to 60 days, but usually signs appear within 15 to 25 days of exposure. The virus travels to the brain along nerve networks. *The further the bite is from the brain, the longer the incubation period.* The virus then travels back along nerves to the mouth, where it enters the saliva.

Signs and symptoms of rabies are due to inflammation of the brain (encephalitis). During the first (or *prodromal*) stage, lasting one to three days, signs are quite subtle and consist of personality changes. Affectionate and sociable cats often become increasingly irritable or aggressive and may bite repeatedly at the site where the virus entered the body. Shy and less outgoing cats may become overly affectionate. Soon, affected animals become withdrawn and stare off into space. They avoid light and may hide and die without ever being discovered.

There are two characteristic forms of encephalitis: the so-called **furious** form and the **paralytic** form. A rabid cat may show signs of one or both.

The *furious* form, or the "mad dog" type of rabies, is the most common. It lasts two to four days. A rabid cat can actually be more dangerous than a rabid dog, springing up suddenly and attacking people about the face and neck. Soon the cat develops muscle twitching, tremors, staggering, hind leg incoordination and violent convulsions.

The *paralytic* form, occurring in 30 percent of cases, causes the swallowing muscles to become paralyzed. The cat drools, coughs and paws at its mouth. As encephalitis progresses, the cat loses control of the rear legs, collapses and is unable to get up. Death from respiratory arrest occurs in one to two days. Because of the rapid course of rabies, paralysis may be the only sign noted.

Public Health Considerations: *Do not pet, handle or give first aid to any animal suspected of having rabies.* All bites of *wild* animals, whether or not provoked, should be regarded as having the potential for rabies. Rodent bites also should be evaluated, although rodents rarely have rabies.

The World Health Organization has established certain guidelines for practitioners to follow in the appropriate management of people who are exposed to a potentially rabid animal. The treatment schedule depends on the type of exposure (lick, bite), the severity of the injury and the condition of the animal at the time of exposure and during a subsequent observation period of ten days.

If there is the slightest possibility that a dog or cat is rabid, and if there has been any human contact, *impound the animal immediately and consult your physician and veterinarian. This is true even if the animal is known to have been vaccinated for rabies.* In the case of a feral cat that can't be trapped or impounded, kill the cat immediately. Should the cat escape, there is no way to prove it was not rabid, and postexposure rabies vaccine may have to be given.

When an animal is killed or dies during confinement, the brain is removed and sent to a laboratory equipped to diagnose rabies from special antibody studies. *The only definite determination of rabies is through autopsy.*

Guide to Postexposure Rabies Prophylaxis. It is of utmost importance to promptly cleanse all animal bites and scratches, washing them thoroughly with soap and water. Studies in animals have shown that local wound cleansing greatly reduces the risk of rabies.

The introduction of inactivated vaccines grown in human diploid cell cultures has improved the effectiveness and safety of postexposure vaccination. When vaccination is indicated, it should begin as soon as possible after the exposure. *Vaccination is not effective once early signs of rabies are present.*

Preexposure Immunization. Preventive vaccinations are available for high-risk groups, including veterinarians, animal handlers, cave explorers and laboratory workers.

Treatment and Prevention: There is *no effective treatment* for cats. Be sure your pet is properly vaccinated. It is important that cats are vaccinated only under the supervision of a veterinarian. Furthermore, a veterinarian can provide legal proof of vaccination should the need arise.

There are two types of rabies vaccines: modified live virus vaccines and killed or inactivated vaccines. Depending on the manufacturer and type of vaccine, booster shots are given annually or every three years. Modified live vaccines should never be given to cats with *feline leukemia, feline immunodeficiency virus disease* and cats that are otherwise immunosuppressed. In these individuals, the vaccine may actually cause rabies. Killed vaccines with a three year duration of immunity are now available and are licensed for use in cats. The three year inactivated preparations may be preferable to all others in that they preclude the possibility of vaccine-induced disease and increase the proportion of immunized cats at any single time.

Regardless of which product is used, give the first vaccination between 3 and 6 months of age. The cat should be revaccinated 12 months later and then annually or every three years, depending on the recommendations of the manufacturer.

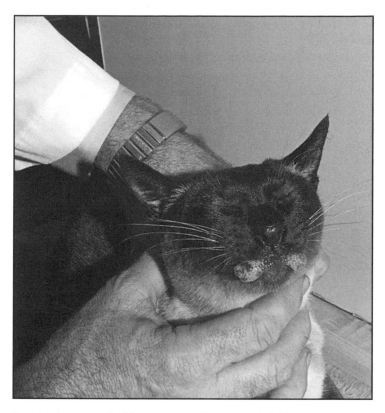

Pseudorabies is typified by excessive drooling and slobbering.

PSEUDORABIES

This disease bears no actual relationship to rabies; however, it can at times be confused with the *furious* form of that disease. It is caused by a herpes virus that infects dogs and cats and is not common in the United States.

Pigs, cows, rats and some other domestic animals appear to serve as a reservoir for the virus. The disease can be produced by eating an infected rat or by consuming infected uncooked beef or pork.

Pseudorabies is an acute, highly fatal disease that involves the nervous system and comes on two to nine days after exposure. The first signs are restlessness followed almost at once by intense pain. In the classic form, the cats meow and crouch down in agony. They may drool excessively and act as though there were something caught in the throat. Intense itching on the head, shoulders or within the mouth develops, sites where the virus apparently entered the cat's system. The cat scratches frantically and turns the area raw. In a short time the animal staggers about, collapses and falls into a coma. An atypical form occurs in which the signs are less noticeable. The cat is able to swallow but exhibits fever and is severely withdrawn.

Cats with the classic form die within 24 to 36 hours; cats with the atypical form may live somewhat longer.

Symptoms of pseudorabies may at first suggest the possibility of rabies, but the shorter course (matter of hours), lack of vicious attacks and the intolerable itching distinguish the two conditions. Pseudorabies does not present a hazard to human health. There is no evidence that the disease is transmitted from cat to cat.

No vaccine is available for the protection of dogs and cats in the United States. The only control is to prevent pets from roaming and coming into contact with infected rats and livestock and eating raw meat.

FUNGUS DISEASES

Fungus diseases can be divided into two categories. In the *first* **the fungus affects just the skin** or mucous membranes. Examples are *ringworm* and *thrush*. In the *second* **the disease is widespread,** involving the liver, lungs, brain and other organs, in which case it is called *systemic*. These diseases are caused by fungi that live in soil and organic material. Spores, which resist heat and can live for long periods without water, gain entrance through the respiratory system or through the skin at the site of a puncture.

Systemic fungal diseases tend to occur in chronically ill or poorly nourished cats. Prolonged treatment with steroids or antibiotics may change an animal's pattern of resistance and allow a fungus infection to develop. Some cases are associated with the immune depressant effects of *feline leukemia, feline panleukopenia* and *feline immunodeficiency virus*.

Fungal diseases are difficult to recognize and treat. X rays, biopsies, fungus cultures, and serologic blood tests are used to make a diagnosis. Suspect a fungus when an unexplained infection fails to respond to a full course of antibiotics. Although many systemic fungal agents infect humans and cats, only *Sporotrichosis* has been shown to infect humans following direct exposure to infected cats.

CRYPTOCOCCOSIS

This disease, caused by the yeastlike fungus *Cryptococcus neoformans*, is the most common fungal infection of cats. It tends to occur in middle-aged cats. It is acquired by inhaling spores found in soil heavily contaminated by bird droppings, especially those of pigeons. The likelihood of infection is increased if the cat has an immune deficiency condition. However, not all cats that develop cryptococcosis are immune depressed.

The two common forms of disease are nasal and cutaneous cryptococcosis.

Nasal infection occurs in 50 percent of cases. Signs are sneezing, snuffling, a mucoid to bloody discharge from one or both nostrils, cough and obstructed breathing. Flesh-colored polyp-like growths may protrude from the nose. The infection may extend to the brain and cause fatal meningitis.

Cutaneous cryptococcosis, which occurs in 25 percent of cases, frequently produces a firm swelling over the bridge of the nose. In other forms nodules, which ulcerate and drain pus, occur beneath the skin of the body.

The diagnosis is made by fungus culture or tissue biopsy. A cryptococcus antigen serology test is available.

Treatment: Oral antifungal drugs of the imidazole group such as Ketoconazole are effective when started early in the course of disease. These drugs are slow acting. Treatment is prolonged. There are no documented cases of transmission from cats to people.

HISTOPLASMOSIS

This disease is caused by a fungus found in the central United States near the Great Lakes, the Appalachian Mountains, Texas and the valleys of the Mississippi, Ohio and St. Lawrence Rivers. In these areas, a nitrogen rich soil facilitates growth of the causative fungus (*Histoplasma capsulatum*).

In the majority of cats histoplasmosis is an insidious disease with fever, loss of appetite, weakness, weight loss and debilitation. Respiratory, eye and skin involvement can occur. Diagnosis is made by fungus culture or tissue biopsy. Successful treatment with antifungal drugs depends on early diagnosis. Despite treatment, most cats succumb to this infection.

SPOROTRICHOSIS

This uncommon skin infection is caused by fungus spores in the soil. These spores usually gain access through a break in the skin. Other routes of infection are by ingestion or inhalation of spores. The disease is most common among male cats that prowl in thorny underbrush or sharp prairie grass. Most cases are reported in the northern and central portions of the United States.

A nodule forms at the site of a skin wound, usually on the feet and legs, face or base of the tail. The hair over the nodule falls out, leaving a moist ulcerated surface. In some cases there is little surface reaction, but you may see several small firm nodules beneath the skin that appear to form a chain.

On rare occasions the disease spreads internally to the liver and lungs. In these individuals the outlook for cure is guarded. The diagnosis is made by removing a piece of tissue and examining it under the microscope; or more conclusively, by growing the fungus in culture.

Treatment: The response to treatment is excellent when disease is limited to the skin and surrounding tissues. Potassium iodide is the agent of choice. Ketoconazole and Itraconazole also have been used. Amphotericin B is used for internal infection. These drugs have toxic potential and require close veterinary management.

Public Health Considerations: Sporotrichosis has been known to infect humans handling cats with infective drainage from nodules and ulcers. Wear rubber gloves and use strict hygienic precautions when handling cats with draining wounds.

ASPERGILLOSIS

This fungus is found in decaying vegetation and organic-rich soils. Aspergillosis has usually been reported in immunodeficient cats with concurrent *feline panleukopenia*. Nasal infection similar to that of *cryptococcosis* and systemic involvement like that of *histoplasmosis* have been described. Treatment involves use of antifungal drugs. It is rarely successful.

BLASTOMYCOSIS

This disease is found along the eastern seaboard, Great Lakes region and Mississippi, Ohio and St. Lawrence River valleys. The fungus has been isolated from cedar trees and pigeon droppings. Cats are more resistant to blastomycosis than are dogs and humans. Most cases of blastomycosis in cats have involved the respiratory system, skin, eye and brain. Diagnosis is established by biopsy of infected tissue or culture of infected drainage. A variety of serologic tests are available.

Treatment: Amphotericin B is the drug of choice. Ketoconazole recently has been used with some success. Treatment is complicated, and drug toxicity is a distinct problem in cats.

The hazard to human health is minimal. Accidental inoculation of organisms is possible. Humans have contracted blastomycosis from dog bites.

PROTOZOAN DISEASES

Protozoans are one-celled organisms invisible to the naked eye but seen under the microscope. A fresh stool specimen is required (fecal flotation).

The life cycle of protozoans is complicated. Basically, infection results from the ingestion of the cyst form (*oocyst*). Cysts invade the lining of the bowel, where they mature into adult forms and are shed in the feces. Under favorable conditions they develop into the infective form.

COCCIDIOSIS

Coccidiosis usually targets young kittens shortly after weaning, although adult cats can be affected. The disease is highly contagious. Immunity following recovery from infection is short lived. Cats that recover often become carriers and shed adult oocysts in their feces.

There are several species of coccidia. Only *Isospora felis* is directly transmitted by fecal contamination from cat to cat. Other species use birds and animals as intermediate transport hosts. These species complete their life cycle when the transport host is eaten by the cat. Kittens acquire *Isospora felis* from mothers who are carriers.

Five to seven days after ingestion of oocysts, infective cysts appear in the feces. *Diarrhea is the most common sign of infection.* The feces are mucus-like and tinged with blood. In severe cases, a hemorrhagic diarrhea may develop. These cases are complicated by weakness, dehydration and anemia.

Coccidia can be found in the stools of kittens, without causing problems, until some stress factor such as overcrowding, malnutrition, weaning problems, an outbreak of roundworms or shipping reduces their resistance.

Treatment: Stop the diarrhea with *Kaopectate*. A severely dehydrated or anemic cat may need to be hospitalized for fluid replacement or blood transfusion.

Supportive treatment is important since in most cases the acute phase of the illness lasts about 10 days and is followed by recovery. Sulfonamides and nitrofurazone are the antibiotics of choice.

Known carriers should be isolated and treated. Cat quarters and runs should be washed daily with Lysol and *boiling* water to destroy infective oocysts.

TOXOPLASMOSIS

This disease is caused by the protozoan *Toxoplasma gondii*. Cats are likely to acquire the infection from consuming infected birds or rodents or by ingesting oocysts in contaminated soil.

Evidence strongly suggest that cats (and people) can also get the disease from eating raw or undercooked pork, beef, mutton or veal that contains toxoplasma organisms. The feces of infected cats present another source of infection. Cats and humans can transmit toxoplasma in utero to their unborn offspring.

Feline toxoplasmosis usually is without symptoms. When symptomatic, it affects the brain, eyes, lymphatic system and lungs. The most common signs are loss of appetite, lethargy, cough and rapid breathing. Other signs are fever, weight loss, diarrhea and swelling of the abdomen. Lymph nodes may enlarge. Kittens may exhibit encephalitis, liver insufficiency or pneumonia. Prenatal infection may be responsible for abortion, stillbirths and unexplained perinatal deaths.

Serologic tests (including an ELISA) will show whether a cat has ever been exposed. A positive test in a healthy cat signifies that the cat has acquired active immunity and is unlikely to be a source of human contamination. The finding of *T. gondii* oocysts in the cat's stool indicates the cat is infective to other cats and people.

The most serious danger to human health is congenital toxoplasmosis. About half the human adult population shows serological evidence of having been exposed in the past. Men and women with protective antibodies probably will be immune to infection. However, the disease is a particular hazard when a pregnant woman without prior immunity is exposed to it. Maternal toxoplasmosis can result in abortion, stillbirth and birth of babies with central nervous system infection. Pregnant women should take precautions to avoid contact with fecal material from cats.

Treatment: Antibiotics are available to treat active infection and prevent the intestinal phase of oocyst shedding.

Public Health Considerations: *Prevent the disease by keeping your cat from roaming and hunting.* Wear disposable plastic gloves when handling the cat's litter. Remove stools from the litter box daily. Dispose of the litter carefully so that others will not come into contact with it. Clean and disinfect litter trays every two or three days using boiling water or 10 percent ammonia solution—or better yet, use disposable liners. Cover children's sandboxes when not in use to keep them from being a potential source of infection. Cook all fresh meat, both yours and your cat's, maintaining a temperature of at least 150°F (medium well). Wash hands with soap and water after handling raw meat. Clean all kitchen surfaces making contact with raw meat.

FELINE CYTAUXZOON

This is a fatal protozoan disease, now known to be transmitted by *ixodid ticks*. It was first described in 1976 in southwest Missouri. Cases have been reported throughout the southern United States, extending from Oklahoma and Texas to Florida. The highest incidence occurs in summer, when ticks are most numerous.

The cytauxzoon organism attacks red blood cells and those of the reticuloendothelial system. Symptoms include high fever, anemia, jaundice and dehydration. Death occurs within two weeks. The diagnosis is made by staining a blood smear and examining it under a microscope, looking for characteristic ring-form protozoans inside red blood cells.

Antibiotics may prolong the course of illness but survival is rare. Infected cats do not transmit the disease to other cats or people. In areas where the disease is known to occur, prevent your cat from roaming and hunting during the tick season.

4

SKIN

GENERAL INFORMATION

Skin disease is a common problem in cats, and the condition of the skin can often tell you a great deal about your cat's general health and condition.

Unlike human skin, your cat's skin is thinner and more sensitive to injury. It is easily damaged by careless or rough handling or with the wrong kind of grooming equipment. Because this skin is loosely applied to the underlying muscle, most bites and lacerations are rather superficial.

There are many functions served by the skin. Without an intact skin, water from the cat's tissues would quickly evaporate, draining the cat of body heat and water and leading to death from cold and dehydration. Skin is a barrier that keeps out bacteria and other foreign agents and is involved in the synthesis of essential vitamins. Skin provides sensation to the surface of the body, gives form to the body and insulates the cat against extreme heat and cold.

The outer layer is the *epidermis*. It is a scaly layer varying in thickness in different parts of the cat's body. It is thick and tough over the nose and foot pads and thin and most susceptible to injury in the creases of the groin and beneath the "arms."

The *dermis* is the next layer inward. Its main function is to supply nourishment to the epidermis. It also gives rise to the *skin appendages*, which are hair follicles, sebaceous glands, sweat glands and toenails. They are modifications of the epidermis to serve special functions.

Longhaired cats need to be brushed every day to keep coat from matting and tangling and to lessen the possibility of hairballs.
—Sydney Wiley

Groom a shorthaired cat once or twice a week to remove loose hair and to keep the skin and coat free of parasites.
—Sydney Wiley

The skin follicles produce three different types of hair. The first, called primary hair, is exemplified by long *guard hair*, which makes up the top coat. Each guard hair grows from its own individual root. Tiny muscles connected to the roots of guard hairs enable the cat to fluff out its coat in cold weather, thus trapping warm air and providing better insulation. Secondary hair or *underfur* is much more abundant. Its function is to provide added warmth and protection. Secondary hair grows in groups from a single opening in the dermis. This type can be further subdivided into awn hair and wool hair. Whiskers, eyelashes and *carpal hair* (found on the backs of the front legs) comprise the third type of hair, which is especially modified to serve the sense of touch. The whiskers are long stiff hairs that can be fanned out to make contact with the surroundings. Along with other tactile hair, they supplement the cat's keen sense of smell and hearing. They aid in the detection of air currents and are of importance in sensing and investigating objects close to the cat.

The function of sebaceous glands is to secrete an oily substance called *sebum*, which coats and waterproofs the hair, giving the coat a healthy shine. Skin oil is influenced by hormone levels in the blood. Large amounts of the the female hormone estrogen reduce oil production, while small amounts of the male hormone androgen increase it.

Specialized *apocrine sweat glands*, found all over the body but particularly at the base of the tail and on the sides of the face, produce a milky fluid whose scent may be involved in sexual attraction.

In humans, the skin is well supplied with *eccrine sweat glands*, which help to regulate loss of heat from the body through evaporation. In the cat, eccrine sweat glands are found only on the foot pads. They secrete when the cat is overheated, frightened or excited, leaving damp footprints.

Moisture at the tip of the nose is not caused by sweat but by fluid secreted from the mucous membrane of the nostrils. A cat cools itself by panting and licking its fur. Cooling results from the evaporation of water.

Nails and foot pads are other specialized structures of the epidermis. The front paws are equipped with five toe pads and five claws plus two metacarpal pads that normally do not make contact with the ground. The back feet have four toe pads and four claws plus a large metatarsal pad. The claws can be retracted beneath the skin folds.

The skin of the foot pads is rough for traction and extraordinarily thick—75 *times thicker than on other parts of the body*. Yet it is remarkably sensitive to touch. A cat will extend one paw and gently feel an unfamiliar object to test the size, texture and distance from the cat's own body. Such tactile sensitivity is because of the numerous touch organs located in the deeper layers of a cat's pads.

A cat's toenails are composed of keratin, a solid protein-like substance encased in a hard sheath (*cuticle*). Beneath it is the *quick*, or pink part of the claw, containing blood vessels, nerves and the germinal cells that are responsible for growth. Nails grow continuously. When not worn down by activity or self-grooming, they should be trimmed.

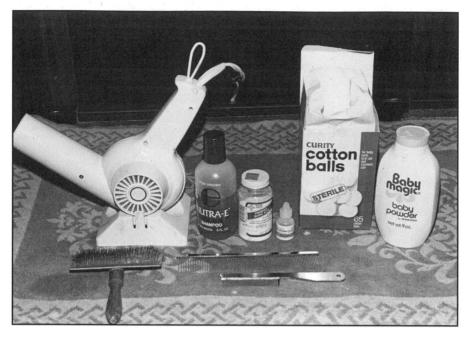

Grooming and bathing equipment.

BASIC COAT CARE

GROWING A COAT

The growth of a cat's coat is controlled by a number of factors. Some cats, by selective breeding, carry a more abundant or more stylish coat.

Cat hair grows in cycles. Each follicle has a period of rapid growth followed by a slower one and then a resting phase. Cat hair grows about one-third of an inch each month. During the resting phase in midwinter, mature hair remains in the follicles but becomes detached at the base. In late spring, the cycle begins anew. Young hair pushes out the old, which is shedding.

Too much female hormone in the system can slow the growth of hair. Too little thyroid hormone often impairs the growth, texture and luster of a cat's coat. Ill health, run-down condition, hormone imbalance, vitamin deficiency or parasites on the cat or within the cat's system may cause the coat to be too thin and brittle. If you suspect that your cat's coat is below par, you should see a veterinarian.

The environment has a definite influence on the thickness and abundance of the coat. Cats living outdoors continuously in cold weather grow a heavy coat for insulation and protection. Some additional fat in the diet is desirable at this time because fat supplies a better source of energy than do protein and carbohydrates. Fat also aids absorption of fat soluble vitamins, provides essential fatty acids for healthy skin and coat and improves the palatability of food. Commercial concentrated fatty acid supplements are available. As an alternative, you can mix equal parts of animal fat (bacon drippings, chicken fat, pork lard) and vegetable oils (safflower, corn oils). Feed one-quarter teaspoon per meal, and increase by one-quarter teaspoon weekly. When stools become soft, the cat's diet is too high in fat.

As a precaution, *do not* add fat supplements to the diet of a cat with pancreatitis, gallstones or malabsorption syndrome. Excess fat supplements can interfere with the metabolizing of Vitamin E. Before making long-term adjustments in the diet's fat content, read the chapter on FEEDING AND NUTRITION and discuss such adjustments with your veterinarian.

SHEDDING

Many people believe that it is the seasonal temperature change that governs when a cat sheds. In fact, shedding is influenced more by changes in surrounding light. The more the exposure to light, the greater the shedding. This applies to both the neutered and the intact cat.

For cats spending all their time outdoors, the longer hours of sunlight in late spring activate a shedding process lasting for many weeks. Cats that go outdoors part of the day normally shed and grow a new coat at the beginning of summer. In fall, as the days grow shorter, the coat begins to thicken for winter. Indoor cats exposed to constant light may shed and grow a coat year-round.

Most cats have a double coat composed of long, coarse outer guard hair and a soft, fine woolly undercoat. The Rex breed is an exception. Rex cats have a single coat made of fine curly hair. These cats shed very little.

When a cat with a double coat begins to shed, its appearance may be quite alarming and at first suggests a skin disease. This is because undercoat is shed in a mosaic or patchy fashion, giving a moth-eaten look. This is perfectly normal. Cats do not shed their coats evenly or in waves.

When shedding begins, prevent skin irritation by removing as much dead hair as possible by daily brushings.

HOW TO AVOID COAT AND SKIN PROBLEMS

GROOMING AND COAT CARE

The cat's tongue has a spiny surface that acts much like a comb. As cats groom themselves, saliva wets the fur, which is then licked dry, catching dirt and pulling out loose hair. Mothers teach their kittens how to do this while still in the nest. When two cats live together, grooming often becomes a mutual activity.

Even though your cat keeps relatively clean, brush it regularly. The more hair you remove, the less can be licked off, swallowed or shed. *This helps to reduce the problem of hairballs.* Frequent grooming also keeps the coat sleek and glowing, free of parasites and other skin problems.

Kittens should be groomed daily, beginning shortly after they are weaned. This is good training. An adult cat unaccustomed to grooming can present a difficult problem when tangles and mats must be removed. Keep the sessions relatively brief.

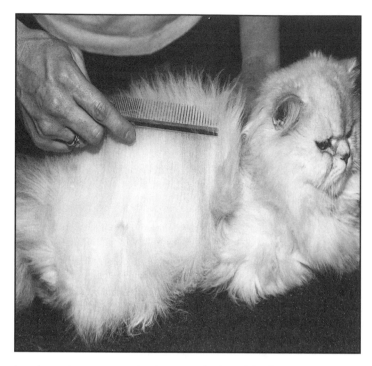

Longhaired cats are combed *against* the lay of the hair.

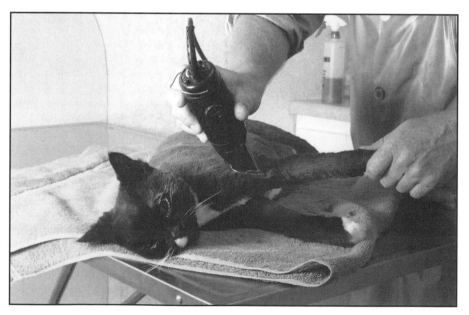

Shearing may be necessary if the coat becomes too matted to comb.

If the kitten learns to dislike the basic routine, then a simple procedure becomes difficult.

How often to groom an older cat depends on the thickness and length of coat and the condition of the hair and skin. Shorthaired cats usually need less grooming. Once a week may be sufficient. Longhaired cats with thick coats—Persians, Himalayans and Angoras—should be combed every day to keep their coats from matting and tangling.

Grooming tools are listed below. The choice depends on the breed or variety of cat and the type of coat.

Grooming Table should be solid with a nonslippery surface. If the table is the correct height, you can work on your cat comfortably without having to bend. Some people prefer to hold their cat on their lap.

Comb should have smooth round teeth designed especially to avoid trauma to the skin. You should have a narrow-toothed comb to remove dirt and fleas. A wide-toothed comb is best for grooming long hair. You can buy a combination comb that has narrow teeth on one side and wide teeth on the other.

Brushes with natural bristles produce less static electricity and broken hair than do nylon ones. A rubber brush is handy for shorthaired cats. For Rex cats, an ultra short-bristled brush is most desirable because this breed is prone to excess hair loss if brushed too vigorously.

Hound Glove is used on shorthaired cats to remove dead hair and polish the coat. A piece of chamois leather or nylon stocking also works well.

Scissors are used to cut out mats. Buy a pair with a blunt tip or rounded bead on the end of the blade.

Nail Clippers come in several types. We prefer those that have two cutting edges, a scissor effect rather than a guillotine.

How to Brush

With a *shorthaired* cat, begin at the head and work toward the tail, drawing a narrow-toothed comb carefully through the coat. Then brush in the same direction with a bristle or rubber brush. Finally, using a hound glove or chamois cloth, polish the coat to give it a sheen.

With a *longhaired* cat, use a wide-toothed comb and begin at the head by brushing or combing toward the head and against the lay of the hair in order to fluff out the coat. Work upward over the legs and sides of the chest, the back, flanks and tail. Then use a brush in the same fashion. The coat around the head is brushed up to form a frame for the face. Should your cat's coat appear greasy, you can use corn starch or baby powder and work the powder into the coat. Allow it to remain for 20 minutes to absorb the oils. A discoloration at the base of the tail, which may be accompanied by loss of hair, is caused by overactivity of large oil-producing glands at the base of the tail. It is most common in the tom but may occur in other cats. It is discussed elsewhere in this chapter (see *Stud Tail*).

Use special care to see that any soft woolly hair behind the ears and under the legs is completely brushed out. These are two areas where clumps of hair form if neglected. Such clumps should be removed. Tangle remover liquids and sprays that may soften these clumps and facilitate removal with a wide-toothed comb are avail-

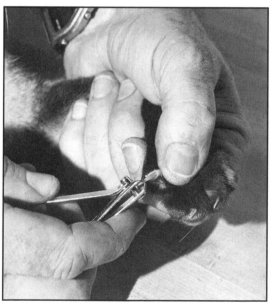

Clipping the nails. Squeeze the toe between thumb and finger to extend the nail. Clip the clear part of the nail ahead of the quick, just in front of the point where it curves down-ward. — J.Clawson

able. In many cases, however, they will need to be cut out. Use sharp scissors and *carefully* cut away from the skin into the hair clump in narrow strips; then ease it out with your fingers. Slide a comb under the mat and cut on top to avoid cutting the skin. Cats with badly matted coats may need to have this done by a professional groomer or veterinarian if skin problems have developed.

Beyond the Brush

The cat's ears should be inspected weekly. To remove dirt and debris, see EARS: *Basic Ear Care*. Routine inspection of the *teeth* will tell you if there is any buildup of tartar or calculus. To learn more about teeth brushing and cleaning, see MOUTH AND THROAT: *Care of Your Cat's Teeth*. Inspection of the anal sacs may disclose a buildup of secretions. To care for the anal sacs, see DIGESTIVE SYSTEMS: *Anal Glands or Sacs*.

A show cat may require special care and grooming. Most breed books provide more information on this subject. If you plan to show your kitten, it is a good idea to ask your breeder to give you a demonstration.

TRIMMING THE CLAWS

Indoor cats should be trained to use a scratching post to keep their front claws worn down (see *Scratching the Furniture* in FELINE BEHAVIOR AND TRAINING). When this is not successful you need to trim them—particularly if the cat is scratching your upholstery or inflicting painful injuries. In such cases the claws should be trimmed as necessary, not necessarily at regular intervals.

Outdoor cats do not need to have their claws trimmed. Activity keeps them worn down. In addition, they may be needed as defensive weapons.

As a rule, you will need to clip only the front nails. Most cats chew their back claws as a natural part of grooming. They split the old nail sheaths and pull them off. This keeps them relatively short. Cats should get used to nail trimming while still kittens. Older cats that have not grown accustomed to the procedure might be difficult to manage. Veterinary assistance may be required.

Nail clippers with *two* cutting edges are the most satisfactory. Lift up your cat's front paw and squeeze one toe between your thumb and finger to extend the nail. Next identify the pink part of the nail (the quick) that contains the nerves and blood vessels. Be sure to cut the clear part of the nail well in front of the pink part. If you can't see the quick, cut the nail just in front of the point where it starts to curve downward. Should you accidentally cut into the quick, the cat will feel some pain and the nail will begin to bleed. Hold pressure over it with a cotton ball. The blood will clot in a few minutes. If it persists, a styptic (such as used for shaving) can be used.

Declawing is an operation that might be considered for indoor cats in whom scratching has not been successfully managed by other methods. It is discussed in the chapter PEDIATRICS.

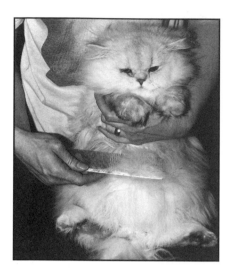

Before bathing, comb out thoroughly.
                                    —Krist Carlson

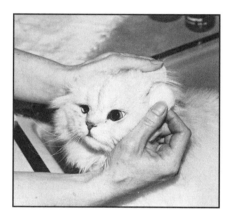

Plug the ears with cotton to keep out
water.   —Krist Carlson

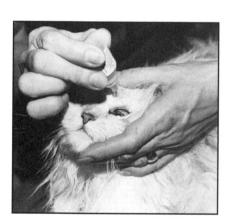

Instill a drop of mineral oil into the eyes
to prevent soap burn.
                                    —Krist Carlson

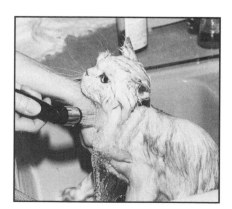

Keep the spray out of the cat's face.
                                    —Krist Carlson

Rinse well to remove all lather.
—Krist Carlson

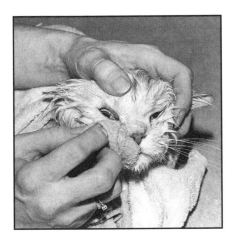

Wrap in towel and pat dry. Wash the face with a damp cloth.
—Krist Carlson

Blow dry with a hair dryer.
—Krist Carlson

Last, fluff out the coat with a brush.
—Krist Carlson

BATHING

While many cats groom their coats and keep themselves relatively clean, there are times when any cat might get dirty and need a bath. Exhibition cats are bathed periodically in preparation for cat shows. If you plan to show your kitten, start this routine early because kittens can be safely bathed after they are three months old.

It is difficult to lay down specific guidelines on bathing since this depends on the coat type and fastidiousness of the individual cat. Overbathing can remove natural oils essential to the coat. Many owners prefer to bathe the cat only for a specific purpose, others as often as once a month. Periodic grooming will keep the coat sleek and glowing and help to eliminate the need for frequent bathing.

However, when the coat is badly stained, has a strong odor or appears oily despite a thorough brushing, the only solution is a complete bath. Cats with skin problems may need to be bathed with medicated shampoos.

How to Give Your Cat a Bath

This can be quite a challenge—particularly if your cat was not bathed as a kitten. Cats basically dislike water, so expect to meet some resistance. If possible, have someone hold and soothe the cat while you give the bath. Occasionally, an unmanageable cat will have to be tranquilized. You can also take the cat to a professional groomer.

Begin by brushing the coat to remove all knots or mats. Matted hair tends to "set" when wet and is more difficult to brush. Plug the cat's ears with cotton to keep out water. Use ointment in the eyes to prevent soap burn. A drop of mineral oil in each eye works well (see EYES: *How to Apply Eye Medicine*).

The next question is what shampoo to use. Commercial pet shampoos now indicate on the label whether they are for dogs or cats. Always use a shampoo that is for cats.

Place a rubber mat or a piece of screen on the bottom of a tub or basin so the cat can have a nonslippery surface to grip. Fill the tub with soapy warm water to a depth of four inches. Holding gently but firmly by the back of the neck, lower the cat into the basin, with its back toward you (so you won't get clawed). Lather the coat with soap, keeping it out of the cat's eyes and ears. Rinse well with warm tap water or a spray, and remove all traces of lather. Soap left behind dulls the coat and irritates the skin. If the coat is especially dirty, you may need to give a second sudsing.

Special creme rinses are sometimes recommended to bring out qualities of the coat for show purposes. If you plan to use one, use it now—then rinse it out completely. *Do not use vinegar, lemon or bleach rinses.* They are either too acidic or too basic and will damage the coat and skin. *Alpha Keri* bath oil (one teaspoon per quart of water) may be added to the final rinse to give the coat luster.

Now dry the coat gently with towels. If your cat does not object to it, you can use an air comb. The coat will take an hour or two to dry, and the cat should be kept indoors until completely dry to avoid chilling.

Cats with an oily coat are especially prone to collect dirt. In such cases, a method of "dry cleaning" the coat between baths is desirable. A number of products have been used successfully as dry shampoos. Calcium carbonate, talcum or baby powder, fuller's earth and cornstarch are all effective. They can be used frequently without danger of removing essential oils or damaging the coat or skin. Work the powder into the coat and leave it for 20 minutes to absorb oils. If you show your cat, all traces of powder must be removed before you enter the judging ring.

Special Bath Problems

Skunk Oil can be removed from a cat's coat by soaking it in tomato juice and then giving a bath as described above.

Tar and Paint. Trim away excess coat containing tar, oil or paint, when feasible. Soak the tarry parts of the coat in vegetable oil overnight, then give the cat a complete bath. If the substance is on the feet, apply nail polish remover and follow with a *good rinsing. Do not* use petroleum solvents such as gasoline, kerosene or turpentine; they are extremely harmful to the skin.

IF YOUR CAT HAS A SKIN PROBLEM

When your cats begin to scratch continuously, lick and bite at their skin and rub against objects to relieve discomfort, they have an *itchy skin disorder,* and you must attempt to determine the cause. See *Table 1.*

There is another group of skin conditions that affect the appearance of the coat and hair. These diseases do not cause your cat much discomfort—at least not at first. *Hair loss* is the main sign. It may appear as impaired growth of new hair, or you may notice a patchy loss of hair from specific areas of the body. At times, the coat does not look or feel right and may be greasy or coarse and brittle. To determine the possible cause, see *Table 2.*

When your cat has a painful skin condition and you see pus and other signs of infection on or beneath the skin, this is *pyoderma.* Some cases are caused by self-mutilation and are late consequences of scratching and biting. Other pyodermas are specific skin diseases that occur by themselves. See *Table 3.*

During grooming, playing or handling your cat, you may discover a *lump or bump* on or beneath the skin. To learn what it might be, see *Table 4.*

If you suspect that your cat is suffering from a skin ailment, conduct a thorough examination of the skin and coat. On shorthaired cats, run a fine-toothed comb against the lay of the hair to expose the skin. On longhaired cats, use a bristle brush. Check the appearance of the skin and examine the scraping found on the comb and brush. In many cases the diagnosis is apparent.

AIDS TO DIAGNOSIS OF SKIN DISEASE
TABLE 1. ITCHY SKIN DISORDERS

(*Crusty Areas Produced by Scratching*)

Fleas: Itching, scratching, and licking along the back, around the tail and hindquarters. Fleas or black and white gritty specks in hair (flea feces and eggs).

Head Mange Mites (*Scabies*): Intense itching around the head, face, neck, edges of ears. Hair rubbed off. Thick gray to yellow crusts. May be complicated by *pyoderma.*

Scratching is a sign of fleas or other *itchy skin disorder.*

—Sydney Wiley

Walking Dandruff (Cheyletiella Mange): Tremendous amounts of dry scaly dandruff over the back, neck and sides. Mild itching.

Chiggers: Itching and severe skin irritation between the toes, around ears and mouth. Look for barely visible red, yellow or orange chiggers (larvae).

Ear Mites (Ododectes): Head shaking and scratching at ears. Excessive brown waxy or purulent material in ear canals.

Ticks: Large insects attached to skin. May swell up to pea size. Often found around the ears, along back and between toes.

Lice: Two-millimeter-long insects or white grains of sandy material (nits) found attached to hair. Found beneath matted hair in poorly kept cats. May have bare spots where hair rubbed off.

Maggots (Myiasis): Soft-bodied legless fly larvae found in damp matted fur. May be complicated by *pyoderma.*

Food Allergy: Severe itching over the head, neck and back. Swelling of eyelids. Often complicated by hair loss and oozing sores from constant scratching and biting.

Feline Miliary Dermatitis: Small bumps and crusts around the head, neck and back felt beneath haircoat. May be associated with fleas. May be complicated by *pyoderma*.

Irritant Contact Dermatitis: Red itchy bumps and inflamed skin at site of contact with chemical, detergent, paint and so forth. May have scales and hair loss.

Allergic Contact Dermatitis: Appearance similar to *contact dermatitis*, but rash may spread beyond area of contact.

Inhalant Allergy (*Atopic Dermatitis*): Appearance similar to *feline miliary dermatitis*. May have symmetric hair loss over body.

TABLE 2. HAIR LOSS DISORDERS

Indolent (Rodent) Ulcer: Red shiny patches of hairless skin. Usually involves the middle of the upper lip; occasionally the lower lip. Not painful.

Ringworm: Scaly, crusty or red circular patches with central hair loss. Sometimes just broken hairs around the face and ears. Highly contagious. May become infected.

Demodectic Mange: Thinning and loss of hair around the eyes and eyelids giving moth-eaten appearance. Rare in cats.

Eosinophilic Granulomas: Raised, red circular plaque on abdomen or inside of thighs (*eosinophilic plaque*); or linear plaques on back of hind legs.

Feline Endocrine Alopecia: Thinning or balding of coat on insides of back legs, lower abdomen and genital area. Distribution is symmetrical (mirror image). Occurs most often in neutered males and spayed females.

Hypothyroidism: Dry skin and thinning of haircoat. Hair becomes dull and brittle. Rare.

Cortisone Excess: Loss of hair in symmetrical pattern over trunk with darkening of underlying skin. May indicate thyroid problem.

Stud Tail: Greasy, rancid-smelling waxy-brown material at top of tail near base.

Psychogenic Alopecia: Thinning of hair in a stripe down the back. Caused by compulsive self-grooming. See FELINE BEHAVIOR AND TRAINING: *Behavior Disorders*.

TABLE 3. PAINFUL SKIN DISORDERS WITH PUS DRAINAGE (PYODERMA)

Feline Acne: Pimple-like bumps on the underside of the chin and edges of lips.

Impetigo: Pus-filled blisters on abdomen and hairless areas of newborn kittens.

Cellulitis or Abscess (*Pyoderma*): Painful, hot, inflamed skin or pockets of pus beneath the skin. Often caused by self-mutilation. Look for underlying cause (i.e., itchy skin disorder, foreign body, puncture wound).

Candidiasis (*Thrush*): Moist white plaques that bleed easily when rubbed. Most common on mucous membranes.

Mosquito Bite Hypersensitivity: Crusty sores with erosions and scabs over bridge of nose and tips of ears.

TABLE 4. LUMPS OR BUMPS ON OR BENEATH THE SKIN

Papillomas and Warts: Grow out from the skin and look like warts or pieces of chewing gum stuck to the skin. Not painful.

Hematomas: Collections of blood beneath the skin, especially on the ears. Caused by trauma.

Tender Knots (*Abscesses*): Frequently found after cat fights. Forms a firm swelling that becomes soft with time. Painful.

Cysts: Smooth lumps beneath the skin. May grow slowly. Can discharge cheesy material and become infected. Otherwise, not painful.

Mycetoma: Mass or nodule beneath skin with an open tract to the surface draining a granular material. Caused by a fungus.

Sporotrichosis: Skin nodule with overlying hair loss and wet surface of pus at site of puncture wound or break in skin. Caused by a fungus. See INFECTIOUS DISEASES: *Fungus Diseases*.

Grubs (*Cuterebra*): Inch-long fly larvae that form cystic-like lumps beneath the skin with hole in center to breathe. Often beneath chin or along abdomen.

When a Lump May Be a Cancer: Rapid enlargement; appears hard or fixed to surrounding tissue; any lump growing from bone; a lump that starts to bleed; a mole that begins to spread or ulcerate; unexplained open sore that does not heal, especially on feet or legs. *Note: The only way to tell for sure is to remove and study the lump under a microscope.* Common surface growths are discussed in the chapter TUMORS AND CANCERS.

INSECT PARASITES

Insect parasites are responsible for the majority of skin ailments encountered by the cat owner and also figure prominently as transmitters of viral, protozoan, bacterial and worm diseases of cats. If you groom your cat regularly, you can prevent many disorders caused by insects. If, despite adequate care, your cat still acquires fleas, mites or some other external parasite, you are in a better position to seek consultation or start treatment before the problem becomes advanced.

Bees, wasps and other insects that sting or bite rather than parasitize the cat are discussed in the chapter EMERGENCIES (see *Insect Stings*).

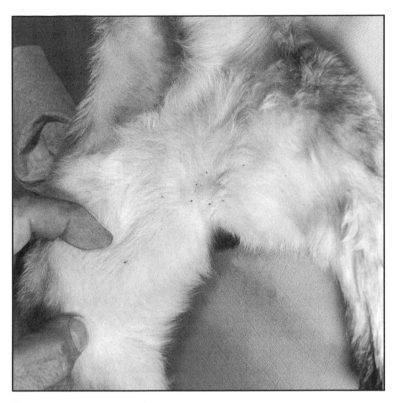

Fleas are easier to see in the groin area.

FLEAS

The ordinary cat flea (C. *felis*) is the most common parasite on the cat's skin. All cats are affected except for those living at higher elevations, because fleas do not live above 5,000 feet. Cats living indoors can have fleas year-round.

Fleas live by feeding on blood. In most cases they cause only a mild itch; but a heavy infestation might cause a severe anemia or even the death of the cat. Fleas also are an intermediate host of the cat tapeworm. Some cats experience hypersensitivity to flea saliva. This produces intense itching and localized or generalized skin reaction. Such cats require special attention (see *Feline Miliary Dermatitis*).

Signs: Flea infestation can be diagnosed by finding fleas on your cat or by seeing salt-and-pepper-like, black-and-white grainlike sand in the coat. These particles are flea feces and flea eggs. Fecal material is made of digested blood. When brushed onto a wet paper, it turns a reddish brown. Look for fleas on your cat's back and around the tail and hindquarters by running a fine-toothed comb through the fur. Fleas are sometimes seen in the groin area, where it is warm and there is less hair. Itching is most pronounced in these areas.

Common products for flea control available through your veterinarian.

The adult flea is a small, dark brown insect that can be seen with the naked eye. Although the flea has no wings and cannot fly, it does have powerful back legs and can jump great distances. Fleas move through the hair rapidly and are difficult to catch. Ticks and lice move slowly and are easy to pick off.

Life Cycle: Fleas need a warm, humid environment to flourish and reproduce. The higher the temperature and humidity, the more efficient the flea's life cycle becomes. The adult flea can live up to 115 days on the cat—but only 1 or 2 days when off the host. A flea's life expectancy is affected by the cat's grooming. A cat that chews and licks at the skin may destroy a large number of fleas and therefore have fewer than expected. Similarly, a cat not as sensitive to fleas may harbor a large number and show few signs of infestation.

Within 48 hours of a blood meal, fleas mate on the cat's skin. A female flea can lay 2,000 eggs in a lifetime. The eggs fall off and incubate under furniture and in carpets, cracks and bedding. Pile or shag carpeting makes an ideal environment. In 10 days the eggs hatch into larvae that feed on local debris. Larvae spin a cocoon and go into a pupal stage lasting for days or months. Under ideal conditions (65° to 80°F, 70 percent humidity, presence of vibration and exhaled carbon dioxide), fleas can emerge in a matter of seconds. After they hatch, fleas search for a host. If one is not found right away, they can live for one to two weeks without feeding.

At any given time, about 1 percent of the flea population is made up of adult fleas; 99 percent remain in the invisible egg, larval and pupal stages. To control fleas on your cat, *it is most important that you destroy a large number of fleas on the premise.*

Unless the yard and house are treated at the same time you treat the cat, they will be a continuous source of reinfestation that no amount of insecticide on the cat can control.

For more information on the selection, safety, use and effectiveness of various classes of insecticide, see *Insecticides* later in this chapter.

Control of Fleas on the Cat: To eliminate all potential sources of reinfestation, it is necessary to treat all animals in the household as described below.

A variety of products is available for killing fleas. Read the label to be certain the product is specifically intended for cats. *Preparations for dogs and other livestock can be toxic to cats.* Many flea preparations should not be used on kittens and pregnant queens. *Check with your veterinarian before using a product if the information on the container is unclear.*

Flea shampoos kill only when they are on the cat. Once rinsed off, they have no residual effect. They are best used for mild to moderate flea infestation after treating the environment thoroughly. A variety of insecticide products are available as flea shampoos. Pyrethrin shampoos are generally safest to use on kittens.

Powders and *dusts* have more residual killing activity but must be worked thoroughly through the haircoat down to the skin. They tend to leave the coat dry and gritty. Dusting must be repeated two to three times a week. Powders are best used with shampoos, sprays or dips.

Sprays and *foams* are most effective when used between shampoos to kill late-hatching fleas that have eluded the living quarters treatment. Most sprays have a residual killing action up to 14 days and use the same insecticides as described for shampoos. Water-based sprays are preferable to alcohol-based sprays, which are flammable and irritate the skin. *Sprays and foams should not be used on kittens under two months of age.* When using a spray, begin near the cat's head and work toward the

A *flea comb* mechanically removes fleas. Flea comb the face as well as the body.

tail. This prevents fleas on the body from escaping the treatment by moving up onto the face.

Insecticide dips applied to the cat's coat and allowed to dry are extremely effective in ridding your cat of fleas. Dips penetrate the haircoat and have the most immediate killing action and longest residual activity. *Organic dips containing d-limonene are among the safest for cats.* Before using an insecticide dip, be sure to read the section on *Insecticides* later in this chapter. Most dips must be repeated every 7 to 10 days, but the product label must be consulted for recommended frequency. Dips should not be used on kittens under four months of age.

Suggested Treatment Program for Eliminating Fleas

On Cats

1. Shampoo with an insecticide product labeled for cats. Note: If infestation is severe, consider dipping in addition to shampooing.
2. For dry skin or flea allergy, use an insecticide cream rinse containing 0.5 percent permethrin.
3. Repeat shampoo every two to three weeks until fleas are eliminated.
4. In between shampoos, use a pump spray product such as *Ovitrol Plus Flea Spray* (contains insect growth regulator), *Mycodex Aqua-Spray*, *Escort Flea & Tick Pet Spray* or *VIP Pet Spray*.
5. Mechanical removal of fleas using a flea comb (32 teeth per inch) is effective on shorthaired breeds and young kittens. Flea-comb the face as well as the body. Kill fleas on comb by immersing in liquid detergent or alcohol. The cat must be combed at least every other day.
6. *Flea collars are only part of the flea-control program and should not be used as the sole source of control.* Use breakaway collars and follow the manufacturer's directions and precautions.

On the Premises

With heavy flea infestation, you may need the services of a professional exterminator recommended by your veterinarian. A most important step in the **indoor** control of fleas is a thorough mechanical cleaning of the household. This must proceed simultaneously with the application of chemicals. For more information see *Disinfecting the Premises*.

Insecticides for indoor flea control come in carpet shampoos, sprays and foggers. In households with young infants, the safest insecticides are pyrethrins and growth regulators.

Foggers usually contain permethrins or synergized natural pyrethrins. Some contain insect growth regulators. Insect growth regulators (IGRs) prevent eggs and larvae from developing into adult fleas. *PreCor* (methoprene) must contact the egg within 12 hours after the egg is laid to be completely effective. Fenoxycarb can contact the egg any time during development and prevent maturation. Both are inactivated by exposure to sunlight. One disadvantages of foggers is that they tend to settle on the top of carpets. Flea larvae and pupae, however, burrow deep into the nap. Foggers also may not settle beneath furniture because of uneven convection. To offset these disadvantages, spray first with a surface product before activating the fogger.

Mechanical cleaning and insecticide applications should be repeated at three-week intervals. It may take nine weeks to eliminate all visible fleas from the environment.

Outdoor control begins with the removal of all decaying vegetation before spraying or dusting. Mow, rake and discard the debris. When applying sprays, give special attention to favorite resting places or flea "hot spots" (e.g., beneath the porch, in the garage). Insecticides effective in outdoor control contain chlorpyrifos or other organophosphate insecticides. Be sure the ground is dry before allowing pets outside. Repeat application every two to three weeks. Observe the manufacturer's *precautions* and follow directions about mixing, preparation and application of the product.

MITES

Mites are microscopic spider-like creatures living on the cat's skin or in the ear canals. Mites cause many skin conditions from simple dandruff to irregular moth-eaten patches of hair loss complicated by draining sores. Collectively, they are called *mange*. Mange can be classified according to the type of mite that causes it.

Demodectic Mange. This noncontagious form of mange is common in dogs, but fortunately, it is extremely rare in cats. The demodex mite is a normal resident of the cat's skin and seldom causes more than mild, localized infection. The exception is the immune-suppressed cat suffering from FeLV, diabetes mellitus, chronic respiratory infection, cancer and the immune-depressant effects of chemotherapy or excessive hydrocortisone.

The *localized* form, most often seen in young cats, is one or more areas of hair loss occurring around the head, neck and ears, progressing to scaly, crusty sores that itch and become secondarily infected. After one or two months the hair begins to grow back. In three months most cases are healed.

The *generalized* form is similar, but the condition extends widely over the body. The cat may be suffering from some other disease that also requires treatment.

Treatment: The diagnosis is confirmed by taking skin scrapings and identifying the characteristic mite under a microscope.

For localized demodectic mange, apply a topical keratolytic and antibacterial agent such as *Pyoben* or *OxyDex* shampoo. Follow with a lime sulfur dip or a local application of *Rotenone*.

Cats with generalized demodectic mange present a difficult problem and should be treated under veterinary supervision. Shampoos are available that remove dead skin, kill mites and treat secondary bacterial skin infection. Treatment is prolonged and repeated applications are necessary. Spontaneous remissions after several months have occurred in some cats.

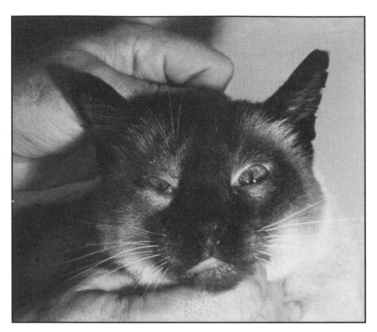

The moth-eaten look of hair loss around the eyes is characterisitc of *localized demodectic mange.*

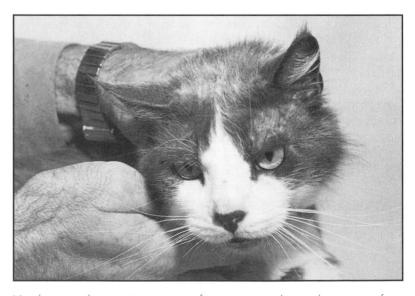

Hair loss over the eyes is common in free-roaming males in whom injuries from cat fights produce a buildup of scar. Can resemble localized demodectic mange.

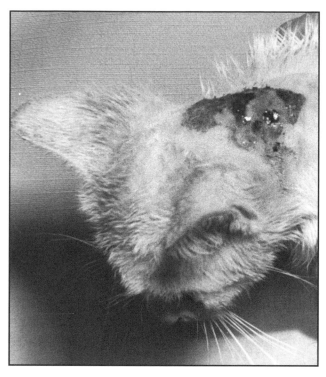

Wet, inflammed infected skin caused by self-mutilation. *Head mange* was the cause of the intense itching and scratching.

Head Mange (Feline scabies). Feline scabies is an uncommon skin ailment caused by the head mite *Notoedres cati*. The first sign is intense itching about the head and neck, along with hair loss and the appearance of bald spots. Due to the incessant scratching, the skin becomes red, raw and excoriated. Typically, you will see thick gray to yellow crusts around the face, neck and edge of the ears. The condition also may involve the skin of the paws and genitalia.

In severe or untreated cases the skin forms scabs, crusts and thickened wrinkled skin on the head that gives the cat an aged look. With intense scratching, wounds become infected.

Severe itching is caused by female mites tunneling a few millimeters under the skin to lay their eggs. Mite eggs hatch in 5 to 10 days. The immature mites develop into adults and begin to lay eggs of their own. The whole cycle takes three to four weeks. The diagnosis is confirmed by skin scrapings, or in difficult cases by skin biopsy (searching for mites).

Head mange is highly contagious. It is transmitted primarily by direct animal-to- animal contact. Dogs and even people can be infested, but only for short periods.

The *Notoedres* mite will reproduce only on cats. It is highly susceptible to drying and cannot live more than a few days off the host.

Treatment: Clip scabies-affected areas on longhaired cats and bathe the entire animal in warm water and soap to loosen crusts. Kittens may be dipped or shampooed but must be dried quickly to prevent chilling. Kill the head mites by dipping the cat in a 2.5 percent lime sulfur dip weekly. Continue for two weeks beyond apparent cure. Lime sulfur dips are safe for use on pregnant queens and kittens over six weeks of age. Other cats on the premise should be dipped once a week for three to four weeks since they may harbor the mite and act as a reservoir for reinfestation.

Mild shampoos can be used between insecticide dips to loosen scales. A cortisone product such as 1 percent *Cortaid*, neomycin with cortisone, *Terra Cortril Anti-Itch Spray* or *Dermagard Hydrocortisone Spray* helps to relieve severe itching. Sores that look infected from self-mutilation should be treated by a soothing topical ointment such as *Panolog*.

Infestation in people produces an itchy skin condition that resolves spontaneously in two to six weeks, providing that all mites have been eliminated from the cat.

Walking Dandruff (Cheyletiella mange). This type of mange is caused by a large reddish mite that lives on the skin and causes mild itching with a tremendous amount of dry scaly material that looks like dandruff. The dandruff is heaviest over the back, neck and sides. This type of mange is not common in cats. The life cycle of the *Cheyletiella* mite is similar to that of the head mange mite. The entire life cycle takes four to five weeks.

Walking dandruff is highly contagious. Humans can become rather easily infested. The signs are itching and the appearance of red, raised bumps on the skin. They look much like insect bites, which in fact they are. The *Cheyletiella* mite cannot live off the cat for more than two weeks. The owner's rash should improve as the cat is treated.

Treatment: The diagnosis is confirmed by finding the mite in dandruff scrapings collected on paper and examined under a magnifying glass. All cats and dogs on the premise should be treated with a lime sulfur insecticide dip or a shampoo containing a pyrethrin insecticide. Continue to treat for two weeks beyond apparent cure. Treat premise like that described for *Fleas*.

Chiggers (Trombiculid mites). Chiggers, also called harvest mites and red bugs, live as adults in decaying vegetation. Only their larval forms are parasitic. Cats acquire the infestation while prowling in forest grasslands and fields where chiggers reproduce. Reproduction occurs in late summer or fall.

Larval mites appear as red, yellow or orange specks barely visible to the naked eye but easily seen with a magnifying glass. They tend to clump in areas where the skin is thin such as the web spaces between the toes or around the ears and mouth, but they can occur elsewhere on the body. The larvae feed by sucking on the skin. The result is severe irritation and the formation of red draining sores with overlying scabs. Patches of raw skin may appear.

Treatment: The larvae can be either seen or identified by skin scrapings. Chiggers in the ear canals are eliminated by treating as you would for *Ear Mites*. Those elsewhere on the body respond to a single application of a lime sulfur dip or pyrethrin shampoo. Corticosteroids may be required to control intense itching. When feasible, prevent reinfestation by keeping your cat confined during the chigger season.

Ear Mites (Ododectes cynotis). These mites are a separate species and should not be confused with *Notoedres cati* causing *Head Mange*. Ear mites are one of the most common problems the cat owner is likely to encounter. These mites live in the ear canals and feed on skin and debris. They are discussed in the chapter EARS.

Sarcoptic Mange Mites. These mites occur frequently in dogs and produce a disease called *Sarcoptic Mange*. Fortunately, they are rarely seen in cats. Their effect and treatment is similar to that of *Head Mange*. Skin scrapings are used to make the diagnosis.

TICKS

Ticks are rarely found on cats because cats keep their coats well groomed. When present, ticks usually are found in inaccessible areas such as the ears, neck, head, back and between the toes.

Ticks have a complicated life cycle. It involves three hosts, including wild and domestic animals and man. The male tick is a small flat insect about the size of a match head. A blood tick is a pea-sized female tick feeding on the host.

Treatment: Since cats rarely have more than a few ticks, simply remove them individually. Grasp the tick with tweezers and gently tease it off the skin. A drop of alcohol or nail polish applied to the tick may cause it to release its hold. If the mouth parts remain fixed to the skin, don't be concerned. In most cases, this causes only a local reaction that clears up in a few days. Only rarely does a tick bite become infected. Ticks can carry diseases dangerous to humans. Do not squeeze or crush a tick with your bare fingers. For outdoor control of ticks, cut tall grass, weeds and brush. Treat the premise with an insecticide preparation as described for *Fleas*.

LICE (PEDICULOSIS)

Lice are uncommon. They occur primarily in malnourished run-down cats that have lost the initiative to keep themselves groomed. Lice are usually found beneath matted hair around the ears, head, neck, shoulders and perineal area. Because of itching and constant irritation, bare spots may be seen where the hair has been rubbed off.

Cats may be infested only with *biting lice* (*Trichodectes felis*) that feed on skin scales. Adults are wingless, slow moving, pale-colored insects about two to three millimeters long. They lay eggs called *nits* that look like white grains of sand and are found attached to hairs. They are difficult to brush off. Nits may look something like dandruff (seborrhea); but cats with seborrhea do not itch as they do with lice. Inspection with a magnifying glass makes the distinction easy because nits are well-formed rounded eggs attached to hair shafts.

Lice are an intermediate host for the common cat tapeworm.

Treatment: Lice show little resistance to insecticides and do not live long when off the cat. They can be killed by giving a thorough bath followed by an insecticide

This senile cat was too weak to keep itself free of *maggots* (the larvae of blow flies), which hatch on dirty and infected skin.

dip effective against fleas (see *Fleas*). Three to four dips must be given at 10-day intervals.

Note: Heavily infested, severely malnourished cats might not be able to withstand the treatment and could go into shock. Consult your veterinarian before using an insecticide dip on such an individual. Infected bedding should be destroyed and the cat's sleeping quarters disinfected (see *Disinfecting the Premises*).

FLIES

Adult flies do not afflict the cat but may at times deposit their eggs on raw or infected wounds or in soil where larvae can penetrate the cat's skin.

Maggots (Myiasis). This condition, called *myiasis*, is a seasonally warm weather disease most often caused by the bluebottle or blow fly that lays eggs in open wounds or badly soiled damp matted fur. The eggs hatch in 8 to 72 hours. In 2 to 19 days the larvae grow into large maggots that produce an enzyme in their saliva that digests the skin, causing "punched-out" areas. The maggots then penetrate the skin, enlarge the opening and set the stage for a bacterial skin infection. With a severe infestation the cat may go into shock. The shock is caused by enzymes and toxins secreted by the maggots.

Treatment: Clip the affected areas to remove soiled and matted hair. Remove all maggots with blunt-nosed tweezers. Wash infected areas with Betadine solution and dry the cat thoroughly. Use a nonalcohol spray or shampoo containing a pyrethrin insecticide. Repeat application as described for *Fleas* and check closely for remaining maggots.

Cats with infected wounds should be treated with an oral antibiotic such as Penicillin. The cat's health and nutrition must be stable to bring about a cure. If the cat exhibits signs of shock, go at once to the veterinarian.

Grubs (Cuterebriasis). The most frequent cause of grub infestation is the large botfly, which has a wide seasonal distribution in the United States. This fly lays eggs near the burrows of rodents and rabbits. The cat acquires the disease by direct contact with infested soil. Newly hatched larvae penetrate the skin forming cystlike lumps that have a small opening to the outside to allow the grubs to breathe. From time to time, inch-long grubs protrude from the skin through the breathing holes. In about a month, they emerge and drop to the ground. More than one grub may be found in the same area (usually along the jawbone, around the face, under the belly or along the sides). In such cases they form large nodular masses.

Treatment: Clip away hair to expose breathing holes. Grasp each grub with a fine-tipped forceps and gently draw it out. Do not crush or rupture the larva during extraction. *This can produce anaphylactic shock.* If necessary, a small incision should be made under an anesthetic to remove the parasite. Grub wounds are slow to heal and often become infected. Antibiotics may be required.

INSECTICIDES

Insecticides are used in shampoos, powders, dusts, sprays and dips for the elimination of insects on the cat. They are also used to disinfect bedding, houses, catteries, runs, gardens, garages and other spots where a cat might be infected by coming into contact with the adult or intermediate insect forms.

Insecticides are poisons! *If you decide to use an insecticide preparation, be sure to follow the precautions and directions on the label.* Otherwise, poisoning may occur from improper exposure.

There are four classes of insecticides in current use: **pyrethrins** (natural and synthetic); **carbamates; organophosphates;** and **natural insecticides.** In addition, there are insect growth regulators (IGRs) that, although not insecticides, act in a manner to prevent insect reproduction.

Pyrethrin. A natural extract of the African chrysanthemum flower, it kills fleas quickly but has little residual activity because it is rapidly degraded in the environment by ultraviolet light. Pyrethrin has low potential for toxicity and is approved for use on both dogs and cats. It is found in many shampoos, sprays, dusts, dips, foggers and premise sprays. **Pyrethroids** are synthetic compounds that resemble pyrethrin in structure but are more stable to sunlight and therefore have longer residual activity. **Permethrin** is the most commonly used synergized pyrethrin, but there are others. Some are incorporated into products that are safe to use on dogs and cats, others only for dogs. Read the label carefully before using a synergized pyrethrin product on your cat.

The insecticidal effects of natural and synthetic pyrethrins can occur when combined with *piperonyl butoxide*, which works by inhibiting the insect's (fleas or ticks) own enzymes.

Carbamates. *Carbyl* (*Sevin*) is an insecticide found in flea and tick powders and shampoos. *Bendiocarb* (*Ficam*) is commonly used by professional exterminators for premise control of fleas. Both are effective and safe when used according to directions. Signs of toxicity are like those of organophosphate poisoning. Carbamates should not be used on kittens under four weeks or on pregnant or lactating queens.

Organophosphates. These insecticides are unstable and do not persist in the environment. They are among the most toxic to mammals and are particularly toxic to cats. *Chlorpyrifos (Dursban), diazinon, dichlorvos (DDVP), and fenthion should be used with extreme caution if at all* on the cat—and should be used on premises via sprays and foggers only in accordance with the manufacturer's precautions and directions. *Malathion* is the only organophosphate safe to use on adult cats.

Natural insecticides. These products are botanical compounds derived from roots and natural extracts of citrus fruit. *Rotenone* and *d-limonene* are moderately effective against fleas, ticks and some species of lice and mites. *D-Limonene* is effective against fleas in all stages, including the egg; however, residual activity is less than synergized pyrethrins. It is used in shampoos, dips and sprays approved for both dogs and cats.

Growth regulators (IGRs). *Methoprene (PreCor) and Fenoxycarb* are two hormone-like compounds that prevent flea larvae from developing into adults. They do not affect the cocoon or adult stages. Both are degraded by sunlight and therefore used mainly for indoor treatment. *PreCor* is used in foggers and premise sprays alone or in combination with *pyrethrins or chlorpyrifos (Dursban)* to provide a spectrum of both egg and adult stage insecticides.

With the development of pyrethrin compounds, natural insecticides and IGRs, the more toxic insecticides are used less often for cats. Environmental concerns also favor use of the natural compounds. Because cats are especially sensitive to insecticide toxicity, it is important to use the least toxic product whenever possible.

Recommendations for specific products used for shampooing, spraying and dipping are discussed in the paragraphs dealing with the specific insect parasites.

Lysol and other household disinfectants are not suitable for washing your cat and should not be used. Like insecticides, they are absorbed through the skin and can cause illness or death.

Insecticide poisoning: An *overdose* of an organophosphate insecticide can cause your cat to twitch at the mouth, foam, collapse, convulse and fall into a coma. Other signs of insecticide toxicity are diarrhea, asthmatic breathing, a staggering gait and muscular twitching and jerking. Many of these same signs are seen with toxicity caused by the other insecticide classes.

If you suspect that your cat might be suffering from an insecticide reaction, give a bath in warm soapy water to remove residual compound from the coat, and keep the animal quiet. *Contact your veterinarian.*

Dips. Dips are insecticide solutions that are sponged onto the body and dry on the hair and skin without rinsing. Choose a dip recommended by your veterinarian, or if you decide to wash your cat with a commercial preparation, check the label to be sure it is effective against the insect in question and *safe for cats.*

CAUTION: Some worm medications contain similar chemicals. If the animal has just been wormed, there could be a sudden accumulation of chemicals in the cat's system from powdering, shampooing, dipping or spraying with an insecticide. Avoid using an insecticide dip within a week of worming the cat.

If your cat's hair is matted, dirty or greasy, first wash with a gentle commercial cat shampoo. Then, while the coat is still wet, rinse thoroughly with an insecticide dip made according to the directions on the package. Apply ointment or mineral oil in the eyes, and plug the ears with cotton so you can treat head and ears with the dip. Immediately after dipping, while the cat is still wet, use a flea comb (32 teeth per inch) to mechanically remove insects.

Most dips must be repeated every 7 to 10 days, but the product label should be consulted for recommended frequency of application. Dips should not be used on kittens under four months of age.

DISINFECTING THE PREMISES

The goal is to prevent reinfestation by ridding the environment of insects, eggs, larvae and other intermediate stages. To eliminate all sources of reinfestation, treat all animals in the household as described in *Control of Fleas on the Cat*.

All blankets, bedding and rugs where the cat sleeps should be washed weekly at the hottest setting. A thorough housecleaning that includes vacuuming of carpets, spraying of furniture, application of insecticide to corners and cracks, will help to eliminate the insects, eggs and larvae. Cleaning usually has to be done two or three times. Floors should be mopped, giving special attention to cracks and crevices where organic debris and eggs accumulate. With severe infestation, steam cleaning carpets is highly effective in killing eggs and larvae. Insecticides can be used in the water of the steam cleaner. Specific products are now available where you rent the cleaner. Vacuum bags should be discarded immediately after use because they provide an ideal environment for flea development. With heavy infestation, it is sometimes better to enlist the services of a professional exterminator.

After a thorough mechanical cleaning, the house and yard should be treated with insecticide applications as described in the section *Suggested Treatment Program for Eliminating Fleas*. At least three applications, at two to three week intervals, are required to eliminate fleas. Afterward, the house should be treated periodically as needed. In warm, humid states, it may be necessary to re-treat every six to eight weeks. The residual activity of outdoor insecticides depends on weather conditions. In dry weather, residual activity may persist for a month; in wet weather, one to two weeks. Re-treat accordingly.

ALLERGIES

GENERAL INFORMATION

An allergic episode is an unpleasant reaction caused by the cat's *immune system*. Without an immune system, any animal would not be able to build up resistance to viruses, bacteria, foreign proteins and other irritating substances that get into the system. Certain foods or substances such as pollens, powders, feathers, wool, house dust and insect bites trigger a reaction typified by itching and sometimes sneezing, coughing, swelling of the eyelids, tearing or vomiting and diarrhea. This occurs in cats as well as in humans.

For a cat to be allergic to something, exposure must occur at least twice. What the cat is allergic to is called the **allergen.** The way the body responds to that allergen is called a *hypersensitivity reaction or allergic reaction.*

There are two kinds of hypersensitivity reaction. The *immediate* type occurs shortly after exposure and produces hives and itching. Hives in the cat are characterized by sudden swelling on the head, usually around the eyes and mouth, and occasionally the appearance of welts elsewhere on the body. The *delayed* reaction produces itching that occurs hours or days afterward. Flea bite dermatitis is an example of both types. This explains why a cat may continue to itch even after successful flea treatment.

Allergens enter the body through the lungs (pollens, house dust); the digestive tract (eating certain foods); by injection (insect bites and vaccination); or by direct absorption through the skin. While the target area in people usually is the air passages and lungs (producing hay fever and asthma), in the cat it is the skin or gastrointestinal tract. The main sign of skin involvement is *severe itching*.

Food Allergy (Hypersensitivity)

Cats may become allergic to certain foods or substances in foods. The most common food allergens are beef, pork, chicken, milk, eggs, fish, corn, wheat and soy. An intensely itchy rash often develops on the head, neck and back and may be accompanied by swollen eyelids. You may see hair loss and oozing sores from constant scratching. Less frequently, food allergy produces diarrhea or vomiting (see *Inflammatory Bowel Disease* in the Digestive System chapter).

Diagnosis is made by exposing the cat to a suspected allergen and then watching for a reaction. Treatment is discussed at greater length in the chapter Digestive System (see *Treatment of Diarrhea*).

Feline Miliary Dermatitis

This skin disease is caused by an allergic skin reaction to a number of agents, including the bites of fleas, mites and lice. Bacterial and fungus skin infection, nutritional disturbances and drug reactions can also produce miliary dermatitis. The affected cat breaks out along the back and around the head and neck with small bumps and crusts about the size of millet seeds beneath the haircoat. Itching may or may not be present.

Flea bite allergy is the most common cause of miliary dermatitis in cats. Other skin parasites, allergic and infectious causes should be considered for cats that have miliary dermatitis without fleas.

Flea-Bite Dermatitis. The skin is severely itchy and may break down, producing raw patches of skin that become infected from intense scratching. Localized or generalized *eosinophilic plaques* may develop as a consequence (see *Eosinophilic Granuloma Complex*). Although cats are especially resistant to flea bites and can harbor many fleas without symptoms, in the allergic reactor a single bite once or twice a week is sufficient to produce the response. Symptoms are most prevalent in the middle of summer (flea season). However, once the cat is exposed, if fleas live in the house, itching may persist year-round.

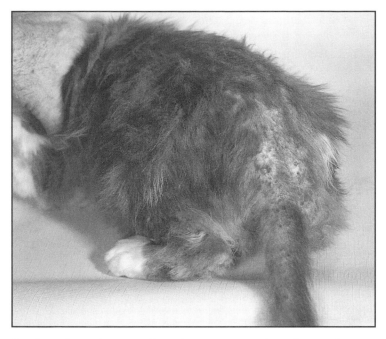

Flea bite allergy dermatitis. Typical appearance with small crusts, bumps and raw patches of skin. Hair loss due to licking and scratching.

The diagnosis is suspected by seeing the characteristic skin rash and by finding fleas on the cat. You can check for fleas by standing your cat over a sheet of white paper and brushing the coat. White and black grains of sandy material that drop on the paper are flea eggs and feces. The diagnosis is confirmed by an intradermal skin test. This is a hypersensitivity reaction of both immediate and delayed type; itching tends to persist long after fleas have been destroyed.

Treatment: When fleas are present, treat infestation as described above (see *Fleas*). In the absence of fleas, an effort must be made to determine the cause of the miliary dermatitis and to treat accordingly.

Cortisone tablets or injections that block the allergic reaction and relieve the itching are useful in long-term management in selected cases. They should be used under veterinary supervision because of potential side effects. Treat sores with a topical antibiotic/steroid ointment such as *Panolog*. Desensitization is not very effective.

IRRITANT CONTACT AND ALLERGIC CONTACT DERMATITIS

Irritant contact dermatitis and allergic contact dermatitis are two different conditions discussed together because they produce apparently similar reactions. Both are caused by contact with a chemical. In contact dermatitis, the skin reaction is caused by a direct irritating effect of the chemical. In allergic contact dermatitis, repeated

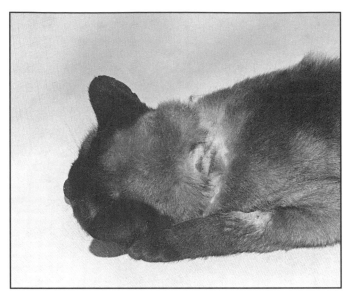

Allergic contact dermatitis produced by the insecticide in a *flea collar.*

contact produces skin sensitization that results in an allergic response from subsequent exposure. Both types of dermatitis are rare in cats owing to their haircoat and self-grooming habits that protect the skin from sustained contact with chemicals. This is especially true for allergic contact dermatitis.

Both irritant and allergic contact dermatitis affect parts of the body where hair is thin or absent, that is, the feet, chin, nose, abdomen and groin. These areas are also the most likely to come in contact with chemicals. Liquid irritants may affect any part of the body. Contact dermatitis of either type produces red itchy bumps along with inflammation of the skin. Scaliness follows, and the hair falls out. Excessive scratching causes skin injury and infected sores. The rash from allergic contact dermatitis may spread beyond the contact area. Chemicals producing irritant dermatitis are acids and alkalis, detergents, solvents, soaps and petroleum by-products.

Substances causing an allergic reaction are flea powders; shampoos (particularly those containing iodine); poison ivy, poison oak and other plants; fibers, including wool and synthetics; leather; plastic and rubber dishes; and dyes in carpets. Neomycin, found in many topical medications, can produce an allergic reaction, as can other drugs and medications.

Flea collar dermatitis is a reaction to the insecticide in the collar. It affects the skin around the neck, producing local itching and redness followed by hair loss and crust formation. This condition may spread to other areas. In addition to causing local hypersensitivity, flea collars may cause toxicity from absorption of chemicals and therefore are not recommended as the sole means of flea control.

Litter box dermatitis affects the skin around the tail and anus.

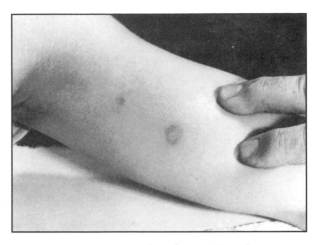

Ringworm is a contagious skin infection. Typical appearance is a round patch with scales at the center and an advancing red ring at the margin.

Treatment: Consider the area of exposure and identify the skin allergen or chemical causing the problem. Prevent exposure. Treat infected skin as you would for *Cellulitis and Abscesses.* Topical or oral corticosteroids help to reduce itching and inflammation. They do not cure the problem. Allergy shots and immune therapy may control the symptoms but do not cure the problem.

INHALANT ALLERGY (ATOPIC DERMATITIS)

This is an allergic skin reaction caused by breathing pollens, house dust, molds and other allergens in the indoor or outdoor environment. It may or may not occur seasonally. Signs and symptoms are variable. They include itching on the head and neck, a rash along the neck and back like that described for *Feline Miliary Dermatitis,* skin eruptions like those described in *Eosinophilic Granuloma Complex* and symmetric hair loss over the body caused by excessive licking and grooming.

Atopic dermatitis is difficult to distinguish from other allergic skin disorders such as those caused by insect bites, food hypersensitivity and chemical contact. Diagnosis is best made by intradermal skin testing.

Treatment: Best results are obtained when the allergen can be identified and eliminated from the cat's environment. Antihistamines or corticosteroids are beneficial in relieving symptoms but do not cure the problem. Allergy shots to desensitize the cat have been effective in some cases.

FUNGUS INFECTIONS

RINGWORM

Ringworm is *not a worm* but a plantlike growth that invades the hair and hair follicles. Most cases are caused by the fungus *Microsporum canis.* A few are caused by other species.

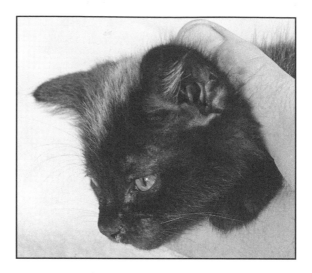

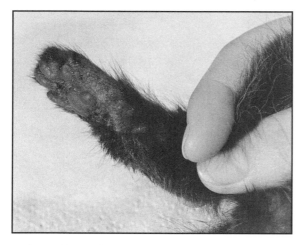

Scaly patches and irregular hair loss on the face and foot of a cat with *ringworm.*

Ringworm gets its name from its appearance, a spreading circle with hair loss and scaly skin at the center and an advancing red ring at the margin. However, the typical form may not be present—especially in cats. Occasionally, you will see only scaly patches, irregular hair loss or just a few broken hairs around the face and ears. (Ringworm of the ear flap is discussed in the EARS chapter.) Ringworm may invade toenails; when the nails grow out they are usually deformed.

Although simple ringworm is not an itchy condition, scabs and crusts can form, leading to draining sores that provoke licking and scratching. There can be extensive skin involvement. This problem usually occurs in young cats, those poorly nourished and cats whose immune system is depressed by disease.

The disease is transmitted by contact with spores in the soil and by contact with the infective hair of dogs and cats typically found on carpets, brushes, combs, toys and furniture. Cats can carry the fungus without showing any apparent infection and may represent a source of infection for other pets in the house. Humans can pick up ringworm from cats and can also transmit the disease to them. Children, who are especially likely to catch the disease, should avoid handling cats with ringworm. Adults, except for the elderly, seem relatively resistant.

Mild cases of ringworm, with just hair loss and local scaliness, often resemble demodectic mange. A diagnosis of ringworm can be made if the skin glows under ultraviolet light. This test is not positive in all cases. Microscopic examination of skin scrapings or fungal cultures are more certain methods of diagnosis.

Treatment: Mild cases often regress spontaneously. Recurrence is uncommon in cats with normal immunity.

For localized infection, clip away the infected hair at the margins of the ringworm patches and cleanse the skin with *Betadine* solution. Apply an antifungal cream, ointment or solution containing miconazole, chlorhexidine, clortrimazole or thiabendazole (e.g., *Conofite, Nolvasan, Lotrimin, Tresaderm*) to the affected areas and surrounding skin and hair once a day. Treat infected sores with a topical antibiotic such as *Triple Antibiotic Ointment*. It is usually necessary to continue treatment for four to six weeks.

Generalized ringworm requires an extensive clip of all infected hair and a twice a week dip with an antifungal solution such as *LymDyp* (lime sulfur), *Nolvasan* (chlorhexidine) or *Captan* (a garden fungicide). Dips should be continued for two weeks beyond apparent cure. For information on dipping, see *Insecticides*.

Oral antifungal drugs are often prescribed for generalized ringworm. Griesofulvin (*Fulvicin*) is the drug of choice. Ketoconazole and fluconazole are also effective but currently not licensed for use in animals. Griesofulvin and ketoconazole should not be given to pregnant queens as it may cause birth defects. Antifungal drugs require close veterinary counseling and supervision.

Prevention: Spores, which can survive for up to one year, should be eliminated from the premises to prevent reinfection. The cat's bedding should be discarded. Grooming equipment should be sterilized in a dilute solution (1:10) of sodium hypochlorite (*Clorox*). The house should be thoroughly cleaned and carpets vacuumed weekly to remove infected hair. Mop and wash hard surfaces (floors, countertops, cattery runs) using dilute Clorox. *Technical Captan* can be used as a spray in 1:200 dilution (in water) to spray a cattery.

Strict hygienic precautions are necessary to prevent human infection. Rubber gloves should be worn while handling and treating infected cats. Boil contaminated clothing and fabrics or wash in Clorox to kill spores.

THRUSH (CANDIDIASIS)

This yeastlike organism affects the mucous membranes of the mouth and ear canals. Skin involvement occurs rarely, almost exclusively among cats that live in moist humid environs.

Prolonged use of antibiotics can alter the natural bacterial flora and improve conditions for growth of yeast. Yeast infections can also occur in cats that are immunosuppressed and in those that are receiving corticosteroids. The yeast produces white elevated plaques that form an exudate and bleed easily when rubbed.

Treatment: Precipitating causes should be identified and corrected if possible. Skin patches are successfully treated with an ointment containing Nystatin (i.e., *Panolog*). Fungus infection of the mouth and ear canals is discussed in the chapters dealing with these areas.

MYCETOMA

Mycetomas are tumor-like masses caused by several species of fungi that enter the body through wounds. The typical appearance is a lump beneath the skin with an open tract to the surface draining a granular material. The color of the granules is white, yellow or black, depending on the type of fungus involved. The condition may resemble a chronic abscess that refuses to heal with antibiotics. Some species of mycetoma can cause a fatal infection.

Treatment: Antifungal drugs are seldom effective. Complete surgical removal is the treatment of choice.

HORMONAL SKIN DISEASES

Hormonal skin diseases are not common. Characteristically they produce a symmetrical hair loss equally distributed along both sides of the body—one side being

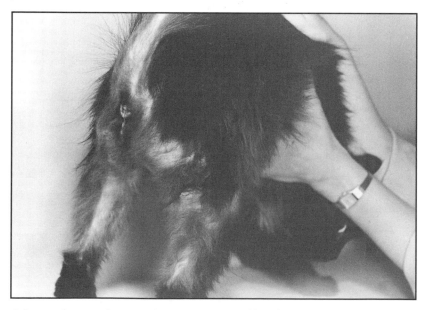

Feline endocrine alopecia, showing symmetrical hair loss with normal skin.

the mirror image of the other. They do not cause itching. The rare exception is the cat whose hormone disorder is complicated by a skin infection.

BALDING (FELINE ENDOCRINE ALOPECIA)

Alopecia is the name given to balding. Feline endocrine alopecia is a type of balding seen most often in neutered males and spayed middle-aged females. A hormone deficiency has long been suspected as the cause of the problem, but hormone assays usually are normal. *Psychogenic alopecia* occurs in the same age range. It is possible that many cases attributed to hormone deficiency actually are cases of compulsive self-grooming. For more information, see the chapter *Behavior Problems*.

Loss of hair occurs in a symmetrical pattern on the lower part of the abdomen, perineum and genital areas and on the insides of the back legs. Only in severe cases is the remainder of the coat affected. Some cats grow back the hair only to lose it again later. Itching is not a problem.

Treatment: This is mainly a cosmetic condition. Treatment with sex hormones is not recommended owing to serious side effects that include liver and bone marrow toxicity.

THYROID DEFICIENCY (HYPOTHYROIDISM)

Hypothyroidism is rare in cats and most commonly follows operations on the thyroid gland. A deficiency of thyroid hormone impairs new hair growth and prolongs the resting phase. Thus there is a gradual thinning of the coat, which may also appear dull and lifeless. Other signs of hypothyroidism include lethargy, constipation, weight gain, mental dullness and a disproportionate type of dwarfism characterized by an enlarged broad head with short neck and limbs. Diagnosis requires a thyroid blood test.

Treatment: Hypothyroidism is usually permanent and requires lifetime treatment with daily hormone replacement therapy.

CORTISONE EXCESS (ADRENAL HYPERFUNCTION)

This condition is due to overproduction of cortisone by the adrenal glands that are located on top of the kidneys. An adrenal gland tumor (or a tumor of the pituitary gland, which acts on the adrenal gland) can cause this problem. Both are extremely rare in cats. Administering cortisone by mouth or injection can, in time, lead to the same effect as if the adrenals were making too much cortisone. This happens infrequently in cats because they have a high degree of resistance to the side effects of cortisone.

The effect of excess cortisone is to produce loss of hair in a symmetrical pattern over the trunk, with darkening of the underlying skin. There is a pot-bellied look. Such cats gain weight, retain fluid and may have associated disorders of the liver, pancreas or urinary system.

Treatment: If your cat is getting cortisone by tablet or injection, your veterinarian may be able to gradually reduce the dosage or stop the medication altogether. Cortisone excess caused by a tumor of the pituitary or adrenal gland is treated by removal of both adrenal glands and daily cortisone replacement tablets.

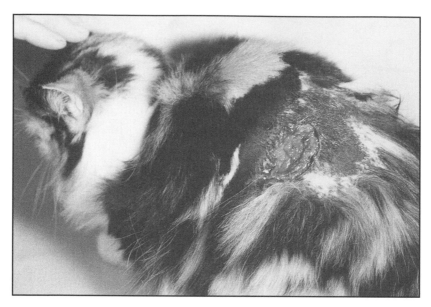

Pyoderma and *skin abscess* caused by a wound inflicted during a cat fight.

PYODERMA (BACTERIAL INFECTION OF THE SKIN)

Pyoderma is a bacterial infection of the skin. Ninety percent of cases are caused by the staphylococcus bacteria. Pyoderma is classified according to the depth of skin involvement.

IMPETIGO

This is an infection of the dermis of the skin that occurs in newborn kittens. It is discussed in PEDIATRICS: *Skin Infection of the Newborn*.

FOLLICULITIS

This is a localized infection of hair follicles. It is often associated with more extensive skin involvement but may occur by itself. Deeper involvement of hair follicles is called *furunculosis*. When numerous hair follicles are affected, a *carbuncle* may form.

FELINE ACNE

Feline acne develops in the sebaceous glands on the underside of the chin and edges of the lips. Blockage of skin pores by excess sebum or keratin is a predisposing cause. It is more common among cats with oily skin. It is not analogous to acne in people.

Feline acne is identified by finding blackheads or pimple-like bumps that come to a head and drain pus. Swelling of the entire chin and lower lips may be seen in severe cases.

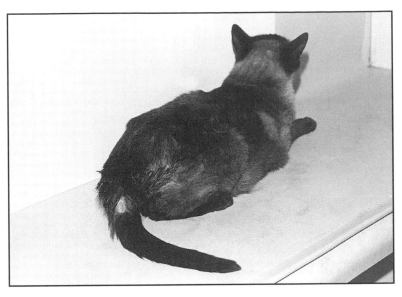

Stud tail is most common in tomcats.

Treatment: The infection usually responds to cleansing of the skin twice a day with an ointment or gel containing 2.5 percent to 5 percent benzoyl peroxide (*OxyDex*), chlorhexidine (*Nolvasan*) or povidone-iodine (*Betadine*). When excess sebum is a factor, the skin should be cleansed with a tar and sulfa shampoo for cats. An extensive or deep infection may require antibiotics. As the underlying condition remains the same, acne often recurs when treatment is stopped.

STUD TAIL

This condition is similar to acne because it is caused by oversecretion of sebaceous glands. As you part the hair on top of the tail near its base you may see an accumulation of waxy brown material. In severe cases the hair follicles become infected. The hair becomes matted and greasy, develops a rancid odor and may fall out. The condition is most common in tomcats but may occur in females and neutered males.

Treatment: Wash the tail twice a day with a tar and sulfa shampoo for cats and sprinkle cornstarch or baby powder. If the skin is infected, treat as you would for *Cellulitis and Abscesses* (below). Neutering may relieve the condition in tomcats.

CELLULITIS AND ABSCESSES

Cellulitis is an inflammation involving the deep layers of the skin. Most cases are caused by animal bites or scratches (i.e., cat fights). Puncture wounds allow skin bacteria to get established beneath the epidermis. Infection can be prevented in many fresh wounds if proper care is taken of them within the first few hours (see *Wounds*, in the chapter EMERGENCIES).

The signs of skin cellulitis are *pain* (*tenderness* to pressure), *warmth* (it feels hotter than normal), *firmness* (it's not as soft as it should be) and *change in color* (it appears *redder* than it should be). As the infection spreads from the wound into the lymphatic system, you may see red streaks in the skin and be able to feel enlarged lymph nodes in the groin, armpit or neck.

A *skin abscess* is a localized pocket of pus beneath the surface of the skin. Pimples, pustules, furuncles and boils are examples of small abscesses. The signs are the same as those for cellulitis except that an abscess feels like fluid under pressure.

If hot packs are applied to an area of cellulitis, the heat and moisture assist the natural defenses of the body to surround the infection and make it come to a head. The skin over the top of an abscess thins out and ruptures, allowing the pus to be evacuated. Then the pocket heals from below.

Treatment: Localize the infection by clipping away the hair and applying warm soaks three times a day for 15 minutes each. Saline soaks, made with a teaspoonful of salt in a quart of water, make a suitable poultice.

Pimples, pustules, furuncles, boils and other small abscesses that do not drain spontaneously need to be lanced with a sterile needle or scalpel. Flush the cavity with dilute *Betadine* solution or a dilute hydrogen peroxide solution (one part to five parts water) to keep it open and draining until it heals from below. Foreign bodies (such as splinters) beneath the skin must be removed with forceps because they are a continuous source of infection.

Antibiotics are used in the treatment of wound infections, cellulitis and abscesses. Most skin bacteria respond well to penicillin, Keflex, Tetracycline or Chloromycetin, but cultures and antibiotic sensitivity tests may be indicated to select a drug.

EOSINOPHILIC GRANULOMA COMPLEX

Eosinophilic granulomas, formerly called *lick granulomas*, are a group of skin diseases producing ulceration and granulation of the skin. Some sores may be associated with an allergic skin disorder such as *Feline Miliary Dermatitis*, *Food Hypersensitivity* or *Inhalant Allergy*. In others an immune-depressant condition such as *Feline Leukemia* may exist.

The *Indolent* (*Rodent*) *Ulcer* is found most commonly on the middle of the upper lip, occasionally on the lower lip, or in the mouth behind the last upper molar. The ulcer is not itchy or painful. It has the potential to develop into cancer. It is discussed in the MOUTH AND THROAT chapter.

The *Eosinophilic Plaque* is an itchy skin condition that occurs in young to middle-aged cats (average age three years). It is characterized by well-circumscribed, raised, red plaques with hair loss. These plaques are found on the abdomen and inside thighs. They are believed to be caused by an allergy. The diagnosis is made by biopsy of a plaque.

Linear Granulomas occur in kittens and young cats (average age one year), more often in females than males. They are circumscribed, raised and red but present a *linear* rather than a circular appearance. They occur on the back of the hind legs, in most cases on both sides, one side being the mirror image of the other. Linear granulomas also involve the foot pads and may occur in the mouth. This condition is also believed to be the result of an allergy. Diagnosis is like that for eosinophilic plaque.

Mosquito Bite Hypersensitivity affects the bridge of the nose and tips of the ears and produces itching of the pads of the feet. Characteristically you will see crusty sores with erosions and scabs. When severe and generalized, it is accompanied by fever and swollen lymph nodes. It disappears in winter. Cats with hypersensitivity to mosquito bites should be prevented from going outdoors in the mosquito season.

Treatment of Eosinophilic Granuloma Complex: Identify the underlying cause of the problem if possible, and treat it accordingly. Chlorpheniramine (*Chlor-Trimeton*), two to four mg by mouth twice a day, helps to relieve itching. Cortisone can be administered directly into the sore by injection. Oral cortisone preparations are required in most cases. Treatment should be vigorous because eosinophilic granulomas are difficult to treat and tend to recur. *Veterinary supervision is essential.*

LUMPS AND BUMPS (NODULES ON OR BENEATH THE SKIN)

Any sort of lump, bump or growth found on or beneath the skin is by definition a tumor, which means literally a swelling. Tumors are classified as **benign** when they are not cancer—and **malignant** when they are.

Classically, a benign growth is one that grows slowly, is surrounded by a capsule, is not invasive and does not spread to other parts. However, there is no good way to tell whether a tumor is benign or malignant without removing it and examining it with a microscope. If the tumor is benign, it won't come back if it is completely removed.

Cancers usually enlarge rapidly (a few weeks or months). They are not encapsulated. They appear to infiltrate into surrounding tissue and may ulcerate the skin and bleed. A hard mass that appears attached to bone or could be a growth of the bone itself is a cause for concern. The same is true for pigmented lumps or flat moles that start to enlarge, then spread out and begin to bleed (*Melanomas*).

A hard gray (or pink) open sore that does not heal, especially on the feet and legs, should be regarded with suspicion. This could be a skin cancer.

Any unexplained nodules or open sores on your cat should be checked by your veterinarian. Most cancers are not painful. Do not delay simply because your cat does not seem to be feeling uncomfortable. To learn more about common surface growths, see the chapter TUMORS AND CANCERS.

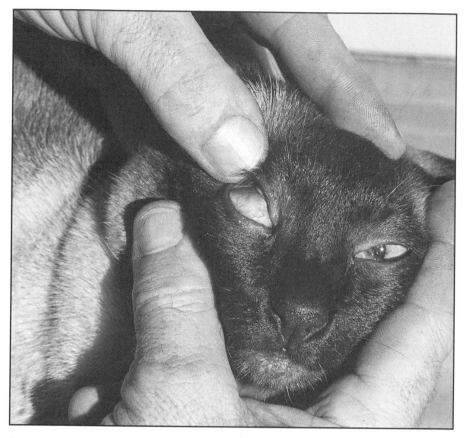

By recessing the eye you can demonstrate a normal third eyelid. —J. Clawson

5

EYES

SPECIAL CHARACTERISTICS

Cats' eyes have some special characteristics that set them apart from those of most other animals. Dogs use a combination of sight, hearing and smell to orient themselves to their surroundings, but cats depend more on their sight, which is uniquely adapted to hunting and stalking.

The eyes of cats are unusually large. In fact, if man had an eye of comparable size, it would measure almost eight inches in diameter. The eyeball is recessed in a fat cushion that protects the eyeball in a bony socket. Because of this deep-seated location, eye movements are restricted. Especially adept at detecting movement out of the corner of the eye, a cat turns its head rapidly to bring the object into focus. The cat is less skillful at identifying stationary objects and will watch them for long periods with an intense, steady, unblinking stare, to detect the slightest movement.

A cat does not see close objects in good focus. This is because the muscles that change the shape of the lens are relatively weak. Near vision is like that of a middle-aged person who is becoming nearsighted and needs reading glasses. The cat compensates for this somewhat by narrowing the pupils into slitlike openings that sharpen the image.

The cat's **retina,** a light sensitive membrane at the back of the eye, contains two types of photoceptor nerve cells called *rods* and *cones.* Rods react to intensities of light. They enable cats to see black, white and shades of gray. Cones provide for color vision. Since the cat's retina has many rods and few cones, the cat is able to see well in dim light but has limited color vision.

The reason cats' eyes appear to glow in the dark is that they have a special layer of cells behind the retina called the *tapetum lucidum.* These cells act like a mirror, reflecting the light back onto the retina, doubly exposing the photoreceptors. It is this reflective process plus the large number of rods in the retina that is responsible for the cat's exceptional night vision, which is superior to that of most other animals.

Another special characteristic of the cat's eye is an extra eyelid or **nictitating membrane,** normally not visible but resting on the eyeball at the inside corner. You can see this extra eyelid by recessing the eye. Press gently on the eyeball through the eyelid with your index finger. The third membrane will immediately slide out across the surface of the eye. The third eyelid has an important cleansing and lubricating function and compensates for the fact that a cat seldom blinks. Like a windshield wiper, the third eyelid sweeps across the surface of the eye, dispersing tears and removing dust and foreign particles. It also helps to protect the eye's surface from injury. By partially closing the upper and lower eyelids and protruding the nictitating membrane, a cat's eyes are protected while going through weeds and brush.

STRUCTURE OF THE EYE

The whole clear front part of the eye, which you can see when you look at your cat's face, is the cornea. It is covered by a layer of transparent cells and surrounded by a white rim called the *sclera.* In the cat, you can see very little of the sclera without drawing back the eyelids. The layer of tissue that covers the white of the eye is called the *conjunctiva.* It reflects back to cover the inner surface of the eyelids and both sides of the nictitating membrane but does not cover the cornea.

The cat's eyelids are tight folds of skin that support the front of the globe. They do not make direct contact with the surface of the eye because there is a thin layer of tears between them. The edges of the eyelids should meet when the eyes are closed. If this does not happen the cornea dries out, causing eye irritation. Normally, cats do not have eyelashes, but when present and misdirected, they are a source of irritation to the surface of the eye.

The tears are secreted by glands found in the eyelids, nictitating membrane and conjunctiva. They serve two functions. They cleanse and lubricate the surface of the eye and contain immune substances that help prevent bacteria from gaining a foothold and causing an eye infection.

A normal accumulation of tears is removed by evaporation. Excess tears are pooled near the eye's inner corner and carried via a drainage system to the nose. Excess tearing or watering of the eye indicates an eye ailment.

The opening at the center of the eye is the **pupil**. It is surrounded by a circular or elliptical layer of pigmented muscle called the **iris**. The iris changes the size and

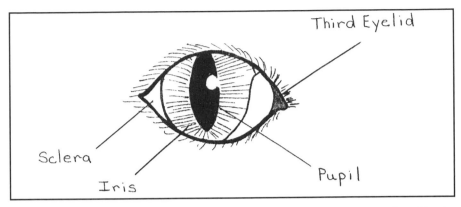

Front view of the eye. —Rose Floyd

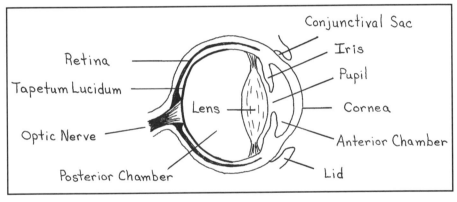

Side view of the eye. —Rose Floyd

shape of the pupil. As the iris expands the pupil enlarges and becomes round. As it contracts, the pupil narrows to a vertical slit.

Cats' eyes come in many colors. Eye color is the result of pigment in the iris. Common eye colors are yellow and green. Some cats have orange, blue, or purplish eyes. Occasionally a cat is born with eyes of different colors. This occurs most often in Persians—one iris is orange and the other is blue. This may be associated with congenital deafness on the side with the blue iris. Congenital deafness can also occur in white-coated cats with blue irises.

The **inner eye** has two chambers. The *anterior chamber* is found between the cornea and the lens. The *posterior* chamber, containing a clear jelly, is the central cavity of the eye between the lens and the retina. Light enters the eye by passing first through the cornea and the anterior chamber and then through the pupil and

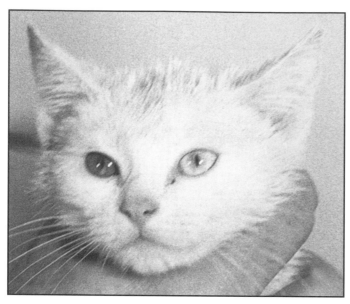

A white cat with a blue left eye. She was deaf in the left ear.

the lens. The *lens* focuses the light, which then passes through the posterior chamber and is received by the retina.

WHAT TO DO IF YOUR CAT HAS AN EYE PROBLEM

Your cat has an eye problem if there is matter in the eye, the eye waters, the cat blinks, squints, paws at the eye or gives evidence that the eye is painful or if the nictitating membrane is visible. The first thing to do is examine the eye and try to determine the cause.

HOW TO EXAMINE THE EYE

The eye examination should be done in a dark room using a single light source such as a flashlight and a magnifying glass. With magnification, you can see fine details on the surface of the eyelids and the eyeball and may be able to inspect some of the inner-eye structures. Most cats need to be restrained. Put the cat in a pillowcase and pin the case around the neck.

You can often get a clue to the cause of the problem by comparing one eye with the other. See if the eyes are of the same size, shape and color. Do they bulge forward or are they recessed back in their sockets? Is there an eye discharge? Is the third eyelid visible over the inside corner of the eye? Does the eye look smoky, hazy or cloudy?

To examine the outer surface of the eyeball, place one thumb just below the eye and the other over the bone just above the upper lid. Gently draw down on the lower thumb and apply counter traction with the other. The lower lid will sag out and you can look in and see the conjunctival sac and most of the cornea behind it. Reverse the procedure to examine the surface of the eye behind the upper lid. Flash a light across the surface of the cornea to see if it is clear and transparent. A dull or dished-out spot is a sign of an injury. The pupils should be equal in size. They should narrow to vertical slits when light is flashed into the eye.

Push gently on the surface of the eyeball through the eyelid to see if one eye feels unusually hard or soft. If the eye is tender, the cat will give evidence of pain.

To test for vision, cover one eye and pretend you are about to touch the other eye with your finger. A cat that has vision will blink when your finger approaches.

SIGNS OF EYE AILMENT

Eye disorders are accompanied by a number of signs and symptoms. Pain is one of the most serious. *A cat with a painful eye should receive prompt veterinary attention.*

Eye Discharge: The type of discharge helps to define the cause. A clear discharge without redness and pain indicates a problem in the tear drainage system (see *The Tearing Mechanism*). Any discharge accompanied by a *painful* eye should alert you to the possibility of CORNEA or INNER EYE involvement. A thick, sticky, mucus or puslike discharge along with a red (inflamed) eye suggests conjunctivitis (*Red Eye*).

Painful Eye: Signs of pain include excessive tearing, squinting (closing down the eye), tenderness to touch and avoidance of light. The nictitating membrane often protrudes in response to pain. The usual causes of a painful eye are injuries to the *Cornea* and diseases of the *Inner Eye*.

Film over the Eye: An opaque or whitish film that moves out over the surface of the eyeball from the inside corner of the eye is a protruded nictitating membrane. Causes are discussed in *The Third Eyelid*.

Cloudy Eye: Loss of clarity or transparency of the eye indicates an *Inner Eye* disorder. When it is entirely opaque, the owner might think the cat has a "blind eye," but this is not necessarily correct.

Hard or Soft Eye: Changes in eye pressure are caused by disorders of the *Inner Eye*. The pupil may become fixed and unable to dilate or constrict. A hard eye with a dilated pupil indicates *Glaucoma*. A soft eye with a small pupil indicates inflammation of the inner structures of the eye (*Uveitis*).

Irritation of the Lids: Conditions that cause swelling, crusting, itching or hair loss are discussed in *Eyelids*.

Bulging or Sunken Eye: Abnormal contours and positions of the eye are discussed in *The Eyeball*.

Abnormal Eye Movements: Eyes that focus in different directions or jerk back and forth are also discussed in *The Eyeball*.

HOW TO APPLY EYE MEDICINE

Steady your cat's head with one hand and draw down on the lower eyelid to expose the inner surface. Rest the other hand containing the applicator against the cat's face as shown in the illustration. Should the cat move suddenly your hand will also move, avoiding injury to the eye. Apply ointment to the inside of the lower lid.

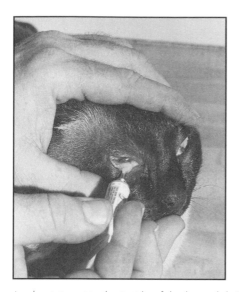 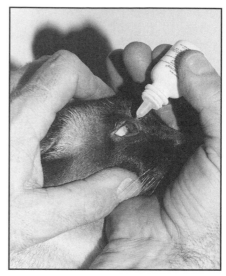

Apply ointment to the inside of the lower lid. Drops are applied to the inner corner of the eye.   —J. Clawson

Direct application of ointment to the eyeball is irritating and may cause the cat's head to jerk.

Eye drops are applied directly to the eyeball. Steady the hand holding the dropper against the side of the cat's head. Tilt the cat's nose upward, then drop the medication into the inner corner of the eye. Rub the eyelids gently to disperse the medicine. Eye drops should be applied frequently since they tend to wash out with tears. Use only preparations specifically labeled for *ophthalmic* use. Check to be sure that the preparation is not out of date. Prolonged administration of antibiotics in the eye can predispose to fungal infection.

Minor eye ailments should not be neglected. If they do not respond to treatment in 24 hours, consult your veterinarian.

THE EYEBALL

EYE OUT OF ITS SOCKET (AN EMERGENCY)

A hard blow to the head or a forceful strain can push the eyeball out of the socket. The lids may snap behind the eyeball, causing it to remain dislocated. This injury tends to occur in short-nosed breeds with large prominent eyes. Shortly after the dislocation, swelling behind the eye makes it extremely difficult to manipulate the eye back to its normal position.

Apply cold compresses to prevent further swelling, and bandage as described in the EMERGENCIES chapter (see *Eye Bandage*). Cover both eyes, as movement of the uninjured eye results in undesired movement of the dislocated eye. Seek immediate veterinary attention. The eyeball must be replaced as soon after the injury as possible.

If unable to obtain veterinary services within one hour, attempt the following: First restrain the cat (see EMERGENCIES: *Handling and Restraint*). Then lubricate the eyeball with a few drops of mineral oil and gently draw the lids outward over the eyeball, allowing the eyeball to drop back into its socket. If unsuccessful, do not persist as forceful manipulation and repeated attempts cause further swelling and lead to greater injury.

BULGING EYE (EXOPHTHALMOS)

In this condition, swelling of tissue behind the eye pushes the eyeball forward. As seen from above, the affected eye appears to be more prominent. Major protrusion prevents closure of the eyelids. If the nerves to the eye are stretched or damaged, the pupil dilates and does not constrict when a light is flashed in the eye. Exophthalmos may occur also after a blow that fractures the bones of the eye socket and causes a sudden buildup of blood or fluid behind the eye.

Infections that spread to the eyeball from the sinus also cause the eye to bulge. They are accompanied by extreme pain when the cat attempts to open its mouth.

A growth behind the eyeball is another cause of eye protrusion. Most are malignant and respond poorly to treatment. You will notice a gradual bulging of the eye that gets worse over a matter of weeks.

Finally, untreated chronic glaucoma can lead to increased size of the eye and protrusion (see *Hard Eye*).

Treatment: All causes of exophthalmos are extremely serious and may cause loss of vision. *They require immediate veterinary attention.* Drugs can be given to reduce the swelling produced by trauma. Antibiotics are required to treat infections behind the eye. Surgery may be indicated to drain blood or pus behind the eye or

A bulging right eye caused by a growth behind the eyeball.

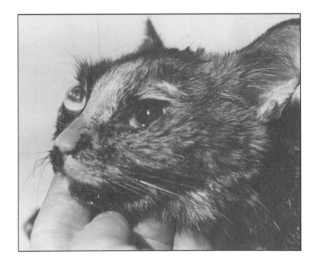

within an infected sinus or to suture an eyelid over a bulging eyeball to protect that eyeball from injury and keep it from drying out.

SUNKEN EYE (ENOPHTHALMOS)

Both eyeballs may recede when there is loss of substance in the fat pads behind the eye, as in dehydration or rapid weight loss.

There is a retractor muscle that, when it goes into spasm, pulls the eye back into its socket. This can occur with a painful injury to the cornea. Tetanus produces retractor muscle spasms of both eyeballs, with characteristic appearance of the third eyelids. Damage to a nerve trunk in the neck can result in a sunken eyeball and a small pupil (*Horner's Syndrome*). This can occur as a consequence of a neck injury or middle-ear infection. Finally, after a severe injury, the eye may atrophy, becoming smaller and sinking into the socket.

As the eye begins to recess, the third eyelid or nictitating membrane becomes visible, and there is an accumulation of mucus in the recessed space formed by the eye's sinking. This gives the eye a peculiar, rolled-back look. Because of the presence of a membrane across the eye, a sunken eye is often mistaken for just a protrusion of the third eyelid.

Treatment: The treatment of enophthalmos is directed at the underlying cause of the problem.

CROSS-EYED GAZE (STRABISMUS)

A cross-eyed look is extremely common among Siamese cats—so much so that many owners accept it as normal. One eye looks ahead while the other eye turns in. This condition is inherited.

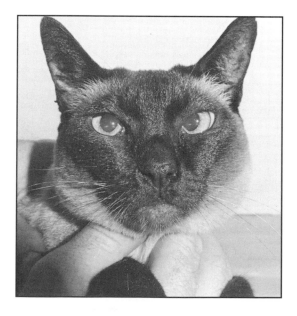

A cross-eyed look is common among Siamese

—J. Clawson

Severe squinting (blepharospasm) associated with a painful eye condition.

Other types of strabismus are caused by eye muscle paralysis. The eye cannot move in a certain direction. Brain tumors and injuries to the nerves and muscles of the eye are predisposing causes. This type of strabismus is rare.

JERKING EYE MOVEMENTS (NYSTAGMUS)

Involuntary movement of the eyes may be irregular side-to-side jerking of the eyeballs or rhythmic pendulum-like swings with a fast and slow phase. They indicate a disorder of the vestibular system (see *Inner Ear* in the EARS chapter).

EYELIDS

SEVERE SQUINTING (BLEPHAROSPASM)

Spasm of the muscles around the eye is induced by eye irritants such as foreign materials. The irritation causes tightening of the eyelid muscles, which partially close the eye and roll the eyelids inward against the cornea. Once rolled in, the rough margins of the lids rub against the eyeball, causing further pain and spasm.

Anesthetic drops can be applied to the eyeball to relieve the pain and break the cycle. The relief is temporary if the underlying irritant is not found and removed.

IRRITATED EYELIDS (BLEPHARITIS)

Blepharitis, or inflammation of the eyelids, occurs often, primarily because of eyelids injured during cat fights. Scratches and surface injuries can easily become infected.

This leads to itching and scratching, crust formation and the accumulation of pus and debris on the eyelids.

Blepharitis can also be caused by *head mange mites* (*Notoedres cati*), *demodectic mange mites* and *ringworm* infection. Head mange causes intense itching. Because of persistent scratching there is hair loss, redness and scab formation. Ringworm affects the hair on the eyelid, causing it to become brittle and break off next to the skin. This is not an itchy condition. The skin may look scaly and crusted but is seldom red or irritated.

Treatment: Protect the eye by instilling mineral oil and then loosen the scabs by soaking them with warm compresses. Keep the eye clean and *seek veterinary attention*. The treatment of ringworm and mange is discussed in the SKIN chapter.

SUDDEN SWELLING (CHEMOSIS)

Sudden swelling of the eyelids and conjunctiva is caused by an allergic reaction. Insect bites and allergens in foods and drugs are the most common causes. For more information, see *Allergies* in the SKIN chapter. The conjunctiva and eyelids are fluid-filled, puffy and soft. Water has passed out of the circulation into the tissues in response to the allergen.

This is not a serious problem. It is of short duration and improves when the allergic agent is removed. Simple cases may be treated with drops or eye ointments containing a corticosteroid that should be prescribed by your veterinarian.

FOREIGN BODIES IN THE EYE

Foreign material such as dust, grass seed, dirt and specks of vegetable matter can become trapped behind the eyelids and nictitating membranes. The first indication is tearing and watering, along with signs of irritation such as blinking and squinting. The third membrane may protrude to protect the irritated eye.

Treatment: First examine the eye as described above (see *How to Examine the Eye*). You might be able to see a foreign body on the surface of the eye or behind the upper or lower eyelid. If not, the foreign body may be caught behind the third eyelid, and the cat will need a topical eye anesthetic before you can lift up the eyelid and remove the foreign matter.

For dirt and loose debris in the eye, hold the eyelid open and flush the eye with cool water for 10 to 15 minutes. Soak a wad of cotton and squeeze it into the eye. If a foreign body can be seen but cannot be removed by irrigation, you may be able to remove it by gently swabbing the eye with a moistened cotton-tipped applicator. The foreign body may adhere to it. Thorns that cling to the eyelid's surface can be removed with blunt-nosed tweezers. Foreign bodies that penetrate the surface of the eye should be removed by a veterinarian. After you have removed a foreign object, apply a triple antibiotic ointment such as *Mycitracin*.

The cat may persist in rubbing the eye after treatment. If so, the foreign body may still be in the eye or a corneal abrasion may have occurred (see *Cornea*). *Get professional help*.

Chemosis. Sudden swelling of the eyelids and conjunctiva caused by an allergic reaction.

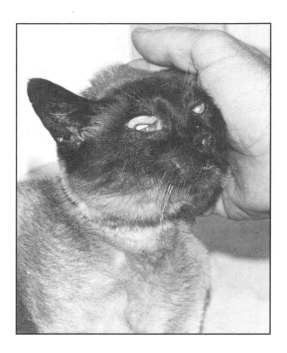

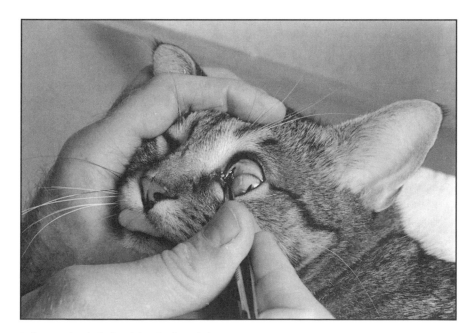

A foreign body behind the third eyelid.

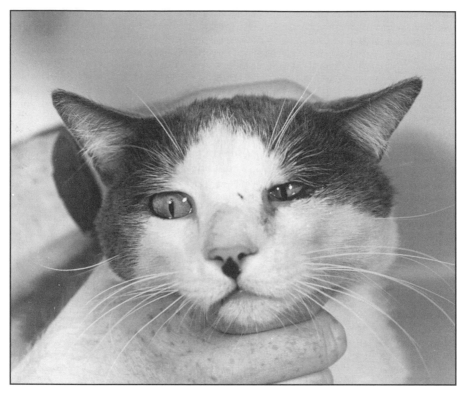

Severe squinting with eye discharge and loss of hair, indicative of chronic eye irritation—here due to *entropion*.

Eye Irritation from Lashes (Trichiais)

Normally cats do not have eyelashes, but there are exceptions. When present, they may grow in from the eyelid and rub against the cornea, producing eye irritation and injury. In such cases the hair should be removed by the roots through surgery or cryotherapy (freezing). Plucking them with blunt-nosed tweezers provides temporary relief.

Eyelid Rolled Inward (Entropion)

This condition occurs sporadically as a hereditary defect in the Persian but can occur in any cat because of scarring of the lower lid following a bout of purulent conjunctivitis or a lacerated eyelid. The rolled-in lid produces eye irritation with tearing and severe squinting. Entropion in the adult cat can be corrected by an operation.

Eyelid Rolled Outward (Ectropion)

In this situation, the lower eyelid rolls out from the face, exposing the surface of the eye to irritants. It may be caused by a birth defect, but in most cases it is due to an

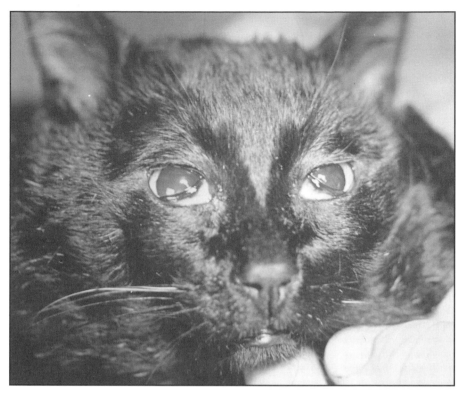

Protrusion of the nictitating membranes, occurring with the Haw syndrome.

improperly healed laceration of the lid. Plastic surgery may be necessary to tighten the lid and protect the eye.

TUMORS

In cats, growths of the eyelids tend to be cancers. Some are a cauliflower-like growth, while others are ulcerated. Eyelid tumors usually occur in older cats. Malignant tumors grow rapidly and spread to lymph nodes in the neck. Squamous cell cancer is the most common malignancy. White-coated cats are predisposed to squamous cell cancer of the eyelids, nose and ears.

All growths of the eyelids should be removed and sent for tissue examination.

THE THIRD EYELID

FILM OVER THE EYE (PROTRUSION OF THE NICTITATING MEMBRANE)

An opaque third eyelid, not normally seen, may become visible in response to illness or injury. The length of time the membrane is exposed may vary, as though blinking, or remain fixed. When the nictitating membrane is visible *over* the inside corner of the eye it is protruding.

When associated with a *bulging eye*, causes of protrusion of the nictitating membrane include infection in the tissue behind the eyeball (abscess), bleeding behind the eye and tumor.

When associated with a retracted or *sunken eye*, causes of protrusion of the nictitating membrane include any painful eye illness resulting in spasm of the muscles around the eye; spasm of these muscles when caused by tetanus; and dehydration or chronic weight loss that reduces the size of the fat pad behind the eye. When only one eye is involved, suspect an illness related to that eye; when both eyes are involved, suspect a systemic illness such as *feline viral respiratory infection*.

The **Key-Gaskell** syndrome is a rare autonomic nervous system disorder of unknown cause, one sign of which is prolapse of the third eyelid.

Horner's syndrome can result in a sunken eye, prolapse of the third eyelid and a small pupil. This can occur as a consequence of injury to (or cancerous involvement of) a nerve in the neck or middle ear infection.

The **Haw** syndrome is a rather common but temporary protrusion of uncertain cause of the third eyelid. It affects healthy cats under two and is frequently preceded by a gastrointestinal illness. The protrusion clears up within a few months without treatment. During this time, if the film interferes with your cat's vision, your veterinarian can prescribe an eye drop solution containing 1 percent or 2 percent Pilocarpine, which reduces the size of the protrusion.

THE TEARING MECHANISM
THE WATERY EYE (EPIPHORA)

There are a number of conditions in which a watery or mucus-like discharge overflows the eyelids and runs down the sides of the face, staining the hair.

First it is important to determine whether the eye is red (irritated). Irritative eye disorders are characterized by excessive tearing along with a red or painful eye. However, if the eye is *not* red, then a tear drainage system blockage is at fault.

Keep in mind that excessive tearing or a sticky puslike discharge from the eyes or nose is frequently associated with *feline viral respiratory infection*. This possibility should be investigated before the eye alone is treated.

Cats do not experience emotional tearing. They do not cry as people do, so this is not a factor to be considered as one of the causes. In all cats with a runny eye, the cause should be determined so that proper treatment can be given.

Inadequate Tear Drainage (*Nasolacrimal occlusion*). This is a factor to be considered if the cat has a persistent eye discharge without redness. The discharge is due to an overflow of tears caused by a blockage in the tear draining system. See *Structure of the Eye*.

A cat may be born with an inadequate tear drainage system. However, in most cases nasolacrimal occlusion is the result of scarring from eyelid injuries acquired in cat fights. Other causes are chronic infection in the duct system and plugging of the ducts by thick secretions, dirt or grass seeds.

To see if the drainage system is open, a veterinarian stains the pool of tears near the inner corner of the eye with Fluorescein dye. If the dye does not appear at the

A clear watery discharge suggests serous conjunctivitis. The eye is not painful.

nostril, the tear duct is blocked on that side. Nasolacrimal probes are inserted into the duct opening, and various flushing techniques are used to show the point of obstruction. The flushing often removes the blockage and opens the duct.

Treatment: Infection in the duct system is treated with antibiotics. In some cases they are instilled into the duct or used to flush the system. The dosage, type and route of administration should be determined by your veterinarian.

Tear Stains in Persians and Himalayans. An overflow of tears accompanied by unsightly staining of the hair below the eyes occurs in some cats with short noses, large prominent eyes and flat faces. The problem is seen most often in Persians and Himalayans. These breeds are subject to chronic eye irritations and infections that produce tearing. Their facial structure usually causes a narrowing of the nasolacrimal duct and a shallow tear lake at the inner corner of the eye. All these factors may contribute to the problem.

Treatment: If there is no correctable cause, symptomatic improvement often results from a broad spectrum antibiotic. Should a chronic infection exist, the antibiotic will treat it. Tetracycline is the drug of choice. It is secreted in tears and also binds that part of the tears that stains the fur. If improvement is only due to the binding action of the drug, the face remains wet but not discolored. Tetracycline is given by mouth for three weeks. If the stain returns after treatment, then long-term administration might be considered. Some owners prefer to add low-dose tetracycline to the cat's food for long-term control. When cosmetic considerations are

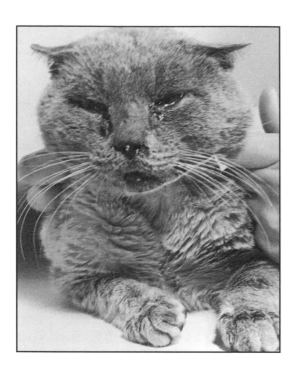

A kitten with feline viral respiratory disease and purulent conjunctivitis.

important, you can improve your cat's appearance by clipping the hair close to the face.

THE OUTER EYE

RED EYE (CONJUNCTIVITIS)

Conjunctivitis is an inflammation of the membrane covering the back of the eyelids and surface of the eyeball up to the cornea. It is one of the most common eye problems in cats. Signs are a red eye, discharge and pawing at the eye to relieve itching. *Conjunctivitis is not painful.* If the eye *is* red, irritated and painful to touch, consider the possibility of *keratitis, uveitis* or *glaucoma. Delay in treating these conditions could result in loss of vision.*

Serous Conjunctivitis is a mild condition in which the membrane looks pink and somewhat swollen. The discharge is clear and watery and is caused by physical irritants such as wind, cold weather, dust and various allergens. Serous conjunctivitis may be the first sign of a *feline viral respiratory disease.*

Purulent Conjunctivitis begins as a serous conjunctivitis that becomes purulent. Thick secretions crust the lids. The eye discharge contains mucus or pus. This suggests secondary *bacterial infection.*

When the discharge involves both eyes simultaneously, suspect a *virus.* When it involves one eye at first and progresses to the other eye several days later, suspect

Chlamydia or *Mycoplasma*. These microorganisms can be detected under a microscope in scrapings taken from the conjunctival membrane. Specific antibiotics are required.

Conjunctivitis due to *fungal infection* is rare and requires special laboratory aid for diagnosis.

Follicular Conjunctivitis is a condition in which the small mucous glands (follicles) on the underside of the nictitating membrane form a rough, cobblestone surface that irritates the eye and produces a mucoid discharge. Various pollens, allergens and infective agents are implicated as causes. After the initiating factor has been removed, these follicles may remain enlarged. The roughened surface of the conjunctiva then acts as a persistent irritant to the eye. A steroid-based eye ointment can be used to decrease the size of the follicles and smoooth the surface. If steroids are not effective, your veterinarian can mechanically or chemically cauterize the follicles.

Treatment of Conjunctivitis: Mild irritative forms of conjunctivitis can be treated at home. The eye should be cleansed with a dilute solution of boric acid for ophthalmic use or a sterile ophthalmic irrigating solution that can be purchased over the counter and used as directed for people. You should expect definite improvement within 24 hours. If not, *have your cat examined by a veterinarian.*

Purulent conjunctivitis requires eye irrigations and sometimes warm soaks to loosen crusted eyelids. Antibiotics are applied to the eye surface several times a day. They should be continued for seven days *beyond* apparent cure. An ointment containing a combination of neomycin, bacitracin and polymyxin works well (*Neosporin Ophthalmic Ointment*). If caused by chlamydia or mycoplasma, eye drops containing tetracycline or chloramphenicol are the antibiotics of choice.

Antiviral eye medications are available for the treatment of viral conjunctivitis. They should be prescribed by a veterinarian.

Deep-seated infections are difficult to clear up. In such cases you should suspect involvement of the tear drainage system. Repeated cleansing of the eye, correction of any underlying problem and specific topical and oral antibiotics tailored to cultures and sensitivities form the primary approach to this problem.

CONJUNCTIVITIS IN NEWBORN KITTENS (OPHTHALMIA NEONATORIUM)

Newborn kittens' eyes do not open until they are 10 to 12 days old. Before they open, there is a closed space behind the eyelids that can become infected if bacteria or other infectious agents gain entrance via the bloodstream or through small scratches about the eyes. The closed eyelids bulge out. A partially opened eye may develop a dry crusty covering. *Any discharge from the eye of a kitten is abnormal.*

Feline herpes virus can cause neonatal infectious conjunctivitis. It is transmitted from the queen to her kittens at birth or shortly thereafter.

Treatment: The eyelids must be teased open with a toothpick to allow the pus to drain out. Otherwise, there can be permanent damage to the forepart of the eye. Once the eyelids have been separated, pus will drain out in large drops. The eyes should be flushed with boric acid eyewash or a sterile ophthalmic irrigating solution

Chronic conjunctivitis with a thick mucus discharge from the eyes.

bought over the counter and used as directed for people. Afterward, medicate with antibiotic drops (e.g., neomycin, gentamicin) four times a day. If herpes virus is suspected, your veterinarian can prescribe antiviral medications. Crusted eyelids *must* be cleansed several times a day to prevent them from pasting shut. Neonatal conjunctivitis usually affects several kittens in the litter.

Eye Worms

Cats can have eye worms transmitted by flies feeding on eye secretions. The adult worms, about one and a half inches long, appear in the conjunctival sac. They can be removed with blunt-nosed tweezers. If left unattended, they can damage the eye.

This disease affects cats living on the West Coast of the United States.

CLOUDY EYE

There are certain diseases that change the clarity of the eye, turning it cloudy or making it seem as if the cat has a "blind eye." This cloudiness can vary from a small localized haziness to complete opacification of the eye. Disorders that can cause a cloudy eye are *keratitis*, *glaucoma* and *cataracts*. They are discussed in the sections below.

A cloudy eye is beyond the scope of home veterinary care. It should receive immediate professional attention.

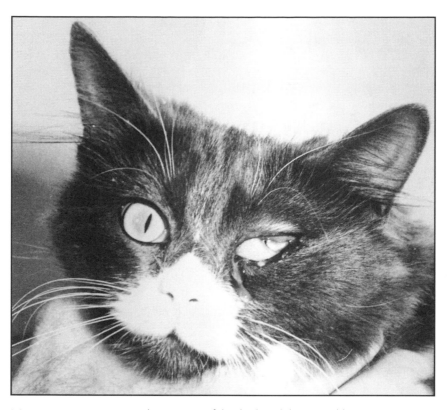

Note tearing, squinting and protrusion of the third eyelid—caused by an extensive corneal abrasion.

CORNEA

The cornea, or clear part of the eye, is covered by a protective layer of surface (*epithelial*) cells. Most destructive processes affecting the cornea begin with an injury to this layer. Any irritative process such as a foreign body or cat scratch can cause a surface injury. Cats with prominent eyes are especially susceptible. Once the continuity of the epithelium has been destroyed, the injury either heals spontaneously or progresses to a more serious problem. The outcome depends on the magnitude of the injury, how quickly it is recognized and whether or not the initiating factor has been identified and removed.

CORNEAL ABRASION

This is defined as an injury to the eye caused by a scratch. Corneal injuries are extremely painful. The cat squints, waters, paws at the eye; and light may hurt the eyes. Often the third eyelid comes out to protect the injured eye. With an extensive injury, the surface of the cornea surrounding the injury becomes swollen, giving it a cloudy, hazy or opacified appearance.

The cause of the corneal abrasion can often be suspected from its location. Abrasions in the upper part of the cornea may be caused by misdirected eyelashes on the upper eyelid. Lower corneal opacities suggest an imbedded foreign body. Abrasions near the inner corner of the eye suggest a foreign body beneath the third eyelid.

Healing of a corneal abrasion usually takes place in 24 to 48 hours by a process in which the epithelium thins and slides over a small defect. Larger and deeper abrasions require more time. A corneal abrasion will not heal if a foreign body is imbedded in the cornea or beneath one of the eyelids. Accordingly, in all but mild cases, examination for foreign bodies under the eyelids should be performed. Delay can lead to *corneal ulcer* or *keratitis*. Removal of foreign bodies is discussed above (*see Eyelids*).

Corneal Ulcers

Corneal ulcers are dangerous and must receive prompt medical attention. Most are caused by an injury to the cornea. Others are associated with an infection (virus, bacteria, fungus) or a nutritional deficiency. In some cases the cause is unknown.

Large ulcers may be visible to the naked eye. They appear as dull spots or dished-out depressions on the eye surface. Smaller ones are best seen after the eye has been stained with Fluorescein. Early treatment is vital to avoid serious complications or even loss of the eye. Cortisone, which is incorporated into many eye preparations used for conjunctivitis, *should not be put into an eye suspected of having a corneal injury.* This can lead to rupture of the cornea and blindness.

Keratitis

Keratitis is an inflammation of the cornea, or clear window of the eye. This is a *painful eye* condition and should be distinguished from *conjunctivitis*. Signs of keratitis include squinting, eye discharge, rubbing the eye and protrusion of the third eyelid. Conjunctivitis, on the other hand, is characterized by a chronic eye discharge with *little*, if any, *pain*. There are different types of keratitis. All result in loss of transparency of the cornea, which may lead to partial or complete blindness in the eye. Keratitis must be managed by a professional.

Ulcerative Keratitis. An injury to the surface of the eye can result in the development of an abrasion or ulcer that does not heal and becomes secondarily infected. Trauma is the most common cause of keratitis in cats.

An infectious form of ulcerative keratitis is caused by feline herpes virus (see Infectious Diseases: *Feline Viral Respiratory Disease Complex*). The signs of respiratory infection occur before or at the same time as eye involvement. One or both eyes may be affected. Treatment involves antiviral eye medications.

Chronic Degenerative Keratitis (Corneal sequestration). This condition, unique to cats, occurs in Persians, Siamese and domestic shorthair breeds. Signs are similar to those of ulcerative keratitis, but in this condition, inflamed tissue forms a

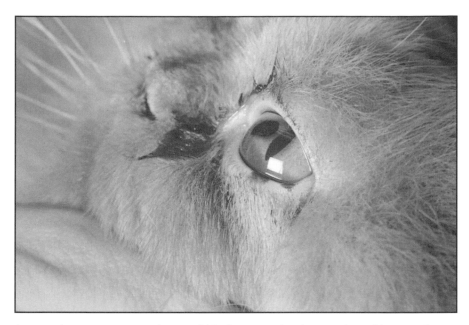

A corneal sequestrum. Note the round black spot on the clear window of the eye. This condition is unique to cats.

brown or black plaque on the corneal surface (sequestrum). The exact cause is unknown, but it has been found in association with entropion, lack of normal tear production (keratitis sicca), and lagophthalmos, a condition in which the eyelids do not completely close. Treatment involves removal of the sequestrum.

THE INNER EYE

THE BLIND CAT

Any condition that prevents light from getting into the eye will impair a cat's vision. Diseases of the cornea (*keratitis*) and of the lens (*cataract*) fall into this category. Inflammations of the deep structures of the eye (*glaucoma, uveitis*) also lead to blindness. Finally, any disease that reduces the sensitivity of the retina to light impulses (*retinal atrophy*) or any disease that affects the optic nerves or the sight center of the brain (*trauma*) can produce various forms of visual disturbance, including blindness. Most cases of blindness are not evident on general observation of the eye itself. Ophthalmologic studies are required to make an exact diagnosis.

Shining a bright light into a cat's eyes to test for pupillary constriction is *not* an exact method of determining whether or not the cat sees. The pupil may become smaller simply because of a light reflex. This won't tell you if the cat's brain has the ability to form visual images. But there are other indications that might suggest your cat is not seeing as well as possible. For example, activities that require eye and body

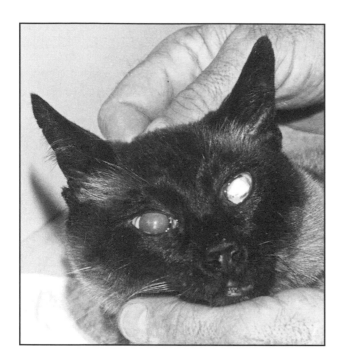

A cataract in the left eye.

coordination such as pouncing on a ball or jumping from a sofa to a chair might be impaired. In a dimly lighted room, cats with little or no vision may bump into furniture or may carry their noses close to the ground and feel with their whiskers.

Quite often, older cats' eyesight begins to fail shortly after the onset of deafness. They then rely more and more on memory to find their way around the house. Many totally blind cats get along surprisingly well when kept in familiar surroundings. However, *one thing they should not do is run free.* They must be kept indoors or in enclosed areas and taken out only under supervision.

CATARACTS

A cataract is defined as any opacity on the lens that interferes with transmission of light to the retina. A spot on the lens that blocks out light, *regardless* of size, technically is a cataract.

Cataracts of all types *are rare in cats.* Most cataracts are caused by eye injuries and infections. Inherited cataracts can be accompanied by other eye birth defects such as *microphthalmia* (small eye) or persistent pupillary membrane. Cataracts can develop in diabetic cats, but this is uncommon.

As a cat gets older, there is a normal aging of the eye. New fibers, continually forming on the lens surface throughout life, push toward the center. The lens also loses water as it ages. These changes lead to the formation of a bluish haze seen on the lens behind the cornea in older cats. Usually this does not interfere with vision and does not need to be treated. This condition, called **nuclear sclerosis,** *should be distinguished from a cataract.*

The bulging eye of chronic glaucoma, complicated by a corneal ulcer.

A cataract is important only when it impairs vision. Blindness can be corrected by removing the lens (cataract extraction). While this restores vision, there is a loss of visual acuity because the lens is not present to focus light on the retina. Accordingly, this operation is reserved for individuals with cataracts in both eyes who are having problems getting around.

GLAUCOMA (HARD EYE)

Glaucoma is due to an increase in fluid pressure within the eyeball. There is a continuous (although very slow) exchange of fluid between the eyeball and the venous circulation. Anything that upsets this delicate balance can cause a buildup of pressure and produce a hard, enlarging eye. When eye pressure becomes greater than the arterial blood pressure, arterial blood cannot enter the eye to nourish the retina.

Inflammations and infections within the eye are the most common causes of acquired or *secondary glaucoma* in cats (see *Uveitis*). Other causes are cataracts, eye injuries and cancers within the eye. *Primary* (congenital) glaucoma is rare but has been observed in the Persian, Siamese and domestic shorthair breeds.

An eye suffering from *acute glaucoma* exhibits mild to moderate tearing and squinting and slight redness to the white of the eye. The affected pupil is slightly *larger* than the opposite pupil. The eye may be painful when gently pressed and feels harder than the other eye. As fluid pressure increases, the eye becomes noticeably larger and the surface begins to bulge. In time, the retina becomes damaged. The lens may be pushed out of alignment (dislocated). *This entire sequence can occur suddenly or over a matter of weeks.* Measurement of intraocular pressure, using an instrument placed on the surface of the eye, and inspection of the interior of the eye are needed for a diagnosis. Some permanent vision may be lost before the disease is discovered.

Every effort should be made to distinguish glaucoma from *conjunctivitis* and *uveitis*, which produce similar signs. It is critical to begin treatment of glaucoma before irreversible injury occurs to the retina.

Treatment: Acute glaucoma may require emergency hospitalization. Various topical and oral drugs are used to lower intraocular pressure. Maintenance drugs are used for chronic glaucoma. Any underlying eye disorder should be treated. Failure to respond to medical management may be an indication for surgery. If there is potential for vision, an operation can be done to decrease the fluid pressure. For an eye that is blind and painful, the best approach is to remove the entire eye. A prosthesis can be inserted for cosmetic appearance.

UVEITIS (SOFT EYE)

Uveitis is defined as an inflammation of the inner pigmented structures of the eye. It is one of the most common inner eye conditions of cats, in part due to a number of feline infectious diseases that can involve the eye. They include feline leukemia, feline infectious peritonitis, feline immunodeficiency syndrome, toxoplasmosis, systemic fungus infections and the larvae of roundworms and heartworms. Uveitis may also be caused by penetrating eye injuries, bloodborne bacterial infections and eye tumors. Uveitis is a serious disorder that can lead to blindness.

Uveitis is painful. The cat squints, and the affected eye waters. Other distinguishing signs of uveitis are surface redness and a *small* pupil. When you push with your finger against the eye against the eyelid, the eye is tender and feels like a soft grape.

Treatment: Any underlying infectious or systemic illness should be treated. Corticosteroids reduce intraocular inflammation. Eye drops dilate the pupil and relieve pain. Treatment must be under veterinary supervision.

RETINAL DISEASES

The retina is a thin delicate membrane that lines the back of the eye and is actually an extension of the optic nerve. In retinal disease, the eye loses the ability to interpret the light it receives. The visual image may be blurred, and part or all of the visual field may be blacked out. Retinal diseases usually begin with loss of night vision. At this point the cat hesitates to go out at night or won't jump onto or off furniture in a darkened room. In cats, retinal diseases usually are not caused by genetic influences, although a hereditary form of *Progressive Retinal Atrophy* occurs in Persians and Abyssinians.

Retinitis is a disease in which inflammation of the retina leads to degeneration and destruction of the light receptors. It occurs in association with *feline toxoplasmosis, feline infectious peritonitis, lymphoma, cryptococcosis* and systemic fungus infections. It may also occur as a consequence of hypertension, of eye injury or for unknown reasons.

The dilated pupils of a blind cat with advanced retinal disease.

A dietary deficiency of the essential amino acid taurine produces a *central retinal degeneration* in cats that initially involves the central portion of the retina. Because this is the area where the cat sees best, the cat is unable to see stationary objects well. The cat retains some peripheral vision and thus is able to detect moving objects seen at the periphery. For more information on taurine deficiency see FEEDING AND NUTRITION: *Nutritional Requirements*.

Treatment of Retinal Diseases: The outlook for useful vision depends on the cause and extent of retinal damage at the time of diagnosis. Medical diseases are treatable. Control or cure can prevent further damage. Taurine deficiency is slowly progressive but dietary correction stops the process. *Progressive retinal atrophy* eventually leads to blindness. However, many totally blind cats get along surprisingly well when kept in familiar surroundings.

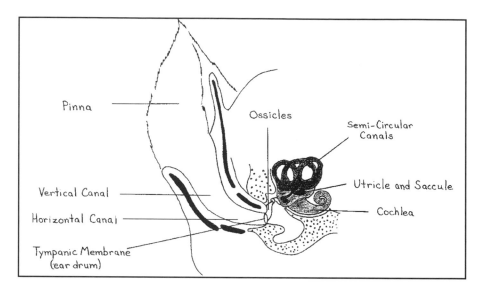

Anatomy of the ear.   —Rose Floyd

6

EARS

SPECIAL CHARACTERISTICS

Hearing is one of a cat's best developed senses. Cats can hear sounds too faint for us to detect. They can also hear noises pitched at a much higher frequency—even beyond the acute range of the dog. A cat's whole head turns toward the source of a sound and cocks from side to side. The ears move forward and backward or in a half circle to locate the angle of direction. The eyes also focus in the same direction.

Cats also have a remarkable sense of equilibrium due to a mechanism in the inner ear that allows the body to adjust with great speed and agility. When dropped from a height in an upside-down position, cats will land on their feet in less than two seconds. This is done by rotating the forequarters ahead of the hindquarters. With the aid of a strong tail, the body twists to bring all four feet down together for the landing. The fact that cats can land on all four feet does not mean they can fall from great heights without sustaining an injury. If you live in an apartment above the ground floor, be sure to keep screens on your windows. Cats may jump with little or no regard for heights.

STRUCTURE OF THE EARS

The ear is divided into three parts. The **outer ear** is composed of the *ear flap* (*pinna*) and *ear canal* (*external auditory canal*). The **middle ear** is made up of the *eardrum* (*tympanic membrane*) and the *auditory bones* or *ossicles*. The **inner ear** contains the *cochlea, bony labyrinth* and *auditory nerves*.

Sound, which is really air vibrations, is collected by the ear flap and directed down the ear canal to the eardrum. Movements of the eardrum are transmitted via a chain of small bones, the ossicles, to the bony canals of the inner ear.

The cochlea is a system of fluid-filled tubes in which waves are created by movements of the ossicles. Here the waves are transformed into nerve impulses and carried via the auditory nerve to the brain.

Cats' ears are carried erect. The skin on the outside is covered by hair and, like the rest of the body, is susceptible to the same diseases. Skin on the inside is pale pink, occasionally with spots of pigment. A small amount of brown waxy secretion in the ear canals is normal.

When a kitten is born, its ear canals are closed. They begin to open at 5 to 8 days. Kittens become oriented to sound at 13 to 16 days. They learn to recognize or distinguish between different sounds at three to four weeks. Knowing this sequence can help you to judge whether your kitten's hearing is developing normally.

The signs of an *Outer Ear* problem are discharge, head shaking, ear scratching and tenderness about the ear. Diseases of the *Middle Ear* produce head tilt and loss of hearing. Diseases of the *Inner Ear* affect the balance center. The cat wobbles, circles, falls and rolls over and has trouble righting itself. The cat may show rapid jerking movements of the eyes (*nystagmus*).

Middle and inner ear disorders should receive prompt veterinary attention.

BASIC EAR CARE

How to Avoid Ear Problems

When bathing your cat, prevent water from getting into its ears by inserting cotton wadding into the ear canals. Wet ear canals can cause ear infections.

DO NOT swab out or irrigate your cat's ears with ether, alcohol or other irritating solvents that cause pain and swelling of the tissues. Use mineral or olive oil instead. If your cat has been in a fight, check the ears for any cuts or bites that may need to be treated (see *The Ear Flap*).

Cleaning the Ears

Routine ear cleaning is not required. Some wax is necessary to maintain health of the tissues. However, ears should be cleaned when there is an excessive amount of wax, dirt or debris in the ear.

To clean a dirty ear, apply a few drops of warm mineral oil or a veterinary ear-cleaning solution such as *Oti-Clens* or *Gent-L-Clens* to the external ear canal and massage the base of the ear to loosen dirt, excess wax and debris. Then gently wipe out the ear with a cotton ball. Ear folds and creases are best cleaned with a cotton-tipped applicator moistened with mineral oil or cleansing solution. *Do not* direct the applicator into the ear canal because this will push the debris deeper into the canal and pack it against the eardrum.

Many cats object to ear cleaning and should be gently restrained as described in the chapter EMERGENCIES: *Handling and Restraint.*

Cleaning the ears. Instill an ear-cleaning solution and massage the base of the ear.

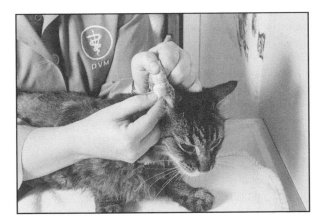

Gently wipe out with a cotton ball.

Clean folds and creases with a cotton-tipped applicator. Do not insert into ear canal.

How to Apply Ear Medicines

Ear preparations should be applied only to clean ear canals.

Some ear preparations come in tubes with long nozzles; others come with medicine droppers. Restrain your cat so the tip of the applicator does not accidentally lacerate the skin of the ear canal. Fold the ear flap over the top of the head. Insert the end of the nozzle or medicine dropper into the ear canal only as far as you can see. Squeeze in a small amount of ointment; or instill three to four drops of liquid. As most infections involve the deep horizontal ear canal, it is important for the medicine to reach this area. Massage the cartilage at the base of the ear for 20 seconds to disperse the medicine. The massaging will produce a squishy sound.

Antibiotic Ear Preparations: Antibiotic preparations commonly used in the treatment of external ear infections are *Panolog, Liquichlor, Tresaderm, Gentocin Otic* and *Nolvamite.* Others are available. All ear preparations can damage the middle ear if the eardrum has been ruptured by disease. Preparations should not be put into ears until a veterinarian has examined the cat and determined that the drums are intact.

Problems associated with the prolonged use of antibiotic ear preparations include allergic skin reaction, the development of antibiotic resistant strains of bacteria and overgrowth of yeast and fungi. Follow the directions of the manufacturer

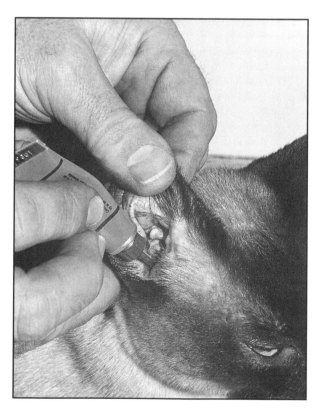

Insert the tip of the nozzle only as far in as you can see and squeeze in a small amount of ointment.

An ear bandage may be required to protect an injured ear after treatment of a bite or laceration.
—J. Clawson

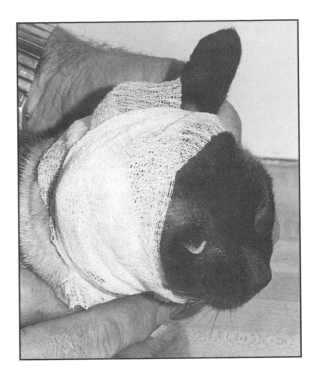

about frequency of application. Expect to see improvement in two to three days. If not, consult your veterinarian because further delay can be harmful.

OUTER EAR DISEASES

Your cat has an ear problem if you notice ear scratching, repeated head shaking, a bad odor emanating from the ear or large amounts of waxy discharge or pus draining. The most likely cause is ear mites—especially in the younger cat—but other diseases do occur. A cat with an itchy ear ailment may scratch so vigorously that the skin behind the ear becomes severely abraded. The abraded skin may become secondarily infected leading to an abscess. Attempts to treat the traumatized ear flap may not be successful until the initiating cause of the itching and scratching has been identified and treated.

The Ear Flap (Pinna)

The pinna is an erect flap of cartilage covered on both sides by a layer of skin. It is fragile and easily damaged.

Bites and Lacerations. Cats give and receive painful bites and scratches that are prone to severe infection. The ear flap is a frequent site for such injuries. Some occur during mating.

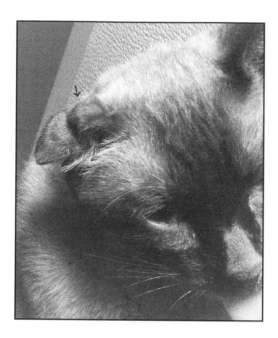

Hematoma of the ear flap, caused by violent head shaking. Note swelling and deformity.

Treatment: All cat bite wounds should be carefully cleaned and inspected. Trim the hair from the edges of the wound. Bathe the wound with one part hydrogen peroxide solution to five parts water to remove dried blood and foreign debris. Omit this bath if there is fresh bleeding. Then apply a topical antibiotic ointment such as *Triple Antibiotic Ointment* or *Neosporin Ointment*. Because claws and teeth produce deep wounds and punctures, injuries caused by cat fights are often complicated by abscesses. Some can be prevented by giving your cat a course of antibiotics by mouth (penicillin). Large lacerations and those involving the margin of the ear or the cartilage should receive veterinary attention. Surgical repair is necessary to prevent scarring and deformity.

Swollen Ear Flap. Sudden swelling about the ear is due to an **abscess** or **hematoma**. Abscesses are the most common. They are caused by an infection of the ear and often occur after a fight. Severe scratching at the ear may produce skin infection and abscess. Abscesses are found below the ear. They are discussed in the SKIN chapter.

A hematoma is a blood clot under the skin of the ear flap. It, too, can be caused by trauma or by violent head shaking and scratching at the ear. Look for an itchy ear disorder such as ear mites or an infection involving the ear canal—which should be treated along with the hematoma.

Treatment: Blood should be expressed from a hematoma to prevent scarring and deformity of the ear. Removing it with a needle and syringe usually is not effective because serum accumulates in the pocket formerly occupied by the blood clot and the pocket fills again. Surgery, the treatment of choice, involves removing a window of skin to provide open and continuous drainage. Sutures are then taken through both sides of the ear to pull the skin down and eliminate the pocket.

Ear Allergies. Allergies are typified by the sudden onset of itching and skin redness without drainage. They can affect the skin of the ear canals as well as the ear flap. An allergic reaction is best treated with a hydrocortisone preparation such as *Cortaid* (1 percent hydrocortisone cream). Because of intense scratching, the cat may traumatize its ears and set the stage for a secondary bacterial infection.

For more information, see *Allergies* in the SKIN chapter.

Frostbite. Frostbite affects the ears of outdoor cats in severe winter weather, particularly high wind and humidity. The ears are especially susceptible because they are exposed and only lightly protected by fur, especially at the tips. Treatment of frostbite is discussed in the chapter EMERGENCIES. Having been frozen, the ear tips of dark-coated or Siamese cats may become rounded and develop white hairs at their tips. Drooping of the ear flap is another condition that follows prolonged exposure to wind and cold.

Sunburn (Solar dermatitis). Cats with white ears are particularly susceptible to solar injury. Hair is lost from the tips and edges of the ears. Then, the underlying skin becomes reddened. Finally, because of scratching at the ear, the skin breaks down and forms an open sore or ulcer. The condition grows worse with each passing summer. In time a squamous cell skin cancer is likely to develop in the ulcerated area.

Treatment: A cat with this condition should be let outdoors only at night. Keeping it inside only on sunny days does not address the entire problem because ultraviolet rays, which are responsible for skin damage, can penetrate clouds.

Surgery is indicated for a non-healing sore. When the ear tips are ulcerated, they are rounded off and removed. Small ulcers can be excised. Large ulcers, which are often malignant, may require removal of the entire ear flap.

Head Mange. This disease is caused by a head mite called *Notoedres cati* that lives on the skin about the head and ears of cats. Itching is the predominant symptom. Clean ear canals help distinguish this condition from ear mite infection caused by *Otodectes cynotis*. Treatment is discussed in the SKIN chapter.

Ringworm. This fungus infection affects the ear flap as well as other body parts. Typically, a dry, scaly, hairless patch of skin appears. Hair is broken off at the skin surface. Ringworm can be told apart from ear mite infection because ringworm does not cause itching and does not produce a dark brown waxy discharge from the ear canals. Treatment is discussed in the SKIN chapter.

Flea Infestation. Fleas frequently feed on the skin of the ear flap. You may be able to see the actual fleas on the ears or elsewhere on the body, or you may see only black, crumbly crusts of dried blood. Treatment is discussed in the SKIN chapter (see *Fleas*).

Tumors. Squamous cell cancers can occur on the ears after prolonged exposure to sunlight (see *Sunburn*). Other tumors also can grow on the skin of the ears. Most are malignant. Any growth on the ear is a cause for concern. Have it examined by your veterinarian.

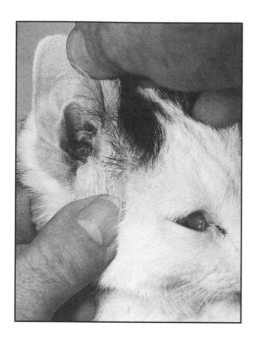

A dark brown, dry, waxy, crumbly discharge is typcial of ear mites.

THE EAR CANAL

Signs of irritation or infection in the ear canals are discharge, head shaking, scratching and pawing at the ear. Common causes are listed below.

Ear Mites (Otodectes cynotis). Ear mite infection is one of the most common health problems seen in cats. Ear mites are tiny insects that live in the ear canal and feed by piercing the skin. Mites are prolific. Most kittens are infected by their mothers while still in the nest. Suspect ear mites when *both* ears are affected.

The most frequent sign is intense itching characterized by scratching and violent head shaking. You will see a dry crumbly, dark brown waxy discharge when you look into the ears. The discharge looks like coffee-ground material and may be foul smelling. Constant scratching at the ears can cause raw areas along with scabs and loss of hair around the ears. The initial problem may be complicated by a chronic bacterial infection.

Ear mites can be identified by removing some ear wax from a fold or crease with a cotton-tipped applicator and examining it under a magnifying glass, against a black background. Mites are white specks, about the size of the head of a pin, which move.

Ear mites can leave the ear canals and travel over the body. They are highly contagious to cats and dogs, but not humans. All pets in the household should be treated.

Treatment: Do not begin treatment until you are sure that ear mites are the cause of the symptoms. Other ear ailments can be complicated by using ear mite preparations.

Clean the ears as described above (see *Cleaning the Ears*). *This is essential.* Dirty ear canals provide wax and cellular debris that shelter mites and make it difficult for ear medications to destroy them.

Medicate the ears as described above, using an ear preparation effective against mites. Some common miticidal ear preparations are *Nolvamite*, *Mitaclear* and *Tresaderm*. Dosages vary according to the product. Follow the manufacturer's instructions. It is very important to complete the recommended course of treatment because a new crop of mites will reinfect your cat if the treatment is stopped too soon. *Ivermectin*, although not approved for use in cats, has been used successfully in the treatment of ear mites. It is given as a single subcutaneous injection.

During treatment, mites escape from the ear canals and temporarily take up residence elsewhere on the cat, causing itching and scratching. It is important to treat the *entire* cat with a topical insecticide preparation as described under *Fleas* in the SKIN chapter. Since most cats sleep with their tails curled up next to their ears, treat the tail as well.

Secondary bacterial infection is treated as described below.

Bacterial Infection (Otitis externa). Bacterial infections are frequently caused by skin scratches and cat bites. Some begin in an ear canal containing excessive amounts of wax, cellular debris or foreign material. Ear mite infections are often complicated by a bacterial otitis.

Signs of an infected ear canal are head shaking, scratching at the ear and an unpleasant odor. The cat may tilt or carry the head down on the painful side and exhibit tenderness when the ear is touched. Examination reveals redness and swelling of the skin folds of the ear canal. There may be an excess amount of wax or a discharge. An otoscope is needed to examine the depth portions of the ear canal looking for a foreign body or other cause of chronic infection. This is best left to a qualified professional.

Bacterial infections that progress over a long period produce thickening and reddening of the ear canal with considerable discomfort and pain. Treatment is prolonged. Inflammatory polyps and tumor-like masses may develop and block the ear passages. Surgery becomes necessary to open the ear and promote drainage.

Treatment: The first step is to determine the cause. Mild cases, that is, those without excessive discharge but perhaps associated with a dirty ear or the buildup of wax, may be treated at home.

Clean the ears as described earlier. Remove crusts and serum with a cotton ball soaked in one part hydrogen peroxide solution with five parts water, being careful not to push the debris deeper into the canal. If there is a buildup of wax, a wax dissolving ear-cleaning solution should be instilled to soften the debris and make it easier to remove (see *Cleaning the Ears*). Afterward, dry the ear canals with a cloth or cotton ball and apply an antibiotic ear preparation as described earlier in this chapter.

Clip the cat's toenails to minimize injuries produced by scratching at the ear.

Fungus/Yeast Infection. A yeast otitis may develop as a secondary infection in an ear with a long-standing bacterial or ear mite infection. The prolonged use of topical antibiotics alters the natural bacterial flora in the ear canal, which improves conditions for growth of yeast and fungi.

Signs and symptoms of a yeast infection are not nearly as pronounced as the infection caused by bacteria. The ear is less inflamed and less painful. The discharge is dark and waxy but not purulent. A rancid odor is characteristic.

Treatment: It is similar to bacterial otitis except that an antifungal agent (nystatin, thiabendazole) is used. *Panolog*, which contains nystatin, is effective against the yeast *Candida albicans*. *Tresaderm*, which contains thiabendazole, is effective against *Candida* and most common yeast invaders. Yeast and fungus infections tend to recur. Treatment is often prolonged.

Foreign Bodies and Ticks. Foreign bodies in the ear canal cause irritation and subsequent infection. Less common in the cat than the dog, they are usually due to plant material (grass seeds, awns) that first cling to hair surrounding the ear opening and then drop down into the canal. Ears should be examined after a cat has been prowling in tall grass, weeds and brush. When a foreign body is near the opening, it can be removed with blunt-nosed tweezers. Foreign bodies deep in the ear canal must be removed with special instruments. This is a sensitive area and requires an anesthetic.

Ticks can adhere to the skin of a cat's ear. If the tick is easily accessible it can be removed. Grasp the tick with tweezers and gently tease it off the skin as described in the SKIN chapter (see *Ticks*). Do not squeeze or crush a tick with your bare fingers. *Ticks deep in the ear canal should be removed by a veterinarian.*

THE MIDDLE EAR

INFECTION (OTITIS MEDIA)

Middle ear infections are not common. Most result from an external ear infection that ruptures the eardrum. Tonsillitis and mouth and sinus infections can travel to the middle ear through the *eustachian tube*, a passage connecting the middle ear to the back of the throat. Rarely, bacteria gain entrance through the bloodstream.

The first signs of middle ear infection are often masked by an ear canal infection that precedes it. However, as the middle ear becomes involved, the cat evidences more severe pain, crouching low and tilting the head down on the affected side. The head is held as still as possible. The gait is often unsteady because balance is affected. An otoscopic examination by a veterinarian may show perforation or loss of the eardrum. X rays may show bone involvement. The face may droop on the affected side if the nerve that crosses the surface of the eardrum is involved.

Middle ear infections can extend to involve the inner ear. *All infections of the middle and inner ear should be treated by a veterinarian.*

THE INNER EAR

INFECTION (OTITIS INTERNA)

Extension of a middle ear infection to the inner ear should be suspected if your cat vomits, staggers or falls toward the affected side, circles toward that side or shows rhythmic jerking movements of its eyeballs (rapid eye movements). These are signs of *labyrinthitis*. Most ear preparations are capable of causing labyrinthitis and some permanent ear damage if they make direct contact with the sensitive structures of the inner ear. For this reason, the ears should not be flushed or medicated without first examining the cat's ear canals to be sure the eardrums are not punctured or ruptured. See *How to Apply Ear Medicines*.

Infections of the inner ear should be managed by a professional.

Other disorders that produce signs like those of an inner ear infection include brain tumor, drug intoxication, poisoning and *Idiopathic Vestibular Syndrome* of cats (see *Vestibular Disorders* in NERVOUS SYSTEM). The idiopathic syndrome is the most common.

You should suspect one of these disorders when a cat shows signs of labyrinthitis without a prior ear infection.

DEAFNESS

Some cats are born without the ability to hear because of developmental defects in the hearing apparatus. This usually occurs in white cats with blue eyes. *Congenitally deaf cats should not be used for breeding.*

Loss of hearing can be caused by old age, middle ear infections, head injury, ear canal blockage by wax and debris and by certain drugs and poisons. In particular, the antibiotics streptomycin, gentamicin, neomycin and kanamycin if used for long periods can cause damage to the auditory nerves, leading to deafness and signs of labyrinthitis.

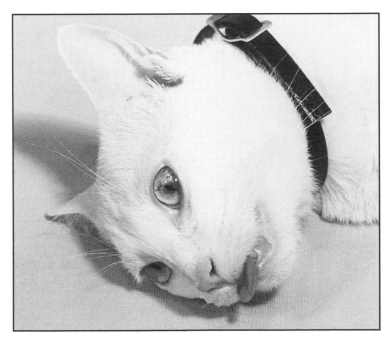

Congenital deafness often occurs in white cats with blue eyes.

It is difficult to tell if a cat is going deaf. The ability to hear must be judged by observing cats' actions and how they use their ears. Cats that hear well cock their heads and look toward the noise. The ears move back and forth to pinpoint the sound. Accordingly, lack of attentiveness is one of the first indications that a cat is not hearing as well as it should. One way to test this is to make a loud noise while a cat is asleep. If the cat does not startle and wake up, you can assume there is a significant loss of hearing.

Gradual loss of hearing occurs in some cats older than 10 years. Senile deaf cats, however, often retain hearing for high-pitched sounds such as a dog whistle. Stamping on the floor will attract their attention as they can feel the vibrations.

Deaf cats get along quite well. They use their senses of sight and smell and the tactile sensations transmitted through their whiskers to compensate for the hearing loss.

7

NOSE

GENERAL INFORMATION

The nasal cavity is divided by a midline partition into two passages, one for each nostril. These passages open into the throat. The cat has two large frontal sinuses that communicate with the nasal passages. The nasal cavity is lined by a mucous membrane (*mucociliary blanket*) rich with blood vessels and nerves. This blanket traps bacteria and foreign irritants, acting as the first line of defense against infection. Exposure to dehydration or prolonged cold stops the motion of the cilia and thickens the layer of mucus. This reduces the effectiveness of the mucociliary blanket.

The nasal cavity is extremely sensitive and bleeds easily when traumatized. Because of their small size, the nasal passages of cats must be examined under sedation or anesthesia.

Although both the cat and the dog have a keen sense of smell, only the dog uses it for tracking. In the cat the sense of smell is used primarily for self-orientation (which includes recognition of threatening odors) and for appetite stimulation. This last is so important that *nasal obstruction is almost always accompanied by loss of appetite*.

Cats also rely on their sense of smell to identify each other. Cats greet each other by first smelling each other's faces and then anal areas.

The cat has an additional odor sensing mechanism that people do not have. It is composed of two small air passages (the *nasopalatine ducts*), located in the roof of the mouth just behind the incisors. These ducts permit air in the mouth to pass up into the nose. When using this accessory scent mechanism, the cat raises its upper lip as if baring the teeth, wrinkles its nose, partially opens its mouth and then draws

Cats have small nasal passages. Internal examination requires anesthesia.

air up into the nose through these ducts. This behavior, called "flehman," can be seen in kittens as early as two months old. It is most commonly seen in adult toms.

Certain odors are uniquely attractive to cats. Catnip, often put in toys, is a variety of mint that acts as a nerve stimulant and seems to cast a spell over cats. They will approach catnip, sniff it, then usually lick or chew it. Afterward, the cat appears dazed, rolls on the floor or rubs against furniture. The immediate effect lasts but a few minutes, but repeated exposure can result in long-term side effects, including confusion and loss of awareness. Catnip sensitivity is hereditary. It affects about two out of three domestic cats.

Cats are also attracted to the odors of garlic and onion. These flavorings are frequently added to pet foods to enhance their appeal. The odor of mothballs and orange peels, on the other hand, is repugnant. This fact can be used to keep cats away from certain spots in the house.

Cats' noses can vary in color from light pink or salmon to blue, brown, black or freckled. Some breed Standards call for a nose of a certain color (e.g., blue for "Blue Point" Siamese; black for "Seal Point"). In showing, points may be subtracted for a mottled or off-colored nose. A cat with a pink nose may temporarily develop a white nose after being in cold weather or excited. A white nose for no explainable reason may indicate anemia.

A warm dry nose could mean that a cat is dehydrated or has a fever. Occasionally, the reverse is true; a sick cat has a runny nose that is cool because of evaporation.

A cat's whiskers are sensitive tactile organs that transmit complex information about prey and surroundings to nerve bundles beneath the skin. Cats know that if their whiskers can pass through a small opening, then the body can also. Whiskers should never be clipped or trimmed.

SIGNS OF NASAL IRRITATION

RUNNY NOSE (NASAL DISCHARGE)

A discharge that persists for several hours is significant. It is important to recognize early signs as professional attention may be required.

- A *watery* discharge with sneezing is caused by *local irritation* or *allergic rhinitis*.
- A *mucoid* discharge is characteristic of *viral respiratory disease* complex.
- A thick yellow *puslike* discharge indicates *bacterial infection*.

A discharge through both nostrils, often accompanied by fever, loss of appetite, eye discharge, drooling, cough or sores in the mouth suggests a *feline viral respiratory disease*. When *both* nostrils are blocked by swollen membranes, the cat sniffles, exhibits *noisy breathing* and *may* breathe through the mouth. As cats avoid *mouth breathing* whenever possible, you may see this only when the cat exercises.

Tumors, fungal infections and chronic bacterial infections erode the nasal membranes producing a blood-tinged or bloody discharge. One or both nostrils may be involved. Veterinary examination is indicated when there is blood in the discharge.

Colds. Human cold viruses do not affect the cat. However, cats are afflicted by a number of viruses that produce symptoms much like those of the human cold. If your cat develops a runny nose along with a discharge from the eyes—and if the cat coughs, sneezes and runs a slight fever—consult your veterinarian.

SNEEZING

Sneezing is one of the chief signs of nasal irritation in cats. It is a reflex that results from stimulation of the lining of the nose. If the cat sneezes off and on for a few hours but shows no other signs of illness, it is most likely a minor nasal irritation or allergy.

Sneezing that persists all day long could be the first sign of *feline viral respiratory disease*. A sudden bout of *violent* sneezing along with head shaking and pawing at the nose suggests a *Foreign Body in the Nose*.

Bacterial infections also produce bouts of sneezing and sniffling. These tend to become chronic.

REVERSE SNEEZING (LARYNGOSPASM)

This uncommon but harmless condition may be a cause of alarm because it sounds as though the cat has something caught in an air passage. During an attack the cat violently pulls in air through the nose. This produces a loud snorting noise.

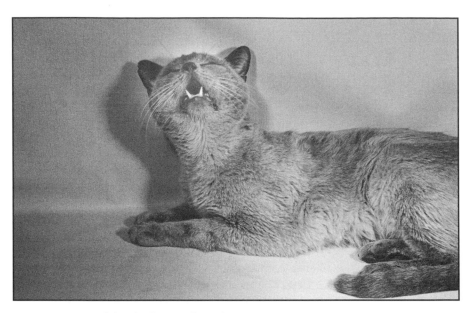

Sneezing is one of the chief signs of nasal irritaton.

Reverse sneezing is caused by a temporary spasm of the muscles of the larynx due to an accumulation of mucus at the back of the throat. The cat is perfectly normal before and after these attacks.

THE NASAL CAVITY

TRAUMA AND NOSEBLEEDS (EPISTAXIS)

Nosebleeds do not occur spontaneously in cats. Most are associated with a blow to the face that damages the nose. Others are due to an erosion of the nasal membrane caused by a foreign body, infection, tumor or parasite.

Rarely, a nosebleed may be a manifestation of a generalized clotting disorder such as that produced by liver disease or *rodenticide anticoagulants*.

When a cat sustains trauma to the nose sufficient to cause bleeding, a midline fracture to the roof of the mouth may also have been incurred. Suspect this if the cat exhibits open-mouth breathing. This fracture can cause misalignment of the teeth, in which case the alignment must be adjusted and the teeth wired together to stabilize the upper jaw until healed.

Treatment: Nosebleeds may be accompanied by sneezing spasms that aggravate the bleeding. Keep the cat quiet and confined. Apply ice cubes or packs to the bridge of the nose to reduce blood flow and aid clotting. Slight bleeding usually subsides quickly, especially if interference is reduced. Persistent bleeding is a cause for concern. Call your veterinarian.

A thick, puslike discharge from both nostrils indicates nasal infection.

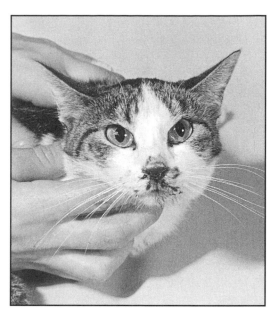

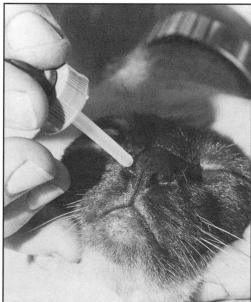

Nose drops help to shrink swollen membranes. This eases breathing and restores appetite.

FOREIGN BODIES IN THE NOSE

Nasal foreign bodies are uncommon in cats because of the small size of their nasal passages. Nevertheless, pieces of straw, grass seeds and awns, fish bones, string, wood splinters and, occasionally, insects can become wedged in the nose.

A noticeable sign is the sudden appearance of *violent* sneezing—at first continuous and later intermittent—along with pawing at the nose. The cat's head may be tilted to the affected side; the eye on that side may squint; or cats may drop their noses to the floor, extend the neck and make deep breathing efforts. Repeated clearing of the throat suggests that the foreign object is trapped at the back of the nasal cavity. Some foreign bodies produce few symptoms and may go unnoticed.

Foreign objects that have been allowed to remain for a day or longer are associated with secondary bacterial infection (see *Nasal Infections*).

Treatment: If the foreign body is visible and close to the opening of the nostril, remove it with tweezers. Usually, it is lodged farther back. If you look down the throat, you may see a piece of string or grass bent over the soft palate projecting into the pharynx.

If the foreign body is not visible and not causing severe symptoms, the cat may yet expel it with time. If the cat is unable to do so or if the foreign body is causing severe symptoms, the cat must be given an anesthetic to locate and remove the object.

A cat with a persistent foreign body should be given prophylactic antibiotics (Chloromycetin, tetracycline) to prevent secondary bacterial infection. The antibiotic should be continued for one to two weeks beyond the time when the foreign body was expelled or removed.

Nasal Allergies (Allergic Rhinitis)

Nasal allergy is characterized by periodic bouts of sneezing that last a short time and tend to recur day to day. Usually, there is a clear watery discharge from the nose. Most cases are caused by contact with environmental irritants and allergens (see *Allergy* in the Skin chapter). This type of rhinitis responds well to medications containing steroids and antihistamines.

Nasal Infections

Nasal infections produce sneezing, nasal discharge, noisy breathing and mouth breathing. When nasal congestion interferes with the ability to smell, the cat loses its appetite and stops eating.

Bacterial infections become established when the lining of the nose has been injured by a foreign body or nasal trauma or by a prior viral respiratory disease. On occasion, infection spreads to the nasal cavity from the frontal sinus (see *Sinusitis*). The chief sign of bacterial involvement is a nasal discharge that is mucoid, creamy yellow or puslike. A bloody discharge indicates deep involvement with ulceration of the nasal membrane.

A common cause of nasal infection relates to the *feline viral respiratory disease complex*. Eighty percent to 90 percent of cats that recover become carriers of herpes virus or calicivirus. During periods of stress, immunity breaks down and the disease is reactivated. In some cases the nasal infection is mild; in others there is a chronic mucopurulent discharge from the eyes and nose.

Treatment: The objectives are to restore breathing, treat and prevent infection and keep the cat as comfortable as possible. Gently wipe the nostrils with a moist cotton ball or linen cloth to remove crusts and secretions. Rub in baby oil or Vaseline to keep nostrils from cracking and drying. Vaporizers loosen secretions and help to restore the integrity of the mucociliary blanket. Encourage eating by feeding aromatic foods such as canned fish.

Shrink swollen nasal membranes by administering *Afrin Children's Strength Nose Drops* (.025 percent). Administer cautiously to prevent rebound congestion and excessive drying out of the mucous membranes. Administer one drop to one nostril the first day. The next day, use the other nostril. Continue to *alternate* between nostrils because the medicine is absorbed and acts on both nostrils simultaneously. Use the decongestant for five to seven days.

A purulent discharge signifies a bacterial infection and indicates the need for an antibiotic (tetracycline, ampicillin). When the discharge persists despite treatment, it should be cultured. *Seek veterinary attention.* An appropriate antibiotic can be selected on the basis of sensitivity testing. In long-standing cases suspect a fungus.

Prevention: It is advisable to treat all nasal cavity injuries (such as those caused by a foreign body) with a prophylactic antibiotic to prevent bacterial infection.

SINUSITIS

The cat has two frontal and two sphenoid sinuses. The small sphenoid sinuses are of little importance. Since respiratory infections are common in cats, secondary infections of the frontal sinuses occur with some frequency. Signs of a chronic bacterial infection are a persistent purulent nasal discharge often just on one side accompanied by frequent sneezing and sniffling. X rays may show increased density of one sinus. The cat may appear to have a headache and sit with eyes partially closed and head hanging. Diminished appetite can lead to rapid weight loss.

An abscessed tooth (usually the root of one of the top premolars) can lead to an abscessed frontal sinus. This produces a painful rising below the eye. It is not common in the cat.

Fungus infections (*cryptococcosis* and *aspergillosis*) are uncommon causes of sinus infection in the cat. These conditions are discussed in the INFECTIOUS DISEASE chapter (see *Fungus Diseases*).

Treatment: Sinusitis can be suspected from the clinical signs and is usually confirmed by an X ray. Trial with an appropriate antibiotic is indicated. Sometimes this is not successful. A surgical procedure, which involves making an opening into the sinus through the skin to aid drainage, may be required.

NASAL POLYPS AND TUMORS

Benign and malignant growths are found in the nasal cavity and sinuses, usually on just one side. Early signs are sneezing and sniffling. They are followed by obstructed breathing. Bleeding can occur through the affected nostril. Large tumors make one side of the face protrude more than the other. When tumors extend behind the eye, that eye will bulge. Such tumors are far advanced. Treatment generally is not possible.

Nasopharyngeal polyps are an uncommon upper respiratory condition unique to cats. Young cats are most often affected. These tumors block the eustachian tube at the back of the throat and produce middle ear infection (see *Otitis Media*). Treatment involves surgical removal.

8

MOUTH AND THROAT (OROPHARYNX)

GENERAL INFORMATION

The mouth is bounded on the front and sides by the lips and cheeks, above by the hard and soft palate, and below by the tongue and muscles of the mouth floor. Four pairs of salivary glands drain into the mouth.

The **pharynx,** or throat, is a space formed by the nasal passages joining with the back of the mouth. Food is kept from going down the wrong way by the **epiglottis,** a flaplike valve that closes off the **larynx** and **windpipe** when the cat swallows.

The average adult cat has 30 teeth. This is 2 fewer than humans and 12 fewer than dogs. Cats' teeth are designed for grasping, cutting, tearing and shredding. They are not designed to grind food. As cats grasp a piece of meat with their front claws, they bite down on it with the 4 canine teeth, scissor the meat between their back teeth and tear off a mouthful that is swallowed without chewing. The back teeth, like those in the front, are pointed and sharp.

The peculiar surface of the cat's tongue, with sharp inwardly directed spikes, makes an ideal comb for self-grooming. However, one disadvantage is that hair clings to the tongue. The only way a cat can get rid of the hair it is to swallow it. This is the reason why hairballs are such a big problem in cats.

A dog may lick wounds, but cats are unlikely to do so because the tongue's rough surface causes pain. This may explain why cat wounds have such a high rate of infection.

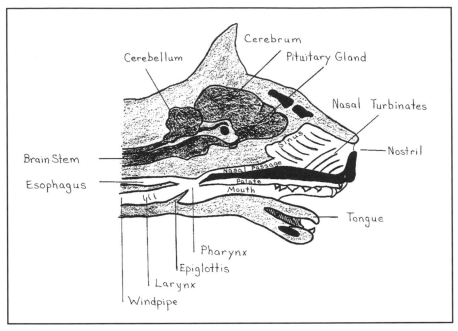

Anatomy of the head. —Sydney Wiley

Cats have sensitive whiskers on their lips, cheeks, and above their eyes. These tactile organs assist them in detecting and avoiding objects in the dark.

How to Examine the Mouth

Most mouth problems can be diagnosed by inspecting the lips, teeth and oral cavity.

To examine the cat's bite, raise the upper lip while drawing down on the lower lip with your thumb. The bite is determined by seeing how the upper and lower incisor teeth meet (see *Incorrect Bite*). This maneuver also displays the gums and teeth.

To open the cat's mouth, with one hand place thumb and forefinger against its upper cheeks and press in gently (see photo). As the mouth begins to open wide, press down on the lower jaw with the index finger of your other hand. To see the tonsils and back of the throat, push down on the back of the tongue. Many cats are reluctant to have their mouths examined and should be restrained to avoid a painful scratch or bite (see EMERGENCIES: *Handling and Restraint*).

Signs of Mouth Disease

One of the first indications of mouth disease is *failure to eat*. This is caused by mouth pain rather than loss of appetite. The cat will often sit beside the food dish, giving every indication of wanting to eat, and may even begin eating, then drop the food

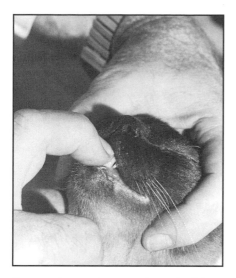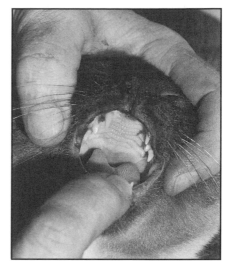

To open the mouth, grasp the arch of the cat's face across the cheekbones and press in. With the index finger of your other hand, press down on the lower jaw.   —J. Clawson

quickly. If you attempt to examine the mouth, the cat draws back and struggles to escape.

Because the mouth is used for coat grooming, an *unkempt appearance* is another indication of a cat with a sore mouth. When grooming is accompanied with drooling, the hair on the cat's chin and chest may be dirty and wet. A painful mouth is one of the main causes for drooling.

A further indication of mouth disease is *bad breath*. The most likely causes are Stomatitis and Gingivitis. Excess tartar on the teeth is another leading cause of bad breath (see *Tooth Decay*). Of course, garlic and onion, added to some pet foods to enhance their appeal, can cause a characteristic odor to the breath. But a persistent disagreeable odor from the mouth is abnormal. The cause should be determined so proper treatment can be given.

Gagging, choking, drooling and difficulty in swallowing suggest a foreign object in the mouth, tongue or throat.

Difficulty opening the mouth or swallowing is characteristic of head and neck abscesses and injuries to the jaws. *Rabies* should be considered if the mouth sags open and the cat drools or foams at the mouth.

LIPS

INFLAMMATION OF THE LIPS (CHEILITIS)

Cheilitis is recognized by serum crusts which form where the hair-covered parts meet the smooth parts of the lips. As the crusts peel off, the area beneath looks raw and

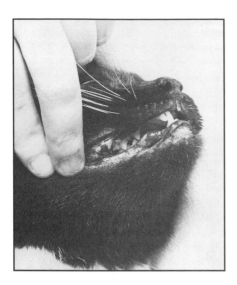

Inflammation of the lips (cheilitis) is often caused by mouth infection.

denuded and is sensitive to touch. Inflamed lips are often caused by an infection inside the mouth which extends to the lips. Other causes are contact with weeds and brush which irritate the lips, giving them a chapped look.

Treatment: Clean the lips with *Benzoyl peroxide* shampoo or dilute hydrogen peroxide (one part to five parts water) daily and apply an antibiotic-steroid ointment such as *Neocort* twice a day. When the infection subsides, apply *petroleum jelly* to keep the lips soft and pliable until healing is complete.

Rodent Ulcer (Indolent Ulcer, Eosinophilic Ulcer)

This unsightly condition is found in cats nine months to nine years old, with an average age of six. It is unique to the cat and occurs three times more often in females than males. In 80 percent of cases it begins on either side of center on the upper lip. Less commonly, it occurs on the lower lip or at the back of the jaw behind one of the last upper molars.

A rodent ulcer begins as a yellow or pink shiny spot that deepens and becomes an open sore. It is not itchy and seems to cause no pain. As the ulcer advances, the lip may be partly eroded by a large ulcerated swelling that exposes teeth and gums. In time, it may undergo malignant transformation to a squamous cell cancer or a fibrosarcoma.

The exact cause of rodent ulcer is unknown. Some cases are associated with dental infection. It has been found in cats exposed to the leukemia virus, suggesting that impaired immunity may be a cause. However, not all cats with rodent ulcer test positive for the leukemia virus, nor does a rodent ulcer necessarily mean that a cat has leukemia. Recently, an allergic cause has been suggested. Note that a similar process involving ulceration and granulation occurs in other body parts (see SKIN: *Eosinophilic Granuloma Complex*).

A rodent ulcer typically begins near the center of the upper lip.

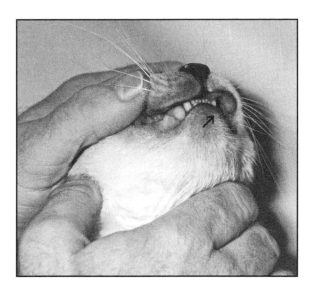

Diagnosis is suggested by the typical appearance and location of the ulcer. In questionable cases, biopsy can be done to rule out malignant transformation. Cats with rodent ulcer should be tested for *Feline Leukemia* (see INFECTIOUS DISEASES).

Treatment: Veterinary supervision is required. Because the ulcer is precancerous, early vigorous treatment is indicated. Cortisone has proven to be the most effective treatment. It is given either as pills (prednisone) or by injection (Depo-medrol). Depo-medrol is a long-lasting injection that is given at two week intervals. Usually three courses are necessary. Alternately, prednisone can be given daily until the ulcer disappears. If the ulcer recurs after either injectable or oral cortisone therapy, the cat is placed on prednisone maintenance—usually one pill every other day.

Megestrol acetate (*Megase*) has been used in some cases of rodent ulcer. However, this progesterone drug is not approved for cats and has undesirable side effects. It is best used as a secondary line of treatment under veterinary protocol.

As some cases of *Eosinophilic Granuloma Complex* are known to respond to antibiotics (especially Trimethoprin-sulfa), an initial trial of antibiotics may be of value. Radiation therapy may be indicated for ulcers that have undergone cancerous change.

LACERATIONS OF THE LIPS, MOUTH AND TONGUE

The soft tissues in the mouth are common sites for cuts. Most are caused by animal and cat bites. Some are due to picking up or licking sharp objects such as the top of a food can. An unusual cause of tongue trauma is freezing to metal in extremely cold weather. When pulled free, the surface of the tongue strips off, leaving a raw bleeding patch.

Treatment: Bleeding can be controlled by applying pressure to the cut for five minutes. Use a clean gauze dressing or a piece of linen. A cat with a painful mouth usually must be restrained (see EMERGENCIES: *Handling and Restraint*).

Cuts on the upper lip are covered with a gauze that is held in position between the fingers. On the lower lip, bleeding is controlled by pressing the gauze directly against the wound. Bleeding from the tongue requires opening the mouth as described above. You may need to pull the tongue forward to see the bleeding site.

Minor cuts that have stopped bleeding do not need to be sutured. Stitching should be considered when the edges of the cut gape open; when lip lacerations involve the borders of the mouth; and when bleeding recurs after the pressure dressing is removed. Puncture wounds are prone to infection. Proper early treatment of these wounds as described in the chapter EMERGENCIES is important.

During healing of the wound, cleanse the cat's mouth twice a day with 0.1 percent Chlorhexidine antiseptic solution (*Nolvadent, Peridex*). Feed a bland diet and avoid dry kibble that requires chewing.

BURNS OF THE LIPS, MOUTH AND TONGUE

Electrical Burns of the mouth are caused by chewing on an electric cord. Although quite painful, most heal spontaneously. In some cases a gray-appearing membrane appears on the surface of the burn and an ulcer develops. Surgical removal of the dead tissue back to healthy tissue will be necessary.

Chemical Burns are caused by a variety of corrosives, including lye, phenol, phosphorus, household cleaners, alkalis and others. Should the substance be swallowed, the throat may be burned, leading to a more serious problem (see DIGESTIVE SYSTEM: *Esophagus*).

Treatment: *Immediately* flush the poison from the cat's mouth using large amounts of water while sponging and rinsing for several minutes. Aftercare for mouth burns is the same as for *Lacerations* above.

GUMS

Healthy gums are firm and pink. There is no room for food and debris to get down between the gums and the teeth. Pockets alongside the teeth are a source of gum infection and tooth decay.

Pale gums are a sign of anemia. Bluish gray gums indicate shock or dehydration.

GINGIVITIS (GUM INFECTION)

Gum infections are caused by dental plaque and calculus and by trapped food and hair between the gums and teeth. Infection may also occur with several diseases, including *feline panleukopenia, feline viral respiratory disease complex*, kidney and liver failure and nutritional disorders.

First, you will notice that the gums appear reddened, painful and swollen and may bleed when rubbed. Next, the edges of the gums recede from the sides of the teeth, allowing small pockets and crevices to develop. These pockets trap food and bacteria that produces infection at the gum line and sets the stage for *Periodontal Disease* and *Tooth Decay*.

Gum infection predisposes the cat to *periodontal disease* and *tooth decay*.

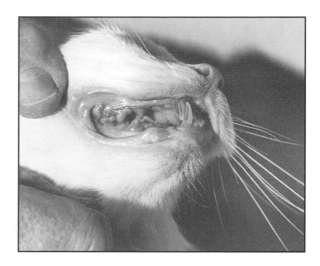

Signs of gum disease are loss of appetite, ungroomed appearance, drooling and halitosis.

Treatment: Once signs of gingivitis have appeared, a significant degree of dental tartar, calculus and gum-pocket infection will be present. The teeth should be professionally cleaned, after which the cat should be placed on a home dental care program as described in the section *Care of Your Cat's Teeth*. Brushing the teeth daily or at least twice weekly will be required to prevent recurrence of the gum infection.

Other diseases that may be contributing to the problem must be treated as a necessary part of restoring a healthy mouth.

GROWTHS ON THE GUMS

Tumors of the gum are rare and tend to occur in elderly cats. Most are malignant, the most common being a squamous cell cancer. Cancers often spread to other structures in the mouth; therefore, treatment is difficult. *Rodent ulcers* can occur on the gums at the back of the jaw behind the last upper molars but are more likely to occur on the upper lip (see *Lips*).

TEETH

Dental problems in domestic cats are due in part to diets. Cats fed soft, canned rations are prone to excess tartar formation, with subsequent periodontal disease and tooth loss. Dry kibble is best for the teeth because it is less likely to become packed in crevices between teeth and gums than is soft food. Also, because kibble is abrasive, it helps remove plaque from the crowns of the teeth.

Teeth can be chipped, broken and lost—usually after a fight with another animal.

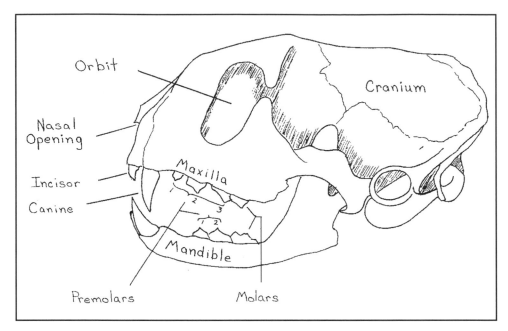

Teeth—side view.   —Rose Floyd

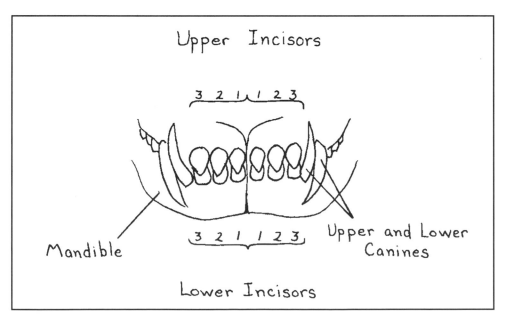

Teeth—front view.   —Rose Floyd

A cat's teeth should be inspected regularly. A good program of home dental care will prevent many problems that would otherwise lead to a poor state of health and nutrition.

How Cats' Teeth Tell Their Age

The method of determining the age of an animal by checking the amount of wear on the cusps of the teeth is relatively reliable for the horse and some other domestic animals but less so for the cat whose teeth are not used for grinding. The general condition of the teeth and gums may allow a guess about the approximate age of the cat, but accurate determinations are possible only for very young cats. They are based on the time of eruption of the deciduous and permanent teeth as described herein.

The dental formulae for cats are

Deciduous (Baby) Teeth: 2 (**I** 3/3 **C** 1/1 **P** 3/2) = 26

Permanent (Adult) Teeth: 2 (**I** 3/3 **C** 1/1 **P** 3/2 **M** 1/1) = 30

For example, there are three upper and three lower incisors; the first number (2) indicates that this is true for both the right and left sides of the mouth.

Deciduous (Baby) Teeth

The average kitten has 26 deciduous (baby) teeth. They are the incisors, canines and premolars. Kittens do not have molars. With rare exceptions, kittens are born without teeth. The incisors are the first deciduous teeth to appear, usually at two to three weeks. They are followed by the canines at three to four weeks and premolars at three to six weeks. The last premolar arrives at about six weeks. This sequence can be used to determine the approximate age of young kittens.

Teething in Kittens (Eruption of Adult Teeth)

Baby teeth are replaced gradually by the permanent teeth. At three to four months the incisors erupt, followed at four to six months by the canines, premolars and molars. By seven months the cat's adult teeth are fully developed. Knowing this sequence can give you an idea of the approximate age of the older kitten.

During teething, which lasts two to three months, a kitten may exhibit some soreness of the mouth. It may be off its feed from time to time but not enough to affect growth and development.

Retained Baby Teeth

Normally, the roots of baby teeth are reabsorbed as adult teeth take their place. When this fails to happen, you will see what appears to be a double set of teeth. The permanent teeth are then pushed out of line, leading to malocclusion, or a bad bite. Kittens at two to three months should be watched carefully to see that their adult teeth are coming in normally. Whenever a baby tooth stays in place while an adult tooth is coming in, the baby tooth should be pulled.

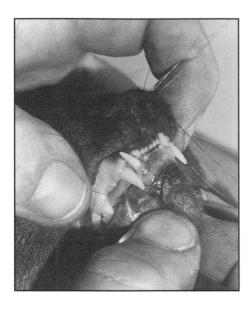

To examine the cat's bite, raise the upper lip while drawing down the lower. In this correct even or level bite, the incisors meet edge to edge.

—J. Clawson

Abnormal Number of Teeth

It is not uncommon to see adult cats with fewer teeth than normal. Some cats are born with missing tooth buds. This has little or no effect on their health.

Rarely, you may find that your kitten has more than the usual number of teeth. This problem can cause the teeth to twist or overlap. One or more of the extra teeth will need to be extracted to make room for the rest.

Incorrect Bite

Most bite problems are hereditary, resulting from genetic factors controlling the growth of the upper and lower jaws. Some incorrect bites are caused by retention of baby teeth that push emerging adult teeth out of alignment.

A cat's bite is determined by how the upper and lower incisor teeth meet when the mouth is closed. In the *even* or *level* bite, the incisor teeth meet edge to edge. In the *scissors* bite, the upper incisors just overlap but still touch the lower incisors.

An *overshot* bite is one in which the upper jaw is longer than the lower jaw, so the teeth overlap *without* touching. The **undershot** bite is the reverse of the above with the lower jaw projecting beyond the upper (like the bulldog). The **wry** mouth is the worst of the malocclusion problems. In this situation one side of the jaw grows faster than the other, twisting the mouth so to give it a wry look. Incorrect bites interfere with the ability to grasp, hold and chew food. Furthermore, teeth that do not align may injure the soft parts of the mouth.

Incorrect bites are much less common in cats than in dogs because cats' (unlike dogs') heads are quite similar in shape despite differences in breeds. Shortnosed breeds such as the Persian are most susceptible to bite problems.

Treatment: The overshot bite may correct itself if the gap is no greater than the head of a match. Retained baby teeth displacing permanent adult teeth should be

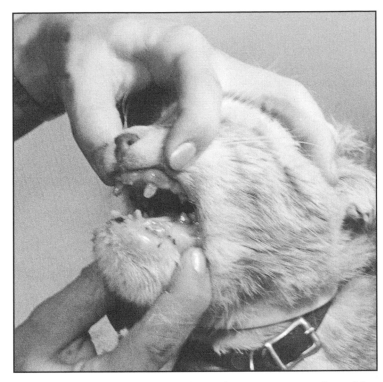

Advanced periodontal disease and root abscesses. Note swelling of the lower jaw because of bone infection.

extracted by four to five months, at which time the jaw is still growing, and there is opportunity for the bite to correct.

PERIODONTAL DISEASE AND TOOTH DECAY

Periodontal disease is a term used to describe infections of the teeth and gums. It is one of the most common problems encountered in veterinary practice. It begins when plaque and calculus are deposited on the teeth near the gum line. This occurs in all cats over two years old and will be found in some cats even before they are one year old.

Plaque is a soft, colorless material not easily seen with the naked eye. It consists of organic and inorganic material plus millions of living and growing bacteria.

Calculus or *tartar* is a mixture of calcium phosphate and carbonate with organic material. These calcium salts are soluble in acid but precipitate in the slightly alkaline saliva of the cat. Calculus is yellow or brown and produces the characteristic tartar stains. Calculus forms irregular surfaces on the teeth, which enhance the deposition of plaque. It begins to accumulate within one week of removal.

One of the first signs of periodontal disease is an offensive mouth odor. It may have been present for some time—perhaps even accepted as normal. Another sign is a change in the cat's eating habits. Since it hurts to chew, the cat may sit by its food dish but decline to eat. Weight loss and an ungroomed appearance are common.

The combination of calculus and plaque presents an ideal media for bacterial growth and subsequent infection of the gums (see *Gingivitis*). It has been suggested that some cats are more susceptible to periodontal disease than others. Increased susceptibility seems to occur among cats that suffer from repeated viral respiratory infections and among those exhibiting past exposure to the feline leukemia virus.

Normal chewing on hard, abrasive material cleans the teeth and reduces the formation of calculus. That is why cats eating dry kibble seem to have stronger teeth than those eating primarily soft, canned foods.

If you look closely you will see tartar deposits on the premolars, molars and canines. Pressure against the gums may cause pus to exude from pockets alongside the teeth, indicating *Gingivitis*.

Many dental problems go undetected until they cause major symptoms. Cats resist examination, particularly when suffering from a painful mouth.

Treatment: The mouth must be thoroughly cleansed and restored to a near normal condition. This involves the removing of dental tartar and calculus, draining pus pockets and polishing the teeth. This can be done by your veterinarian. Afterward, the cat should be placed on an antibiotic for 7 to 10 days. At this time it is important to begin a good home dental program as described below in *Care of Your Cat's Teeth*.

Cavities (Dental caries): Cavities are not common, primarily because a cat's diet is quite low in carbohydrates and sugars. Cavities account for only a small percentage of lost teeth. When present, they develop along the gum line in association with periodontal disease and not on the crown of the tooth as they do in humans. However, a crown can be broken by trauma. Infection can then erode into the pulp. A broken tooth should be pulled, or its pulp sealed, to prevent a tooth abscess.

Loose teeth (Periodontitis): Loose teeth occur as a sequel to unchecked periodontal infection. Teeth are held in their bony sockets by a special kind of connective tissue cement called the *periodontal membrane*. Infection in this membrane and the underlying bone leads to root infection. In time, the teeth begin to loosen and may have to be extracted. A surprisingly large number of teeth will reattach to the bone if treatment is started before the condition is too far advanced. In fact, as long as 50 percent of the root is anchored in bone, effective treatment may still save the tooth.

CARE OF YOUR CAT'S TEETH (HOME DENTAL CARE)

Most cats need preventive dental care by age two or three. Frequency of dental examination, scaling and polishing will depend on the rate at which calculus forms on the cat's teeth. A program of dental hygiene will limit the rate at which this happens and help to prolong the health and life of your pet. For best results you should:

1. Feed a dry kibble diet. Dry foods are abrasive and help to keep the teeth clean and sharp. However, if your cat suffers from *Feline Urologic*

Syndrome, you may need to take special precautions as outlined in the chapter FEEDING AND NUTRITION (see *Types of Cat Food*).

2. Start regular brushing when the cat is one or two years old, while gums are still healthy. Less effort is required to prevent gum disease than to treat it. You can maintain disease-free gums by brushing once or twice a week. However, once the cat develops periodontal disease, *daily* brushing is necessary to keep the condition in check.

3. Do not give objects to chew that are harder than the cat's teeth. High impact rubber balls and rawhide chew toys are less likely to split or break teeth than are nylon or knuckle bones.

Many toothpastes and dental products designed for people are *not* appropriate for cats. However, pastes, gels sprays and solutions are now available for pets. Some products contain abrasives such as calcium and silicates; for example, *DVM Toothpaste* and *Pet Dent*. Others use oxygenating substances to limit growth of anaerobic bacteria (*CET* dental products and *Oxyfresh*). *Nolvadent* and *Peridex* contain 0.1 percent Chlorhexidine, which is both antibacterial and antiviral. *Maxi/Guard* contains zinc ascorbate, which promotes healing of diseased gums. Your veterinarian may suggest one of these products especially if your cat has gum disease.

For routine cleaning, a satisfactory dentifrice can be made by mixing one tablespoon of baking soda with one teaspoon of water. If the cat is on a salt-restricted diet, substitute a salt replacer (potassium chloride) for the baking soda.

Some cats may resist having their teeth brushed. However, a step-by-step approach usually will lead to acceptance. Begin by rubbing the cat's muzzle over the teeth. This is easily accepted as it mimics natural behavior when cats rub against people. Then raise the lip and massage the gums with your finger. When this becomes routine, wrap a cloth or gauze around your finger and gently rub its teeth and gums. The next step is to introduce a toothbrush. Begin with a *soft, small toothbrush*, first using the water from a can of tuna as a "dentifrice." Before using the toothpaste, introduce it to the cat by offering it on the tip of your finger.

The most important part of the gum to brush is the gingival sulcus, where the gum attaches to the teeth (see the illustration of teeth). Move the brush forward and backward, parallel to the gum line, with the bristles in the gingival sulcus. It is not necessary to brush the tongue side. The cat's rough tongue will help to distribute the dentifrice on the inside of the teeth.

TONGUE

SORE TONGUE (GLOSSITIS)

Inflammation and infection of the tongue is called glossitis. Glossitis often accompanies immunodeficiency states such as *feline leukemia*, *feline immunodeficiency virus syndrome* and *feline viral respiratory disease complex*.

Cats can irritate their tongues while removing burrs or other abrasive substances from their coats. Tongue burns can be caused by licking caustic material off the feet or by licking a metal surface in freezing weather. Burns, scratches and cuts on the tongue can become infected.

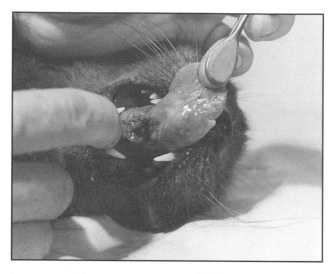

String around the tongue, cutting into the base.

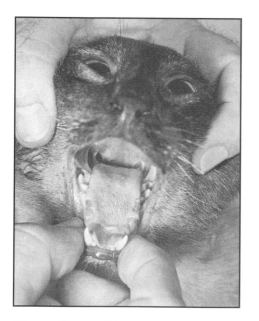

Glossitis. The tip of the tongue appears smooth and shiny. This condition is often associated with feline upper respiratory infection.

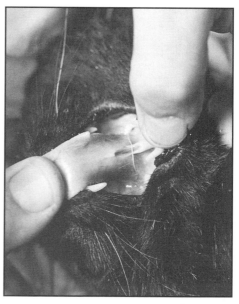

An ulcerating sore beneath the tongue, produced by a penetrating foreign body.

A cat with a sore tongue has an ungroomed appearance. The fur on its neck may be dirty and wet from drooling and frothing. As the inflamed surface of the tongue is shed, the rough spikes are lost, causing the tongue to appear red and shiny. Ulcers and open sores may be present.

Treatment: Flush out the cat's mouth twice a day with 0.1 percent Chlorhexidine solution or a weak solution of hydrogen peroxide and water. Ulcers should be cauterized with a silver nitrate stick. An antibiotic such as Ampicillin should be given twice a day. A cat with a painful tongue may have difficulty eating or drinking. Feed soft, canned food diluted with water to a liquid consistency.

FOREIGN BODIES IN THE TONGUE

Small plant awns, burrs, splinters and needles can become imbedded on the surface of the tongue. Signs are like those of *Foreign Bodies in the Mouth*. A common place for a foreign body is the underside of the tongue. On lifting the tongue, you may see a grapelike swelling or a draining tract, which means the foreign body has been present for some time. If a foreign body is visible and easily accessible, it can be removed with tweezers. A thread attached to a needle should not be pulled out because it can be used to locate the needle. Foreign bodies that have been present for some time are difficult to remove and require an anesthetic. Afterward, the cat should be place on a prophylactic antibiotic (penicillin) for one week.

STRING AROUND THE TONGUE (STRANGULATION)

In this condition, as the cat swallows one end of a piece of string, the other end loops around the tongue. The more the cat swallows, the harder the string cuts into the base of the tongue. Eventually, the string may cut off the blood supply and cause strangulation.

It may be difficult to locate the cause of this problem. The cat will be difficult to examine and the string could be as small as a thread. Close inspection is necessary to find and remove the cause of the constriction.

MOUTH

SORE MOUTH (STOMATITIS)

Mouth inflammation should be suspected when you see drooling, refusal to eat, difficulty chewing, head shaking, pawing at the face and reluctance to allow mouth examination. The inside of the mouth looks reddened, inflamed, swollen and tender. The gums may bleed when rubbed. Bad breath is present. Lack of self-grooming is evident.

In some cases mouth infection is directly attributable to periodontal disease or a foreign object caught between the teeth or imbedded in the tongue. Other cases are associated with an immune deficiency disease such as *feline immunodeficiency virus, feline leukemia, feline viral respiratory disease complex* or kidney failure.

Cases caused by a specific infection follow.

Trench Mouth (Vincent's stomatitis): This is an extremely painful stomatitis caused by a bacteria-like germ. There is a characteristic offensive mouth odor, usually accompanied by a brown, purulent, slimy saliva that stains the front of the legs. The gums are beefy red and bleed easily. Trench mouth occurs in cats with severe periodontal disease and in those that are run-down because of chronic illness or dietary deficiency. Frontal sinus infection can occur as a complication of trench mouth (see NOSE: *Sinusitis*).

Treatment: Your veterinarian may elect to thoroughly cleanse the cat's mouth under anesthesia. This affords the opportunity to treat decayed roots, loose teeth and dental calculus when present. Ulcers are cauterized with silver nitrate. Infection is treated with an antibiotic. Afterward, the cat is placed on soft, canned food diluted with water to a liquid consistency. After care involves daily mouthwashes, using either 0.1 percent Chlorhexidine solution or dilute hydrogen peroxide, accompanied by a home program of good oral hygiene (see *Care of Your Cat's Teeth*).

Ulcerative (Viral) Stomatitis: This is an extremely painful stomatitis in which ulcers form on the tip of the tongue and hard palate. The saliva is at first clear, then becomes blood tinged and foul smelling. A yellow puslike exudate forms on the surface of the ulcers. Ulcerative stomatitis is seen most often with the *feline respiratory disease complex*.

Treatment: It is the same as for trench mouth, except that antibiotics are not recommended unless the problem is complicated by secondary bacterial infection. Cats with viral stomatitis should be examined by a veterinarian.

Thrush (Yeast stomatitis): This is an uncommon stomatitis seen chiefly when a cat has been on a prolonged course of a broad-spectrum antibiotic that alters the normal flora of the mouth and allows the growth of yeast. It also occurs in immunodeficiency states associated with chronic illness. The mucous membranes of the gums and tongue are covered with soft white patches that coalesce to form a whitish film. Painful ulcers appear as the disease progresses.

Treatment: Nystatin is the drug of choice. Large doses of B-complex vitamins are recommended. Correction of all predisposing causes is essential.

FOREIGN BODIES IN THE MOUTH

Foreign bodies that can lodge in the mouth include bone splinters, gristle, slivers of wood, sewing needles, pins, porcupine quills, fish hooks and plant awns. Some penetrate the lips, gums and palate; others become caught between the teeth or wedged across the roof of the mouth. Pieces of string can become wrapped around the teeth and tongue.

Suspect a foreign body when your cat paws at the mouth, rubs the mouth along the floor, drools, gags, licks the lips or holds the mouth open. Occasionally, the only signs are loss of pep, bad breath, refusal to eat and an ungroomed appearance.

Foreign bodies in the tongue and back of the throat are discussed elsewhere in this chapter.

Treatment: Obtain a good light source and gently open your cat's mouth as described earlier in this chapter. A good look may reveal the cause of the problem. The direct removal of some foreign bodies is possible. Others will require a general anesthetic.

Ulcerative stomatitis. Note the shiny ulcerative appearance of the top of the tongue and the thick, slimy saliva.

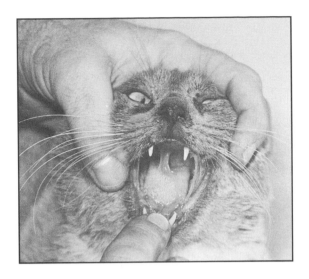

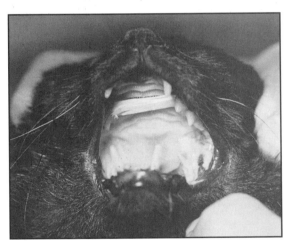

A foreign body wedged across the roof of the mouth.

To remove a fishhook, push the barbed end through the lip. Cut the shank and remove the hook in two pieces.

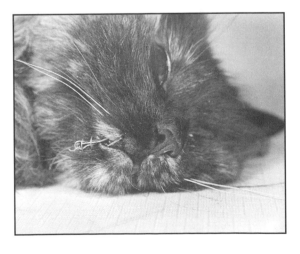

To remove a fishhook when the barb is free, cut the shank next to the barb with wire cutters and remove the fish hook in two pieces. If the barb is embedded in the tissue, try to push the hook through until the barb is free.

Foreign bodies left in place for a day or longer may cause infection. A broad-spectrum antibiotic (penicillin) is recommended for one week.

Porcupine Quills. Porcupine quills can penetrate the face, nose, lips, oral cavity, feet and skin of the cat. If you decide to remove quills at home, restrain the cat. Using a surgical hemostat or needle-nosed pliers, grasp each quill near the skin and draw it straight out in the long axis of the quill. If the quill breaks off, a fragment will be left behind to work in further, causing a deep-seated infection.

Quills inside the mouth are difficult to remove and require a general anesthetic.

GROWTHS IN THE MOUTH

Any solid tumor growing in the mouth is a cause for concern. The majority are cancers. They require immediate professional attention.

Growths of the gums and salivary glands are discussed elsewhere.

THROAT

SORE THROAT (PHARYNGITIS)

Isolated sore throats are not common in the cat. Most are associated with a viral illness or mouth infection. The signs of sore throat are fever, coughing, gagging, vomiting, pain in the throat when attempting to swallow and loss of appetite.

Foreign bodies in the throat give symptoms much like those of sore throat and tonsillitis. This possibility should be considered.

Treatment: Veterinary examination and treatment of the basic disease process is required. Cats with a sore throat should be placed on soft, canned foods diluted with water to a liquid consistency. Administer penicillin antibiotic for one week.

TONSILLITIS

This also is rare in cats. The tonsils are aggregates of tissue much like those of lymph nodes, located at the back of the throat as they are in people. Usually, they are not visible unless they are inflamed. Infected tonsils cause symptoms much like those of a sore throat, except that fever is more pronounced (over 103°F), and the cat appears more ill. Most cases are caused by a bacteria.

Treatment: The treatment is the same as for sore throat. Removal of chronically inflamed tonsils is seldom necessary.

FOREIGN BODIES IN THE THROAT (CHOKING AND GAGGING)

Some cats, especially kittens, may try to eat or swallow string, tinsel, cloth, fishhooks and other small objects or toys. Depending on how far down the throat an object is lodged, the cat will exhibit gagging, neck extension on swallowing and choking on swallowing.

Note: If the signs are forceful *coughing* and the cat is having difficulty taking in air, the foreign body has passed into its larynx. Proceed at once to RESPIRATORY SYSTEM: *Foreign Object in the Voice Box.*

Treatment: Cats are extremely difficult to restrain when panicked. Struggling with them may cause a foreign body to work deeper into the throat. Do not try to open the mouth. Calm the cat and proceed directly to the nearest veterinary hospital.

However, if the cat has fainted, the foreign body will have to be removed at once to re-establish the airway. Open the mouth. This is now easily accomplished because the cat is unconscious. Take hold of the neck in back of the object and apply enough pressure to keep the object from passing down while you hook it with your fingers. Work it loose as quickly as possible. Then administer *Artificial Breathing* (see EMERGENCIES).

Prevention: Watch your cat carefully and do not let it play with small, easily torn toys. Do not feed chicken bones or long bones that can splinter.

SALIVARY GLANDS

There are four main salivary glands that drain into the cat's mouth. Only the parotid gland, located below the cat's ear at the back of the cheek, may be felt from the outside. The salivary glands secrete an alkaline fluid that lubricates the food and aids in digestion.

DROOLING (HYPERSALIVATION)

Healthy cats do not drool like some dogs. However, it is common for cats to drool when they know they are going to be given an unpleasant-tasting medicine or receive a shot. This is psychological.

Keep in mind that an animal that drools excessively and acts irrationally could have rabies. Exercise great caution in handling such an animal.

Drooling accompanied by signs of ill health such as watering of the eyes is quite likely due to a feline viral respiratory infection. Mouth infections and foreign bodies in the mouth are accompanied by drooling. Heat stroke can cause excess salivation, as can certain poisons (e.g., insecticides, arsenic).

Treatment is contingent on identifying the cause of the drooling.

SALIVARY GLAND TUMORS AND CYSTS

The salivary glands can be injured as a result of a cat fight or some other trauma to the head or neck area. The damaged gland may leak salivary fluid into the surrounding tissue, producing a cyst called a **mucocele.** When this occurs in the floor of the mouth on one side of the tongue, it is called a **ranula.** Mucoceles can enlarge and interfere with eating or swallowing. Treatment involves drainage of the cyst into the mouth or, for a more certain cure, removal of the entire salivary gland.

Growths of the salivary gland are rare and occur in old cats. Most are cancers. They present as a slowly enlarging firm swelling or lump in the neck or on the side of

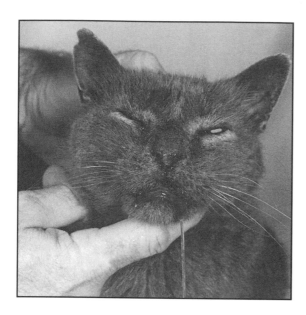

Drooling caused by severe mouth infection.

the face. Surgical cure is possible if undertaken before the tumor has spread to other body parts.

SWOLLEN HEAD

ALLERGIC REACTION

Sudden swelling of the face, lips, ears and eyelids can be caused by a hivelike allergic reaction called **urticaria.** The cat's head may appear strangely out of proportion to the body, and the eyes may be swollen shut. Common causes are food allergy, contact and inhalation allergy, and the bites and stings of insects. Swelling appears about 20 minutes after exposure to the allergen.

Treatment: Most reactions subside in three to four hours. Your veterinarian may choose to administer adrenaline or an antihistamine. You should try to find out what caused the allergic reaction so you can prevent your cat from coming into contact with that allergen again.

Note: The addition of wheezing, respiratory distress, vomiting or diarrhea indicates a potentially serious allergic reaction (see *Anaphylactic Shock* in DRUGS AND MEDICATIONS). *Snakebite* is another possibility. *Seek immediate veterinary attention.*

HEAD AND NECK ABSCESSES

Head and neck abscesses appear suddenly and are accompanied by fever. They are extremely tender and may give a lopsided look to the head, face or neck. Opening the mouth causes extreme pain in some cases. These cats refuse to eat or drink. Most head and neck abscesses are caused by infected animal bites, mouth infections that

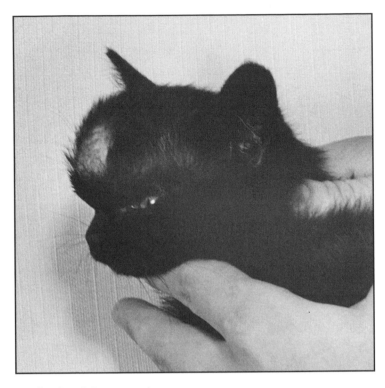

Swollen head due to an abscess.

spread to the frontal sinuses or the space behind the tonsils and sharp foreign bodies such as wood splinters and quills that have worked back into the soft tissues.

Retrobulbar abscesses behind the eye cause tearing and protrusion of the eye. **Submandibular** abscesses cause swelling beneath the chin. An abscess in the frontal sinus causes swelling beneath the eye. Ear flap abscesses are discussed in the chapter EARS.

Treatment: In nearly all cases, incision and drainage will be necessary when the abscess becomes soft (fluctuant). Your veterinarian may suggest application of warm saline packs for 15 minutes four times a day to localize the infection before draining. Antibiotics are required. After incision and drainage, a wick of gauze may be used to keep the edges apart so that the wound can heal from the bottom. You may be required to change and dress the wound at home.

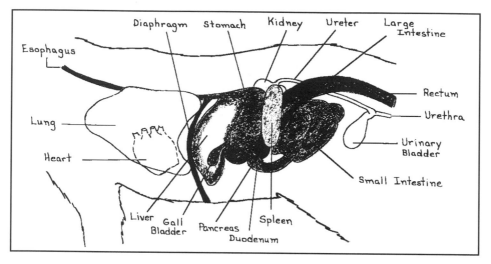

Anatomy of the gastrointestinal system.   —Rose Floyd

9

DIGESTIVE SYSTEM

GENERAL INFORMATION

The digestive tract is a complex system beginning at the mouth and ending at the anus. The lips, teeth, tongue, salivary glands, mouth and pharynx are considered elsewhere. The remaining digestive tract organs are the esophagus, stomach, duodenum (first part of the small bowel), small intestine, colon, rectum and anus. The organs that aid in the digestion and absorption of foodstuffs are the pancreas, gall bladder and liver.

The *esophagus* is a muscular tube that carries the food down to the stomach by rhythmic contractions. The lower esophagus is equipped with a muscular ring that enters the stomach at an angle. This helps to prevent reflux of foods and liquids back into the mouth.

Food remains in the *stomach* for three to six hours and then passes down through the *small intestine* and into the *colon.* Digestive juices in the small intestine break down food into amino acids, fatty acids and short-chain sugars. The products of digestion then pass through the wall of the bowel and into the bloodstream. Blood from the intestines flows to the liver. The liver has numerous functions connected with metabolism. Here the cat's meal is converted into stored energy.

The function of the colon is to remove water and store waste products until they are eliminated.

Because of the cat's relatively relaxed abdominal wall, it is possible to feel many of the organs within the abdomen. Your veterinarian usually can tell whether the liver and spleen are enlarged and may be able to feel other swellings that could indicate a problem in the gastrointestinal or genitourinary systems.

ESOPHAGUS

The esophagus transports food and water from the mouth to the stomach. Regurgitation, painful and difficult swallowing, drooling and, in long-standing cases, weight loss are signs of disease in the esophagus.

REGURGITATION

Regurgitation is the passive or relatively effortless expulsion of undigested food without retching. It occurs when there is a complete esophageal blockage or a breakdown in the swallowing mechanism. It should not be confused with *vomiting*, the *forceful* expulsion of stomach contents preceded by retching. Vomited food appears digested, or at least partly digested, and is mixed with yellow bile.

Bouts of severe coughing and gagging can be mistaken for either regurgitation or vomiting. It is important to distinguish between all three conditions because each denotes a disease in a different system.

PAINFUL SWALLOWING (DYSPHAGIA)

If there is a partial blockage, swallowing can be difficult and painful, but the cat does not necessarily regurgitate. A cat with a painful esophagus makes repeated attempts to swallow the same mouthful and eats slowly. There may be noticeable weight loss, and as the condition becomes more painful, the cat may stop eating altogether. Painful swallowing can be associated with mouth infections, dental infections, a sore throat and tonsillitis. In these conditions it is often accompanied by drooling and halitosis.

MEGAESOPHAGUS (DILATED ESOPHAGUS)

When food is retained in the esophagus for an extended period, the esophagus becomes a storage organ and enlarges like a balloon. This process, called megaesophagus, is accompanied by regurgitation, loss of weight and recurrent episodes of aspiration pneumonia caused by reflux of food into the breathing tubes. There are two main causes of megaesophagus. One is a motility problem characterized by failure of the esophagus to contract normally and to propel food down into the stomach. The other is due to a physical blockage in the esophagus.

Congenital megaesophagus: A hereditary form of megaesophagus occurs in Siamese and other kittens. As the kitten swallows, the esophagus does not contract and does not propel food into the stomach. This is due to a developmental defect in the nerve plexus in the lower esophagus. In time, the upper esophagus begins to dilate and balloon. This can be demonstrated by lifting up the kitten's back legs and looking for a bulging of the esophagus at the side of the neck.

Kittens with megaesophagus begin to show signs shortly after they start to eat solid food. They begin to eat eagerly but, after a few bites, back away from the food dish. They often regurgitate small amounts of food, which they eat again. After repeatedly eating, the food becomes quite liquid and often passes into the stomach. Recurrent episodes of pneumonia are common.

Another type of congenital megaesophagus occurs in kittens with retained fetal arteries in the chest (*aortic arch anomalies*). These arteries constrict the esophagus and cause physical blockage. Regurgitation and difficult swallowing appear as kittens are weaned from liquid to solid food. These kittens become malnourished and exhibit stunted growth. Surgery can correct some of these obstructions.

Adult-onset megaesophagus is seen in older cats. It can be a late manifestation of congenital megaesophagus but also can be caused by esophageal foreign bodies, tumors, strictures, nervous system diseases, autoimmune diseases and heavy metal poisoning.

Treatment of megaesophagus: The problem can be confirmed by a barium swallow X ray. Treatment of congenital megaesophagus is directed at maintaining and improving nutrition. Food and water should be given from a raised bowl to maximize the effect of gravity. A semiliquid or gruel mixture is easier for some cats to swallow; others do better with solids. Determine this by trial and error. A kitten may eventually outgrow this condition. Older cats with acquired megaesophagus may respond to treatment of the stricture, tumor or medical condition responsible for the symptoms.

Foreign Body in the Esophagus

If a cat becomes suddenly distressed, drools, swallows painfully or regurgitates food, suspect a foreign body such as a needle or bone splinter caught in the esophagus. A history of regurgitation and difficulty swallowing for several days or longer does not rule out a foreign body.

Perforations of the esophagus can occur with sharp objects such as bone splinters, needles and fishhooks. Early diagnosis is important.

Treatment: Removal of a foreign body requires an instrument called an *endoscope*. The cat is first given an anesthetic and the instrument is passed through the mouth and into the esophagus. The object is viewed through the endoscope and removed with a long forceps. Difficult foreign bodies and injuries to the esophagus may require surgery.

Strictures

A stricture is a circular scar that develops after an injury to the esophagus. Esophageal injuries can result from foreign bodies and swallowed caustic liquids. The most common cause of stricture is esophageal injury caused by reflux of stomach acid into the lower esophagus when a cat is under anesthesia.

Treatment: Most early strictures can be treated by stretching the wall of the esophagus with endoscopic dilators. Following dilatation, some cats swallow normally. Those that do not because *megaesophagus* has developed may require surgical removal of the stricture.

In a cat with a stricture, *overloading the esophagus with large meals aggravates the problem*. Feed several small, semisolid meals a day from a raised food dish.

GROWTHS

When a cancer (usually *Lymphosarcoma*) involves the lymph nodes around the esophagus, these enlarged nodes can press on the esophagus, creating a physical blockage. Tumors of the esophagus are not common, but when present, they are usually malignant and occur in older cats.

STOMACH

VOMITING

A number of diseases and upsets in the cat are associated with vomiting. It is one of the most common nonspecific symptoms you are likely to encounter.

Cats vomit more easily than most other animals. Some cats seem to do so almost at will, at times for no apparent reason. A cat may vomit undigested food immediately after eating, then eat it again. A mother vomits food so her kittens will have a predigested meal.

All vomiting is the result of stimulation of the vomiting center in the brain by numerous receptors located in the digestive tract and elsewhere. As the need to vomit is perceived, the cat appears anxious and may seek attention and reassurance. You will also see the cat begin to salivate and make repeated efforts to swallow.

As vomiting starts, a simultaneous contraction of the muscles of the stomach and abdominal wall occurs. This leads to an abrupt buildup in intra-abdominal pressure. At the same time the lower esophageal ring relaxes. The stomach contents travel up the esophagus and out the mouth. As the cat vomits, it extends its neck and makes a harsh gagging sound. This sequence should be distinguished from the passive act of *regurgitation* described earlier.

Vomiting unrelated to eating is frequently associated with an infectious disease, kidney or liver disease or a central nervous system disorder.

The most common cause of vomiting is swallowing hair or some other indigestible foreign material such as grass that is irritating to the stomach. Most cats experience this at one time or another. Another common cause is overeating—or eating too fast. When kittens gobble their food and exercise immediately, they are likely to vomit. This after-meal vomiting is not serious. It may be due to feeding several kittens from a single pan, which encourages rapid eating. Separating kittens or feeding smaller meals more often eliminates this problem.

If the cat vomits once or twice but appears perfectly normal before and after, the problem is not serious and can be treated at home (see *Gastritis*).

Diseases frequently associated with vomiting include *feline panleukopenia, tonsillitis*, sore throat and infected uterus (*acute metritis*). Other signs of illness will be present. In young cats, sudden vomiting with fever is suspicious of panleukopenia.

Another serious cause of vomiting is the ingestion of a poison such as antifreeze or a drug such as aspirin. Poisons are discussed in the chapter EMERGENCIES. A most serious cause of vomiting is associated with *peritonitis*. *This is an emergency.* Causes are discussed in the chapter EMERGENCIES under *Painful Abdomen*.

It is often possible to understand your cat's problem by noticing *how* and *when* it vomits.

Repeated Vomiting. The cat vomits, then continues to retch, bringing up a frothy, clear fluid. This suggests spoiled food, grass, hairballs, other indigestibles and certain diseases such as *infectious enteritis* which irritate the stomach lining. If the vomiting is accompanied by diarrhea, consult the paragraphs on diarrhea later in this chapter.

Sporadic Vomiting. The cat vomits off and on but not continuously. There is no relation to meals. Appetite is poor. The cat has a haggard look and appears listless. Suspect a disease of an internal organ such as the liver or kidneys. Other possibilities are *chronic gastritis*, a heavy worm infestation or *diabetes*. A thorough checkup is in order.

Vomiting Blood. Fresh blood indicates a break in the intestinal lining somewhere between the mouth and the upper small bowel. This is most commonly caused by a foreign body. Other causes are tumors and ulcers. Material that resembles *coffee grounds* is partly digested old blood. This indicates that the bleeding point lies in the stomach or its outlet. Some cases may be due to swallowed blood.

If a cat vomits blood, the condition is serious and warrants a trip to the veterinarian.

Fecal Vomiting. If a cat vomits material that looks and smells like stool, suspect *intestinal obstruction*. Blunt or penetrating abdominal trauma is another cause of fecal vomiting. In both cases *professional treatment is required.*

Projectile Vomiting. This is a forceful vomiting in which the stomach contents are ejected suddenly, often a considerable distance. It indicates a complete blockage in the upper gastrointestinal tract. Foreign bodies, hairballs, tumors and strictures are possible causes. Brain diseases that cause increased intracranial pressure also produce projectile vomiting. They include brain tumor, encephalitis and blood clots.

Vomiting Foreign Objects. Hairballs may form wads too large to pass out of the stomach. Other foreign objects that cats may vomit include pieces of cloth, bone splinters, sticks and stones. For more information, see *Intestinal Foreign Bodies*. Kittens with a heavy roundworm infestation may vomit adult worms. These kittens should be treated.

Motion Sickness. Many cats suffer from car sickness and may become seasick when traveling by boat or air. The signs are restlessness followed by salivation, yawning, nausea and then vomiting. Motion sickness is caused by overstimulation of the labyrinth system in the inner ear. Most cats will get over it once they adjust to traveling. If you suspect your cat is going to be sick, a veterinarian may suggest that you give *Dramamine*, 12.5 mg for the average-sized cat, one hour before traveling. Withhold food before taking a trip. Cats travel best on an empty stomach.

Vomiting in kittens is discussed in the PEDIATRICS chapter.

INFLAMMATION OF THE STOMACH (GASTRITIS)

Gastritis is an inflammation of the lining of the stomach. The principal sign is vomiting. The vomiting may be sudden and *acute* or *chronic* and sporadic.

Acute Gastritis. Severe and continuous vomiting that comes on suddenly is most likely caused by swallowing an irritant or poison. Common stomach irritants are grass, hair, bones, spoiled food and garbage. *Certain drugs, notably* aspirin, *but also cortisone, butazolidin and some antibiotics produce gastric irritation. Common poisons are antifreeze, fertilizers, plant toxins, crabgrass killers and rat poisons. When any of these is suspected, notify your veterinarian.*

A cat with an acute gastritis vomits shortly after eating and later stops eating altogether and appears lethargic, sitting with head hanging over the water bowl. The temperature remains normal unless the cat has an acute enteritis, usually accompanied by diarrhea.

Treatment: When the stomach responds promptly, the foreign material is expelled. Afterward, rest the stomach. Withhold food and water for 24 hours. If your cat appears thirsty, allow the animal to lick ice cubes. After 24 hours, offer sips of water. If the water is well tolerated, advance to a strained meat baby food (low in fat). Offer four to six small feedings a day for the next two days. Then return to a regular diet.

Consult your veterinarian if vomiting persists for more than 24 hours, if the cat becomes dehydrated or if vomiting recurs.

Chronic Gastritis Cats with a chronically upset stomach vomit sporadically (not always after meals), appear lethargic, carry a dull hair coat and lose weight. The vomitus sometimes contains food eaten the day before.

A common cause of chronic gastritis is swallowed hair that forms a hairball or bezoar in the stomach. Prevention is discussed in the section *Intestinal Foreign Bodies.* Other causes of chronic gastritis are persistent grass eating, the ingestion of cellulose, plastic, paper, rubber and other irritating products and a diet of poor-quality or spoiled food.

Aspirin, when given to cats regularly, produces thickening and peptic stomach ulceration, a condition that may be complicated by gastrointestinal bleeding. Aspirin and other nonsteroidal anti-inflammatory drugs should be given only under veterinary supervision. See DRUGS AND MEDICATIONS.

Finally, if there is no apparent explanation for the sporadic vomiting, the cat may be suffering from an internal disorder such as liver disease, kidney failure, diabetes, tonsillitis, infected uterus, pancreatitis, hyperthyroidism or heartworm disease.

Treatment: This depends on finding and correcting the underlying cause. A cat with chronic vomiting should be examined by a veterinarian. Special diagnostic studies may be required. Cats with chronic vomiting often require a low fiber, semisolid or canned food diet (such as Hill's *Feline c/d* or *d/d*) to fit the particular disease causing the vomiting.

OTHER CAUSES OF UPSET STOMACH

Some cats are unable to tolerate certain foods or specific brands of commercial cat food. This is determined by trial and error. Special diets can be prescribed by the veterinarian.

If your cat vomits about two hours after eating, the problem could be **Food Hypersensitivity**. This is usually accompanied by watery, mucus-like or even bloody diarrhea (see *Diarrhea*).

Stomach ulcers are not common in cats. They are usually caused by drugs and medications—especially aspirin, the nonsteroidal anti-inflammatory agents such as ibuprofen and butazolidin and steroids. Vomiting is the most frequent sign and often contains old blood (coffee-ground material) and occasionally fresh blood. Weight loss and anemia are accompanying features. Diagnosis is made by upper gastrointestinal X rays or by endoscopy. Treatment involves discontinuing all ulcer-producing medications. Drugs are available to treat ulcers in cats. They are the same as the drugs used for people.

BLOAT (ABDOMINAL DISTENSION)

Several disorders cause the abdomen to appear bloated or swollen. Overeating, eating fermented foods and constipation can give a cat a somewhat bloated or pot-bellied look. Worm infestation can do this in kittens.

Sudden swelling accompanied by pain and signs of distress in the abdomen indicates an urgent condition such as a bowel obstruction, bladder outlet obstruction, abscessed uterus or peritonitis (see *Painful Abdomen* in the EMERGENCIES chapter, and *Intestinal Obstruction* below). *Acute gastric dilatation* or *volvulus*, which occurs in dogs, is extremely rare in cats but is an emergency when it occurs. The signs are sudden abdominal swelling, a shocklike state, and peritonitis. *Rush your cat to the veterinary hospital.*

An abdominal swelling that comes on gradually over several days or weeks is most likely due to **ascites,** a condition in which fluid accumulates in the abdomen. Feline infectious peritonitis should be suspected. Other causes are right-sided heart failure and liver disease.

Keep in mind that pregnancy and false pregnancy are common causes of abdominal enlargement in queens.

Treatment depends on determining the exact cause. *Veterinary examination is indicated.*

INTESTINES

Cats have relatively short intestines. Much of their nutrition comes from meat which requires less surface area for digestion. Problems in the small and large bowel are associated with three common symptoms: diarrhea, constipation, and the passage of blood.

Diarrhea in kittens is discussed in the PEDIATRICS chapter.

DIARRHEA

Diarrhea is the passage of loose, unformed stool. In most cases there is a large volume of stool and an increased number of bowel movements. A common cause of loose stools is overfeeding. Dietary overload presents the colon with more volume than it can handle easily.

Food in the small intestine takes about eight hours to get to the colon. During this time the bulk of it is absorbed. Eighty percent of water is absorbed in the small bowel. The colon concentrates and stores the waste. At the end, a well formed stool is evacuated. A normal stool contains no mucus, blood or undigested food.

When food passes rapidly through the small intestine, it is incompletely digested and arrives at the rectum in a liquid state. This results in a loose unformed bowel movement. Transit time in the intestinal tract can be speeded up by a variety of *irritating substances*, including

> dead animals, rodents, and birds;
>
> garbage and decayed food;
>
> rich foods, gravies, salts, spices, and fats;
>
> sticks, cloth, grass, paper, plastic.

Some *toxic substances* causing diarrhea are

> gasoline, kerosene, oil, or coal tar derivatives;
>
> cleaning fluid, refrigerants;
>
> insecticides, bleaches (often in toilet bowls);
>
> wild and ornamental plants, toadstools;
>
> building materials (cement, lime, paints, caulks).

Toxic diarrhea is not common in cats. They are quite careful of what they eat and tend to eat slowly. However, toxic substances can be ingested when cats clean their feet or groom their coat. Many of these substances are also toxic to the stomach and cause vomiting.

Some adult cats (and occasionally kittens) are unable to digest milk and some milk by-products. This is because they lack adequate amounts of the enzyme *lactase*, which aids in the digestion of milk sugars. The unabsorbed sugar, called *lactose*, holds water in the small intestine, producing increased motility and a large volume of stool. Other foods that some cats may be unable to tolerate or be allergic to are beef, pork, chicken, horse meat, fish, eggs, spices, corn, wheat, soy, people foods and some commercial cat foods. At times, even a minor deviation from the customary diet can cause diarrhea.

Cats can experience emotional diarrhea when excited or upset—for example, when going to the veterinary hospital or a cat show.

To narrow the search for the cause of the diarrhea, begin by examining the color, consistency, odor and frequency of stools:

Color (A normal stool is brown.)

> Yellow or greenish stool—indicates rapid transit.
>
> Black tarry stool—indicates bleeding in the upper digestive tract.
>
> Bloody stool—red blood or clots indicates lower bowel (colon) bleeding.
>
> Pasty, light-colored stool—indicates lack of bile (liver disease).
>
> Large, gray rancid-smelling stool—indicates inadequate digestion.

Cats with severe diarrhea dehydrate quickly and should be given intravenous fluids to prevent shock and collapse.

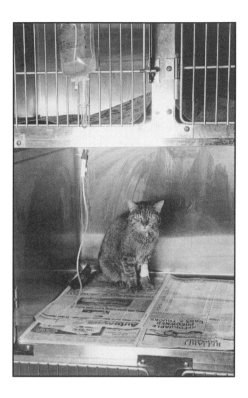

Consistency

Soft bulky stool—often seen when cats are overfed or receive poor-quality food high in fiber.

Watery stool—indicates bowel wall irritation (acute enteritis, ingested toxins) with rapid transit and impaired absorption.

Foamy stool—suggests bacterial infection.

Greasy stool (often with oil on the hair around the anus)—indicates malabsorption syndrome.

Odor (The more watery the stool, the greater the odor.)

Foodlike or smelling like sour milk—suggests both incomplete digestion and inadequate absorption (for example, overfeeding, especially in kittens).

Putrid smelling—suggests intestinal infection or blood in the stool (i.e., feline panleukopenia).

Frequency

Several in an hour, each small with straining—suggests colitis.

Three to four a day, each large—suggests malabsorption syndrome or inflammatory bowel disease.

Diarrhea that persists for a week or longer suggests a chronic ailment such as *colitis, inflammatory bowel disease*, parasite infestation, or *malabsorption syndrome*.

TREATMENT OF DIARRHEA

Diarrhea is a symptom—not a disease. The first step is to find and remove the underlying cause.

If a cat has a *lactase* enzyme deficiency, thereby making the animal unable to convert milk and dairy products, these can be removed from the diet without causing a nutrient deficiency because they are not a necessary part of an adult cat's diet.

Diarrhea caused by **overeating** (characterized by several large, bulky, unformed stools) is controlled by cutting back the overall food intake and feeding three small meals instead of one large meal a day. When **unfamiliar drinking water** is the problem, carry an extra supply. When irritating or **toxic substances** have been ingested, identify the agent because specific antidotes may be required (see *Poisoning* in the chapter EMERGENCIES).

Food allergy is treated by placing the cat on a homemade or commercial hypoallergenic diet prescribed by your veterinarian for about eight weeks. If the diarrhea disappears, the cat can remain on this diet, or various foods can be added one by one until the offending food allergen is detected by return of symptoms. This food substance is then eliminated from the diet.

Diarrhea that persists for more than 24 hours is potentially serious. *Consult your veterinarian without delay.* A cat dehydrates quickly when fluid losses go unchecked, and this can lead to shock and collapse. Other indications to consult your veterinarian are bloody diarrhea and diarrhea accompanied by vomiting, fever and signs of toxicity. The cause of a chronic diarrhea over a week's duration is difficult to diagnose and requires laboratory analysis and close professional monitoring.

Diarrheas of short duration without excessive fluid loss can be treated at home. Withhold all food for 24 hours. If the cat appears thirsty, give very small amounts of water, or give ice cubes for licking. As the cat begins to recover, introduce food gradually, feeding three to four small meals a day. Begin with a diet high in fat and poultry protein. Strained meat baby food, *Purina Tender Vittles* and Hill's prescription diet *Feline c/d* are good examples. Avoid high-carbohydrate diets. Cats have a low tolerance for starch. High-starch diets are likely to prolong diarrhea. Return to the ususal ration when the cat has fully recovered.

Some specific disorders of the small and large intestine associated with diarrhea are listed below.

INFLAMMATORY BOWEL DISEASE (IBD)

There are three bowel diseases in cats characterized by chronic and protracted diarrhea, malabsorption and, in long-standing cases, weight loss, anemia and malnutrition. They are somewhat treatable but seldom cured.

Although the cause of IBD is unknown, evidence suggests that certain bacteria or food proteins may prime the immune system, causing cats to produce antibodies that attack the cells of their own intestinal tract.

In each disease a different type of inflammatory cell (plasma cell, eosinophil, lymphocyte, macrophage) accumulates in the mucous lining of the small or large intestines. These cell types distinguish the three diseases. Diagnosis is made by endoscopy or exploratory surgery, during which biopsies are taken of the intestinal wall.

Eosinophilic Enterocolitis: Eosinophils may be found in the stomach, small intestine or colon. A persistent eosinophilia (increased blood eosinophil count) also may exist. Some cases of eosinophilic enterocolitis are thought to be associated with the tissue migration of roundworms and hookworms. Treatment involves the use of high-dose corticosteroids that are tapered as symptoms are controlled. The cat should be tested for food allergy and intestinal parasites and treated accordingly. This form of IBD is the most difficult to treat successfully and has the poorest outlook.

As a general measure, the cat should be placed on a hypoallergenic diet, either homemade (baby foods or boiled chicken) or commercially obtained (e.g., Hill's Pet Products). The diet should be highly digestible and low in fat. If *colitis* is present, fiber may need to be added.

Lymphocytic-Plasmacytic Enterocolitis: Lymphocytes and plasma cells are the predominant inflammatory cells seen on biopsy of the small and large intestines. This is the most common form of IBD in cats. The disease has been associated with **giardiasis, food allergy** and an overgrowth of **intestinal bacteria**. Vomiting is a common symptom but is not present in all cases. An antibiotic (metronidazole) is given to treat bacterial overgrowth and giardiasis. Immunosuppressant drugs such as azathioprine (*Imuran*) or prednisone are a secondary line of treatment.

Granulomatous (Regional) Enteritis: Macrophages, which are tissue white cells, are found in the lower small intestine and colon. This rare disease in cats is similar to *Crohn's disease* in humans. There is thickening and narrowing of the bowel due to inflammation of surrounding fat and lymph nodes. Biopsies are processed with special stains to exclude *histoplasmosis* and intestinal *tuberculosis*. Corticosteroids and immunosuppressive drugs are employed to reduce inflammation and scarring. A course of metronidazole may be of benefit. Surgery may be required for a strictured bowel.

Acute Enteritis (Infectious Diarrhea)

The parvovirus that produces *feline panleukopenia* is a common cause of infectious diarrhea in cats. Less commonly infectious diarrhea is caused by bacteria (salmonella, camphylobacter); protozoa (coccidia, giardia, toxoplasma); and intestinal parasites (roundworms, tapeworms, hookworms). These diseases are discussed in the chapter INFECTIOUS DISEASES.

Colitis

This is an inflammatory disease of the large bowel or colon, usually occurring as a manifestation of **inflammatory bowel disease,** occasionally as a manifestation of **acute enteritis.**

Signs of colitis are urgent straining, painful defecation, prolonged squatting, flatulence and the passage of many small stools mixed with blood and mucus. These signs should be distinguished from *constipation*.

The administration of antibiotics can upset the normal flora of the colon and result in an overgrowth of virulent bacteria that then produce an acute *pseudo-membranous colitis.* This is common in people but uncommon in cats.

Colitis is complicated and requires veterinary diagnosis and management. High-fiber diets as described for the treatment of chronic constipation are beneficial.

MALABSORPTION SYNDROME

Failure to digest or absorb food in the small intestine leads to loose, unformed stools containing large amounts of fat. The absorption of nutrients requires both the presence of digestive enzymes and a healthy bowel lining. Liver and pancreatic disease can be associated with failure to produce or secrete digestive enzymes, while inflammatory disease of the small intestine may permanently damage the intestinal lining. The crowding out of normal cells in the bowel wall by malignant cells, which occurs with intestinal lymphosarcoma, is another consideration.

Cats with malabsorption syndrome are thin and malnourished despite a large appetite. The stool contains large amounts of undigested fat, giving it a rancid odor. The hair around the anus is oily or greasy.

The exact cause of malabsorption can usually be determined by specific tests or intestinal biopsy. Treatment is then directed at the underlying disease. When pancreatic disease is the problem, the cat can be given the missing pancreatic enzymes by mouth with its meals.

Cats with malabsorption should be placed on a low-fat diet. Suitable homemade diets include boiled chicken or lamb. Prescription diets are available through your veterinarian (Hill's Pet Products). Supplemental B-complex and fat-soluble vitamins should be given.

INTESTINAL OBSTRUCTION (BLOCKED BOWEL)

The most common cause of intestinal obstruction is a swallowed foreign body (discussed below). Other causes are tumors and strictures of the small and large intestine, adhesions following abdominal surgery, navel and groin hernias and *intussusception*—a condition in which the bowel telescopes in upon itself, much as a sock pulled inside out. On occasion, obstruction of the colon may be caused by a fecal impaction or tumor. An intestinal blockage can be partial or complete.

Partial or intermittent *obstruction* such as that caused by a tumor or stricture may cause signs that come and go. These signs include weight loss, intermittent vomiting or diarrhea. Tumors tend to occur in older cats, and most of them are malignant. They often become large before being discovered, usually by feeling a mass in the abdomen.

Signs of *complete blockage* are vomiting, dehydration, and swelling of the abdomen. When the blockage is high, projectile vomiting occurs shortly after eating. When low, there is progressive distention of the abdomen followed by vomiting of

Do not allow your cat to play with string or other objects it could swallow.

dark brown material having a fecal odor. A cat with a complete obstruction passes no gas or stool through the rectum.

Intestinal obstruction leads to death unless treatment is instituted. The cat's condition is most urgent when there are signs of strangulation or interference with the blood supply to the bowel. This is characterized by sudden distress, an extremely tender "boardlike" abdomen to touch, shock and prostration. Strangulation requires immediate surgical relief. A dead segment of bowel must be removed and the bowel restored by an end-to-end hookup.

Intestinal Foreign Bodies

Hairballs rank as the number one cause of symptoms produced by foreign material in the gastrointestinal tract. As cats groom their coat, they pick up and swallow hair. The hair forms tubular, brownish, castlike wads. Other material such as wool may be incorporated into the wad of hair, resulting in the formation of a *bezoar*. Eventually the bezoar becomes too large to pass out of the stomach and produces bouts of vomiting and symptoms like those of *chronic gastritis*. Hair that passes into the colon contributes to constipation. If you find that your cat vomits wads of hair or if the stool has quite a bit of hair in it, anticipate a problem and take the preventive measures described below.

Objects sometimes swallowed by cats include pins and needles, wood splinters, nylon stockings, rubber bands, feathers, cloth, plastic and string. Most pass through the intestinal tract without causing problems, although sharp objects have the potential for perforating the bowel. Fortunately, this is not common, even when a pin is swallowed. Should perforation occur, it leads to signs of *painful abdomen*. Seek immediate professional attention.

Surgery is indicated to remove string. One end of the string often knots while the other gets caught in food. Tension on the string causes it to cut through the wall of the bowel.

Note: If your cat swallows a sharp object or any object that you suspect may be too large to pass through its intestinal tract, do not induce vomiting. Consult your veterinarian.

Prevention: Do not allow your cat to play with string, cloth or plastic toys it could tear and swallow. Brush the coat more frequently, especially at shedding time. Administer a commercial hairball preparation (cat laxative) available at pet supply stores. A safe and effective home remedy for hairballs is white petroleum jelly. Apply one-half teaspoon to the cat's nose, and it will be licked off. The jelly melts in the stomach and lubricates the hairball for easier passage. Use once or twice a week. Mineral oil is effective. Add it to the cat's food once or twice a week at a dose of one teaspoon per five pounds body weight. Do not give by mouth because of the potential for inhalation. Keep in mind that mineral oil and petroleum jelly may decrease the absorption of fat-soluble vitamins, if given in large doses or for a prolonged period.

CONSTIPATION

Constipation is defined as the infrequent passage of small, hard, dry stools. When feces are retained in the colon for two to three days, they become dry and hard. This results in straining and pain during defecation. Most cats have one or two stools a day. However, some cats have a bowel movement every two or three days. These cats are quite likely to be constipated.

Straining also occurs with **colitis** and the **feline urologic syndrome** (FUS). Be sure the cat is not suffering from one of these conditions before treating for constipation. An overlooked bladder outlet obstruction, for example, is especially serious since it can produce damage to the kidneys and death. FUS is discussed in the chapter URINARY SYSTEM.

CHRONIC CONSTIPATION

Diets low in fiber and those high in concentrated meat protein are common causes of constipation. These diets produce stools that are dry or gummy and difficult to pass. The problem is intensified if the cat does not drink enough water. In fact, the intake of water among cats is generally low compared with most other animals. Cats eating canned food, which is 75 percent water, may not experience the urge to drink for one or two days.

Hairballs are a common cause of hard stools, particularly in long-coated breeds. Suspect this if your cat vomits hair or if you see hair in the stool. The prevention of hairballs is discussed above (see *Intestinal Foreign Bodies*). Other nondigestible substances such as grass, cellulose, paper and cloth can lead to constipation or a fecal impaction.

The urge to defecate can be voluntarily overridden. Many cats will not defecate when in strange surroundings; others may refuse to use dirty litter pans. Older less active cats experience reduced bowel activity and have weakness of their abdominal wall muscles. Either condition can lead to prolonged retention and increased hardness of the stools.

Occasionally, chronic constipation is due to or results in an enlarged, sluggish, poorly contracting colon. This condition is called **megacolon.** These cats require lifelong treatment with stool softeners and special diets. Veterinary supervision is necessary.

A chronically constipated cat may have a bloated look, seem lethargic and pick at its food. Cats with a fecal impaction often pass blood-tinged or watery, brown stool. This may be mistaken for diarrhea. What is actually happening is that liquid stool is being forced around the blockage. Fecal impaction is confirmed by digital examination using a well-lubricated glove.

Constipation and fecal incontinence can occur in Manx breed cats having developmental deformities of the spine.

Treatment: Remove predisposing factors to assure long-term success.

Cats with chronic or recurrent episodes of constipation benefit from high-fiber diets. In general, this is best accomplished by feeding a commercial cat food formulated for senior cats. These contain less fat and more fiber than maintenance food. If not successful, replace the commercial product with Hill's *Science Diet Feline Light* (a dry food only) or Hill's *Feline w/d* or *Feline r/d* (canned and dry). The canned formula has a higher fiber content than the dry.

For mild constipation, the addition of *bulk-forming laxatives* is beneficial. These laxatives absorb water in the colon, soften feces and promote more frequent defecation. Wheat bran (one tablespoon per day) or *Metamucil* (one to three teaspoons per day mixed into wetted or liquid food) is recommended. Bulk laxatives can be used indefinitely without causing a problem.

Stimulant laxatives are effective for simple constipation, but repeated use may interfere with colon function. Several products are available. They include *Kat-a-lax* and *Laxatone*. The latter is especially effective for hairballs.

Kitty litter should be cleaned at least once daily and changed two or three times a week (see FELINE BEHAVIOR AND TRAINING: *Housebreaking*). Daily exercise is beneficial.

Fecal impaction: The removal of impacted feces requires the use of both a laxative and a small volume enema. For a severe impaction associated with dehydration, fluid replacement is necessary before attempting to remove the impaction. Veterinary treatment is necessary. Enemas are given through a rubber catheter connected to a plastic syringe or enema bag. Lubricate the tip and insert it one to two inches, which is far enough to retain the enema without risking an injury to the rectum. Appropriate enema solutions are:

- Tap water at room temperature (2.5 ml per pound body weight);
- Tap water (5 to 10 ml) to which is added 1 ml (10 mg) *Colace Liquid* 1 percent;
- Mineral oil 5 to 10 ml total.

Mineral oil prevents the absorption of water into feces and should be used only *after* tap water enemas. Enemas may be repeated as necessary to evacuate all fecal material. Soap suds enemas and *Fleets'* enemas should not be used because of potential toxicity in cats.

If a fecal impaction is too large or hard to evacuate with enemas, manual extraction with forceps (under anesthesia) will be required by your veterinarian.

PASSING GAS (FLATULENCE)

Cats that continually pass gas embarrass or distress their owners. This condition, called flatulence, is caused by eating highly fermentable foods such as onions, beans, cauliflower, cabbage and soybeans; drinking large quantities of milk; and swallowing large amounts of air during meals. Diets high in carbohydrates and fiber contribute to it. Flatulence also occurs with malabsorption. This is related to incomplete digestion of carbohydrates. If your cat has a robust appetite and passes a large amount of soft stool, see *Malabsorption Syndrome* earlier in this chapter.

Treatment: If dietary manipulation fails to control the problem, switch from commercial rations to a highly digestible prescription diet such as Hill's *c/d*. Free feed to prevent greedy eating and air gulping. A medication combining simethicone and activated charcoal (*Flatulex*) is available for people and can be used in cats. The feline dose is one-half tablet once or twice a day (preferably after meals).

LOSS OF BOWEL CONTROL (FECAL INCONTINENCE)

Loss of bowel control follows a spinal cord injury, especially one which occurs when a car runs over a cat's tail. The bladder may also be paralyzed. The sacral or coccygeal vertebrae are pulled apart, damaging the nerves to the rectum, bladder and tail. An injured cat with a limp tail should be X-rayed to see if it has a spine injury.

Loss of function may be temporary or permanent, depending on the severity of the nerve injury (see NERVOUS SYSTEM: *Spinal Cord Diseases*). Loss of the ability to urinate or defecate (void) is particularly serious. If untreated, it leads to kidney failure and death.

ANUS AND RECTUM

Signs of anal and rectal disease are pain when defecating, severe straining, scooting, passing bright red blood and licking repeatedly at the rear. Cats with anal and rectal pain often try to defecate standing.

Bleeding from the anus or rectum is recognized by finding blood on the outside of the stool rather than mixed in with it.

Scooting along the ground is a sign of anal itching. It can be caused by flea bites, inflammation of the anus, anal sac disease, roundworms and tapeworm segments.

PROCTITIS (INFLAMED ANUS AND RECTUM)

Maceration of the skin around the anus is often caused by feces adhering to the hair over the anus.

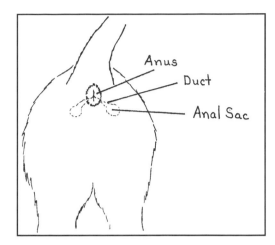

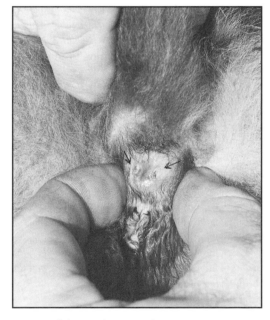

Position of the anal sacs and openings.

Irritation of the anal canal itself is produced by passage of bone chips, sharp objects and hard, dry stools. Repeated bouts of diarrhea, especially in kittens, cause an inflamed anus and rectum. Other causes are insect bites and worms.

Straining is the most common sign of proctitis. Other signs are scooting, biting and licking at the rear. The rough surface of the cat's tongue may aggravate the problem, causing further ulceration and extreme discomfort.

Treatment: Clip away any matted stool if present to let air get to the skin. An irritated anus can be soothed by applying ointment such as *Triple Antibiotic Ointment* or *Cortaid* (hydrocortisone preparation). Put your cat on an appropriate diet. See *Constipation* if the cat has hard dry stools. See *Diarrhea* if this is a contributing factor. Feed smaller amounts of the ration more often until the condition is healed.

Cats may be kept from licking their rears by applying bad-tasting repellent medication obtained from a veterinarian or by using an Elizabethan collar.

PROTRUSION OF ANAL TISSUE (ANAL AND RECTAL PROLAPSE)

With forceful and prolonged straining, a cat can force the lining of the anal canal to protrude. A *partial prolapse* is confined to the mucous membrane. In a *complete prolapse*, a segment of intestine two to three inches long may protrude. This difference is quite evident. Protrusion of anal tissue could be taken for hemorrhoids, but hemorrhoids do not occur in cats.

Conditions that produce forceful straining and predispose to prolapse include *infectious enteritis, fecal impaction, prolonged labor, colitis* and *feline urologic syndrome.* Kittens younger than four months have the highest incidence of prolapse. Manx cats also have a higher incidence.

Treatment: The underlying cause of straining must be identified and treated. A partial prolapse is treated in the same manner as described for proctitis above.

A complete rectal prolapse should be replaced manually. Clean the tissue and lubricate it with petroleum jelly. Then gently push it back through the anus. To prevent recurrence, your veterinarian may suggest taking a temporary purse-string suture around the anus to hold it in place until healed. The cat should be placed on a stool softener such as *Colace Liquid* 1 percent. Add 1 ml (10 mg) daily to food. Feed a highly digestible *low-residue* diet such as Hill's *Feline c/d.*

ANAL GLANDS OR SACS

The cat has two anal glands or sacs located at about four o'clock and eight o'clock in reference to the circumference of the anus. A cat's anal glands are about the size of peas. They are smaller than the dog's and therefore less likely to cause problems. The openings of the anal sacs are found by lifting up the cat's tail, drawing down on the skin of the lower part of the anus and looking for the openings in the described locations.

These sacs are sometimes referred to as "scent" glands. In the skunk they serve a protective purpose. In the cat they mark the stool with an odor that identifies that particular individual and establishes territory.

The anal sacs are emptied by rectal pressure during defecation. The secretions are liquid, malodorous and light gray to brown. At times they may be thick, creamy or yellow looking. It is not necessary to express the anal glands unless there is some medical reason to do so. However, when frequent odor poses a problem (for example, in a cat with overactive anal sacs), you can control it by expressing the sacs yourself.

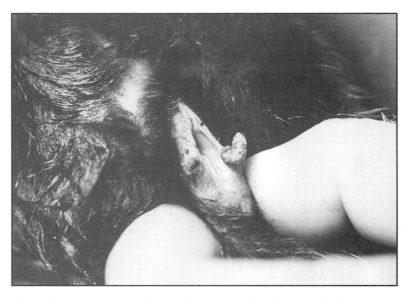

The anal sacs are emptied by pinching the anal skin between the fingers.

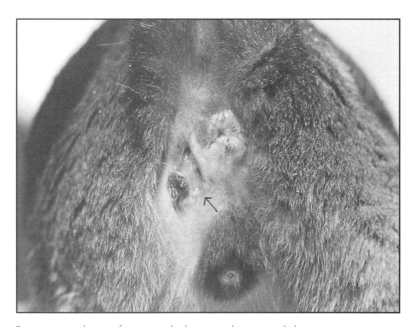

Recurrent anal sac infection with draining abscess and skin tracts.

How to Empty the Anal Sacs

Raise the cat's tail and locate the openings as shown in the illustration. You can feel the sacs as small pea-sized lumps in the perianal areas at the four o'clock and eight o'clock positions. Grasp the skin surrounding the sac with your thumb and forefinger and squeeze together. As the sac empties, you will note a pungent odor. Wipe the secretions away with a damp cloth. If the discharge is bloody or purulent, *anal sac infection* is present and you should treat it as described below.

Impaction of Anal Sacs

Impaction is uncommon and occurs when the sacs fail to empty normally. This may be caused by plugging of the small ducts by their pasty secretions. Often it is not recognized until infection is present.

Uncomplicated anal sac impaction is treated by manual emptying.

Anal Sac Infection (Anal Sacculitis)

This condition complicates impaction. Signs are the presence of blood or pus in the secretions, swelling on one or both sides of the anus, and the presence of anal pain and scooting. These signs also occur with *anal sac abscess.*

Treatment: The anal sacs should be expressed and emptied weekly, after which an antibiotic is put into the sac through the opening. *This procedure is difficult and should be performed by a veterinarian.* You can help to resolve infection by applying warm wet packs to the anal area for 15 minutes three times a day for seven to ten days. An antibiotic (amoxicillin) might be prescribed by your veterinarian.

Cats with recurrent anal gland infections should have the glands removed.

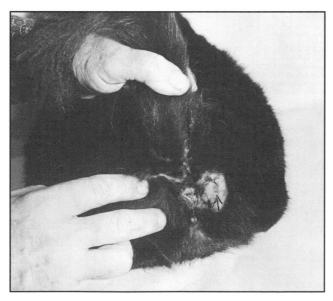

Anal sac abscess—a painful swelling next to the anus.

Anal Sac Abscess

An abscess is recognized by the signs of infection and swelling at the site of the gland. The swelling is at first red then turns a deep purple.

Treatment: An abscess is ready to drain when it becomes soft and fluid-like. At this point it should be lanced so that pus and blood will drain out. The abscess cavity must heal from the bottom up. Keep the edges apart by flushing the cavity twice a day with a topical antiseptic such as dilute (tea colored) *Betadine* solution for 10 to 14 days, and apply warm packs as described above. An oral antibiotic is administered (amoxicillin). Culture and antibiotic sensitivity test may be warranted.

Polyps and Cancer

Polyps are grapelike growths that occur in the rectum and protrude from the anus. They are not common and should be removed.

Cancer of the anal canal is not common. It appears as a fleshy growth that ulcerates and bleeds. Signs are like those of a prolonged proctitis—straining being one of the most common. The diagnosis is made by obtaining a fragment of tissue for microscopic examination.

LIVER

The liver has many vital metabolic functions, including the synthesis of proteins and sugars, removal of wastes from the bloodstream, manufacture of blood-clotting factors and detoxification of many drugs and poisons.

A common sign of liver disease is *jaundice*, in which bile accumulates in the tissues, turning the skin and whites of the eyes yellow and the urine tea colored.

Ascites is the accumulation of fluid in the abdomen. It is caused by increased pressure in the veins of the abdomen. A cat with ascites has a swollen or bloated look to the abdomen. *Feline infectious peritonitis* is the most common cause of ascites.

Spontaneous bleeding is a sign of advanced liver disease. Common sites of bleeding are the stomach, intestine and urinary tract. Pinhead-sized areas of hemorrhage occur in the mouth (especially on the gums).

Cats with impaired liver function appear weak and lethargic and exhibit loss of appetite and weight. They may also suffer from vomiting and diarrhea, drink excessively and experience pain in the abdomen. Signs of central nervous system involvement in the form of head pressing, intermittent apparent blindness, stupor, seizure and coma indicate advanced liver failure.

Causes of Liver Failure

The most common cause of liver disease in cats is *idiopathic hepatic lipidosis*, discussed below. Infectious diseases that involve the liver are *feline infectious peritonitis* and *toxoplasmosis*. *Feline leukemia* and cancers that begin in the liver or spread there from other locations are other causes of liver insufficiency.

A blockage of the bile ducts by gallstones or parasites (liver flukes) is not common but becomes a consideration when a cat has unexplained jaundice.

Chemicals known to produce liver toxicity are carbon tetrachloride, insecticides (e.g., the chlorinated hydrocarbons *Chlordane* and *Dieldin*) and toxic amounts of copper, lead, phosphorus, selenium and iron.

Drugs adversely affecting the liver include acetaminophen (*Tylenol*), inhaled anesthetic gases, antibiotics, diuretics, sulfa preparations, anticonvulsants, arsenicals and some steroid preparations. Most drugs cause problems only when recommended doses are exceeded or when administered for long periods.

Treatment of liver insufficiency depends on making the diagnosis. Special laboratory studies (ultrasound, CT scan, liver biopsy) may be needed to determine the exact cause. Prognosis for recovery is related to the duration and extent of damage and to whether the cause can be corrected.

IDIOPATHIC HEPATIC LIPIDOSIS (IHL)

This disease, unique to cats, is a common cause of liver failure. Although the precise cause(s) is unknown, this syndrome appears to be a type of **anorexia nervosa** that occurs when a cat has a sustained loss of appetite and stops eating. Usually the loss of appetite is for two to three weeks; but cases do occur in which anorexia is present for just a few days.

The liver plays a major role in fat (lipid) metabolism. With starvation, fat accumulates in liver cells. The liver becomes yellow, greasy and enlarged. Signs of liver failure (especially jaundice) appear as liver function deteriorates.

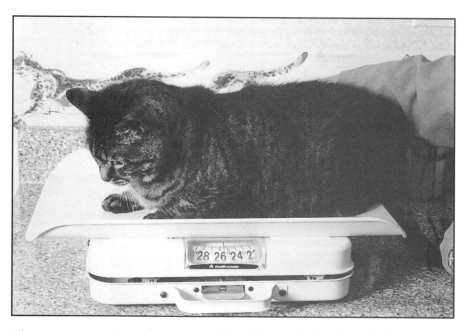

Obese cats are predisposed to many health problems, including idiopathic hepatic lipidosis.

IHL occurs in cats of both sexes and all ages. Being overweight is a predisposing cause. Often, stress is the initiating factor, but frequently the cause of the anorexia is unknown. Diagnosis is confirmed by liver biopsy.

Treatment: Early intensive fluid replacement and forced feeding offer the best chance for reversing the process. Appetite stimulants can be prescribed by your veterinarian. In most cases nutritional support involves special diets and formulas administered by stomach tube or gastrostomy, an operation in which a feeding tube is placed into the stomach through a small incision in the abdominal wall. Nutritional support is continued until the cat recovers and begins to eat on its own. This may take two to three months and requires home nursing care and complete dedication by the owner.

When cats stop eating for extended periods they are prone to liver disease. Seek veterinary attention whenever your cat refuses to eat for several days.

PANCREAS

The pancreas has two main functions. The first is to provide digestive enzymes, the insufficiency of which causes malabsorption syndrome. The second is to make insulin for sugar metabolism.

Sugar Diabetes (Diabetes Mellitus)

Sugar diabetes is a commonly diagnosed disease in cats that affects all organs. It is due to inadequate production of insulin by the pancreas. Insulin is secreted directly into the circulation. It acts upon cell membranes, enabling sugar to enter the cells, where it is metabolized to form energy. Without insulin, the body can't utilize sugar. This results in elevated blood sugar levels (*hyperglycemia*). Excess sugar is eliminated by the kidneys, producing frequent urination. There is a need to compensate for the increased urination by drinking unusual amounts of water.

Glycosuria is the name given to sugar in the urine. When a urine sugar test is positive, suspect diabetes.

Acids (ketones) are formed in the blood of diabetics because of inability to metabolize sugar. High levels lead to a condition called *ketoacidosis*. It is characterized by acetone on the breath (a sweet odor like nail polish remover); rapid, labored breathing; and eventually diabetic coma.

In the early stage of diabetes, a cat will try to compensate for the inability to utilize blood sugar by eating more food. Later, with the effects of malnourishment, there is a drop in appetite. Accordingly, the signs of early diabetes are frequent urination, drinking lots of water, a large appetite and unexplained weight loss. The laboratory findings are sugar and acetone in the urine and a high blood sugar.

In more advanced cases there is loss of appetite, vomiting, weakness, ketone breath, dehydration, labored breathing, lethargy and finally coma. Unlike dogs, diabetic cats rarely develop cataracts.

Treatment: Dietary control and daily injections of insulin can regulate most diabetic cats, allowing them to lead normal lives. The amount of insulin *cannot be* *predicted* on the basis of weight and must be established for each individual. It is important for success of initial therapy that each cat be hospitalized to determine the daily insulin requirement.

Dietary Management. Obesity greatly reduces tissue responsiveness to insulin and makes diabetes difficult to control. Accordingly, overweight cats should be put on a diet until they reach their ideal body weight. A prescription diet such as Hill's *Feline r/d* is available for weight reduction. Occasionally, an obese diabetic cat responds to dietary management alone and does not require insulin to keep its blood sugar well controlled.

Daily caloric requirements are determined by the weight and activity of the individual. Once established, the quantity of food can be determined by dividing the daily caloric requirements by the amount of calories per cup or can. To prevent high levels of blood sugar after eating, avoid feeding the whole day's calories at one meal. Divide the daily ration by the number of feedings, and feed a percentage each time. For cats on once daily insulin, feed three meals a day; for cats on twice daily insulin, feed four meals a day.

Hyperglycemia is less likely to occur if the cat is fed a special prescription diet that is high in fiber and low in fat. If obesity is not a problem, prescription diet Hill's *Feline w/d* or *Science Diet Feline Light* is recommended. *Science Diet Light* is a dry ration with high fiber content. Dry diets are preferable to soft, canned products but may not have the same taste appeal.

Because insulin requirements vary with the diet, it is important to keep the cat's caloric intake constant from day to day. It is equally important to maintain a strict schedule for insulin injections and exercise. Insulin is sold in concentrations of 40 and 100 units per ml. Cats require small amounts, so it is necessary to dilute the insulin for accurate dosing. *How to prepare and inject the insulin will be explained to you by your veterinarian.*

Many cats go through periods when the diabetes seems to correct itself, and they do not require insulin. They may remain in this state of spontaneous remission for varying periods before again needing insulin to control their diabetes. It is important to regularly check the cat's urine for sugar to assist in the early detection of this transient nondiabetic state to avoid insulin overdose. Insulin substitutes by mouth similar to those used for people have been unsuccessful in treating diabetic cats.

INSULIN OVERDOSE

An overdose of insulin drops the blood sugar well below normal. This is called **hypoglycemia**. Suspect this if your cat appears confused, disoriented, drowsy, shivers, staggers about, collapses, falls into a coma, or has seizures.

Treatment: If the cat remains conscious and is able to swallow, give a sugar solution (corn syrup, honey). If the cat is not able to swallow, rub the solution into the mucous membranes of the cat's cheeks. Recovery occurs within minutes. Then *immediately take your cat to a veterinarian.*

10

RESPIRATORY SYSTEM

GENERAL INFORMATION

The cat's respiratory system is made up of the nasal passages, throat, voice box, windpipe, bronchial tubes and lungs. The bronchial tubes branch out to become progressively smaller until they open into the air sacs. Here the air exchanges with the blood.

Lungs are composed of breathing tubes, air sacs and blood vessels. The ribs and muscles of the chest, along with the diaphragm, function as a bellows, moving air into and out of the lungs.

A cat at rest takes about 25 to 30 breaths per minute, about twice as many as a human. It takes a cat about twice as long to exhale as it does to inhale. The respiratory motion should be smooth, even, unrestrained. Rapid breathing at rest, coarse breathing, wheezing, rasping, coughing and bubbling in the chest indicate an abnormal state. Causes are discussed below.

ABNORMAL BREATHING

RAPID BREATHING

Rapid breathing can be caused by pain, emotional stress, fever and overheating. Other conditions to consider are shock and dehydration, lung and heart disease and a buildup of acid or toxic substance in the blood (diabetes, kidney failure, poisoning). An increased rate of breathing at rest suggests a diseased state, and veterinary examination is necessary.

SLOW BREATHING

A very slow rate of breathing is found in narcotic poisoning, encephalitis or a blood clot pressing on the brain. In late stages of shock or collapse it usually signifies a terminal condition.

PANTING

Panting is a normal process after exercise. It is one of the chief means by which a cat lowers body temperature. This is accomplished by the evaporation of water from the mouth, tongue and lungs and by the exchange of warm air for cool. Cats also cool themselves by licking their fur and by perspiring through the pads of the feet.

When panting is rapid, labored and accompanied by anxiety, heat stroke should be considered.

NOISY BREATHING

Noisy breathing indicates obstructed breathing and is a cardinal sign of upper respiratory disease.

CROUPY BREATHING

This refers to the high, harsh sound caused by air passing through a narrowed voice box. When the onset is sudden, the most likely diagnosis is a foreign body in the voice box or swelling in the throat.

WHEEZING

A wheeze is a whistling sound that occurs when a cat breathes forcefully in or out. It indicates narrowing or spasm in the breathing tubes. Tight deep-seated wheezes are best heard with a stethoscope. Causes of wheezing are *feline asthma, lungworms, and tumors or growths in the airways*.

SHALLOW BREATHING

Shallow breathing is seen in conditions restricting the motion of the rib cage. In most cases, shallow breathing is associated with splinting. To avoid the pain of a deep breath, a cat breathes rapidly but less deeply. Pain of pleurisy and rib fracture causes splinting.

Blood, pus or serum in the chest produces restricted breathing but without pain. This condition, called *pleural effusion*, is the most common cause of respiratory distress in cats.

MEOWING (CRYING)

A cat that meows continuously is most likely in pain. You should determine the cause of this anxiety. *Seek veterinary attention.* Excessive meowing can lead to voice strain (*laryngitis*).

Purring

Cats' purring is unique. Breathing in and out alternately tenses and relaxes the muscles of the voice box and diaphragm, creating pressure effects resulting in turbulent air flow through the trachea. These cyclic and rapid pressure changes are superimposed on normal breathing and create the characteristic vibrations of purring. Purring is an instinctual act. Kittens purr as early as two days of age.

A common misconception about purring is that it always indicates a state of pleasure. In fact, cats also purr when they are hungry, upset or in pain. Cats have been known to purr just before dying.

COUGH

Coughing is a *reflex* initiated by an irritant in the airway. It can be caused by a respiratory infection; inhaled irritants such as smoke and chemicals; foreign objects such as grass seeds and food particles; pressure from tight collars; and growths arising in the air passages. Some coughs are triggered by an allergic reaction. The type of cough often suggests the location and probable cause:

- A cough accompanied by sneezing and watery red eyes suggests *feline viral respiratory disease complex.*
- A deep, paroxysmal cough with neck extended and production of phlegm suggests *chronic bronchitis.*
- A sudden coughing attack accompanied by wheezing and difficulty breathing suggests *feline asthma.*
- Sporadic coughing with weight loss, listlessness and depressed appetite is seen with *heartworms, lungworms* and *fungus diseases.*
- Spasms of coughing that occur after exercise suggest *acute bronchitis.*

Coughs are self-perpetuating. Coughing irritates the airways, dries out the mucous lining and lowers resistance to infection—leading to further coughing.

The diagnostic workup of a cat with a chronic cough includes a chest X ray and transtracheal washings. These washings are obtained through a sterile tube placed into the windpipe with the cat under light anesthesia. Microscopic examination of recovered cells leads to a specific diagnosis. *Bronchoscopy* is an excellent method of evaluating airway disease. A fiberoptic instrument is passed into the trachea, again with the cat under anesthesia. The breathing tubes can be viewed directly, biopsies taken and phlegm removed for microscopic exam and culture/sensitivity testing.

Treatment: Only minor coughs of brief duration should be treated at home. Coughs accompanied by fever, difficulty breathing, discharge from the eyes and nose or other signs of a serious illness should be seen by a veterinarian.

It is important to identify and correct contributing problems. Air pollutants such as cigarette smoke, aerosol insecticides, house dust and perfumes should be eliminated from the atmosphere. Nose, throat, lung and heart disorders should be treated if present.

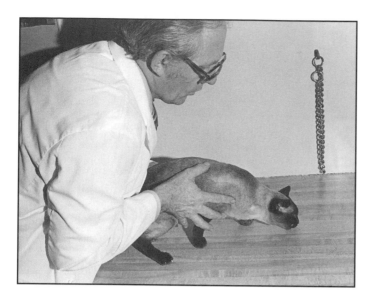

The cough of brochitis. Note the typical posture with hunched-up shoulders, lowered head and stretched neck.

—J. Clawson

A variety of cough suppressants used in children are available at drugstores for the treatment of mild coughs. However, *preparations containing acetaminophen (Tylenol), codeine and other narcotics are toxic to cats and must be avoided. Robitussin* is an example of a safe and effective cough preparation for cats. It contains an expectorant that does not suppress the cough reflex but liquefies mucus secretions so they can be coughed free. The dosage is one-half teaspoon per 10 pounds weight every four hours. *Robitussin-DM* contains the cough suppressant dextromethorphan, the only cough suppressant safe for cats. The dosage is one-half teaspoon per 10 pounds weight every six hours as necessary.

While cough suppressants decrease the frequency and severity of the cough, they do not treat the disease or condition causing it. Overuse may delay diagnosis and treatment. Cough suppressants (but not expectorants) should be avoided when phlegm is being brought up or swallowed. These coughs are clearing unwanted material from the airway.

VOICE BOX (LARYNX)

The larynx is a short, oblong box located in the throat above the windpipe. It is composed of cartilage and contains the vocal cords. In the domestic cat the voice box is connected directly to the base of the skull by the hyoid bone. In lions, tigers, leopards and other members of the large cat family, the hyoid bone is partly replaced by cartilage. As a result, the vocal apparatus of large cats is able to move freely and produce the characteristic full-throated roar. In contrast, small cats can make only weak cries.

The larynx.
—Rose Floyd

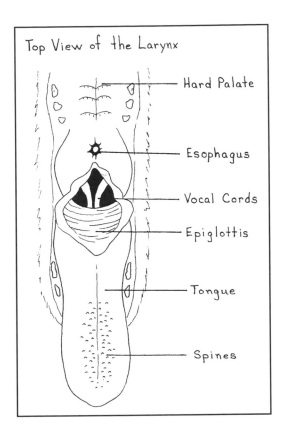

Top View of the Larynx

- Hard Palate
- Esophagus
- Vocal Cords
- Epiglottis
- Tongue
- Spines

The larynx is the most sensitive cough area in the body. At the top of the larynx is the epiglottis, a leaflike flap that closes during swallowing, keeping food from going down the windpipe. Disorders of the larynx give rise to coughing, croupy breathing and loss of voice.

LOSS OF VOICE (LARYNGITIS)

Laryngitis is an inflammation of the mucous membranes of the voice box. Signs of laryngitis include hoarseness and loss of voice. The most common causes of loss of voice are excessive meowing and a chronic cough. Both produce vocal cord strain.

Laryngitis can be associated with tonsillitis, throat infections, tracheobronchitis, pneumonia, inhalant allergies and (rarely) tumors in the throat. The lining of the larynx is not coated with cilia. Therefore, mucus frequently accumulates in the larynx. Exaggerated throat clearing is needed to dislodge it. This further irritates the larynx and lowers resistance to infection.

Treatment: Laryngitis due to excessive meowing usually responds to removing the cause of the cat's anxiety or distress. If caused by prolonged coughing, seek veterinary attention to investigate and eliminate the cause of the chronic cough.

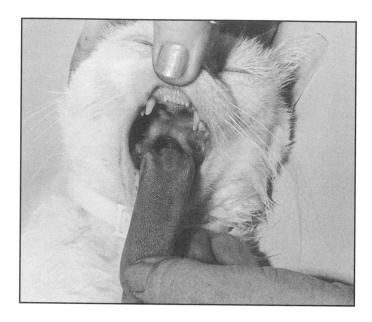

Pull the tongue out to inspect the back of the throat for an obstructing foreign body.

FOREIGN OBJECT IN THE VOICE BOX

The sudden onset of forceful coughing, pawing at the mouth and respiratory distress in a healthy cat suggests a foreign body caught in the larynx. This is an emergency. If the cat is conscious and able to breathe, go at once to the nearest veterinary clinic.

If the cat collapses and is unable to breathe, lay the cat on the side with its head lower than the body. Open the mouth, pull out the tongue, take hold of the cat's neck in back of the object and apply enough compression to keep the object from passing down. Work the object loose as quickly as possible.

If unsuccessful, proceed to the *Heimlich maneuver:*

- Place one hand along the back and the other just below the sternum or rib cage.
- With both hands in position, give four forceful thrusts by pressing in and up.
- Next check the mouth for the foreign body with a finger sweep.
- Then give two breaths (mouth to nose) as described in EMERGENCIES: *Artificial Breathing.*
- Repeat cycles of compression and *artificial breathing* until the object is dislodged.

Foreign bodies caught in the larynx are not common. Most food particles are of little consequence because the resulting cough expels them.

Note: If your cat is *choking* with gagging, retching and respiratory distress, assume there is a foreign body such as a bone splinter or rubber ball caught in the cat's throat. See *Foreign Bodies in the Throat* in the MOUTH AND THROAT chapter.

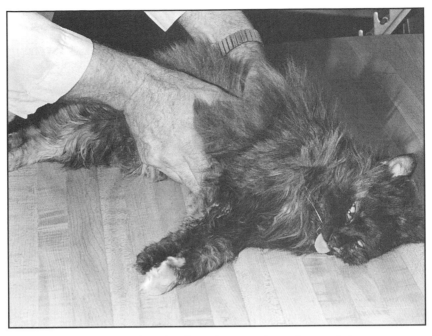

The *Heimlich Maneuver.* Place hands as shown and give four quick thrusts pressing
up and in. —J. Clawson

BREATHING TUBES (TRACHEA AND BRONCHI)

FOREIGN BODIES IN THE WINDPIPE

Grass seed and food particles are the most common foreign material of sufficient size
to lodge in the windpipe or bronchus when inhaled by the cat. Most of these are
quickly coughed up. If the object becomes fixed in the airway, it causes intense
irritation and swelling.

Sudden attacks of coughing after a cat has been prowling in weeds or long grass
or immediately after vomiting suggest aspiration of a foreign body.

Treatment: *Have the cat examined by your veterinarian.* Cough medicines should
be avoided since they serve no purpose and delay treatment. Foreign objects can be
located by chest X ray or located and removed by bronchoscopy.

BRONCHITIS

Inflammation of the smaller breathing tubes is called bronchitis. It is characterized
by repeated coughing, which further irritates the lining of the breathing tubes and
spreads infection to the trachea. For this reason the term **tracheobronchitis** may be
more accurate.

The **trachea** and **bronchi** have a protective layer of mucus that traps foreign
material and infectious agents. Along with hairlike cilia that move foreign material
toward the mouth, it serves as a major defense system against infection. Conditions

that interfere with the function of the mucociliary blanket—such as chilling, breathing cold dry air and dehydration predispose to bronchial infection.

Acute Bronchitis. The major cause of acute bronchitis in cats is upper respiratory infection (see *Feline Viral Respiratory Disease Complex* in the chapter INFECTIOUS DISEASES). Secondary bacterial infections are common and frequently lead to persistent cough and chronic bronchitis. The cough of acute bronchitis is harsh, dry and hacking and is aggravated by exertion and cold dry air. Therefore, warm humid air and restricted exercise are of great therapeutic value.

Chronic Bronchitis. Bronchitis that persists for several weeks is referred to as chronic. Many cases begin as acute bronchitis; others occur as a sequel to *feline asthma*. After a period of chronic coughing, secondary bacterial infection becomes established. The cough of chronic bronchitis is moist or bubbling and often ends with retching and the expectoration of foamy saliva.

Chronic bronchitis can severely damage the breathing tubes and infected mucus and pus can accumulate in partially destroyed bronchi. This condition is called *bronchiectasis*. Chronic coughing can lead to a breakdown and enlargement of the air sacs, a condition called *emphysema*. These conditions are not reversible. For these reasons, chronic coughs require veterinary examination and professional management. The diagnostic workup is similar to that described for *Cough* earlier in this chapter.

Treatment: Rest and proper humidification of the atmosphere are important. Confine your cat in a warm room and use a home vaporizer. Cough suppressants interfere with host defenses and prevent the elimination of purulent secretions. They should not be used in chronic bronchitis. Expectorants may help. Bronchodilators (*Theophylline*) relax breathing passages and reduce respiratory fatigue. Phlegm should be cultured and specific antibiotics selected by the veterinarian.

Cortisone preparations reduce the inflammatory response caused by coughing. However, cortisone is contraindicated in the presence of bacterial infection and should be used only under professional supervision.

FELINE ASTHMA (FELINE ALLERGIC BRONCHITIS)

An acute respiratory disease occurs in cats which in many ways resembles bronchial asthma in humans. Some of these cats present as an acute emergency with severe respiratory distress; others have a chronic history characterized by coughing and wheezing.

In some cases asthmatic attacks may be triggered by exposure to inhaled allergens such as tobacco smoke, kitty litter dust, sprays and carpet deodorizers. In many cases the initiating cause is unknown.

An acute attack begins with the sudden onset of difficulty breathing accompanied by wheezing and coughing. The wheezing is heard as the cat exhales, and usually it is loud enough to be heard with the naked ear. With a severe attack the cat may sit with shoulders hunched or lie chest down with mouth open, straining to breathe. The mucous membranes show a bluish color due to lack of oxygen (*cyanosis*). Only two other conditions produce similar signs and symptoms. They are *pleural effusion* and *pulmonary edema* (see CIRCULATORY SYSTEM: *Heart Failure*).

Treatment: *Immediate veterinary attention* is needed to relieve bronchial spasm and ease respiratory distress. Bronchodilators and cortisone are effective in the acute attack. Antihistamines and cough suppressants should not be used because they interfere with the cat's ability to clear its secretions. Asthmatic cats may have to be hospitalized for sedation and to remove them from an allergenic environment.

Feline asthma is a chronic condition with recurring attacks. These attacks are best controlled with maintenance corticosteroid therapy (prednisone). To avoid dependency, the medication is usually given every other day. Some cats may respond favorably to tapering the drug, whereas others experience an immediate relapse and require lifelong support.

LUNGS

PNEUMONIA

Pneumonia is an infection of the lungs and is classified according to cause: viral, bacterial, fungal, parasitic or inhalation.

Pneumonia can follow one of the feline viral respiratory illnesses when the natural defenses of the host are weakened by the primary infection. This allows secondary bacterial invaders to gain a foothold. Individuals most likely to be affected by pneumonia are kittens, old cats, cats that are malnourished or immunosuppressed and cats with long-standing respiratory diseases such as *chronic bronchitis*. Aspiration of foreign material during vomiting (perhaps while the cat is under anesthesia) and the unskilled administration of medications or supplemental feedings account for occasional cases. Tuberculosis and systemic fungus infections are infrequent causes of pneumonia. These illnesses are discussed in the chapter INFECTIOUS DISEASES.

The general symptoms of pneumonia are high fever, rapid breathing, splinting, cough, fast pulse, rattling and bubbling in the chest. When severe enough to cause oxygen lack, you will notice a blue cast to the mucous membranes of the mouth.

Treatment: *Pneumonia is a serious illness requiring urgent veterinary attention.* The diagnosis is confirmed by laboratory tests and chest X ray. Until veterinary help is

Pneumonia can occur with a severe case of feline viral respiratory disease.

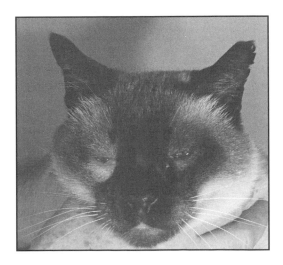

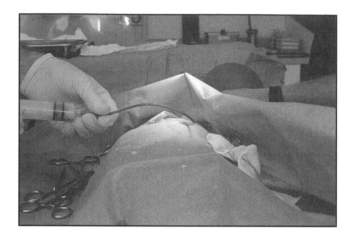

An infected pleural effusion (empyema) requiring surgical drainage.

available, move your cat to warm, dry quarters and humidify the air. Give plenty of water. *Do not use cough medications.* Coughing in pneumonia helps to clear the airways.

Pneumonia usually responds to an antibiotic specific for the causative agent. Your veterinarian can select the proper antibiotic.

PLEURAL EFFUSION (FLUID IN THE CHEST CAVITY)

The most common cause of difficult breathing in cats is fluid accumulation in the pleural space surrounding the lungs. The fluid compresses the lungs and keeps them from filling with air. This condition is much more common in cats than other animals. The reason is that cats suffer from two specific diseases that produce pleural effusion. They are *feline infectious peritonitis* and *feline leukemia* (see INFECTIOUS DISEASES). Other causes of pleural effusion are congestive heart failure and liver disease.

Infections in the pleural space follow puncture wounds of the chest, often acquired in fights with dogs. The infection leads to pus formation, a condition called *empyema.*

Bleeding into the chest cavity and lungs often follows chest trauma. A severe blow to the abdomen can rupture a cat's diaphragm, allowing the abdominal organs to enter the chest cavity and compress the lung. These cats show evidence of shock.

Signs of pleural effusion are those of respiratory insufficiency. Cats often sit or stand with elbows out, chest fully expanded and head and neck extended to draw in more air. The animal may be unable to lie down. The least effort produces sudden distress or collapse. Breathing is open-mouthed, and the lips, gums and tongue may look pale or appear blue or gray. The blue-gray color, called *cyanosis,* is due to insufficient oxygen in the blood. Depending on the cause of the fluid accumulation, other signs of illness may include weight loss, fever, anemia, signs of heart or liver disease.

Treatment: *When fluid builds rapidly in the chest, urgent veterinary attention is required to prevent respiratory failure and sudden death.* The fluid will need to be drained. The cat should be hospitalized for further studies.

11

CIRCULATORY SYSTEM

The circulatory system is composed of the heart, the blood vessels and the blood. The amount of blood in the cat's circulatory system is about one half pint or 35 ml per pound body weight.

HEART

The heart is a pump made of four chambers: the right atrium and right ventricle, and the left atrium and left ventricle. The two sides are separated by a muscular septum. Blood cannot pass from one side to the other without first going through either the general or the pulmonary circulation. Four valves are present. Their function is to keep blood flowing in one direction. When the valves are diseased, blood leaks backward, causing the heart to pump less effectively.

PHYSIOLOGY

Blood is pumped out of the left ventricle into the aorta. It passes through progressively smaller arteries until it reaches the capillary beds of the skin, muscle, brain and internal organs. Blood is carried back to the heart through progressively larger veins, finally reaching the right atrium via two large veins called the *vena cavae*.

The blood then passes into the right ventricle and out into the pulmonary circulation through the pulmonary artery. The pulmonary artery branches into smaller vessels and finally into capillaries around the air sacs, where gas is exchanged. The

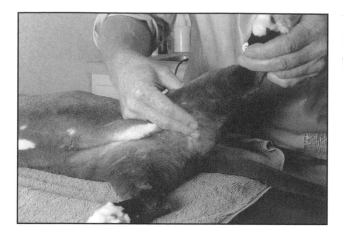

Taking the femoral pulse. Feel along the inside of the thigh. Press with your fingers to locate the pulsation.

Taking the pulse with the cat standing.
—J. Clawson

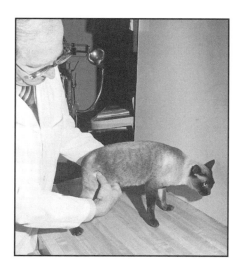

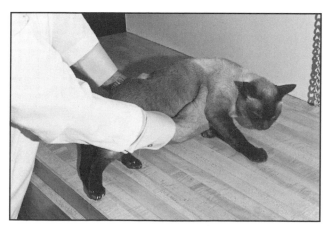

Another way to take the pulse is to feel for the heartbeat behind the elbows.
—J. Clawson

blood then returns to the left atrium via the pulmonary vein and then enters the left ventricle—thus completing the circle.

The arteries and veins are under nervous system and hormonal controls. They can expand or contract to maintain a correct blood pressure.

The heartbeat is controlled by an internal nerve system that releases electrical impulses. This system is responsive to outside influences, so the heart speeds up when the cat exercises, becomes frightened, overheats, goes into shock or requires greater blood flow to tissues.

Heart rhythms follow a fixed pattern that can be seen on an electrocardiogram (EKG). Whether the beat is fast or slow, the sequence in which the various muscle fibers contract remains the same. This sequence causes a synchronized beat, allowing both ventricles to empty at the same time. *Arrhythmia*, an absence of rhythm, upsets this normal pattern, causing inefficient pump action.

There are physical signs that help to determine if a cat's heart and circulation are working properly. Familiarize yourself with the normal findings so you can recognize abnormal signs if they appear.

Pulse

The pulse, a transmitted heartbeat, is easily detected by feeling the *femoral* artery in the groin. With your cat standing or lying underside up, feel along the inside of the thigh where the leg and body are joined. Press with your fingers until you locate the pulse. Alternately, take the pulse by pressing against the rib cage over the heart. With the cat standing, feel the pulse just behind the elbow. If the heart is enlarged or diseased, you may be able to detect a buzzing or vibration over the chest wall. The pulse can be determined by counting the number of beats in a minute. Adult cats run a rate of 140 to 240 beats per minute. The pulse should be strong, steady and regular. A fast pulse indicates excitation, fever, anemia, blood loss, dehydration, shock, infection, heat stroke or heart (and lung) disease. A slow pulse indicates heart disease, pressure on the brain or an advanced morbid condition causing collapse of the circulation. *An erratic, irregular pulse indicates an arrhythmia.* Various drugs can affect the rate and rhythm of the heart.

Heart Sounds

Veterinarians use a stethoscope to listen to the heart. You can listen to the heart by placing your ear against the chest.

The normal heartbeat is divided into two separate sounds. The first is a LUB, followed by a slight pause; and then a DUB. Put together, the sound is LUB-DUB. . . in a steady, even-spaced manner. When the heart sounds can be heard all over the chest, the heart is enlarged.

Murmurs

Murmurs are caused by a turbulence in the blood flow through the heart. Serious ones are due to feline cardiomyopathy and birth defects. Hypothyroidism can cause heart murmurs.

Not all murmurs are serious. Some are *functional*—that is, there is no disease, just a normal degree of turbulence. Your veterinarian can determine whether a murmur is serious or of little consequence.

THRILLS

A thrill is caused by turbulence of such a degree that you can feel a buzzing or vibration over the heart. It suggests an obstruction to the blood flow—for example, a narrowed valve or a hole in the muscular wall between two chambers. A *thrill indicates a serious heart condition*.

CIRCULATION

By examining the gums and tongue, you can determine both the adequacy of a cat's circulation and the presence or absence of anemia. Deep pink is a sign of normal red blood cell volume. A gray or bluish color is a sign of inadequate oxygen in the blood (*cyanosis*). It can be seen in heart and lung failure.

The adequacy of the circulation can be tested by noting the time it takes for the tissues to pink up (or refill) after the gums have been pressed firmly with a finger. With normal circulation the response is immediate (one second or less). More than two seconds suggests poor circulation. When the finger impression remains pale for three seconds or longer, the cat is in shock.

HEART FAILURE

Heart failure is defined as the inability of the heart to pump enough blood to provide adequate circulation and meet the body's needs. It is the result of a weakened heart muscle. The liver, kidneys, lungs and other organs eventually become affected, causing a multiple organ-system problem. When a diseased heart begins to weaken, signs of right- or left-sided failure occur. Treatment of heart failure is discussed below (see *Feline Cardiomyopathy*).

LEFT HEART FAILURE

As the left ventricle starts to fail, pressure backs up in the pulmonary circulation. This results in lung congestion and accumulation of fluid in the air sacs (*pulmonary edema*). In the late stages of pulmonary edema, the cat is extremely short of breath, coughs up a bubble of red fluid and can't get enough oxygen. Pulmonary edema is likely to be brought on by exercise, excitement or any stress that causes the heart to accelerate. Fluid may accumulate around the lung in the chest space, pressing on the lungs and causing further breathing difficulties. This is called *pleural effusion*, a common cause of respiratory distress in cats. It is discussed in the chapter RESPIRATORY SYSTEM.

The two early signs of left-sided heart failure are fatigue and rapid breathing with exercise. They are less apparent in sedentary cats. In advanced cases, breathing is labored and the cat assumes a characteristic sitting position with elbows apart and

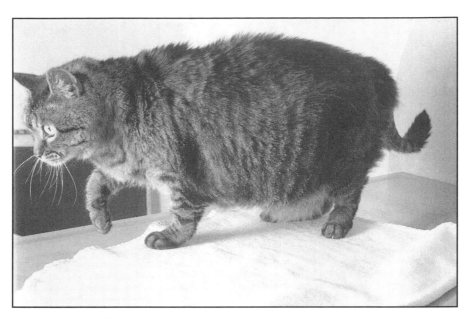

The swollen pot-bellied abdomen of *ascites*.

head extended to take in more air. The pulse is rapid, weak and irregular. Murmurs or thrills may be detected over the chest. Arrhythmia can cause fainting, which may be mistaken for a seizure.

RIGHT HEART FAILURE

Right heart failure is less common than left-sided failure. When the right ventricle starts to fail, pressure backs up in the veins of the general circulation, causing *congestive heart failure*. You will observe fluid beneath the skin of the abdomen and swelling of the limbs (dropsy).

Fluid also builds in the abdominal cavity, giving a pot-bellied look. This is called *ascites*. It may suggest lymphosarcoma or the wet form of feline infectious peritonitis. Fluid retention is augmented by the kidneys, which respond to the sluggish blood flow by retaining salt and water.

FELINE CARDIOVASCULAR DISEASE

Coronary artery disease, for all intents and purposes, does not occur in cats.

Cardiomyopathy is the major cause of heart disease in cats. Congenital heart disease accounts for about 15 percent of cases. Valvular heart disease and heartworms account for the occasional case. Congenital heart defects usually produce heart failure by 10 months of age. In contrast, cardiomyopathy affects young to middle-aged cats. Occasionally, symptoms will not become apparent until a cat is older.

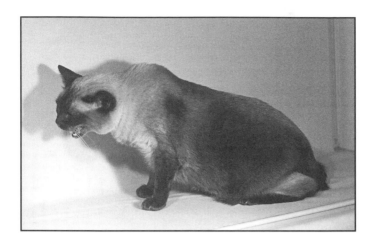

Feline cardio-myopathy, showing the typical appearance of heart failure with the head and neck extended straining to breathe.

Birth Defects of the Heart (Congenital Heart Disease)

The most common congenital defects are those involving the heart valves and the septum that separates the two sides of the heart. **Septal defects** are windows that allow blood to go from one side to the other without passing through the circulation. Siamese, Burmese and domestic shorthaired breeds are affected most often.

The extent and severity of the symptoms depend on the type and location of the defect. More than one defect may exist at the same time. Examination of the asymptomatic kitten will disclose a murmur. However, the first indication usually is the appearance of heart failure. Most kittens with congenital heart disease die within the first year. Early detection in some cases may allow for surgical repair.

Feline Cardiomyopathy (Heart Muscle Disease)

Cardiomyopathy refers to impaired function of the heart muscle. There is more than one cause. Thus, cardiomyopathy is not a specific disease but the result of some disturbance affecting the muscle of the heart. All causes of cardiomyopathy in cats are not known.

Cardiomyopathy exists in two forms called **dilated cardiomyopathy** and **hypertrophic cardiomyopathy.** The difference rests in how the disease process affects the walls of the ventricles.

Dilated cardiomyopathy occurs when the heart muscle loses its tone and becomes flaccid. The heart chambers overfill, the walls of the ventricles become thinner and the chambers enlarge. One cause of dilated cardiomyopathy is *taurine deficiency*. Taurine is an essential amino acid present in high concentration in animal tissue. Feeding dog food or vegetable grain cat food could lead to taurine deficiency. Most commercial cat foods are supplemented with taurine. Dog foods are not.

Another cause of dilated cardiomyopathy is *myocarditis*, which is inflammation of the heart muscle. Virus diseases and autoimmune diseases have been implicated in the cause of myocarditis in humans.

A form of dilated cardiomyopathy occurs in elderly cats suffering from *feline hyperthyroidism* (see GERIATRICS).

Hypertrophic cardiomyopathy tends to affect cats one to five years of age. In this condition the walls of the ventricles become thick. However, because the muscle fibers are replaced by fibrous connective tissue (scar), the thicker heart wall does not translate into increased pumping power. In fact, the heart is actually weak. The wall of the heart becomes less elastic and the heart chambers contract.

Early signs of hypertrophic cardiomyopathy are vague and indefinite. Loss of pep and appetite and reduced exercise tolerance may go unnoticed. Cats are unique in their ability to recognize their limitations and restrict activities accordingly. It is unusual to detect heart disease before signs of failure. Coughing is rarely a sign of heart disease in cats. A chronic cough is more likely to indicate *bronchitis* or *feline asthma.*

Dilated cardiomyopathy, in contrast, is often a rapid onset disease that progresses over two or three days as the heart begins to fail. The most frequent sign is labored breathing at rest. The cat often sits with head and neck extended and elbows out, straining to take in air. Coolness of the feet and ears and a below normal body temperature are signs of poor circulation. Heart murmurs are common. The pulse is often rapid and thready and may be irregular or at times even slow. Loss of appetite, rapid weight loss, weakness, fainting attacks and crying out spells often accompany the above signs of illness.

The appearance of a blood clot in an artery, as described below, may be the first indication of cardiomyopathy of either type.

Treatment: Accurate diagnosis is necessary to establish which form of the disease is present to provide the proper therapy. Chest X ray, electrocardiogram, ultrasound of the heart and thyroid function tests are utilized.

The treatment of dilated cardiomyopathy is directed at correcting taurine deficiency when present and controlling fluid retention. The latter is best managed by *Digoxin* and diuretics such as *Lasix.* Cats are especially sensitive to the dangerous side effects of *Digoxin,* and close veterinary management is required. A restricted mineral and sodium diet such as Hill's Prescription Diet *Feline h/d* is recommended. Antithyroid drugs are used to treat hyperthyroidism when present.

Hypertrophic cardiomyopathy requires the use of drugs that relax the heart and increase its efficiency. Most of the drugs used in treating heart disease in people are used for similar purposes in small animals. The choice depends on the stage of illness and presence or absence of complicating factors such as arrhythmia.

Restricting the cat's activity reduces the strain on the heart. Your veterinarian may prescribe a period of cage rest. These measures often yield substantial results in a longer, more comfortable and active life for your cat.

BLOOD CLOT IN AN ARTERY (ARTERIAL THROMBOEMBOLISM)

This is characterized by passing of a blood clot (*embolus*) from the left side of the heart into the general circulation, where it becomes lodged in an artery. The resulting obstruction to the flow of blood leads to clotting of the artery (*thrombosis*).

The most common site for blockage is the point at which the abdominal aorta branches into the main arteries to the legs. Arteries elsewhere in the body can be

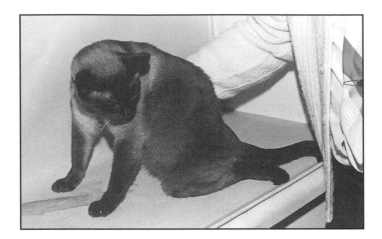

Sudden onset of paralysis in the rear legs. Conditions to consider are arterial thromboembolism and ruptured disc.

affected. Diagnosis is difficult and requires special techniques usually available at veterinary medical centers.

Formation of a blood clot in the heart and subsequent arterial thromboembolism occur in about half of all cats suffering from feline cardiomyopathy. It may be the first indication of heart disease. Suspect this possibility if your cat experiences the sudden onset of weakness in the rear legs. Look for the following signs: cold legs, bluish skin, faint or absent pulses in the groin. One leg may be more severely blocked than the other. The colder leg with the weaker pulse is the more severely affected.

Treatment: This depends on the severity of the blockage. Medications can be given to try to dissolve the clot. In some cases surgery is considered.

ACQUIRED VALVULAR DISEASE

Acquired valvular heart disease, as opposed to *congenital* valvular heart disease, is rare in cats. It is due to bloodborne infection. Bacteria lodge on the heart valves, forming clumps of infective material containing fibrin and debris and damaging the valves. Heart failure develops as a consequence of impaired valve function.

The disease can be prevented by treating skin abscesses and other infections likely to invade the bloodstream.

HEARTWORMS

Heartworm disease, so named because the adult worms live in the right side of the heart, is *common in dogs, but rarely occurs in cats*. In fact, cats may be accidental hosts only. The heartworm, *Dirofilaria immitis*, is spread by the bite of a mosquito that harbors infective larvae in saliva. The larvae burrow into the cat's tissues and undergo several changes that lead to the development of small, adult worms that then make their way to a vein and move to the heart. This process takes a few months. In dogs, mature heartworms produce larvae that circulate in the bloodstream. This rarely happens in cats.

Because of the small size of the cat's heart, one or two worms may be enough to cause serious heart trouble or even sudden death.

Signs of heartworm infestation include a cough made worse by exercise, lethargy, loss of weight and coat condition and bloody sputum. Labored breathing and congestive heart failure appear late in the disease. Worms may be discovered at autopsy following sudden unexplained death.

Treatment: Treatment is complex and potentially dangerous. Drugs are available to kill the adult worms. Treatment of the larval stage is seldom necessary.

Areas of most frequent heartworm infestations are along coastal regions where swamps or other brackish water provide ideal conditions for mosquitoes to breed. Since mosquitoes have a flight range of one-quarter mile, in many cases spraying around catteries can be partially effective. In theory, the best way to prevent heartworms is to keep your cat from being bitten by a mosquito. Cats can get reasonable protection if kept indoors during late afternoons and evening, when mosquitoes are feeding.

ANEMIA

Anemia is a deficiency of red blood cells in the circulation. Red blood cells carry oxygen to the tissues; therefore, the symptoms of anemia are due to insufficient oxygen in the blood and tissues. In adults, anemia exists when there are fewer than five million red cells in one milliliter of blood or when the percentage of red cells in whole blood is less than 25 percent by volume. Normal values are somewhat lower in young kittens. Once anemia is identified, its cause can be determined by other tests.

Causes of Anemia

Anemia can be caused by blood loss or inadequate red cell production. In some cases the body produces red cells rapidly but not fast enough to keep up with the losses. It may take three to five days for the bone marrow to respond to the blood loss by producing new red cells.

Blood Loss. Rapid blood loss is caused by trauma and major hemorrhage. Shock will ensue. Treatment of shock by intravenous salt solutions and transfusions is directed at the control of bleeding and the restoration of fluid volume and red blood cells. Shock is discussed in the EMERGENCIES chapter.

A less obvious blood loss takes place through the gastrointestinal tract as a result of hookworm or coccidia infestation, tumor or ulceration. External parasites such as fleas and lice can produce surprising amounts of blood loss in the unkempt cat.

The average life span of red cells in the cat is 66 to 78 days. A shortened life span occurs when red cells are prematurely destroyed within the circulation. This condition, called *hemolysis*, can occur with autoimmune hemolytic anemias, toxic drugs and infectious microorganisms. **Feline infectious anemia** and **feline cytauxzoon** are two diseases that produce red blood cell hemolysis.

Inadequate Blood Production. The majority of feline anemias (80 percent) are due to inadequate red cell production. Iron, trace minerals, vitamins and essential fatty acids are incorporated into red blood cells, so a deficiency in building materials will result in failure to manufacture the final product.

Iron deficiency is a prominent cause of anemia. Some cases are caused by diets low in iron and other essential nutrients. However, most cases are caused by chronic blood loss. Each milliliter of blood lost contains 0.5 mg iron.

A number of diseases and toxic agents interfere with the production of formed elements in the bone marrow. They include the viruses of feline leukemia and feline infectious peritonitis, drugs such as *Chloromycetin*, kidney failure with uremia and various chemicals and poisons. In fact, *any chronic illness can depress the bone marrow and lead to anemia.*

SIGNS OF ANEMIA

Signs may be overshadowed by a chronic illness. In general, anemic cats lack appetite, lose weight, sleep a great deal and show generalized weakness. The mucous membranes of the gums and tongue are pale. With severe anemia the pulse and breathing rate are rapid. These signs also occur with heart disease. These two conditions can be confused.

Treatment: Uncomplicated nutritional anemia responds well to replacement of the missing substances and to restoring the cat to a nutritionally complete diet.

Iron deficiency anemia should alert you to the possibility of chronic blood loss. A stool check will show whether there are ova and parasites or traces of blood in the feces. Treat external parasites, especially fleas. Complicated anemias require professional diagnosis and management.

12

NERVOUS SYSTEM

GENERAL INFORMATION

The central nervous system of the cat is composed of the cerebrum, cerebellum, midbrain (which includes the brain stem) and spinal cord.

The **cerebrum** is the largest part of the brain and is composed of two hemispheres. This area controls learning, memory, reasoning and judgment. It initiates a cat's voluntary actions. Diseases affecting the cerebrum are characterized by changes in personality and learned behavior. A well-socialized cat may begin to make mistakes in the house or perhaps grow irritable or become aggressive, exhibit compulsive pacing, circling or apparent blindness. Seizures are frequently associated with cerebral disease.

The **cerebellum** is extremely large and well developed in the cat. It is also a bilobed structure with the main function of integrating the motor pathways of the brain to maintain coordination and balance. Injuries or diseases of the cerebellum result in uncoordinated body movements such as jerking, stumbling, falling and overreaching with the paws.

In the **midbrain** and **brain stem** are the centers that control the respiratory rate, heart rate, blood pressure and other activities essential to life. At the base of the brain are centers for primitive responses such as hunger, rage, thirst, hormone activity and temperature control. Closely connected to the midbrain and brain stem are the **hypothalamus** and **pituitary gland.**

A special set of 12 nerve pairs called the **cranial nerves** pass directly out from the midbrain into the head and neck through special holes in the skull. Especially important in the cat are the optic nerves to the eyes, auditory nerves to the ears and olfactory nerves to the scent organs.

The **spinal cord** passes down a bony canal formed by the arches of the vertebral bodies. The cord sends out nerve roots that combine with one another to form the *peripheral* nerves, which carry motor impulses to the muscles and receive sensory input from the skin and deeper structures.

In the assessment of brain and nerve diseases, history is of the greatest importance. Your veterinarian will ask if your cat has been in an accident or has received a blow to the head. Was there a history of poisoning? Is the cat taking any drugs? Has the animal been exposed to other cats with illness? When did you first notice the symptoms? Have the symptoms progressed? If so, has the progression been rapid or gradual? These are all important points to consider. To further evaluate a neurological disorder, special tests may be of assistance. They include X rays, electroencephalography (the EEG), CT scan and the spinal tap—a procedure in which fluid is removed from the spinal canal and submitted for laboratory analysis.

HEAD INJURIES

Forty percent of cats hit by a car suffer a head injury. Other causes of head injury are falls and blows to the skull. Since the brain is not only encased in bone but also surrounded by a layer of fluid and suspended in the skull by a system of tough ligaments, it takes a major blow to fracture the skull and injure the brain. Injuries of sufficient magnitude to fracture the skull are often associated with bleeding into the brain from ruptured blood vessels.

SKULL FRACTURES

Skull fractures can be linear, star shaped, depressed, compound (open to the outside) or closed. Fractures at the base of the skull often extend into the ear, orbit, nasal cavity or sinuses, creating openings for brain infection. In general, the magnitude of a fracture is an indication of the severity of brain injury. Nevertheless, even head injuries without skull fracture can cause severe brain damage.

BRAIN INJURIES

Brain injuries are classified according to the severity of the damage to the brain.

Bruising (Contusion). This is the most mild sort of injury in which there is no loss of consciousness. After a blow to the head the cat remains dazed, wobbly or disoriented. This condition then clears gradually.

Concussion. By definition, a concussion means that the cat was knocked out or experienced a *brief* loss of consciousness. Upon returning to consciousness, the cat exhibits the same signs as contusion.

Brain Swelling or Blood Clot. Following severe head injury, there may be swelling of the brain or the formation of a blood clot from ruptured vessels. Both produce *increased intracranial pressure (pressure on the brain).*

Brain swelling, technically called **cerebral edema,** is always accompanied by a depressed level of consciousness and often coma. Since the brain is encased in a bony skull, brain swelling leads to pressure on the brain stem. As the cerebellum is forced down through the spinal cord opening at the base of the skull, the vital centers in the midbrain become squeezed and compressed. When this happens suddenly, it leads to death of the cat.

Death also occurs when the brain is deprived of oxygen. Complete interruption of the oxygen circulation for only five minutes produces irreversible damage to the cells of the cerebral cortex. This could happen with suffocation, drowning and cardiac arrest.

A blood clot on the brain produces localized pressure symptoms that do not, at least initially, compress the vital centers. There is a depressed level of consciousness. Often one pupil is dilated and will not constrict down when a light is flashed in the eye. A paralysis or weakness may be present on one side of the body.

Signs of Increased Intracranial Pressure

Following a blow to the cat's head, you should watch for signs of brain swelling or the development of a blood clot. These signs can appear anytime during the first 24 hours.

Coma. The most important thing to observe is the level of consciousness. This cat cannot be aroused.

The most important thing to observe is the level of your cat's consciousness. An *alert* cat is in no immediate danger. A *stuporous* cat is sleepy but still responds to the owner. A *semicomatose* cat is sleepy but can still be aroused. A *comatose* cat cannot be aroused. After physical or emotional stress, cats tend to sleep as the excitement wears off. Awaken your cat every 2 hours for the first 24 hours to check on the level of consciousness. Also look for these other signs:

Slight Pressure on the Brain. The cat is stuporous and may stumble or stagger. Breathing is normal. The pupils remain small and constrict when a light is flashed in the eyes.

Moderate Pressure on the Brain. The cat is reclining and difficult to arouse. Breathing is rapid and shallow. The cat is generally weak. Eye movements and pupils are normal.

Severe Pressure on the Brain. The cat is in a coma. All four legs are rigid, then become flaccid. Breathing is gasping or irregular. Pupils are dilated and do not react to light. The heart rate is slowed. Eye movements are slight or absent.

All signs of increased pressure are serious. Even slight pressure suggests that symptoms are evolving. **Notify your veterinarian without delay.** Early treatment, preferably within the first hour, greatly influences the prognosis for successful recovery. When treatment is delayed for just a few hours, the opportunity to prevent irreversible brain damage is lost.

TREATMENT OF HEAD INJURIES

Treatment of shock takes precedence over management of the head injury. If the cat is unconscious, establish an open airway by extending the head and pulling the tongue forward.

With severe brain injury the cat may exhibit few if any signs of life. Signs of death are no pulse, no effort to breathe, dilated pupils and a soft eye. Whether sudden "death" is caused by a head injury or a state of shock from internal bleeding is usually impossible to know. It is wise to administer cardiopulmonary resuscitation immediately on suspicion of death (see EMERGENCIES: *CPR*).

At the scene of an accident, follow these instructions for transporting the cat to the nearest veterinary hospital:

- Control bleeding as described in EMERGENCIES: *Wounds*.
- Place the cat on a flat stretcher as described in the treatment of *Spinal Cord Injuries*.
- Stabilize all fractures if possible (see MUSCULOSKELETAL SYSTEM: *Broken Bones*); cover with a warm blanket.
- Record baseline neurologic exam (level of consciousness; limb movement; pupil size).
- Transport with head higher than rear; this helps to lower intracranial pressure.

Cerebral edema is treated with steroids, oxygen and diuretics (mannitol) to reduce brain swelling. Severely depressed and open skull fractures require surgical

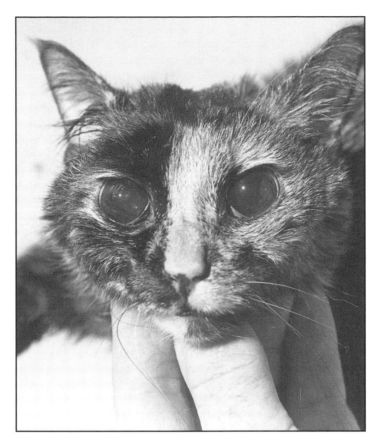

The dilated pupils of terminal brain injury.

cleansing and removal of devitalized bone or elevation and replacement of a depressed fragment to relieve pressure on the brain. Antibiotics are indicated to prevent infection. Uncomplicated skull fractures can be observed.

The outlook following head trauma depends on the severity of the injury and whether treatment is successful. When both pupils are fixed and dilated, the injury is usually irreversible. When a coma persists for more than 24 hours, the outlook is poor. However, if the cat shows steady improvement throughout the first week, the outlook is good. Cats that recover from brain injuries may exhibit permanent behavior changes, head tilt, blindness or seizures.

BRAIN DISEASES

Central nervous system disorders affect less than 1 percent of cats. The most frequent is head trauma. Next in frequency are drug intoxication, poisoning, cerebrovascular disease and brain infection. Other conditions seen less frequently are tumors, vitamin deficiencies and congenital malformations.

Brain Infections (Encephalitis)

Inflammation of the brain is called encephalitis. Symptoms are caused by the destructive effect of the infectious agent and by secondary brain swelling. They include fever, behavioral and personality changes (especially aggression), loss of coordination, unstable gait, stupor, seizures and coma.

Viruses that produce encephalitis include *feline infectious peritonitis, panleukopenia, feline leukemia, rabies* and *pseudorabies*. Rabies is of the greatest concern. It is discussed in the chapter Infectious Diseases. Panleukopenia is a problem in the newborn kitten when it produces *cerebellar hypoplasia*.

Bacteria also can produce encephalitis. Most bacteria gain entrance to the brain via the bloodstream or by direct extension from an infected sinus, nasal passage, eye or head and neck abscess. Fungal brain infection (*Cryptococcus*) is a rare cause of encephalitis, as is the protozoan *Toxoplasmosis*.

Treatment of encephalitis is directed at the primary cause. Steroids are used to reduce brain swelling.

Stroke (Feline Cerebrovascular Disease)

Strokes in cats are caused by ruptured blood vessels with bleeding into the brain. There may have been a recent upper respiratory infection or an illness producing a fever prior to the stroke. However, in most cases the initiating cause of cerebral hemorrhage is unknown.

Signs that often come on suddenly include spasms of the face and limb muscles, paralysis, loss of coordination and blindness. Usually, only one side is affected. Residual signs include behavior changes, pacing and circling and seizures. Diagnosis of a stroke can be made from the history and physical findings. However, it can be confirmed only by special studies that are not generally available to most practitioners.

Tumors

Brain tumors are rare. **Lymphosarcoma** is the most common tumor of the central nervous system. It affects the spaces around the brain and the spinal cord. Signs of brain tumor are like those of *stroke*, except they tend to come on gradually as the tumor grows.

Other Causes of Central Nervous System Disease

Hypoglycemia, or low blood sugar, can produce seizures, a depressed level of consciousness and coma. It is sometimes associated with prolonged chilling. Insulin overdose is a common cause (see Digestive System: *Sugar Diabetes*).

Hypocalcemia causes signs and symptoms much like those of hypoglycemia. It is discussed in the chapter Pregnancy and Kittening (see *Milk Fever*).

Thiamin deficiency occurs when a cat fails to eat regularly or is fed an unbalanced diet containing large amounts of raw fish. Raw fish contains an enzyme that destroys Vitamin B_1. Signs of brain involvement are similar to those described for *Vestibular Disorders* and are frequently accompanied by seizures. When lifted up, cats

One dilated pupil suggests *brain tumor* or *blood clot* on the brain.

often flex their necks, dropping chin to chest. When the deficiency is discovered and treated before the cat becomes comatose, injections of thiamin and the establishment of a balanced diet lead to recovery.

Inherited Metabolic Diseases are a group of genetically determined feline disorders that produce degenerative changes in the central nervous system. In

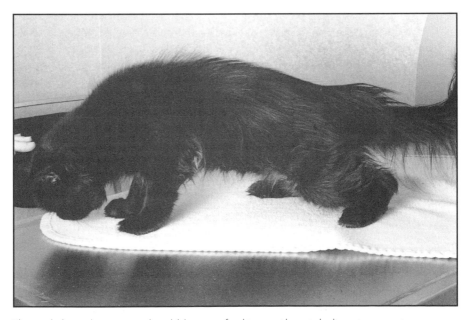

The wide-based stance and wobbly gait of a kitten with metabolic nervous system disease.

Using the head to keep its balance.

each case, a specific enzyme required for nerve cell metabolism is missing. Although these diseases are quite rare, the cat breeder should recognize that such progressive neurological diseases do exist.

Metabolic nervous system diseases are inherited as homozygous recessive traits. Siamese and Domestic Shorthair cats are most often affected. Both parents must carry the gene and each must pass it on to an affected kitten. Littermates that do not show signs of the disease may carry the trait. Accordingly, when one of these diseases is discovered in a family or bloodline, carriers should be identified by special enzyme tests so that steps can be taken to eliminate the trait.

Signs first appear at weaning or shortly thereafter. They include muscle tremors and loss of coordination. The kitten's gait may be wobbly and unstable. As the disease progresses the kitten develops late signs that include weakness, paralysis of the back limbs, blindness and seizures.

Inherited metabolic diseases should be distinguished from *cerebellar hypoplasia* that follows intrauterine exposure to the virus of feline panleukopenia.

Other congenital malformations do occur. They are rare. *Hydrocephalus* is an enlargement of the dome of the skull due to a blockage in the cerebral spinal fluid circulation. *Lipodystrophy* is due to an enzyme deficiency that allows accumulation of fatty material in several body organs, notably the brain. These conditions produce a variety of central nervous system signs.

SEIZURE DISORDERS (FITS)

A seizure is a sudden and uncontrolled burst of activity that may include one of the following: champing and chewing, foaming at the mouth, collapse, jerking of the legs, loss of urine and stool. An altered level of consciousness is followed by a gradual return to normal.

Some "fits" are atypical. Instead of the classic convulsion, the cat exhibits strange and inappropriate behavior such as sudden rage or hysteria. Cats may lick and chew themselves, scratch or bite the owner. This is called a *psychomotor seizure*.

Most classic seizures in cats are caused by acute poisoning. Seizures after head injury may occur at the time of the accident, but in most cases appear several weeks later as a result of scar tissue on the brain. Stroke and epilepsy are other causes of seizures.

Common poisonings that induce seizures are strychnine, antifreeze (ethylene glycol), lead, insecticides (chlorinated hydrocarbons, organophosphates) and rat poisons. Poisons are discussed in the chapter EMERGENCIES. Organophosphates characteristically produce seizures that are preceded by drooling and muscle twitching. A history of exposure to an insecticide (spray, dip, premise treatment) suggests this diagnosis (see SKIN: *Insecticides*).

Kidney and **liver failure,** accompanied by the accumulation of toxins in the blood, can cause seizures and coma.

Epilepsy is a recurrent seizure disorder of cerebral origin. It is far less common in cats than in dogs. To establish a diagnosis of epilepsy, the attacks must be recurrent and similar. Toward this purpose your veterinarian will ask you to provide a complete description of your cat's behavior—before, during and after the seizures.

There are a number of conditions that, while not true seizures, can easily be mistaken for them. **Bee stings,** for example, can cause shock and collapse. Fainting spells associated with advanced heart or lung disease may look like seizures.

Narcolepsy-Cataplexy is a rare condition in which the cat suddenly falls asleep and drops to the ground. The cat may have one or dozens of such attacks in a day lasting a few seconds or up to 20 minutes; the attacks can be reversed by petting the cat or making a loud noise. The cat is completely normal when awake.

Treatment. If having a classic seizure, cover your cat with a blanket and stand aside until the animal quiets down. Do not put your fingers in the cat's mouth or try to wedge something between the teeth. Then call your veterinarian to examine the cat to determine the cause of the seizure.

Seizures lasting over five minutes (continuous seizures) are dangerous. They must be stopped to prevent permanent brain damage. Valium is given intravenously to stop a continuous seizure. Recurrent seizure disorders can often be controlled with medications. These are the same drugs used in treating seizures in people. However, in cats they can be quite toxic and require close veterinary supervision.

COMA

Coma is a depressed level of consciousness. It begins with confusion, progresses through stupor and ends in complete loss of consciousness. Following a blow to the head, coma can occur without progressing through the earlier stages. For signs and symptoms associated with coma, see *Brain Injuries*.

Coma is associated with oxygen deprivation, brain swelling, brain tumor, encephalitis, poisoning and death. Disorders that cause seizures can also cause coma. What happens depends on whether the brain is made more or less excitable. Another cause of coma is prolonged chilling. The cat's temperature is subnormal—well below the level on the thermometer. Treatment involves slow warming and intravenous glucose.

Coma with high fever or heat stroke is a grave sign. Vigorous efforts to bring down the fever are needed to prevent permanent brain damage (see EMERGENCIES: *Heat Stroke*). Likewise, coma is ominous when it is associated with brain trauma or when it occurs in the late stages of kidney and liver disease. Coma associated with insulin overdose is discussed in the DIGESTIVE SYSTEM (see *Sugar Diabetes*).

If found in a coma for which there is no apparent explanation, your cat may have been poisoned. Common poisons that cause coma are ethylene glycol, barbiturates, turpentine, kerosene, arsenic, cyanide, dinitrophenol, hexachlorophene, amphetamines and lead salts. A cat transported in the trunk of a car or left too long in an airtight space may have smothered or developed carbon monoxide poisoning. These conditions are discussed in the chapter EMERGENCIES.

Treatment. First determine the level of consciousness and whether the cat is alive. An unconscious cat can inhale its own secretions and strangle on the tongue. Pull the tongue forward and clear the airway with your fingers. Lift the cat by the rear legs and set the animal on a table with head hanging over the side. If alive, wrap the cat in a blanket and go at once to a veterinarian. If the cat shows no signs of life, begin CPR (see EMERGENCIES).

VESTIBULAR (EAR) DISORDERS

Vestibular disorders are common.

The vestibular apparatus (*labyrinth*) is a complex sense organ composed of three semicircular canals, the utricle and saccule (see EARS: *Structure of the Ears*). The labyrinth is stimulated by gravity and rotation movements. It plays an important role in balance and normal attitude of the body. Inflammation of the labyrinth is called *labyrinthitis*.

Cats with labyrinthitis have a problem with balance. The animal wobbles, circles, falls and rolls over and has trouble righting itself. It may lean against the wall for support and crouch low to the floor when walking. The cat often shows rapid jerking eye movements (*nystagmus*), and the head will usually tilt down on one side. When picked up and turned in a circle, the cat will act more dizzy.

A common cause of labyrinthitis is **inner ear infection** (see EARS). Other causes are **stroke, brain infection** (especially Toxoplasmosis), **drug intoxication** (especially by the aminoglycoside antibiotics) and **thiamin deficiency.**

The Idiopathic Vestibular Syndrome is the most common cause of labyrinthitis in cats. The onset is sudden and the cause is unknown. The cat exhibits head tilt and a vibrating movement of the eyeballs (nystagmus) and may have difficulty walking. In two to three days the cat begins to recover. In most cases the cat is well in three weeks, although some cats retain a permanent head tilt.

SPINAL CORD DISEASES

Injuries and diseases of the spinal cord produce a variety of neurologic signs.

Following injury, there may be neck or back pain, weakness or paralysis of one or more legs, a stumbling uncoordinated gait, loss of pain perception in the limbs and urinary or fecal incontinence.

Other conditions producing limb weakness or *paralysis* that may be mistaken for a spinal cord problem are **Arterial Thromboembolism,** nerve injury and broken leg. Arterial thromboembolism can be distinguished by absent or reduced pulses in the groin (see CIRCULATORY SYSTEM).

A pelvic fracture is frequently mistaken for a broken back. In both cases the cat is unable to use the back legs and will show pain when handled in the area of the injury. It might appear that the outlook is poor, even though cats with a broken pelvis usually recover completely.

Acute abdominal pain (peritonitis, FUS, kidney or liver infection) produces a peculiar hunched appearance that can be mistaken for a back problem. The acute abdomen will show signs of pain when pressure is applied to the abdominal wall (see *Painful Abdomen* in EMERGENCIES).

Ruptured discs are common in older cats but seldom produce weakness or paralysis as they do in dogs. Most of them are the result of trauma. Spinal arthritis, called **spondylitis,** is a condition in which spurs of calcium develop on the backbones. They can exert pressure on the spinal cord or roots of the spinal nerves, occasionally causing pain and rarely weakness of a limb.

Paralysis of both rear legs. Consider spinal cord injury and arterial thromboembolism.

SPINAL CORD INJURIES

Traumatic spinal cord injuries are usually caused by automobile accidents and falls. A cat can get caught in the blades of an automobile fan when the car is started because solitary cats frequently will huddle up next to a warm radiator in cold weather.

A very common injury occurs when a car runs over a cat's tail, pulling apart the sacral-lumbar or coccygeal vertebrae and stretching the nerves to the bladder, rectum and tail. The signs are paralysis of the tail (which hangs loosely like a rope) and urinary or fecal incontinence. The anal sphincter is completely relaxed. The bladder is paralyzed and greatly overdistended. If the condition is not recognized and treated shortly after the accident, bladder paralysis remains even though nerve function is restored. As a result, *any cat with a limp tail must be seen by a veterinarian and x-rayed for sacral injury.*

Treatment: A cat with spinal cord trauma may have other life-threatening injuries that take precedence and require *immediate* attention (see *Treatment of Head Injuries*). All cats unconscious or unable to stand should be considered to have spinal cord injury and must be handled with great care to protect the spine. At the scene of the accident, *move the cat as gently as possible onto a flat surface such as a plywood board and transport to the nearest veterinary clinic.* Sliding the cat onto a blanket or large towel and lifting the corners is a satisfactory means of transporting.

Spinal cord injuries are treated with corticosteroids and diuretics to prevent the cord from further swelling. A cat with a mild contusion or bruising of the spinal cord will begin to recover in a few days. However, if the cord has been severed, it cannot regenerate and paralysis will be permanent.

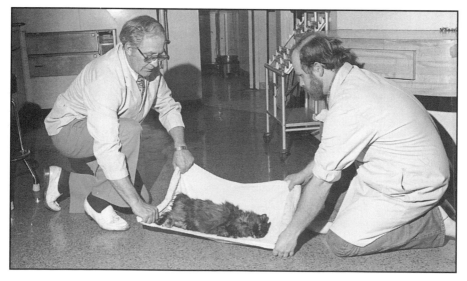

Protect the spine. Use a blanket or towel to lift the cat onto a flat surface before transporting.   —J. Clawson

INFECTIONS

Spinal cord infections are not common. Most of them are due to a neighboring abscess, caused by a penetrating wound such as a bite or laceration. **Meningitis** is an infection of the lining of the spinal canal and brain. On rare occasions it may be caused by bloodborne bacteria.

MALFORMATIONS

Spina bifida is a developmental defect in the closure of the bones in the lower back. It is common in the Manx breed. Signs include lack of bladder and bowel control. These cats can exhibit weakness of the hind legs and a peculiar gait that resembles a "bunny hop."

NERVE INJURIES

An injury to one of the peripheral nerves results in loss of sensation and motor function in the distribution of that nerve. Common injuries are stretches, tears and lacerations.

Brachial and radial nerve injuries involve one of the front legs. They are usually caused by an auto accident during which the leg is jerked backward away from the trunk. The leg hangs limp. With partial paralysis, the cat can often stand but will stumble when taking a step.

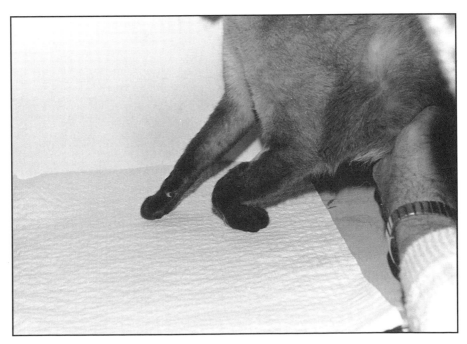

Paralysis of the front leg due to nerve injury.

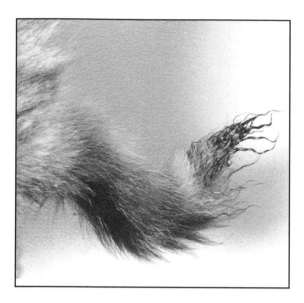

Self-mutilation of a paralyzed, desensitized tail. Amputation was beneficial.

   Paralysis of the tail occurs when a car runs over the tail while the cat is trying to escape. This is a common injury, discussed above. Amputation of the tail may be indicated if movement and sensation do not return after six weeks. The paralyzed tail tends to remain soiled, gets caught in doors and presents a significant handicap to the cat.

   Lacerated nerves must be repaired. Stretched nerves may (but often do not) return to normal. Those that do recover begin to improve in three weeks and may continue to improve for six months. If recovery does not occur, cats often benefit from amputation of the flail leg.

   Another cause of temporary nerve paralysis is the injection of an irritating medication into the tissue surrounding a nerve. This problem is infrequent but can be a source of concern. The correct procedure for giving injections is described in the chapter DRUGS AND MEDICATIONS.

13

MUSCULOSKELETAL SYSTEM

GENERAL INFORMATION

The cat's skeleton is made up of 244 individual bones, about 40 more than humans. Nearly half the difference is made up by the cat's tail, which contains 19–28 small vertebrae. The Japanese Bobtail and Manx breeds are exceptions.

The outside of the bone is called the *cortex*. It gives the bone rigidity. Nutritional deficiencies can result in demineralization of the cortex, making fractures more likely. Inside is the *marrow cavity*, which is important in red blood cell production.

Bones are held together by connective tissue called *ligaments*. The union of two bones is called a joint (*articulation*). In some joints a cushioning pad of *cartilage* (meniscus) is interposed between the two surfaces. Although cartilage is tough and resilient, it still can be damaged by joint stress and trauma. Once damaged, it may deteriorate and become calcified, acting as a foreign body and irritating the joint surfaces.

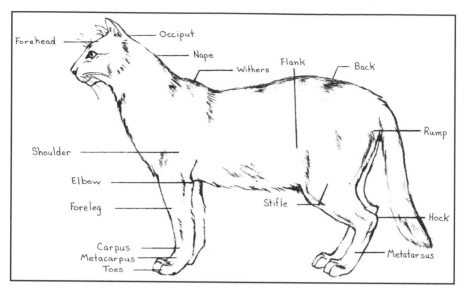

Topographic anatomy. —Sydney Wiley

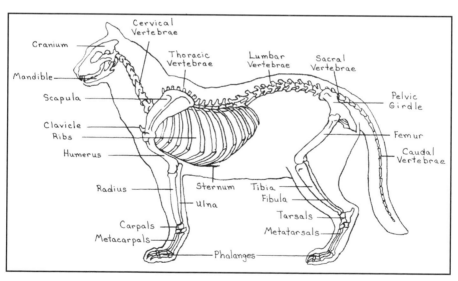

Skeletal anatomy. —Sydney Wiley

Joint position is maintained by ligaments, tendons and a tough fibrous capsule around the joint. These combine to provide stability and tightness. Joint laxity, caused by loose ligaments or a stretched capsule, causes slippage of the articulating surfaces and leads to cartilage injury and later arthritis.

Cats owe much of their flexibility to their extremely mobile vertebrae. These bones are less tightly connected than in most other animals. While the degree of movement between individual vertebrae is small, when taken together, the flexibility of the vertebral column is considerable. A cat can bend, twist and rotate front and back body parts independently. When dropped on its back, a cat will turn right side up and land feet first in less than two seconds.

The skeletal anatomies of humans and cats have much in common, including similar terminology, but there are significant differences in angles, lengths and position of bones. The cat's hock is our heel. Whereas we walk on the soles of our feet, cats walk on their toes. The collar bone (*clavicle*) is only slightly developed in the cat and may even be absent. This narrows the chest and enables cats to keep their legs and feet close together—thereby providing speed, flexibility and the ability to squeeze through tight spaces.

Congenital bone defects occur with some frequency in cats but seldom produce a physical handicap. They include absent or kinked tail, extra toes and cleft foot.

Veterinarians, cat breeders and judges use certain terms to describe a cat's overall composition and structure. *Conformation* is the manner in which various angles and parts of the animal's body agree or harmonize with one another. Standards for purebred cats describe the ideal conformation for each particular breed. At one end of the scale is the strong, sturdy, blocky structure typified by the American Shorthair, Persian, British Shorthair and Maine Coon. At the other end is the lithe, sleek, fine-boned silhouette, exemplified by Oriental breeds such as the Siamese. Other breeds such as the Abyssinian embody characteristics of both. Standards also describe head features, length of coat, color and points, balance and personality of the breed. To some extent standards are based on esthetic considerations but also account for the breed's utility and purpose.

Another term, *soundness*, is used to assess the physical attributes of an animal. When applied to the musculoskeletal system, soundness means the cat is one in which all the bones and joints are in correct alignment and functioning efficiently.

LIMPING (LAMENESS)

Limping indicates pain or weakness in the involved leg. It not only is the most common sign of bone or joint disease but also of muscle or nerve damage.

Determining the Cause

Determine which leg is involved by observation first. A cat will take weight off a painful leg when standing. When moving, animals will usually take a shorter step on a painful or weak leg. You may notice that cats' heads "bob" or drop as weight comes down on the affected leg. Having identified which leg is involved, attempt to identify the site and possible cause. Flex and extend all joints looking for guarding and resistance. If present, this indicates a painful leg problem. Carefully feel the leg from the toes up. Locate a point of tenderness by applying pressure. Having located a site of pain, see if it is caused by movement of a joint or tenderness in a muscle. Check for swelling and discoloration in the area. With this information consider the following:

Infected areas are tender, reddened, warm to touch and often associated with a skin laceration or puncture wound. The limp grows steadily worse. Fever is often present. Infected cat fight wounds are the most common cause of lameness.

Sprains and strains (of joints, tendons and muscles) are of sudden onset and frequently show local swelling and discoloration. They gradually improve. The cat usually has partial use of the leg. Pain is mild. There is no fever.

Fractures and dislocations are associated with severe pain and inability to put weight on the leg. Deformity is present. Movement of the involved part produces a gritty sound. Tissues are swollen and discolored from bleeding.

Spinal cord injuries and peripheral *nerve injuries* produce weakness or paralysis of one or more limbs but *do not produce pain*. These conditions are discussed in the Nervous System chapter.

Arthritis is a joint disease. Pain in the joint sometimes produces lameness, which gets better as the day wears on.

INJURIES TO BONES AND JOINTS

SPRAINS

A sprain is a joint injury caused by a sudden stretching or tearing of the ligaments. The signs are pain over the joint, swelling of the tissues and temporary lameness. If the cat refuses to put weight on a leg, have the animal examined by a veterinarian to rule out a fracture or dislocation. The same is true for any injury that fails to improve in four days. X rays should be taken.

Treatment: The primary treatment is to rest the part. Ice packs help to reduce pain and swelling. Use for 30 minutes every hour for the first three hours. Add crushed ice to a plastic bag. Place the bag over the injured joint and hold in place with an elastic bandage. **Pain medication is not safe to use in cats.**

TENDON INJURIES

A tendon may be stretched, partly torn or completely separated (ruptured). An irritated or inflamed tendon is called *tendonitis*. Strained tendons follow sudden wrenching or twisting injuries. The tendons in the front and back paws are strained most often. Signs of tendonitis are temporary lameness, pain on bending and straightening the joint, tenderness and swelling over the course of the tendon.

Rupture of the *Achilles* (heel) tendon that attaches to the hock joint is caused by sudden and extreme flexion. This tendon is most often injured by auto accidents and cat fights.

Treatment: Stretched ligaments are treated in the same manner as *Sprains*. A ruptured tendon requires immediate veterinary attention.

MUSCLE STRAINS AND CONTUSIONS

A bruised or torn muscle is caused by (a) sudden stretching of the muscle fibers; (b) overexertion from prolonged usage; or (c) a blow to the muscle. Signs are lameness, a knotting of the muscle, tenderness over the injured part and discoloration caused by bleeding.

Treatment: Rest and cold packs are recommended (see *Sprains*).

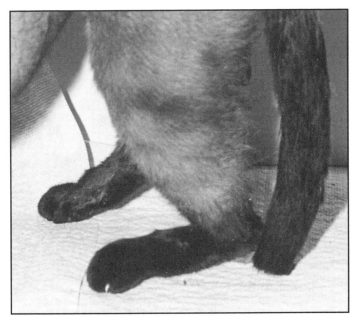

With a ruptured Achilles tendon, the cat walks on the heel instead of the toes.

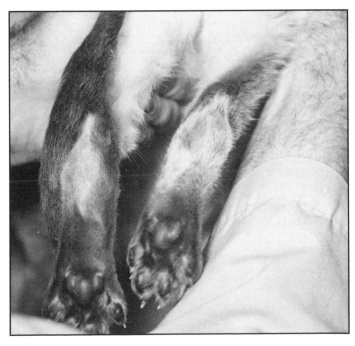

A dislocated hip joint, showing the affected right leg shorter than the left.

Rubber Band Around the Leg

Children occasionally put a rubber band around a cat's leg and forget to remove it if parents are not alerted to this. In time, the rubber band cuts through the skin. This condition may not be noticed until the cat exhibits pain at the site of injury and has trouble putting weight on the leg.

Treatment: Surgical removal of devitalized tissue and repair of the wound, which may involve muscle and tendon, are required.

Dislocated Joint (Luxation)

Major force is necessary to rupture a joint and displace the bones. Such injuries usually are the result of falls, fights with dogs or car accidents. The cat may also have shock and internal bleeding from injured organs. Signs of dislocation are sudden pain with inability to bear weight on the limb. There is an observable deformity (shortening) when compared with the opposite side.

The hip is the most commonly dislocated joint in the cat. It can be recognized by signs of pain on movement of the hip, a gritting sensation and shortening of the leg by about one inch. Other joints less frequently dislocated are the kneecap, hock and jaw. A dislocated kneecap occurs with some frequency in the Devon Rex, in whom there is a hereditary predisposition. Torn knee ligaments, a special circumstance, are discussed below.

Treatment: Veterinary examination is necessary to rule out an associated fracture and to replace the joint in its socket. The treatment of other injuries may take precedence.

Torn Knee Ligaments (Ruptured Cruciates)

The knee is stabilized by two internal cruciate ligaments that cross each other in the middle of the knee joint. A pad of cartilage (*meniscus*) is found within the joint. The knee ligaments are sometimes ruptured, and the meniscus torn, after a car accident or a fall from a building. Signs of injury are joint swelling, pain on flexing and extending the knee and looseness of the joint. You may be able to detect a click in the joint, which is a torn meniscus.

Treatment: Immediate surgical repair of a badly damaged knee joint is the treatment of choice. A mild injury, perhaps limited to the meniscus, can be treated by cage confinement for three to five weeks to rest the joint and allow it to heal by itself. If lameness persists, surgery should be considered. Degenerative arthritis follows trauma to the knee joint. Scar tissue develops in and around the joint, causing pain and stiffness. These arthritic problems are less likely to occur if the joint is repaired surgically.

Broken Bones (Fractures)

Most broken bones are caused by automobile accidents and falls. Falls from apartment windows usually occur during hot weather. The bones most commonly broken are the femur, pelvis and skull. Fractures of the jaw and spine occur less frequently.

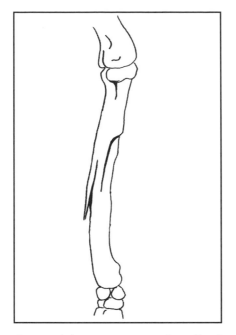

Greenstick fracture.   —Rose Floyd

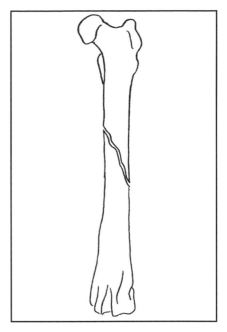

Oblique fracture.   —Rose Floyd

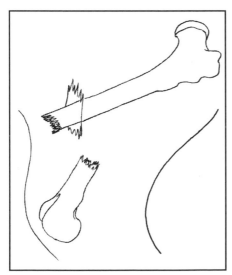

Open fracture.   —Rose Floyd

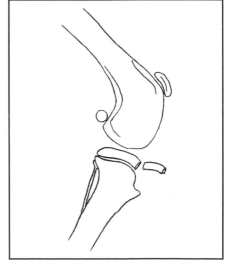

Joint fracture.   —Rose Floyd

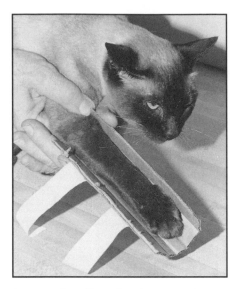 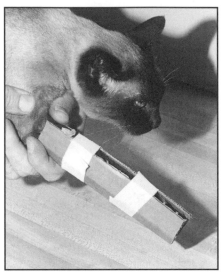

A piece of cardboard makes a good temporary splint for fractures of the front leg below the elbow. —J. Clawson

A rather common type of fracture occurs when a car runs over a cat's tail. It is discussed in NERVOUS SYSTEM: *Spinal Cord Injuries*.

Fractures are classified by type and whether the injury involves a break in the skin. Young bones tend to crack and are called *greenstick fractures*, whereas the bones of elderly cats are brittle and more likely to break. Complete *breaks are classified as open* or *closed*. In an open or *compound fracture* the bone makes contact with the outside, either because of a deep laceration exposing it or because the point of the bone protrudes through the skin. Open fractures are associated with a high incidence of bone infection. In a closed fracture the bone does not break through the skin.

Treatment: Many of these injuries are associated with shock, blood loss and injuries to other organs. Control of shock takes precedence over treatment of the fracture. See *Shock* in the EMERGENCIES chapter. Cats with injury or pain should be handled gently, as described in EMERGENCIES: *Handling and Restraint*. Take precautions to avoid a painful scratch or bite.

Fractures should be immobilized to prevent further injury during the cat's movement to a veterinary hospital. *Splint the involved limb*. A satisfactory splint is one that crosses the joint above and below the injury. When the fracture is below the knee or elbow, immobilize the limb by folding a magazine or piece of thick cardboard around the leg. Then wrap it with roller gauze, a necktie or tape. Limb fractures above the knee or elbow are immobilized by binding the leg to the body.

If the bone is completely broken and the ends are displaced, your veterinarian will need to reduce the fracture and return the ends of the bones to their original

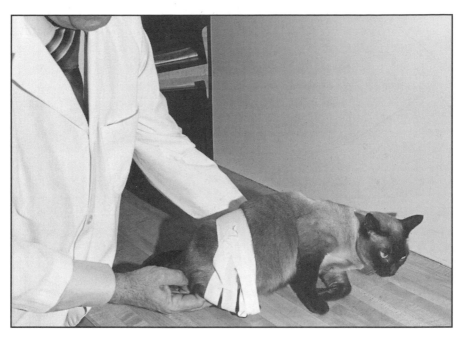

Fractures above the knee joint can be immobilized by taping the leg to the body.
—J. Clawson

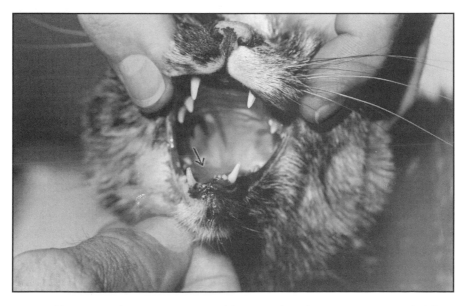

Fractured lower jaw showing separation of the two sides. These injuries commonly follow blows to the head.

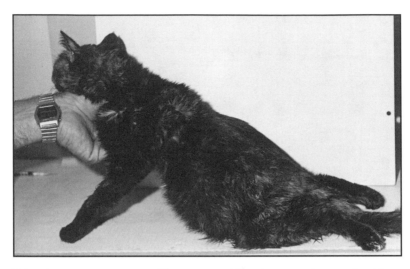

Pelvic fractures are common. The cat is unable to bear weight on its hind legs. This might be confused with a spinal cord injury or arterial thromboembolism.

position. Reduction is accomplished by pulling on the limb to overcome the muscle spasm that caused the shortening. This requires a general anesthetic. Once reduced, the position of the bones must be maintained. In general, fractures above the knee or elbow are stabilized with pins and metallic plates, while those below are immobilized with plaster splints and casts.

Displaced jaw fractures can cause malposition of the teeth. The jaw should be adjusted and the teeth wired together to maintain the position until healing is complete. Skull fractures may require surgery to elevate the depressed fragment. For more information see *Head Injuries* in the chapter NERVOUS SYSTEM.

BONE INFECTION (OSTEOMYELITIS)

Bone infection is more common in cats than in dogs because cat bites, being puncture wounds, are more likely to become infected and progress to involve the bone. Other causes of bone infection are open fractures and surgical operations on bones.

The signs of osteomyelitis are lameness, fever, pain, swelling and discharge through a sinus tract connecting the bone to the skin. The diagnosis is confirmed by X ray and bone biopsy.

Treatment: Bone infection is difficult to eliminate. Bacterial cultures aid in the selection of an appropriate antibiotic combination. Surgical cleansing with removal of devitalized bone and overlying tissue and wide open drainage are indicated in some cases. Treatment is prolonged.

ARTHRITIS (DEGENERATIVE JOINT DISEASE)

Arthritis can affect one or more joints. *Osteoarthritis*, also called *degenerative arthritis* or *degenerative joint disease*, is the most common form of arthritis in cats. Still it is less common in cats than in dogs and produces milder symptoms. In degenerative joint disease, the cartilage covering the articulating surface of a joint wears out and the underlying bone develops a roughened surface that damages the joint.

Degenerative joint disease occurs in joints that have been severely stressed, dislocated or fractured. Months or years after the injury, bone spurs develop in and around the joint, causing pain and restriction. Proper early care of joint injuries may reduce the severity of subsequent lameness. Although degenerative arthritis may begin during the first half of life, symptoms generally do not appear until much later. The signs are mainly those of stiffness and lameness. Lameness is usually worse on arising but gets better as the day wears on.

Vertebral column involvement is called **Spondylitis.** In spinal arthritis, developing bone spurs can create pressure points on the nerve roots. This is the most frequent cause of significant arthritic symptoms in the cat. An unusual cause of spondylitis is a dietary intake of excessive amounts of Vitamin A (see *Overdosing with Vitamins*).

Congenital Hip Dysplasia does occur in cats but is not diagnosed frequently because it seldom produces pain or lameness. In the occasional cat with a painful limp, joint surgery may be considered.

Feline Progressive Polyarthritis is an inflammation involving a number of joints. One or more viruses have been implicated. The feline leukemia virus is the one identified most often.

Septic arthritis is more common in cats than dogs. Cats are more likely to acquire deep bacterial infections from bite wounds that penetrate joints. Treatment of a septic joint is like that described for *Bone Infection*.

Treatment: Aspirin and related drugs used to relieve pain and joint inflammation in people are potentially toxic to cats and should not be used without veterinary approval (see DRUGS AND MEDICATIONS). *Tylenol*, in particular, must *never* be used. Fortunately, pain or severe lameness in cats is infrequent and seldom produces significant disability.

METABOLIC BONE DISORDERS

PARATHYROID BONE DISEASES

There are four small glands in the neck of the cat, located in proximity to the thyroid. They are the *parathyroid glands*. They secrete a substance called *parathyroid hormone*, which is essential to bone metabolism and blood calcium regulation.

As the blood calcium level falls, the parathyroid glands compensate by releasing more parathyroid hormone, which raises the serum calcium level by drawing calcium *out* of the bones. Another stimulant to parathyroid secretion is a high serum phosphorus level. Accordingly, either a low serum calcium or a high serum phosphorus will cause an excess of parathyroid hormone in the blood. When this situation goes unchecked, the bones become demineralized, thin and often look cystic (small holes in the bone) on X-ray. Minor stress can cause a fracture.

The following conditions are related to abnormal parathyroid gland metabolism:

Primary Hyperparathyroidism. This rare condition is due to a parathyroid gland tumor that produces excess hormone. Surgical removal of the affected gland is the only possible treatment.

Renal Secondary Hyperparathyroidism. This condition is the result of long-standing kidney disease that creates retention of phosphorus. The high serum phosphorus stimulates the parathyroid glands to produce excessive amounts of hormone. Effects on bone are the same as those of Nutritional Secondary Hyperparathyroidism (discussed below). However, the symptoms are usually dominated by the kidney picture (*uremia*). Treatment is directed at correcting the kidney problem.

Nutritional Secondary Hyperparathyroidism (Paper bone disease). The cause of this nutritional bone disease is a diet consisting primarily of meat products such as beef heart, liver or kidney. Such a diet is too high in phosphorus and too low in calcium and Vitamin D. (Vitamin D is necessary for calcium to be absorbed from the small intestine).

Kittens are at a particular risk because they require large amounts of calcium for growth and development. The daily calcium, phosphorus and Vitamin D requirements for young kittens and adult cats are found in Table 3 in the chapter FEEDING AND NUTRITION.

When a kitten's sole source of nourishment is eight ounces of meat a day, the animal would receive only 20 mg of calcium but 800 mg of phosphorus. This would result in overactivity of the parathyroid glands.

Symptoms appear after the kitten has been on a high meat diet for about four weeks. Affected kittens are reluctant to move, develop an uncoordinated gait and lameness in the back legs. The front legs are often bowed. Thin bones are paper-like and easily fractured. These fractures, often multiple, tend to heal rapidly and may even go unrecognized. Because the meat diet supplies adequate calories, kittens often appear well-nourished and have a healthy hair coat despite their metabolic bone disease.

The adult form of this disease is called **osteoporosis.** It occurs in older cats that receive large quantities of meat at the expense of other nutrients. Since adult calcium requirements are lower than those for kittens, bone demineralization takes longer to occur (5 to 13 months). The first sign of demineralization is thinning of the jaw bones with exposure of the roots of the teeth. The loose teeth are expelled. Other feeding practices that can lead to osteoporosis include all-vegetable diets; cornbread diets; and feeding leftover table scraps (which are frequently just vegetables).

Treatment: Dietary correction is required. Diets that meet all the nutritional requirements for growing kittens and adult cats are discussed in the chapter FEEDING AND NUTRITION. Calcium and Vitamin D supplements should not be given to kittens unless prescribed by a veterinarian for a specific deficiency. Kittens with paper bone disease should be kept quiet and confined to prevent bone fractures.

Older cats with advanced periodontal disease or fixed eating habits that do not include a balanced ration should be evaluated by a veterinarian and considered for nutritional supplements.

RICKETS (OSTEOMALACIA)

Rickets (called *osteomalacia* in adults) is caused by a deficiency of Vitamin D. Since this vitamin is active in the absorption of calcium and phosphorus from the intestine, these minerals may be deficient also. Disease in the cat is rare because only small amounts of Vitamin D (50 to 100 I.U.) are required as a daily allowance. Many cases classified as rickets are probably due to nutritional secondary hyperparathyroidism.

Signs: There is a characteristic enlargement of the joints where the ribs meet the cartilage of the sternum (*richettic rosary*). Bowing of the legs and other growth deformities in the kitten, along with fractures in the adult, are common in severe cases.

Treatment: It is the same as for nutritional secondary hyperparathyroidism.

OTHER NUTRITIONAL DISORDERS

OVERDOSING WITH VITAMINS

Contrary to popular belief, growing kittens do not need supplemental vitamins and minerals for correct health and development. Modern name-brand commercial kitten foods supply the needed vitamins and minerals to sustain normal growth, provided the kitten or young cat consumes the food as the main or sole source of calories. Vitamins and minerals in excess of those needed for growth and development will not add more coat or substance to the growing animal.

When calcium, phosphorus and Vitamin D are given beyond the animal's capacity to use them normally, growth and development can be adversely affected. Overdosing with Vitamin D causes bones to calcify unevenly. Also, calcium may be deposited in the lungs, heart and blood vessels.

High levels of Vitamin A can cause the development of bone spurs in and around joints, particularly those of the neck and back. These spurs result in loss of flexibility and produce pain on joint movement. Symptoms include joint swelling, lameness, pain in the neck and back and hypersensitivity of the skin to touch. In addition to oversupplementing with Vitamin A, diets containing high levels of Vitamin A (liver and milk diets) have been found to cause this problem. Treatment involves dietary correction and the discontinuation of Vitamin A supplements. However, once bone spurs have developed, symptoms will not disappear.

Vitamin and mineral supplements are most efficacious when given to queens in late pregnancy and during lactation (see PREGNANCY AND KITTENING) and to elderly cats with poor eating habits who may have developed a dietary deficiency.

To avoid complications associated with vitamin overdosing, the exact amounts of calcium, phosphorous and Vitamin D should be determined by a veterinarian.

Yellow fat disease (Pansteatitis)

This disease is caused by a deficiency of Vitamin E. It is one of the most important vitamin deficiency diseases of cats. It occurs among cats fed excessive amounts of unsaturated fatty acids, found especially in red meat tuna. Fatty acids oxidize and destroy Vitamin E. In addition, canned tuna for human consumption is not supplemented with this vitamin.

Vitamin E deficiency causes a yellow pigment to be deposited in fat that acts like a foreign body, producing inflammation. Affected cats run a fever, are reluctant to eat and move and exhibit pain when handled or stroked. Digestive disturbances caused by inflammation and degeneration of fat in the abdomen may dominate the picture. The disease is difficult to diagnose but can be suspected by the feeding history. A fat biopsy confirms the diagnosis.

Treatment: The disease is reversed by giving a daily dose of Vitamin E. Corticosteroids can be administered to decrease the inflammatory reaction. Full recovery takes one to four weeks. Pansteatitis can be prevented by feeding a complete cat ration and by feeding fish products only as occasional treats.

14

URINARY SYSTEM

GENERAL INFORMATION

The urinary system is composed of the kidneys and ureters, bladder, prostate and urethra.

The **kidneys** are paired organs located on each side of the backbone just behind and below the last rib. Each kidney has a renal pelvis or funnel that siphons the urine into a *ureter*. The ureters pass on down to the pelvic brim and empty into the bladder. The passageway that connects the neck of the bladder to the outside is called the *urethra*. The opening of the urethra is found at the tip of the penis in the male and between the folds of the vulva in the female. In the male, the urethra also serves as a channel for semen.

The chief function of the kidneys is to regulate water, mineral and chemical balance and excrete the wastes of metabolism. This is accomplished by *nephrons*, the basic working units of the kidneys. Damage to nephrons leads to kidney failure. Normal urine is yellow and clear. Its color can be altered by the state of hydration and by various drugs and diseases.

The act of voiding is controlled by the central nervous system. A cat can decide when to void. This is the basis for successful litter box training. But once the decision to void is reached, the actual mechanism of bladder emptying is carried out by a complicated spinal cord reflex.

URINARY TRACT INFECTIONS

Bacterial urinary tract infections are not nearly as common in cats as they are in dogs, yet *urinary tract inflammation is one of the most frequent problems encountered in cats.* The reason for this is that the **Feline Urologic Syndrome** accounts for the great majority of feline urinary tract symptoms, and although the signs of FUS might suggest a bladder or urethra infection, studies have shown that in most cases a bacterial infection is not part of this disease—at least not initially. Therefore, veterinarians have had to revise their thinking about the association of bacterial infections with urinary tract symptoms in the cat. The following points should be considered in this regard:

1. There is a normal bacterial flora limited to the terminal portion of the cat's urethra. Accordingly, cultures taken from voided urine specimens are contaminated and show growth of bacteria even though the bladder urine is sterile. Cultures taken by catheter or bladder puncture are more accurate.

2. The lining of the cat's urethra and bladder contains antibodies and immune substances that destroy harmful bacteria. The process of emptying the bladder "flushes" out the lower system and keeps the channel clean.

3. Valves at the junction of the ureters with the bladder prevent reflux of infected urine up into the kidney.

4. The concentrated urine of cats contains acids, urea and other substances that create an unfavorable living environment for most bacteria. Dilute urine is more supportive of bacterial growth. However, heavily concentrated urine that contains sediment is not desirable and may predispose to FUS.

Some breakdown in either local immunity or normal bladder function must occur for a cat to develop a bacterial urinary tract infection. This breakdown allows harmful invaders to gain a foothold. Some processes that lead to a breakdown are:

1. Repeated attacks of obstruction, which scar the urethra and further obstruct bladder outlet. The primary cause of this is FUS.

2. Repeated catheterization of the male, which produces injury to the lining of the urethra and affords the opportunity to introduce bacteria into the bladder.

3. Tumors or growths in the bladder and strictures of the urethra—which impair the flushing effect of urination and leave a residual pool of urine for bacterial growth.

4. A prior urinary tract infection, which leads to tissue injury and reduced local resistance. Cats that have had one urinary tract infection are more likely to have others.

In summary, urinary tract inflammation in cats does not always mean infection. Infections are preceded by some process that damages the cat's normal defense mechanisms and sets the stage for bacterial invasion. Once established, recurrent infections are common. Failure to promptly correct the initial problem makes repeated infections almost a certainty.

SIGNS OF URINARY TRACT DISEASE

Most urinary tract diseases are associated with a disturbance in the normal pattern of voiding. Signs are:

Painful Urination (dysuria): Characterized by distress during urination with prolonged squatting and straining; failure to pass urine after many tries; and passage of mucus, blood clots or bloody urine. Pain and swelling within the lower abdomen suggest an overdistended bladder.

Blood in Urine (hematuria): When accompanied by painful urination, blood indicates a problem in the urethra or bladder. A uniformly bloody urine without pain suggests kidney disease.

Excessive Urination (polyuria): Frequent voiding of normal amounts of urine suggests kidney disease. A cat compensates for a high urine output by drinking large amounts of water. You may notice this first. *Diabetes mellitus* is another cause of excessive thirst and urination.

Urinary Incontinence: This is characterized by loss of voluntary control over voiding or by inappropriate urination. The cat may void frequently, dribble and urinate in unusual places. Because of overlapping symptoms and possibly more than one problem existing at the same time, it is difficult to make an exact diagnosis by symptoms alone.

In the diagnosis of urinary tract disease, the laboratory is of considerable help. Routine tests are blood chemistries and urinalysis.

How to Collect and Test Urine. Your veterinarian may request a sample of your cat's urine. The procedure for collecting a urine sample is as follows:

- Replace the normal kitty litter with an inert substance such as styrofoam packing or aquarium gravel (which does not absorb urine and can be washed between samples).
- After the cat has voided, pour the urine from the litter pan into a small, clean, sealable plastic or glass container.
- You may be asked to test the urine pH with a laboratory strip provided by your veterinarian. Follow instructions.
- If necessary, to store the sample, place it in the refrigerator in the sealed container. The sample should be checked within two hours.

Additional studies are often indicated. They include urine cultures and X ray examinations of the abdomen. The intravenous pyelogram is an X ray examination in which a dye is injected into the circulation. It is excreted by the kidneys and outlines much of the urinary tract. Abdominal ultrasound is another good way to visualize the kidneys and bladder. Other selective studies may be performed when indicated. They include CT scan, surgical exploration and biopsy.

DISEASES OF THE BLADDER AND URETHRA

FELINE UROLOGIC SYNDROME (FUS)

FUS, also called *feline lower urinary tract disease* or the plugged-penis syndrome, is the most common disorder affecting the lower urinary tract in cats. It is by far the major health concern of cat owners despite its affecting only about 1 percent of cats. One reason is that FUS has a 50 percent to 70 percent rate of recurrence.

Although FUS can occur in cats of all ages, it is seen most commonly in those over one year. It occurs with equal frequency in both sexes, but the anatomy of the male makes the disease more symptomatic and increases the likelihood of bladder obstruction. It is more common in obese cats due to mechanical interference with voiding.

The chief signs of FUS are prolonged squatting and straining. Symptomatic cats urinate frequently, pass bloody urine, urinate in unusual locations, lick the penis or vulva excessively and cry out during the act of voiding.

Major obstructions can occur with the first episode or during subsequent attacks. With partial or complete obstruction of the urethra, the lower abdomen becomes distended and painful to touch. As pressure increases in the upper urinary tract, the kidneys stop making urine. Toxic wastes build in the blood, leading to *uremia*. The cat loses its appetite, acts sluggish and begins to vomit. If unrelieved, irreversible kidney damage occurs, leading to death. Thus, it is of vital importance to relieve the obstruction as soon as possible. Keep in mind that cats often seek seclusion when ill or in pain; therefore, a cat with symptomatic FUS should not be allowed outdoors.

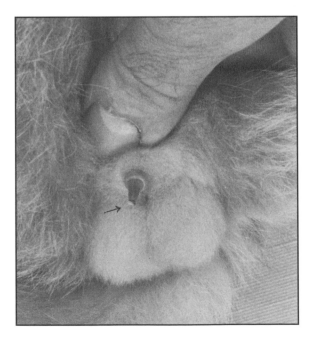

Feline Urologic Syndrome. Note the mucus plug at the tip of the penis.

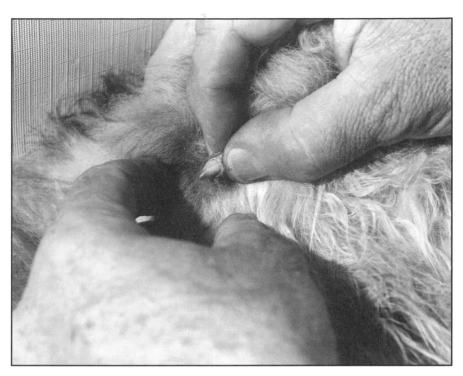

Rolling the penis between finger and thumb may crush the plug and clear the passage.

Causes of FUS. There are a number of important contributing reasons that explain why some cats get FUS, but no one circumstance accounts for all cases. It is known that

1. FUS is caused by plugging of the urethra by a pastelike, gritty or sandy material, composed primarily of mucus and struvite crystals (magnesium-ammonium-phosphate), which are about the size of salt. Although struvite crystals constitute a major part of most plugs, other crystals may be found. Some plugs are composed primarily of mucus, blood and white cells.

2. Two factors of primary importance in crystal formation are high concentrations of magnesium in the urine and a urine with an alkaline pH (over 6.8).

3. Factors influencing urine magnesium concentration are high levels of magnesium in the diet, infrequent urination caused by a dirty litter box, reduced physical activity and reduced water intake occasioned by nonavailability or poor quality water.

4. Cat urine is normally slightly acidic. Factors that favor an alkaline urine are the type of food eaten and the presence of bacterial urinary tract infection. Acid urine is theoretically protective and also has

antibacterial properties. Despite this observation, some cases of FUS occur in cats with acid urine.

5. Bacterial cystitis and urethritis have long been accepted as basic causes. Current research indicates that bacteria are not involved in most cases, at least not at first. However, bacterial cystitis may be a very important cause of recurrent attacks. Also, keep in mind that the potential for infection increases with obstruction.

6. Diet and water intake have been proposed as contributing factors. Cats that eat dry food take in less water with their meals and also lose more water in their stools. Presumably, dry cat food leads to a more concentrated urine and a greater amount of sediment.

In summary, no one theory accounts for all cases. It does seem likely that reduced water intake, dietary consumption of sediment precursors, obesity and perhaps currently unknown factors all contribute. Bacterial infection, once established, is an important cause of recurrent attacks.

Treatment of FUS. A cat with a plugged urethra needs immediate attention. An obstructed male often protrudes the penis. You can massage the penis by rolling it between your thumb and index finger. This may crush the plug and allow the material to be expelled. If not successful, *immediate veterinary attention and hospitalization are*

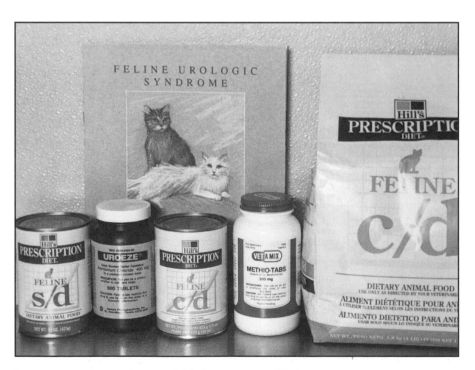

Some prescription products available for treatment of FUS.

In perineal urethrostomy, the penis is removed to enlarge the urethral opening. The cat now is able to control urine.

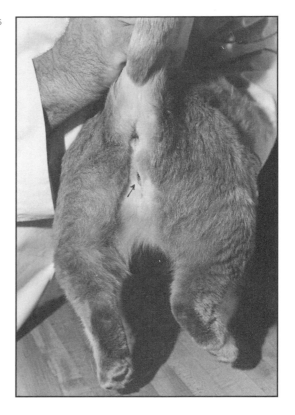

required. In most cases, a small soft rubber or flexible polyethylene catheter is inserted through the urethra into the bladder to relieve the obstruction. This usually is done under sedation or anesthesia. Intravenous fluids are given to rehydrate the cat and increase the flow of urine. Antibiotics may be prescribed to prevent or treat an associated bladder infection (*Cystitis*). The cat will remain hospitalized until it is able to urinate normally.

Following discharge, the cat should be placed on a special diet (e.g., Hill's Prescription Diet *Feline s/d*) to dissolve any residual struvite crystals or stones in the urinary bladder. This food is low in magnesium and aids in maintaining a normal acid urine. In cats fed this special diet exclusively, signs associated with FUS will normally cease within the first five to seven days. To completely dissolve all residual struvite crystals or stones, the diet should be followed for one to two months. This diet, however, is high in salt and ordinarily is not used for maintenance (see *Prevention of FUS*). It is important to feed only the prescribed diet. Do not feed fish, shellfish, cheese, vitamin-mineral supplements or table scraps. These foods contain magnesium and also produce an alkaline urine.

During and immediately after the dissolution process, you may be asked to monitor your cat's urine pH at home (see *How to Collect and Test Urine*) or to bring in a urine specimen to be checked for struvite crystals under the microscope.

For those plugs or stones that consist of nonstruvite compounds, surgery as described below may be necessary.

Prevention of FUS. Many cats experience a recurrence of FUS when they return to their former food. To prevent recurrence, your veterinarian may suggest feeding a prescription diet (Hill's Feline *c/d*) for six to nine months. This diet is low in magnesium. Other suitable substitutes low in magnesium include *Friskies Buffet* Beef & Liver and *Friskies Buffet* Turkey & Giblets. Switch to the prevention diet when your veterinarian has determined that your cat is free of symptoms and the urine is free of struvite crystals. The procedure for introducing a new diet is to gradually mix it in over 10 days with the old diet until only the new diet is fed.

If the cat remains free of symptoms and urinary struvite crystals for six to nine months, your veterinarian may suggest Hill's *Science Diet Feline*, a moderately restricted magnesium diet, or some combination of prescription diets that produce an acid urine. The cat's urine should be checked every six months. If the cat develops new signs of illness while on *Science Diet Feline*, switch back to one of the prescription diets mentioned above.

The following additional steps should be taken to eliminate excessive urinary sediment or infection:

1. Keep the litter box clean. It should be changed every day. Some cats refuse to use a dirty litter box. This can result in voluntary retention.

2. Encourage water consumption by keeping clean, fresh water available at all times.

3. Prevent obesity. Maintain normal body weight by restricting food intake as discussed in the chapter FEEDING AND NUTRITION. Encourage your cat to exercise.

4. Occasionally, a cat will not consume a prescription diet. In such cases, urine acidifiers added to the cat's favorite food aid in reducing crystal formation. Ammonium chloride and DL-Methionine are urinary acidifiers available through your veterinarian. They must be added to feed to work. (*Caution:* Avoid urinary acidifiers if the cat is uremic. This could lead to an acid/base imbalance.)

Cats with repeated attacks that don't respond to the preventive measures listed above should undergo complete veterinary evaluation, searching for bladder stones or other abnormalities in the urinary tract. If no correctable condition is found, your veterinarian may suggest an operation in which part of the penis is removed to enlarge the opening of the urethra. The operation is called *perineal urethrostomy*. It is often quite successful, especially when FUS is complicated by an overdistended, poorly contracting bladder. Upon recovery, cats are still able to control urination and use the litter pan.

The question arises about whether all adult cats should be placed on a magnesium restricted diet as a prophylactic measure to prevent FUS. Considering that 99 percent of cats are not affected by FUS irrespective of diet and that other factors besides diet are important in the etiology of this syndrome, feeding a severely restricted magnesium diet to all cats probably is not justified. Recently, a number of cat food manufacturers have reduced the levels of magnesium in their products and added L-Methionine, a urinary acidifier. These rations should provide some protection against FUS. They are available at some pet supply outlets and natural food stores. Your veterinarian will have information on which products are available in your area.

CYSTITIS

Cystitis is inflammation of the bladder. Most cases of cystitis in males and females are associated with FUS.

Bacterial infection is rarely a problem during the first bout of FUS but becomes increasingly important with recurring attacks. Inserting a catheter into the urethra to relieve an obstruction may introduce bacteria and lead to secondary bacterial cystitis. Bacterial cystitis may complicate *perineal urethrostomy*.

Signs of cystitis are indistinguishable from those of FUS but are more noticeable in males because of the longer urethra. A female with cystitis may exhibit a vaginal discharge and lick at her vulva.

Treatment: It is like that for FUS. In addition, if the urine specimen reveals bacterial infection, an antibiotic selected on the basis of culture and sensitivity testing is administered for three weeks. Wait one week and then reculture. If the second culture is positive, administer another course of antibiotic.

BLADDER STONES

Most bladder stones in cats are related to FUS. The same process that causes small crystalline material to plug the urethra also causes stones to form in the bladder. Stones are more likely to form in a persistently infected bladder and in a bladder that is partially obstructed. Stones irritate the bladder wall, prolong infection and produce symptoms like those of FUS.

Kidney stones, which are common in people, are almost unknown in cats.

Treatment: Struvite stones will usually dissolve in one to three months under the same treatment protocol as described for FUS. Abdominal X rays are taken to monitor the progress of dissolution. Associated bacterial infection is treated as described for *Cystitis*. Stones that do not dissolve are removed surgically. Following treatment, a cat should be placed on the same protocol as described for the *Prevention of FUS*.

URINARY INCONTINENCE

Incontinence is defined as abnormal voiding behavior showing a loss of voluntary control over the act of voiding with inappropriate urination. It should be distinguished from housetraining laspses and psychological causes, which are discussed in the chapter FELINE BEHAVIOR AND TRAINING (see *Inappropriate Elimination*).

When urinary incontinence is associated with FUS, the cat may at first experience sudden urges to void, urinate in locations other than the litter box and void frequently in small amounts. These symptoms are caused by urgency, but the cat retains some control over the act of voiding. However, as the disease progresses, the repeatedly overdistended bladder loses the ability to contract and empty. A more or less constant dribbling of urine occurs from the inert, overloaded bladder. *Perineal urethrostomy*, as described in *feline urologic syndrome*, is most beneficial when used in the treatment of this complication.

Spinal cord injury, especially that associated with a pulling apart of the sacral-lumbar or coccygeal vertebrae when a car runs over a cat's tail, is a common cause of bladder paralysis, overdistension and subsequent urinary incontinence. Spinal cord diseases and brain diseases can also lead to loss of bladder and bowel control.

Treatment of incontinence is directed at finding the underlying cause and correcting it if possible. Drugs that act on the bladder muscle may be useful in selected cases.

KIDNEY DISEASES
INFECTION OF THE KIDNEY AND RENAL PELVIS (PYELONEPHRITIS)

Pyelonephritis, a bacterial infection of the kidney and urinary collecting system, usually ascends from an infection in the bladder. Infrequently, it is bloodborne.

Acute pyelonephritis begins with fever, vomiting and pain in the kidney area. A stiff-legged gait and a hunched posture are characteristic signs. The urine is often bloody.

Chronic pyelonephritis is an insidious disease that may or may not be preceded by signs of acute infection. When the disease is of long duration, you will see weight loss and signs of *kidney failure*. If found before irreversible changes occur in the kidneys (e.g., during a periodic health checkup), treatment may prevent complications.

Treatment: The urine should be cultured. Antibiotics that concentrate in the urine are selected on the basis of bacterial sensitivity testing. Chronic pyelonephritis should be treated for at least six weeks.

NEPHRITIS AND NEPHROSIS

Nephritis is an inflammation of the kidneys regardless of cause. **Chronic interstitial nephritis** is perhaps the most common form, but even this may not be a single disease but the result of various toxins, drugs, poisons or viruses.

Glomerulonephritis is an inflammatory disease affecting the filtering mechanism of the kidneys. The disease appears to be related to a malfunction of the cat's immune system and is found in association with *feline leukemia, feline infectious peritonitis, feline progressive polyarthritis* and certain types of cancer.

Amyloidosis is a rare disorder in which a substance called *amyloid* is deposited in the cat's kidneys and other organs.

Nephrosis refers to kidney diseases accompanied by destruction of nephrons and loss of functioning kidney cells. In the *nephrotic syndrome*, protein leaks through the kidney filtering system in a large amount and is lost in the urine. This results in abnormally low serum proteins. Protein in the serum maintains osmotic pressure that keeps fluid from passing out of the bloodstream into the cat's tissues. Because of low serum protein, there is fluid accumulation beneath the skin of the legs (*edema*) and inside the abdomen (*ascites*). The signs are like those of *right heart failure*. Laboratory studies will distinguish between these conditions.

Treatment: Nephritis and nephrosis are not usually recognized until a cat develops signs of uremia. Abdominal ultrasound and a kidney biopsy may be required to make an exact diagnosis. Steroids and special diets may be of temporary help (see treatment of *Kidney Failure*).

KIDNEY FAILURE (UREMIC POISONING)

Kidney failure is defined as inability of the kidneys to remove waste products from the blood. The buildup of toxic wastes produces the signs and symptoms of uremic poisoning. Kidney failure can come on acutely or occur gradually over weeks or months.

Causes of *acute* kidney failure include

1. A blockage in the lower urinary tract associated with *Feline Urologic Syndrome* or congenital bladder defect.

2. Trauma to the abdomen, especially when accompanied by pelvic fracture and rupture of the bladder or urethra.

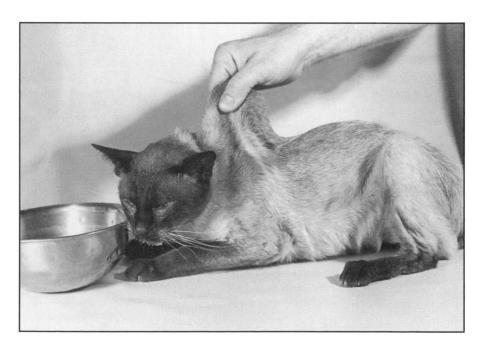

Kidney failure, showing weight loss, dehydration, depression and mouth ulcerations.

3. Shock, when due to sudden blood loss or rapid dehydration.

4. *Arterial thromboembolism* (a blood clot blocking the artery), particularly when both renal arteries are obstructed.

5. *Heart failure*, when associated with a persistently low blood pressure and reduced blood flow to the kidneys.

6. Poisonings, especially that caused by ingestion of antifreeze.

Causes of *chronic* kidney failure include

1. Nephritis and nephrosis.

2. Infectious diseases, especially feline infectious peritonitis and feline leukemia.

3. Toxins. Antibiotics that are poisonous to the kidneys when given for prolonged periods or in high doses are Polymyxin B, Gentamicin, Amphotericin B and Kanamycin. The heavy metals mercury, lead and thallium are nephrotoxic.

4. The aging process. Most elderly cats if they live long enough will have some degree of kidney insufficiency.

Cats with kidney diseases do not begin to show signs of uremia until 70 percent of their nephrons are destroyed. Thus, a considerable amount of damage occurs before any signs are noted.

One of the first signs of kidney failure is an increase in the frequency of voiding. Because the cat is voiding frequently, it might be assumed that the kidneys are functioning properly. Actually, the kidneys are no longer able to conserve water. Cats will go to the litter box several times a day and may begin to make mistakes in the house. This large urine output must be compensated for by increased fluid intake, and the cat will drink a lot more than usual. As renal function continues to deteriorate, the cat begins to retain ammonia, nitrogen, acids and other waste products in the bloodstream and tissues (*uremic poisoning*). Blood chemistries will determine the exact levels of these metabolic products.

Signs of uremia are apathy and sluggishness, loss of appetite and weight, dry hair coat, a brownish discoloration to the surface of the tongue and ulcers on the gums and tongue. The breath may have an ammonia-like odor. Vomiting, diarrhea, anemia and episodes of gastrointestinal bleeding can occur. Terminally, the cat falls into a coma.

The outlook for a cat with kidney failure depends on a number of factors. *Acute* kidney failure can be reversed if the underlying cause can be corrected before it produces permanent damage to the nephrons.

Treatment: Your veterinarian may want to make an exact diagnosis by ordering special tests, including abdominal ultrasound, or by performing exploratory surgery and biopsy. This helps to determine whether the disease is potentially reversible.

Most cases of chronic kidney failure occur in cats that have sustained irreversible damage to the kidneys. However, these cats may still have many happy months or years of life ahead with proper treatment. It is extremely important to be sure these cats take in enough water to compensate for large urine outputs. A supply of fresh, clean water should be available at all times.

The diet of a uremic cat should be of high quality but lower in protein to minimize the amount of nitrogen that must be excreted by the kidneys. Special diets (such as Hill's *Feline k/d*) are available through your veterinarian. Large amounts of B vitamins are lost in the urine of uremic cats. These losses should be replaced by giving Vitamin B supplements. Sodium bicarbonate tablets may be indicated to correct an acid/base imbalance. A phosphorous binder such as *Amphogel* may be prescribed to lower the serum phosphorous.

A uremic cat that becomes ill, dehydrated or fails to drink enough water may suddenly decompensate (*uremic crisis*). The cat should be hospitalized and rehydrated with appropriate intravenous fluids and balanced electrolyte solutions.

Some exercise is good for a uremic cat, but stressful activity should be avoided.

TUMORS

Kidney tumors are rare in cats. *Lymphosarcoma* is the most common. The majority of cats with lymphosarcoma of the kidney are FeLV positive. Therefore, when a growth or mass occurs in the kidney, the prime consideration is *feline leukemia*.

CONGENITAL DEFECTS

Cats may be born with malformations of the kidneys. They include cystic kidneys, malpositions and incomplete development. Such defects are often accompanied by abnormalities in the reproductive tract. Severe defects produce neonatal death. Others do not produce symptoms until later in life, when kidney damage reaches the point of failure.

Congenital obstructions in the urinary tract can cause swollen or infected kidneys. It may be difficult to tell whether the condition is congenital or acquired without special examinations. This could make a difference in treatment. Veterinary workup is desirable.

The popular Persian with a long fine-textured coat, full mane and tail, massive rounded head with short nose and small wide-set ears gives the impression of strength and dignity.   —Sidney Wiley

15

Sex and Reproduction

BREEDING

Pedigreed Cats

The majority of cats living as household pets are not pedigreed. They are born of parents who are themselves unregistered and, in most cases, are of mixed ancestry. Such cats are called mixed breeds or freebreds. But certainly, a freebred kitten is every bit as likely to be a pleasing companion as one with blue-ribbon ancestry.

For pedigreed cat owners, there is the distinction of owning a cat with a very distinguished family background and one that conforms to a set standard, *which is essential if serious breeding is anticipated*. There are also those who are attracted to the body, form, expression, coat coloring or some other characteristic of a particular breed. What constitutes a cat breed can be a matter of interpretation. In a practical sense it is a group of cats having in particular a unique body conformation and structure, color or pattern of coat, hair type and geographic origin.

Whereas the selective breeding of dogs for many centuries has resulted in the establishment of well-defined breeds based on similarities of head type, size and body structure, the physical differences among cats are not so pronounced because until the middle of the last century, cats were kept primarily for companionship and general utility. Little regard was given to selecting for features that would set one cat breed apart from another.

The Siamese is an elegant breed with a long wedge-shaped head, slanted vivid blue eyes and large pointed ears.

—Sidney Wiley

The first breed of cat recognized in America was the Maine Coon, developed from a hardy farm cat originally brought to New England by early British immigrants. The citizens of Maine were proud of these large, handsome longhaired cats and kept pedigree records of parentage long before cat registries were started.

The Himalayan is a "manufactured" breed having the head type and full coat of the Persian along with the pale coloring and darker parts of the Siamese.

—Sidney Wiley

The Burmese also is a created breed derived from Siamese and Asiatic crosses. The short rounded head, wide-set ears and almond-shaped eyes give the breed a distinctive expression.
—Sidney Wiley

The advent of cat exhibitions in Great Britain and North America provided further incentive for breeding cats to meet certain physical and aesthetic requirements. As the merits of an individual animal were judged against those of another of the same general type, the need to develop new Standards to describe the ideal for each breed was realized. Later, cat fanciers became dedicated to maintaining these Standards. There are at least 37 recognized cat breeds and as many color varieties and patterns. Features that distinguish one breed from another can be found in the

The tailless Manx has a distinctive appearance. The breed originated on the Isle of Man in the Irish Sea as a result of a spontaneous mutation. Lack of a tail is no handicap. The Manx is known as a fast runner and agile climber.
—Sidney Wiley

The American Shorthair is an exceptionally strong and hardy breed. Popular as a dependable mouser, this breed has been a permanent resident of American farms for hundreds of years. Its ancestors may have reached America aboard the Mayflower.
—Sidney Wiley

Scottish Folds first appeared in Scotland as the result of a spontaneous mutation in the 1960s. The uniquely folded ears, short nose and large round eyes give the head an almost completely round look, much like the British Shorthair.   —Sidney Wiley

Abyssinians are said to be direct descendants of the Sacred Cats of Egypt. With a medium-sized, lithe and graceful body, the cat has a structure that is midway between compact and lengthy. —Sidney Wiley

shape of the face and ears; the length and character of the coat; the color and distribution of the markings; and the differences in body length, size and bone structure.

Registration. While the American Kennel Club serves as the largest official registry for dogs in the United States, in the cat fancy there are a number of such organizations, both here and abroad, which recognize and register various cat breeds. Many countries, such as Great Britain, have a single official organization (the *Governing Council of the Cat Fancy*)—while other countries have several, at times formed on regional lines or by fanciers who disagree with the policies of a particular organization. In the United States there are several such organizations. They are listed in the APPENDIX. *The Cat Fanciers' Association* (CFA) is the largest and oldest in the United States. The CFA has a large membership, as does the *International Cat Association (TICA)*.

Each organization has separate registering procedures. Cross recognition of pedigrees and Standards for particular breeds may vary from one organization to another. In addition, the organizations do not always agree with each other about what constitutes a distinct breed as opposed to a color variety within a breed. You can write to these organizations to receive further information. Cat clubs, breeders and veterinarians also can provide advice.

Cat registration statistics from CFA show that the Persian is the most popular breed with 48,000 registered during the past year, followed, in order, by the Maine Coon (3,500), Siamese (3,000), Abyssinian (2,400), Exotic (1,400), Scottish Fold (1,300), Oriental Shorthair (1,200), American Shorthair (1,150) and others. The breed with the fewest registrations was the Selkirk Rex (30). If you wish to register your cat with the CFA or some other organization, the individual must have a pedigree, usually four generations, showing that all ancestors are registered and thus attested to be representative specimens of the breed. If you purchase a pedigreed kitten, the breeder should provide you with such a pedigree. He or she may already have registered the litter. In that case you should receive a form that can be filled out and sent to the registering agency, a step necessary to enroll your individual kitten.

GENETICS AND PLANNED BREEDING

The domestic cat has 38 chromosomes, and each chromosome contains more than 25,000 genes. Although this permits a vast array of potential combinations, only a small number are actually concerned with the bodily features that together define a breed or variety. The great majority are simply responsible for the smooth functioning of the many aspects of the cat's physiology.

Heredity is the random combination of countless genes. The smallest combination of genes that can determine an inherited trait is a *pair*. A pair is called an **allele.** One gene is inherited from each parent. When they combine to form the allele, the *dominant* gene is the one that determines the expression of the trait. The other gene is called a *recessive*.

For example, if a kitten inherits a dominant gene for black coat and a recessive gene for blue, the coat will be black. *Recessive genes can determine a trait too, but only when paired together.* A kitten inheriting *two recessive* genes for a blue coat will be blue. Still other genes are *additive*, the trait being expressed by the combined effects of two or more.

When both genes in an allele are identical, the cat is said to be *homozygous* for the physical trait the allele determines. When they are different, the cat is *heterozygous.* The stud and queen are equally responsible for determining the inheritance of their kittens. When both parents have identical homozygous alleles, either dominant or recessive, it does not matter how the genes sort becasue all the kittens will inherit the same allele, and all will express the same physical traits as their parents.

In essence, this is the strategy behind most planned breeding programs. The relationship between the various breeding individuals is kept rather close to concentrate the desired genes in the breeding stock. The method is called **inbreeding.** Close inbreeding involves the mating of parent to offspring and brother to sister. Less close is the mating of half-blood relations such as half-brother and sister, grandparent and grandchild, and cousins. *Inbreeding is neither good nor bad. It is a process that exposes both good and bad qualities in the stock.* If the strain does carry a mutant recessive gene (more likely to be harmful than beneficial), it more likely to become apparent with inbreeding. This might be a disaster in the short term, but the negative trait's exposure in the long term is in the best interest of the breed.

A number of different breeds and varieties of the domestic cat have evolved through the accidental or spontaneous appearance of *mutant genes*. Mutant genes occur rarely, perhaps once in one million offspring. Accordingly, it is not surprising that cat breeders have pursued only about 20 such mutations as breeds despite the large number of cats bred each year. When mutant genes do occur, they are passed along like any others and follow the same rules. Most, but not all, are recessive. The most important mutant genes for breeders are those producing distinctive coat colors. There are only 12 of these, but in various combinations they are responsible for a wide range of cat breeds and varieties. The length and texture of the coat is another essential feature of many breeds. There are at least five such coat-determining mutants that have been adopted. A few breeds are based on a bodily characteristic caused by a single mutant gene. Best known is the Manx breed in which a dominant gene causes the tail to be shortened or absent.

Desirable and undesirable traits can be caused by both dominant and recessive genes. The Scottish Fold breed, for example, is based on the expression of a single dominant gene that causes the tip of the ear to bend forward, giving the characteristic look. A completely unrelated dominant gene affecting all breeds is the gene for extra toes (*polydactyly*). Extra toes, sometimes as many as seven, are usually found on the front feet.

A dominant gene that may be associated with deleterious side effects is the gene for the completely white coat. This gene also predisposes to a form of deafness that affects one or both ears. Although deafness is more common in white cats with blue eyes, it also occurs in white cats with orange ones.

In the typical short-coated cat, the length of the guard hair is about five centimeters. In contrast, the silky abundant coat of a longhaired show specimen may exceed twice that length. This difference is caused by a recessive gene that appears to prolong the period of growth in hair follicles, so the hair reaches a greater length before entering the resting phase. Selective breeding over many generations for this longhaired homozygous recessive coat trait has resulted in the fuller and silkier coat in Persians and other long-coated breeds.

An example of the *additive effect of multiple genes* is seen in the range of eye colors typical of many cats. The colors orange, yellow, hazel and green are determined by additive genes. In the Siamese and white breeds, however, eye color is determined by single genes. Body structure and conformation is another multiple-gene effect. In various combinations, polygenes influence the rate of bone growth, the development of muscle and deposition of fat.

Breeding cats to a high degree of excellence demands careful attention to detail and great patience. The modern breeder has far more information on cat genetics than in the past and also has the product of many generations of selective breeding on which to base a successful program.

The object of any breeding program is to preserve the essential qualities and distinct attributes of the breed. Accordingly, a thorough understanding of the breed Standard is a basic requirement. Pedigrees are important because they are the means to study bloodlines and learn the relationships between the various individuals. They are of the greatest value when the individual cats are known or actually have been seen. *A pedigree only assures that the animals are registered specimens of the breed. It does not testify to the quality of the cats in question.*

Championships do indicate merit and do give some indication of quality. However, they are not always completely informative about the overall superiority of the individuals listed. Some championships are won through the accident of less than normal quality in the competition. The opposite is also true; some cats do not win their medals because of lack of exposure. Since it is the genetic potential of ancestors that determines success, they should possess outstanding qualities worthy of being passed on to offspring. The breeder should possess a knowledge of the virtues and faults of all cats in the pedigree for at least three generations. He or she should have the judgment and experience to pick the best kittens and the willingness to eliminate, as breeding stock, all defective or substandard specimens.

Close inbreeding for three to four generations generally leads to fixing of type, after which further improvement becomes more difficult. At this point the vitality of the strain may begin to suffer. There could be increased incidence of reproductive failure or a lessened resistance to disease. Most breeders have found that it is wise to bring in new blood. The use of a tom from a different bloodline may be considered. This produces an *outcross* litter and "reshuffles" the genes that have tended to become fixed in a more or less predictable manner through previous inbreeding. An improvement in the health and vigor of the resulting kittens may be apparent from the time they are born without the risks of breeding from unknown ancestry. These kittens are then bred back into the original strain. A single outcross can be advantageous—but the continuous use of outcrosses or the mating of animals who are not related with the hope of finding complimentary qualities is rarely rewarding. It merely breaks up a carefully built genetic constitution and nullifies any progress that has been made in improving the strain.

THE QUEEN

Queen is the name given to a breeding female. If you are planning to breed pedigreed cats, it is best to get a good female kitten with an outstanding pedigree. *It is not a good idea to start with the stud.* The management of a stud requires considerable experience and expertise; if he does not have a reputation and at least a grand championship, it is not likely that he will attract many good queens for breeding. It is equally unwise to buy unrelated male and female kittens hoping that when they mature, they will be suitable breeding partners.

Before making the decision to breed your female, give careful thought to the effort and expense in producing a litter of healthy and active kittens. It can be both time consuming and expensive. Many pedigreed kittens cannot be sold locally. This means advertising and the effort and cost of finding just the right home for them. *If your queen is not the quality to be bred, she should be spayed* (see *Birth Control*).

It is safe to breed a queen on her second heat, *after* she is 10 to 12 months old. At this age she is physically and emotionally mature enough to adjust to motherhood. The repeat mating of a queen depends on the size of her litters, her general health and nutrition, the adequacy of her quarters and the demand for her kittens. Overweight queens and those who are depleted by improper diet, excessive breeding and unsanitary living conditions are unsuitable brood matrons. Often, they do not come into season regularly, are difficult to breed, experience problems during delivery and are unable to properly care for their kittens.

Once you decide to mate your queen, take her to your veterinarian for a physical checkup. She should be examined to see that her vaginal opening is of normal size and that there are no obstructions to successful mating. Be sure to have her checked for periodontitis and dental infections. Bacteria from the queen's mouth can be transmitted to newborn kittens during biting of the umbilical cord. This is one cause of serious navel infections.

A brood queen, if not vaccinated within a year, should be given a *feline panleukopenia, feline viral rhinotracheitis* and *feline calicivirus* booster shot *before* being bred. Her *rabies vaccination* should be current. If she has not been tested for *Feline Leukemia* (FeLV) and *Feline Infectious Peritonitis* (FIP), you should have these tests performed. Indications to test for and vaccinate against these diseases are discussed in the INFECTIOUS DISEASES chapter. A stool test will show whether she has intestinal parasites. If found, they should be vigorously treated. A queen with active worm infestation is less likely to give birth to healthy kittens.

Part of the breeding preparation is to choose the stud well in advance. The show record of a prospective stud may include a Championship or a Grand Championship. If he is a proven producer, his offspring's quality becomes a matter of considerable importance. If he has sired outstanding kittens, particularly out of several different queens, you have strong evidence of his dominance. The number of show

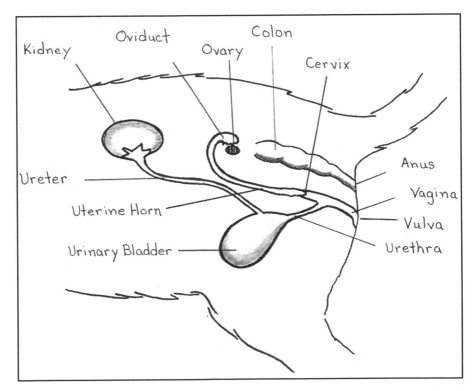

Female genitourinary system.   —Rose Floyd

winners he has produced is also important. However, as there can be a lapse of several years before a mating and a championship, some of the best producers are often not recognized until well after they have stopped producing.

If your queen came from a breeder, it is a good idea to talk to that breeder who should be familiar with the strengths and weaknesses that lie behind your queen before making a final selection. This knowledge can be vitally important in choosing a compatible mate. Some breeding catteries offer stud services. If you have an outstanding queen from that bloodline, you may give serious thought to using a stud from that same strain to reinforce the best qualities of your queen.

It is the responsibility of the breeder (the owner of the queen) to come to a clear understanding with the stud owner concerning breeding terms. Usually a stud fee is paid at the time of mating, or the stud's owner may take the pick of the litter, a kitten of his or her own choosing. The age of the kitten should be agreed on. If the queen does not conceive, the stud's owner may offer a return service at no extra charge. However, this is not obligatory. Terms vary with the circumstances and the policies of the stud owner. If these are in writing, there will be no misunderstandings later.

THE STUD

Stud (or *Tom*) is the name given to a breeding male. The age at which a male cat reaches sexual maturity and begins to produce sperm varies from 6 to 18 months, the average being about 9 months. Two months later, sperm is present in the collecting tubules, so the male has reached sexual maturity and can now fertilize a queen.

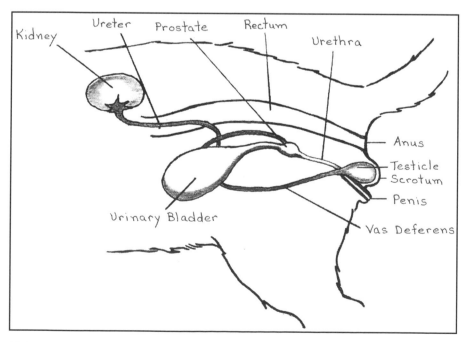

Male genitourinary system.   —Rose Floyd

Ordinarily, a stud should not be used for breeding before he is a year old. If he is going to be shown, it may be two years before he is available.

An active tom has a natural instinct to spray his surroundings with strong smelling urine. A pen with a house and spacious run is therefore highly desirable. A stud should be maintained in top physical condition with regular exercise, routine health checkups and a sound diet. All tests and vaccinations, as described for the queen, should be up to date for the tom.

First matings should be with queens who have already had a litter. The mating of two inexperienced animals can be fraught with difficulty and frustration. A stud can be used for breeding for three consecutive days or three times in one week.

If you own a male cat that is not of breeding quality, he should be neutered (see *Birth Control*).

THE HEAT CYCLE (ESTRUS)

Queens vary in the age at which they first *call* or *go into heat*. Some breeds (such as the Siamese) may call as early as five months. Others, particularly the longhaired breeds such as Persians are not sexually mature until 10 months or older.

Mating Season and Length of Heat Cycles. The mating season in cats is determined by a number of factors, among them the length of daylight, temperature and presence of other cats. When there are 12 hours of daylight and other conditions are optimal, the hormonal system is activated, and the queen begins the reproductive cycle. The mating season of cats in the Northern Hemisphere is from March to September. Cats in the Southern Hemisphere cycle in calendar months opposite to those in the Northern.

Throughout the breeding season, queens go into and out of heat several times but do not always display estrous behavior at regular intervals. Often they exhibit continuous heat cycles in early spring (averaging 14 to 21 days from the beginning of one cycle to the beginning of the next), followed in late spring by cycles that are farther apart. Each queen establishes her own normal rhythm. Abnormal heat cycles are discussed in the section *Infertility*.

Signs of Heat. The estrous or reproductive cycle of cats has four distinct stages. Signs of one may overlap those of the next. Furthermore, there is individual variation in length of stages from one queen to another. Accordingly, it is not always possible to ascertain when a queen is most likely to conceive. Vaginal cytology, analyzed by those experienced in the technique, is helpful in predicting the moment of peak fertility in the difficult queen (see *Shy Breeders—Cats That Won't Mate*). The following are the four stages of the heat cycle:

Proestrus. This stage of heat is the first, lasting from one to two days. You may notice that the vulva enlarges slightly and appears somewhat moist, but this usually is not apparent. The queen shows increased appetite and restlessness, utters short low calls and displays more than usual affection for her owner. At this time she begins to attract toms—but refuses to mate. Proestrus has been described as a period of courtship during which exposure to the male acts as a hormonal stimulus that brings on full heat. This belief stems from the observation that in street matings, where male companionship is common, the conception rate is higher than in catteries, where courtship is less spontaneous.

Estrus. The characteristic stance of a queen in heat.

If you do not want your queen to become pregnant, take steps at the first sign of proestrus to prevent unwanted pregnancy (see Accidental Pregnancy).

Estrus. The second stage is the period of sexual receptivity. It is what breeders refer to as *heat*, or the *call*, lasting four to six days. The queen begins to make more noise and her meow is louder and more frequent. There is an obvious change in her behavior: She becomes much more affectionate toward people, weaves in and out and rubs against their legs, shakes her pelvis and rolls about on the floor. As the urge to mate becomes pronounced, her cries become alarming—sounding like those of an animal in pain. This is the call, which attracts toms from near and far.

To determine if your queen is receptive to mating, hold her by the scruff of the neck and stroke her down the back toward the base of her tail. If in heat, she will raise her hindquarters, switch her tail to the side and tread up and down with her hind feet.

Interestrus (Metestrus). The third stage lasts 7 to 14 days. During this stage the queen refuses to mate and aggressively rejects the male if mating is attempted.

What happens during interestrus depends on what happened during estrus: If a mating did not occur, the queen will remain in interestrus for 7 to 14 days and then start a new cycle beginning with proestrus. If sexual intercourse induced ovulation but the queen did not conceive, she will enter a period of pseudopregnancy lasting 36 days. See *False Pregnancy.* If sexual intercourse resulted in a pregnancy, her kittens will be delivered in 63 days.

Anestrus. The fourth stage of the sexual cycle is reproductive rest. In the Northern Hemisphere, this is a 90-day period from November through January.

HORMONAL INFLUENCES DURING ESTRUS

Pituitary Influence. Proestrus begins when the brain (*hypothalamus*) signals the pituitary gland to release FSH (*follicle stimulating hormone*), which causes the ovaries to produce the egg follicles that begin to make estrogen.

Physical stimulation of the queen's vagina by the male's penis during mating triggers another signal to the pituitary gland, causing it to release LH (luteinizing hormone). LH stimulates the ovaries to release the eggs (ovulation).

Ovarian Influence. Before ovulation, the ovarian follicles produce the female hormone estrogen, which prepares the queen's reproductive tract for mating and fertilization. Estrogen accounts for the physical and behavioral changes of the queen in heat.

After ovulation, the egg follicles become corpus luteum cysts and produce the pregnancy hormone *progesterone*. An important function of progesterone is to prepare the lining of the uterus to receive and support embryos. Removal of the ovaries during the first 50 days of pregnancy or inadequate output of progesterone from the ovaries during this period will result in abortion (see *Fetal Loss During Pregnancy*).

Ovulation. Cats are unusual in that they are *induced ovulators*. This means that unlike the dog and most other mammals, including women, cats do not ovulate spontaneously. Indeed, ovulation is induced by the act (or more accurately the multiple acts) of sexual intercourse, during which the vagina is stimulated by barblike projections on the penis.

Ovulation takes place 24 to 30 hours after intercourse. The time is variable. Some queens ovulate as early as 12 hours after intercourse. In most cases, four eggs are released from the ovaries, but this too is variable. Up to 18 kittens have been reported in a single litter.

It is possible to artificially induce ovulation by stimulating the queen's vagina with a plastic rod. This simulates a mating and induces a false pregnancy lasting 36 days. It is one method of bringing the queen out of heat (see *Birth Control*).

After the queen ovulates, she loses interest in sex and refuses to mate.

FERTILIZATION

Fertilization occurs in the fallopian tubes that lead from the ovaries to the uterus. The embryos implant in the wall of the uterus some 14 days after mating. While only one sperm can fertilize each egg, a queen that has mated with a number of different toms could produce a litter of kittens having different fathers. This phenomenon is called *superfecundity*.

Although ovulation and pregnancy normally suppress the estrous cycle, about 10 percent of queens go back into heat and may even be willing to breed. The act of mating may again induce ovulation, conceiving a second litter. The two litters can subsequently be born at the same time (in which case the second is premature and seldom survives), or the second litter can be born alive a few weeks after the first. This phenomenon is known as *superfetation*.

MATING

GETTING READY

Once the signs of estrus are confirmed, the owner of the stud should be notified. He or she may want the queen at once. This has the advantage of letting the queen settle into her new surroundings before the mating. If possible, take the queen to the stud yourself, transporting her in a suitable container or cage. If the distance is great, you may have to ship her by air. However, an airplane ride can be nerveracking and may upset the queen, putting her out of heat. A current rabies vaccination is required to ship a cat across state lines. The stud's owner may require a certificate showing that the queen has tested free of feline leukemia and feline infectious peritonitis.

Normal Mating Procedure

The method of introducing the cats can be modified to suit the circumstances. Ideally, the queen's container is placed in a pen close to the stud's. The door of her cage is opened to allow her to come out as she chooses and explore her surroundings. Once the queen approaches and begins to show interest in the stud, a gate is opened to allow the two to greet each other. A sexually receptive queen will allow the stud to approach her, touch noses, lick her face and investigate her genital area. This necessary ceremony of greeting and foreplay helps to initiate sexual arousal. In most cases it provides sufficient stimulus for a mature queen to adopt a characteristic position in which she crouches down, raises her pelvis and switches her tail to the side.

It is most important that the stud's owner (or someone familiar with the mating of cats) be present to observe the mating. Even when both cats are experienced, their courtship and mating can become quite violent. Some cats refuse to mate when a person is present. The owner should stay out of sight but in a position where he or she can observe the mating and step in quickly if it seems the pair is having a problem. If the queen is not aroused or not far enough along in estrus to be willing to breed, she will growl at the male and attempt to bite. The stud, on the other hand, may become quite aggressive if unable to get the queen into position for mounting. In either case the pair should be separated. A traumatic experience can be a serious setback to future attempts.

Once the female assumes the receptive position, the stud will approach from the rear and mount, clasping her sides with his front legs. He then seizes her neck with his teeth and treads up and down with his back feet. Insertion of the penis is

A protruded penis, showing the characteristic spines.

The mating sequence, showing the position of the receptive queen. The male mounts and seizes her by the nape of the neck. At the moment of ejaculation, the queen screams piercingly. The cats separate, and the queen srikes out with her claws.   —Sydney Wiley

accomplished with a few deep thrusts. Ejaculation takes place in 5 to 15 seconds. At the moment of ejaculation the male utters a low growl, and the queen screams piercingly. This dramatic sequence is followed by an almost explosive separation, in which the queen may turn and strike out at the stud with her teeth and claws as he jumps back and to the side. The aggressive behavior of the queen at the end of ejaculation may be caused by the withdrawal of the penis. There are numerous barblike projections on the penis that produce an intense and possibly painful stimulation of the queen's vagina. The stimulation appears necessary to trigger the mechanism that causes ovulation to occur 24 hours later (see *Ovulation*).

After the first mating, subsequent matings may occur. The second usually occurs within a few minutes. Others follow at more extended intervals. As ovulation usually does not occur with the first mating, it is recommended that the pair be left together and allowed to mate freely for one to two hours a day, for three consecutive days. (Among free-roaming cats, this pattern of courtship and mating might be repeated many times over several hours for up to three days.) After each mating episode, the queen exhibits an after-reaction. She rolls over a few times, relaxes and then begins to groom herself, paying special attention to her genital area.

After the mating session, the queen should be returned to her container or placed in a separate pen but not until she has passed through the rolling over and self-grooming stage. If disturbed too soon, she may inflict a painful scratch or bite on her handler. At this time, you should check the stud to be sure that his penis has returned to its sheath (see *Penis That Can't Retract*). Most breeders agree that two to three mating sessions are necessary to ensure success of ovulation and conception.

SHY BREEDERS—CATS THAT WON'T MATE

The most common cause of sexual reluctance is breeding at the wrong time in the estrous cycle (usually during proestrus). If the queen is sent to the stud, the resulting stress may send her off call. Most queens call again in one to two days, but some may take longer. If mating is attempted too early in the cycle, the queen will growl and attempt to bite the male. This is normal proestrus behavior, but some breeders might see it as a sign that the mating isn't going to take place.

If the queen is in the correct stage of her breeding cycle yet refuses to mate, the problem is most likely psychological. A pampered female raised as a house pet may be a shy breeder because of inadequate prior social contact with members of her own species. Mate preference, too, can be a determining factor. Some females will not mate with a timid stud; others prefer studs of a certain breed or even a specific coat color.

Sexual aggression in the male fluctuates at different times of the year, usually in association with the breeding season of the female. Male cats are territorial and mark their territory with the scent of urine. A male cat in unfamiliar surroundings may feel less dominant and show less interest in sex. Similarly, a gentle and friendly tom may lack the sexual aggressiveness to mate a dominant queen. Less commonly, a tom with a low libido may be suffering from impotence or a hormone deficiency. Obesity, whether caused by hormone disease or overfeeding, may be associated with reduced sex drive and may also interfere with the mechanics of mating. These subjects are discussed in *Diseases of the Male Genital Tract*.

Unsuccessful attempts to introduce the penis into the vagina can be associated with incompatible body lengths. The male's body is normally shorter than the female's. If this discrepancy is too great, the stud, while grasping the nape of the queen's neck with his teeth, may not be able to align his penis with her vulva and vagina. Occasionally, an inexperienced stud will grasp a female too far back (not at the nape of her neck) and thus will be too far away to accomplish intercourse. Similarly, a cat with dental disease or a sore mouth may be unable to take firm hold of the queen's neck.

If a stud appears unwilling to mate a receptive queen, examine his penis. It must be capable of fully protruding from its sheath to enter the vagina. Protrusion of the penis can be restricted by a ring of hair caught in the spines and wrapped around the shaft of the penis (see *Paraphimosis*).

Treatment: When the queen refuses to accept the stud, she should be tried again in 24 hours. A successful mating may take place. If not, a hormone or psychological problem may exist. Hormone problems are discussed in the section *Fertility Problems in the Female*. Vaginal cytology can be used to determine if the heat cycle is normal. The process of taking the smear may induce ovulation but only if the queen is in estrus. If the result is positive (showing estrus, the correct stage for mating), the pair should be mated at once. If intercourse occurs, a pregnancy should result. However, if the queen still won't mate, a psychological block can be inferred. Then, a decision is needed about whether to proceed with a forced mating or turn instead to AI (see *artificial insemination*).

A forced mating can take place if the queen is held by her owner and is *well tranquilized*. However, forced matings do not always result in kittens. The required sedation may depress the stimulus to ovulate. Forced matings and those accomplished by AI must be timed to coincide with the estrous phase. Vaginal cytology is essential.

INFERTILITY

When the queen fails to conceive kittens after a successful mating, either the stud or the queen can be at fault.

FERTILITY PROBLEMS IN THE MALE

A common cause of reduced fertility in the male is excessive use. Most virile toms can be bred three times a week. If bred more often, they should be rested for a week. When a stud is much in demand, a single mating and low fertility may be the cause of a missed pregnancy. A stud used at regular intervals should receive a high-protein balanced diet.

High fertility tends to be inherited. Some strains produce studs that for generations are known to sire large healthy litters. Toms that have not been used at stud for some time may have a low sperm count due to sexual inactivity. During a second mating, 48 hours after the first, the quality of semen is often much better. It is better to use a stud at regular intervals. Infrequent matings, instead of saving up sperm, often lead to decreased production. If a stud is known to have a low sperm count, it may be better to use him at least twice a week on the queen.

As a stud grows older (beyond eight years), his fertility may diminish because of a reduction in sperm number and quality. This may result in smaller litters, but the quality of the kittens will not be affected. After 12 years of age, testicular atrophy with absence of sperm is common. A male whose testicles fail to descend into the scrotum or in whom descent was delayed will have an absent or reduced sperm count (see *Undescended Testicles*).

Prolonged elevation of body temperature depresses sperm production. A tom recovering from a serious febrile illness may take several months to regain his normal sperm count. Some cats are less fertile in summer, especially when the weather is hot. An excess or deficiency of Vitamin A can induce sterility. Signs of deficiency are weight loss, loss of hair and night blindness. Vitamin A excess occurs among cats fed large amounts of raw liver.

Other causes of reduced fertility are close confinement, boredom, improper diet and lack of exercise. These factors assume importance in the marginally fertile individual.

Genetic and chromosomal abnormalities are infrequent causes of infertility. Male tortoise-shell cats (a rare mutation) are almost always sterile, as are male calico cats.

Other chromosome abnormalities are difficult to diagnose. Genetic investigations must be carried out at a school of veterinary medicine.

Infertility caused by *Diseases of the Male Genital Tract* is discussed later in this chapter.

Treatment: A semen analysis will determine if sperm are of normal number and quality. The procedure for collecting the sample is described in *Artificial Insemination*. Absence of sperm may be congenital or acquired. When some sperm are present, the stud's potency can often be improved by treating the underlying problem.

Impotence. In most cases, impotence, or lack of the male sex drive or libido, is caused by psychological factors (see *Shy Breeders—Cats That Won't Mate*). Many toms that live as household pets and receive lots of human affection lose interest in breeding. This is one reason why pedigreed-cat breeders prepare living quarters separate from the house for their breeding animals.

Hypothyroidism is a treatable condition that causes lack of vitality and sex drive; it can also lower a cat's sperm count. It is managed by thyroid replacement therapy.

The male sex drive is under the influence of *testosterone*, which is produced by the testicles. Rarely, impotence is caused by failure of the testicles to produce this hormone. One explanation is that just before or after birth the male kitten receives a surge of testosterone that conditions or masculinizes his brain. If this surge does not occur, the male kitten develops a female behavior pattern and responds to the female hormone instead of the male. Serum testosterone levels can be used to determine if impotence is caused by a deficiency of testosterone. A semen analysis will only indicate if the testicles are sexually developed and able to produce sperm. *Cells that make the sperm are not the same ones that make testosterone.* Therefore, a fertile male can be impotent, and a sterile male can be quite willing and able to mate with a queen.

Treatment: Impotency due to hormonal rather than behavioral causes may improve with the administration of testosterone when given before breeding. Unfortunately, the dose that activates the male libido also depresses sperm production. It should be used with caution.

Catnip may increase the sexual aggressiveness of some males.

Fertility Problems in the Female

Infertility in the female can be caused by abnormal estrous cycles. Fetal loss during pregnancy is another cause of infertile outcome.

Abnormal Heat Cycles

Heat cycles of queens are quite variable. In general, each queen establishes her own normal rhythm. As a queen grows older, heat periods become less regular and in some cases will not be accompanied by ovulation. Other factors that adversely affect a queen's estrous cycle are improper diet, environmental stress, and ill health.

Anestrus. If a queen remains in anestrus and does not cycle during the breeding season, consider one of the following:

Lack of photostimulation. As discussed above, the length of daylight hours triggers the beginning of the estrous cycle. Less than twelve hours of light per day is often insufficient to initiate the cycle. Insufficient photostimulation is more likely to occur with indoor cats.

Male factor. Queens that live alone may not exhibit estrous behavior due to lack of social exposure to others of their kind, especially males.

Silent estrus. Many cases thought to be lack of heat are really a normal heat in which the queen does not exhibit estrous behavior. A queen low in the social hierarchy of a group of cats, for example, may fail to exhibit estrous behavior until or unless she is removed from the group. Silent heat is diagnosed by vaginal cytology and blood estrogen levels.

Hypothyroidism. This is an uncommon cause of anestrus in cats. When present, other indications of thyroid deficiency may or may not be observed. The diagnosis is established by a blood test. It is treated by giving thyroid hormone.

Absence of ovaries. A previous hysterectomy with removal of the ovaries is a possibility when the prior medical history is unknown. An uncommon cause of estrogen deficiency is *ovarian dysgenesis*, in which the ovaries do not develop to sexual maturity. The vulva and vagina remain small and undeveloped. Heat does not occur because of low estrogen level.

Cystic Ovaries (Cystic ovarian follicles). This condition is caused by excess output of estrogen from the ovaries. A queen that is permitted to call repeatedly but is never mated can, after several heat cycles, develop cysts on her ovaries. These cysts produce an abnormally high estrogen level that suppresses ovulation and also produces *cystic endometrial hyperplasia*, which prevents implantation. The queen may enter a continuous or prolonged heat. She becomes irritable, inclined to fight other cats (both male and female) and refuses to mate—or conversely, will mate frequently (nymphomania) but be unable to conceive.

Ovarian cysts are treated by removing the ovaries or the cysts. When kittens are desired, removing the cysts may be sufficient to correct the problem. The queen may subsequently become pregnant. If breeding is not desired, both ovaries and the uterus should be removed (see *Spaying*).

The administration of estrogen-containing preparations used in the treatment of some skin diseases and feline behavior disorders can produce the same effects as cystic ovaries.

Failure to Ovulate. A common cause of failure to ovulate is breeding too late in the estrous cycle. As a rule, a queen should be bred no later than the middle of her estrus: that is, by day 4 of her period of receptivity to the male. It is equally important to breed the queen several times during this time of receptivity since a single mating is rarely sufficient to induce ovulation. Ovulation is followed by a rise in the serum progesterone level. This test is positive 7 days after estrus and remains so until day 40. If the rise did not occur, ovulation did not take place.

Treatment of Abnormal Heat Cycles: A female slow to come into heat may do so if exposed to light for 14 hours a day or when placed with another queen in estrus. In such cases, the estrus of one may cause the other to call. Their heat cycles may even become synchronized. Exposure to the male through a period of socialization and foreplay is an important initiator of estrus.

Failure to come into heat can sometimes be treated successfully by giving follicle stimulating hormone (FSH) for four to five days. If follicle development occurs and the queen goes into heat and accepts the male, ovulation will usually occur. The queen should be bred several times during the induced estrus. Human chorionic gonadotropin (HCG) is sometimes used after mating to insure the likelihood of ovulation.

Further treatment depends on identifying the cause. A complete workup includes physical examination, vaginal cytology, hormone assays and possible exploratory surgery. A feline leukemia virus test is essential in all cases of feline infertility.

Fetal Loss During Pregnancy

Fetal loss may take place even before implantation of the embryos in the wall of the uterus because of unfavorable conditions in the lining of the uterus or genetic defects in the fertilized eggs. Early embryonic death is most commonly associated with the *Feline Leukemia Virus. Cystic endometrial hyperplasia* can cause early embryonic deaths as well as poor conception rates. *Taurine deficiency* causes abortions and the delivery of low birth weight kittens.

Pregnancy can be detected at three to four weeks by palpating the queen's abdomen (see PREGNANCY AND KITTENING: *Determining Pregnancy*). A blood or urine test, commonly used to diagnose early pregnancy in women, is not available for cats. If the queen is found to be pregnant and subsequently does not deliver kittens, one of two things must have happened: She either miscarried (aborted) or resorbed her kittens.

Signs of *abortion* are vaginal bleeding and the passage of tissue. These signs may not be observed if the queen is fastidious. Her owner will not be aware that she has lost her litter until later.

Fetal resorption occurs before the seventh week of gestation. The developing kittens are absorbed back into the mother's body and no longer felt in the abdomen. Occasionally, you may notice a slight pinkish vaginal discharge.

Death of kittens in utero can be due to inadequate output of progesterone. During the first half of pregnancy, developing kittens are supported by progesterone made in the ovaries. At about day 40 of gestation, this function is taken over by the placenta. Should this transition fail to occur, there is insufficient progesterone to support the pregnancy. Placental insufficiency tends to occur with subsequent pregnancies and becomes a consideration when a queen repeatedly loses her litters.

A well recognized cause of *habitual fetal loss* is the *feline leukemia virus* (FeLV). This is particularly important when an entire breeding colony is affected. Reproductive failure in a cattery may be the first indication of such infection. Most stud owners will not accept a queen for breeding unless she has a certificate showing she has been tested and found free of feline leukemia.

The virus of *feline infectious peritonitis* (FIP) has been implicated as a cause of an entire spectrum of reproductive failure that includes repeated abortions, fetal resorption, stillbirths and kittens that sicken and die shortly after birth.

Causes of *sporadic miscarriages* include emotional upsets, violent exercise (such as jumping from heights), a blow to the abdomen and improper feeding and prenatal care. Care and feeding of the pregnant queen is discussed in the chapter PREGNANCY AND KITTENING.

Treatment of Habitual Fetal Loss: Loss of kittens during pregnancy is an indication for a thorough medical evaluation. The queen should be screened for *feline leukemia virus* and *feline infectious peritonitis*—if these tests results are not current. Other causes of habitual abortion should be investigated including those related to *Diseases of the Female Genital Tract*. Queens with progesterone insufficiency can be treated during the next pregnancy by giving a weekly injection of long-acting progesterone, beginning a week before the anticipated abortion.

DISEASES OF THE MALE GENITAL TRACT

There are several disorders of the male genital tract that can lead to mating problems and, in some cases, cause infertility. Among them are orchitis, balanoposthitis, phimosis, paraphimosis, testicular hyperplasia and undescended testicles.

EXAMINATION OF THE PENIS

This is best carried out by raising the tail to expose the perineum below the anus. A cat's penis points backward. The glans or head of the penis can be exposed by retracting the sheath that covers it. Grasp it between your thumb and forefinger and slide it forward (toward the cat's head). The tip will protrude. Reverse the process to cover the glans.

In a fully mature tom, the shaft of the penis has barblike projections that slant toward the base. After ejaculation, as the stud begins to withdraw his penis, these barbs cause intense stimulation of the queen's vagina. This initiates the release of a hormone, causing the queen to ovulate (see *Ovulation*). In the young tom and the neutered male, the penis is smooth.

INFECTION OF THE PREPUCE AND HEAD OF THE PENIS (BALANOPOSTHITIS)

Irritation of the foreskin and head of the penis can be caused by hair caught in the spines during mating. Frequent sexual activity can irritate the penis and foreskin. Awns or pieces of straw may become caught beneath the sheath. The irritation may be complicated by infection and abscess of the sheath. This makes intercourse painful or impossible.

On occasion, flies lay eggs in the infected tissue. The eggs hatch in a few days, producing maggots.

A cat suffering from balanoposthitis licks his penis and will have a purulent, foul-smelling discharge from his sheath.

Treatment: First, clip away hair near the foreskin. Push back the foreskin to expose the tip of the penis. Cleanse the area with dilute hydrogen peroxide solution or dilute *Betadine* solution and apply an antibiotic ointment (*Neomycin*; *Triple Antibiotic Ointment*). Slide the foreskin back over the tip of the penis. Repeat until all signs of discharge and inflammation are gone. If infection persists seek veterinary attention. Antibiotics or surgical cleansing under anesthesia may be required.

A ring of hair around the penis may prevent it from retracting back into the sheath.

Cats with balanoposthitis should not be used at stud. The infection can be transmitted to the female during mating.

STRICTURED FORESKIN—PENIS CAN'T PROTRUDE (PHIMOSIS)

In this condition, the opening in the foreskin is too small to let the penis extend. It may be so small that urine can escape only in small drops. Some cases are due to infection; others due to a birth defect.

When the problem is related to infection of the sheath, treatment of the infection, as previously described, may correct the phimosis. If not, surgery is necessary.

PENIS THAT CAN'T RETRACT (PARAPHIMOSIS)

In this condition the penis is unable to return to its former position inside the sheath. Long hair on the skin around the sheath may cause the foreskin to roll under so that it cannot slide. The barbs on the glans penis may collect hair from the queen during the mating process, forming a ring of hair that prevents the penis from retracting and also inhibits mating.

Paraphimosis can be prevented by cutting long hair around the prepuce before mating. A stud usually licks the tip of his penis after intercourse and removes any attached hair. A persistent ring of hair should be removed. Check the male after mating to be sure the penis has returned to its sheath.

Treatment: The penis should be returned to its normal position as quickly as possible to prevent permanent damage. Push the prepuce back on the shaft of the penis toward the cat's head, while rolling it out so the hairs are not caught. Lubricate the surface of the penis with mineral oil or olive oil. With one hand, gently draw the head of the penis toward you. With the other hand, slide the prepuce forward. If these measures are not immediately successful, notify your veterinarian. In most cases, it will be necessary to medicate the sheath twice a day as described under the treatment of *Infection of the Prepuce and Head of the Penis.*

Undescended Testicles

The testicles in kittens are thought to be descended into the scrotum at birth. Usually, they can be felt by six weeks of age.

Testicles that do not descend are called *cryptorchid*. A male with one cryptorchid testicle may be fertile. If both testicles are cryptorchid, the cat is sterile. The testicles should be of similar size and feel rather firm. Since much of the testicle's size is due to sperm-producing tissue, soft or small testicles in the sexually mature cat may to be deficient in sperm. Even though a tom with one undescended testicle may be capable of fertilizing a queen, he should not be used for breeding because the trait has a hereditary basis.

Cryptorchid cats should be neutered. An abdominal operation may be necessary to find and remove the testicles.

Testicular hypoplasia is the absence of sexual development of the testicles. If both testicles fail to develop, the cat is sterile and does not exhibit sexual behavior.

Infection of the Testicle (Orchitis)

The most frequent cause of orchitis is an infected cat bite wound of the scrotum. However, infections can be caused by penetrating wounds, frostbite, chemical and thermal burns, *feline infectious peritonitis* and *infections* involving the bladder, urethra and sheath of the penis.

Signs of orchitis are swelling and pain in the testicle. The testicle becomes enlarged, hard and tender to touch. The cat assumes a spread-legged stance with his belly tucked. Later the diseased testicle shrinks and becomes small and firm.

Since most cat bites and other puncture wounds are quite likely to become infected, even relatively minor-appearing injuries should be examined and treated by a veterinarian.

DISEASES OF THE FEMALE GENITAL TRACT

Vaginal Infection

Inflammation and infection of the vagina are rare in queens. Signs of vaginitis are licking of the vulva and discomfort when the vagina is examined. There may or may not be a vaginal discharge. Toms are sometimes attracted to queens with vaginitis, thereby giving the impression that the queen is in heat.

Bacterial infection of the vagina may spread to the bladder or uterus. Veterinary examination is necessary to confirm the diagnosis and determine the cause. An appropriate antibiotic is selected on the basis of culture and sensitivity tests. A queen with vaginitis should not be bred until her infection has been successfully treated.

Uterine Infection

Uterine infection in cats begins with a disease called *cystic endometrial hyperplasia*. The disease changes conditions inside the uterus and creates the potential for secondary bacterial infection: either *endometritis* or *pyometra*.

Cystic Endometrial Hyperplasia. In this condition, the *endometrium*, a layer of tissue lining the wall of the uterus, becomes thick and forms bubble-like cysts. These alterations are caused by the prolonged stimulatory effect of estrogen, produced by the ovarian follicles during estrus (see *Hormonal Influences During Estrus*). Queens who are allowed to cycle repeatedly during one or more breeding seasons but in whom ovulation is not induced by mating or artificial stimulation of the vagina are at increased risk as well as are queens over five years old who have never been pregnant.

Uncomplicated cystic endometrial hyperplasia causes few signs, although some queens may exhibit a bloody vaginal discharge.

Treatment: Pregnancy protects against cystic endometrial hyperplasia. When breeding is no longer desired, the treatment of choice is spaying.

When it is important to preserve fertility but interrupt breeding for one to two years, the queen can be housed in an artificial environment in which she is not exposed to the seasonal influences of daylight. Less than 10 hours of light in a 24-hour period prevents activation of the estrous cycle. The estrous cycle can also be suppressed by birth control drugs (see *Birth Control*).

Endometritis. Most cases are a sequel to cystic endometrial hyperplasia. The infection is limited to the lining of the uterus. Little pus is produced, but the endometrium becomes inflamed and infected. Endometritis occurs in an acute or chronic form:

A queen with *acute* endometritis exhibits listlessness, loss of appetite, fever and a bloody or puslike vaginal discharge. A severe infection may be life threatening.

A queen with *chronic* endometritis often appears in excellent health, has a normal heat period and is mated successfully—yet fails to conceive or loses her kittens during pregnancy—because the chronic infection creates unsuitable conditions for embryo implantation and growth. Suspect this condition when the queen is bred at the right time but fails to conceive on two or more cycles and when she is pregnant but fails to deliver healthy kittens.

Treatment: The vaginal discharge of *acute endometritis* is cultured and antibiotics are prescribed on the basis of sensitivity tests. They should be continued for three to four weeks. *Chronic* endometritis is difficult to diagnose and requires smears and cultures taken from the cervix. A uterine biopsy may be required.

Pus-filled Uterus (Pyometra). Like endometritis, pyometra usually develops from an underlying cystic endometrial hyperplasia complicated by bacterial infection. Pyometra differs from endometritis in that the inflammation of the wall of the uterus is less but the amount of pus in the cavity of the uterus is much greater.

An additional factor in the development of pyometra is the stimulatory effect of progesterone. This is why pyometra is more likely to occur in queens with cystic endometrial hyperplasia who subsequently ovulate and go on to develop corpus luteum cysts. These cysts produce high levels of progesterone (see *Hormonal Influences During Estrus*).

Pyometra is a life-threatening infection that occurs most often in queens over five years old; the average is seven or eight. Signs appear four to six weeks after the queen goes out of heat. A queen with pyometra refuses to eat, appears dull and lethargic, loses weight, runs a fever (but may have a normal temperature), drinks a great deal of water and urinates frequently. The abdomen is quite markedly distended and firm. This may suggest the possibility of either pregnancy or *feline infectious peritonitis* (the wet form of FIP), but the combination of a *severe illness* with a *distended abdomen* after a *heat period* will suggest the diagnosis of pyometra. An enlarged uterus can usually be detected by abdominal palpation. In the unusual case of abdominal enlargement without signs of illness, X rays and abdominal ultrasounds will usually confirm the presence of an enlarged uterus and distinguish between pyometra and pregnancy.

Two types of pyometra occur: open and closed.

In the *open* type the cervix relaxes, releasing a large amount of pus that is often cream, pink or brown. In the *closed* type, there is very little vaginal discharge. As pus collects in the uterus, the cat becomes more toxic, vomits, runs a high fever and quickly dehydrates.

Treatment: *A veterinarian should be called at once.* Hysterectomy is the treatment of choice. It is much safer to do this operation before the cat becomes toxic.

If it is especially important to preserve the fertility of the queen, prostaglandin therapy along with antibiotics may be attempted. Prostaglandin PGF2[a] relaxes the cervix, stimulates uterine contractions and evacuates the pus. It is administered by subcutaneous injection daily for several days. The discharge is cultured, and the queen is placed on an appropriate antibiotic, selected on the basis of sensitivity tests. Antibiotics should be continued for three to four weeks. *Prostaglandin therapy is accompanied by a number of dose-related side effects, including shock.* Uterine rupture may occur when the cervix is closed. Many veterinarians regard closed pyometra as a contraindication to the use of PGF2[a]. PGF2[a] is not currently approved in the United States for use in cats but is widely used by veterinarians for this purpose.

Queens who recover are at increased risk for pyometra in subsequent heat cycles. They should be bred as soon as possible after complete recovery since their reproductive potential will be limited by recurrence of disease.

Uterine drainage and flushing techniques are available but usually are reserved for queens who fail to respond to prostaglandin.

A disease similar to pyometra, *acute metritis*, occurs in the postpartum queen (see *Postpartum Problems* in the chapter PREGNANCY AND KITTENING).

ARTIFICIAL INSEMINATION (AI)

Artificial insemination is a technique in which semen is collected from the male and introduced into the female's reproductive tract. The procedures for AI are now well standardized in the cat. In the matter of selecting equipment, collecting semen and inseminating the queen, a strict protocol is important to insure a successful pregnancy. For this reason, veterinary supervision, at least initially, is recommended. When performed by experienced personnel, the conception rate is 75 percent. AI has its widest application when natural mating is contraindicated or impossible. Usually this is for psychological reasons, anatomical reasons or fear of transmitting a disease.

Atificial stimulation of the vagina is a method of bringing the queen out of heat.

The queen's behavior will indicate when she is in estrus and receptive to successful fertilization. When for psychological reasons she does not display signs of sexual receptivity, vaginal cytology must be used to stage the heat cycle.

Semen can be collected from the male by using an artificial vagina. A tom can be trained to use this devise in three weeks. A teaser female in estrus is needed to stimulate the male. As an alternative, semen can be collected from an anesthetized tom by using an electroejaculator.

Once collected, the semen is diluted with sterile saline and introduced into the queen's vagina. The queen must be hormonally prepared to ovulate in conjunction with the insemination. Best results with AI will be obtained by inseminating the queen two to four times over 24 hours.

After AI, the queen should be confined until she goes out of heat. If she mates with another male, a mixed litter may result.

Frozen semen has been used successfully. However, conception rates are not as high as they are when fresh semen is used. Advanced reproductive techniques using embryo transfer have a low success rate at this time.

FALSE PREGNANCY (PSEUDOCYESIS)

When ovulation occurs but the eggs remain unfertilized, a pseudopregnancy (false pregnancy) results. The condition is caused by progesterone, which is manufactured by the corpus luteum cysts in the ovaries following ovulation (see *Hormonal Influences During Estrus*). A false-pregnant queen seldom exhibits signs of a true pregnancy. Occasionally, a queen will have an increased appetite, gain weight or exhibit nesting behavior. Milk production is rare. False pregnancy can be easily confused with true pregnancy in which kittens have been aborted or reabsorbed (see *Fetal Loss During Pregnancy*).

Treatment: No treatment is necessary. Signs disappear in 35 to 40 days after estrus.

A false-pregnant queen is likely to have other false pregnancies. When breeding is no longer desired, the queen should be spayed. This is best done after the false pregnancy is over.

ACCIDENTAL PREGNANCY

Accidental pregnancies are common. A queen in heat will go to great lengths to get to a tom. Her vocal call and the potent chemical substances in her urine (pheromones) attract toms from miles around. If the queen is left outdoors for just a few minutes, an unwanted pregnancy can occur.

Once your queen is in heat, keep her indoors. Do not let her out of your sight. Queens must be isolated throughout the entire estrous cycle, which begins with the signs of proestrus and continues for 10 to 14 days. If a valuable breeding queen has been mismated, it may be best to let her go through with the pregnancy. She will be perfectly able to breed true to type during a subsequent heat cycle.

If you do not have the time and facilities to care for a litter of kittens or if the queen is not of breeding quality, consider alternatives. One is spaying. This operation can be performed during the first half of pregnancy without added risk to the female. During the second half of pregnancy, a hysterectomy becomes more difficult. Another alternative is to prevent the pregnancy by an estrogen injection. Estradiol cypionate (ECP), the mismate shot, works by preventing implantation of the fertilized ova into the wall of the uterus. If you choose this method, take your queen to a veterinarian as soon as possible. The injection must be given *within 40 hours* of mating. Adverse side effects include prolonged estrus, development of bone marrow suppression (which may be permanent) and risk of producing *pyometra. ECP is not approved in the United States for use in cats for any purpose.*

A safer approach, but one that requires hospitalization, is to induce abortion with the prostaglandin PGF2[a]. It is given by injection for two or more days, after 30 days of gestation. PGF2[a] currently is not approved in the United States for use in cats but has become standard treatment for this purpose in many veterinary clinics.

BIRTH CONTROL

The best method to prevent conception in the female is spaying. Tubal ligation has almost the same risks as spaying and is only slightly less expensive in most veterinary clinics. It won't stop the queen from going into heat and attracting the male. It does not have the health benefits of ovariohysterectomy. Most veterinarians recommend ovariohysterectomy as the operation of choice for sterilization.

If it is important to preserve the fertility of the queen for future breeding, *artificial stimulation of the vagina* and *birth control drugs* can be used to postpone pregnancy.

Two operations **to sterilize the male** are **castration** and **vasectomy**. Sterilizing the male is not an effective population control measure. Another male can fertilize a queen in heat.

Spaying (Ovariohysterectomy)

In this operation, the uterus, tubes and ovaries are removed. Spaying prevents the queen from coming into season and eliminates the problems of cystic ovaries, false pregnancies, uterine infection, irregular heat cycles and confinement during the mating season. Spaying also reduces the frequency of breast tumors.

A **queen does not need to have a litter of kittens to be psychologically fulfilled.** The operation will not change her basic personality, except perhaps to make her less irritable at certain times of the year. Nor will the operation affect her hunting instincts. A spayed female makes an outstanding house pet. She is able to devote herself exclusively to her human family.

Spaying does not make a cat fat and lazy. Obesity is caused by overfeeding and lack of exercise. By coincidence, a queen is usually spayed as she enters adulthood, at which time she requires less food. If she continues to eat a high-calorie kitten ration and puts on weight, the tendency is to blame the operation.

The best time to spay a female is at five to seven months of age, before she goes into her first heat. The operation is easy to perform at this time, and there is less chance of complication.

Having made arrangements to have your female spayed, be sure to withhold all food and water starting the evening before surgery. The operation is done under general anesthesia. A full stomach may result in vomiting and aspiration during induction of anesthesia. Check with your veterinarian concerning other special instructions or precautions to be observed before and after the operation.

Artificial Stimulation of the Vagina

A queen can be brought out of heat by artificially stimulating her vagina. The reasons for this are discussed in the section *Hormonal Influences During Estrus*. Ovulation lengthens the interval between heat cycles from 7 to 14 days to 30 to 40 days. This method is best used to postpone breeding for several weeks.

With an assistant holding the cat by the scruff of her neck, raise her tail and insert a smooth, blunt-ended plastic rod or cotton-tipped applicator one-half inch into her vagina and rotate it gently. The queen should exhibit all the signs of actual mating, including the crying out and postcoital rolling-over behavior. If the queen does not exhibit these signs, the procedure may not have been effective and should be repeated. However, there is risk of injury to the vagina with repeated manipulations to induce ovulation. It may be best to enlist the assistance of your veterinarian.

After successful artificial stimulation of the vagina, the queen will cease to call in three to four days. She should not be allowed outdoors while still in heat. If she should mate a tom, pregnancy will almost certainly result. Many queens will go back into heat in about 44 days, when her ovaries stop manufacturing progesterone.

BIRTH CONTROL DRUGS

Megestrol acetate (*Ovaban*), a long-acting progesterone, is effective in inhibiting the estrous cycle and in preventing estrus when given daily. It is not approved in the United States for use in cats. It should be prescribed under veterinary supervision. Adverse side effects include *pyometra, mammary gland hypertrophy*, breast tumors, *diabetes mellitus* and suppression of adrenal gland activity.

Delmadinone acetate (DMA), currently not available in the United States, shows promise as a safe and effective drug for estrous prevention. It can be given orally once a week or by subcutaneous injection every six months.

Chlorophyll tablets, which you can buy from your veterinarian or at pet stores, may help to mask the odor of a female in heat but are not effective for birth control.

MALE CASTRATION

Castration is an operation in which both testicles are removed. The operation is not difficult or invasive, and the cat can go home the same day.

Castration does not change a male cat's personality except to tone him down and reduce or eliminate his sexual impulses and the aggressive behavior that accompanies them. His hunting instincts are not affected. He often becomes more affectionate and more oriented to the company of people. A neutered male is less likely to wander and become involved in cat fights. *Spraying*, with its accompanying unpleasant smell of cat urine, is often eliminated.

Most veterinarians believe that the best time to castrate a male is when he is six or seven months old. At this time, he is sufficiently mature so that his growth and bone structure are not adversely affected, but sexual behavior, if present at all, has not yet become ingrained. If the male is castrated before six months of age, or more specifically, before the development of secondary sexual characteristics, his penis may remain small. This can predispose to the plugged penis syndrome. See *Feline Urologic Syndrome* in the chapter URINARY SYSTEM.

If an older male is castrated after he has mated queens, he may retain his sex drive. This is not common.

The precautions to take before surgery are the same as those described for *Spaying*.

VASECTOMY

Bilateral vasectomy is the treatment of choice when sterilization *alone* is desired. In this operation, a segment of the right and left vas deferens is removed. These tubes transport the sperm from the testicles to the urethra. A vasectomized tom is able and willing to mate with a queen but is unable to get her pregnant.

Vasectomy does not disturb the hormone function of the testes and does not influence the mating urge or territorial aggressiveness of toms. Nor does it reduce spraying.

Breeders who house a number of queens may keep a vasectomized tom. By mating with a queen, he takes her out of heat without the risk of pregnancy. The effects are similiar to those described in *Artificial Stimulation of the Vagina*.

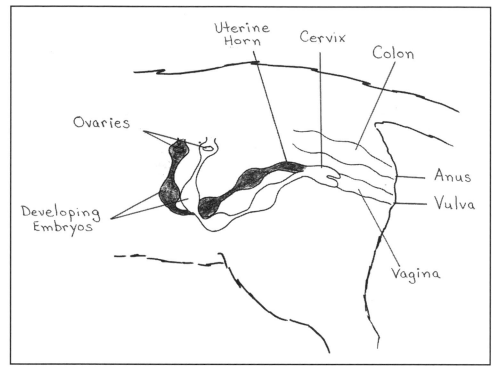

Female reproductive system.

—Rose Floyd

16

PREGNANCY AND KITTENING

PREGNANCY

GESTATION

Gestation is the period from conception to birth. From the first day of a *successful* mating, it averages 65 days. Kittens born on the 63d or 69th day fall within the normal range. Siamese cats may carry their kittens 71 days. However, if the kittens are born before day 60, they usually will be too young to survive.

DETERMINING PREGNANCY

At present, there is not the type of pregnancy test available for cats that there is for people.

During the first few weeks of gestation few signs are detectable except for a slight gain in weight. An occasional queen exhibits signs of morning sickness. By 35 days, the nipples become pink and obvious, and the belly is increasing. As the time of birth approaches, the breasts enlarge and a milky fluid may be expressed from the nipples. However, many queens have breast enlargement after a normal heat, so this alone should not lead to a pregnancy diagnosis.

The cat's uterus is Y shaped with a horn on each side. The kittens grow and develop in the uterine horns. Twenty days after conception, the growing embryos can be felt by abdominal palpation as evenly spaced swellings about the size of unshelled peanuts. By day 35, the fetuses are floating in capsules of fluid and can no longer be detected by palpation. By day 49, the kittens are sausage shaped, and their heads are large enough to be felt as separate structures.

Abdominal palpation requires experience and gentleness. There are other structures in the abdomen that may feel lumpy. Excessive poking and prodding can damage the fetal-placental units and cause a miscarriage.

Abdominal ultrasound can detect kittens as early as 15 days into gestation. Fetal heartbeats, detectable at day 20, provide absolute indications of life. An abdominal X ray will show fetal bone structure at about day 43. They are used as an alternative to ultrasonography when it is necessary to distinguish between pregnancy, false pregnancy and pyometra. They should be avoided in early pregnancy.

Late signs of pregnancy are an obvious pear-shaped abdomen and fetal movements, easily detectable during the last two weeks.

Morning Sickness

Cats, like people, can suffer from morning sickness. This usually happens during the third to fourth week of pregnancy and is due to hormonal changes plus stretching and distention of the uterus. You may notice that your queen appears apathetic. She may be off her feed and vomit from time to time. Morning sickness lasts only a few days. Unless you are particularly attentive, you may not even notice it.

Prenatal Checkups

Preparations to be taken *before breeding* are described in *The Queen* (see Sex and Reproduction).

The first prenatal visit should be scheduled two to three weeks after mating. You will be given pregnancy instructions. Any further tests deemed necessary can be scheduled at this time. Intestinal parasites, if present, should be treated by your veterinarian.

Vaccinations, most medications and many deworming products are not recommended once pregnancy is established. This includes some of the flea and insecticide preparations, dewormers and certain hormones and antibiotics. Tapeworm medications, in particular, can be quite toxic. *Droncit* is a tapeworm preparation safe for use in pregnant queens. Live virus vaccines (e.g., feline panleukopenia, feline respiratory virus) should not be given to pregnant females. Check with your veterinarian before starting a pregnant queen on any drug or medication.

One week before the expected kittening date, make an appointment to have the queen checked once again. Your veterinarian will want to discuss with you the normal delivery procedures, alert you to signs of potential problems and give you instructions for care of the newborn.

Be sure to ask where you can get help (emergency service) if needed after hours.

CARE AND FEEDING DURING PREGNANCY

A pregnant queen needs little special care. It usually is not necessary to restrict her activity. Moderate exercise, in fact, is beneficial, helping to prevent undue weight gain and poor muscle tone. Climbing can be dangerous in late pregnancy because the weight of the uterus alters the queen's center of gravity and affects her balance. If she is given to climbing, jumping from high places and roughhousing with children and pets, you will need to prevent such activity.

During the first four weeks of pregnancy, feed a commercial ration formulated for growing kittens. These products are appropriate for pregnant and nursing queens because they contain extra protein, calcium and other essential nutrients including *taurine*. See the chapter FEEDING AND NUTRITION. *Avoid supplementing* the diet with treats, table scraps and choice cat foods because the queen may not eat enough of the pregnancy ration to get all the nutrients she and her kittens need for a successful and healthy pregnancy. Additionally, vitamin/mineral supplements are not needed and may even be harmful. The only exception is the queen who may be below par from an earlier pregnancy or recovering from an acute illness. Discuss this with your veterinarian.

Protein requirements begin to increase during the second half of pregnancy. Increase the pregnancy ration by one-half unless the queen is overweight. Obesity should be avoided at all costs. Overnourished queens are quite likely to carry fat kittens, which can complicate labor.

A queen may lose her appetite a week or two before kittening. Her abdomen is crowded, and she may have difficulty eating a normal-sized meal. Feed several smaller meals spaced throughout the day.

KITTENING PREPARATIONS

Queens should deliver at home, where they feel secure. They are easily upset by strange people and unfamiliar surroundings. This can delay or interrupt labor. The best place to deliver and care for newborn kittens is in a kittening box. It should be located in a warm, dry, out-of-the-way spot, preferably rather dark—and free of distracting noises.

A suitable box can be quickly fashioned from a strong cardboard container. It should be large enough for the queen to move about. A rectangular box 24 inches long, 20 inches wide, and 20 inches tall is ample. The box should have a lid, so you can clean it and see the kittens. At one end, cut out a doorway about chest high to the queen, so she can step in and out without jumping.

A reusable box can be made of wood. This has the advantage that inside ledges (two inches high and two inches wide) can be nailed to all four sides. Kittens will crawl under these ledges instinctively, where they are protected from being rolled on by their mother.

Lay several sheets of newspaper in the bottom of the box to absorb moisture. This also gives the queen something to dig and scratch, which she will do instinctively in the way of making her nest. Do not use loose bedding such as straw or wood chips. These materials can be inhaled by the kittens and block their nostrils.

Cold, damp quarters are a leading cause of early kitten mortality. The kittening room should be draft-free and kept at a temperature of 85°F for the first seven days following delivery. Thereafter, it should be lowered five degrees each week until it is 70°F. Keep a constant check on the temperature by using a thermometer placed on the floor of the box. Additional heat can be supplied by using 250-watt infrared heat bulbs, either suspended above the floor of the open-topped box or mounted in photographer's floodlight reflectors (or plant lights). Leave an area of the nest out of the direct source of heat so the mother can rest in a cooler area.

The following is a list of other kittening accessories that should be available in case they are needed:

- a small box in which to place newborn kittens
- sterile rubber surgical gloves
- an eyedropper or small syringe to aspirate mouth and nose secretions
- artery forceps to clamp a bleeding cord
- dental floss or cotton thread for ties
- an antiseptic to apply to the umbilical stumps
- scissors
- clean laundered towels
- plenty of fresh newspapers

KITTENING

SIGNS OF IMMINENT DELIVERY

One week before a queen is due to give birth, she begins to spend a lot more time self-grooming, with special attention to her abdomen and genital areas. She may exhibit increased restlessness or irritability and begin to search for a place to have her kittens. Queens often rummage in closets, rearrange clothes in an open drawer, scratch up the owners' bed and go about in a flurry of activity that is the ritual of making their nests.

Now is a good time to introduce your queen to the kittening box and encourage her to sleep in it. A queen who has had kittens will usually take to it without difficulty. But if the queen decides to have her kittens in some other not acceptable spot, move the entire family to the kittening box as soon as she finishes delivering.

After the 61st day of gestation, it is a good idea to take the queen's rectal temperature each morning. Twelve to 24 hours before she is due to deliver, the rectal temperature may drop from a normal of 101.5°F to 99.5°F or below. This two-degree drop may not occur, and if it does, it is easily missed. Therefore, do not assume that if her temperature is normal, she won't be delivering soon.

As the day of confinement approaches, she should be restricted to the house. If allowed outside, she might decide to run off and have her kittens in a haystack or tool shed.

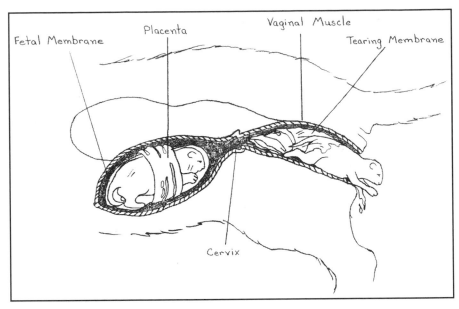

Birth of kittens.

—Sydney Wiley

LABOR AND DELIVERY

The uterus of a cat has two horns that communicate with a central uterine cavity. The outlet or cervix communicates with the vaginal birth canal. Developing kittens, encircled by their placentas, lie within the uterine horns.

There are three stages of labor. In the first stage the cervix dilates, opening the birth canal. In the second stage kittens are delivered. In the third stage the placenta (afterbirth) is delivered. The entire birthing process is seldom difficult and usually proceeds without human intervention.

The **first stage,** which may last 12 hours or more, begins with panting and rhythmic purring, which increases as the moment of birth approaches. The queen becomes noticeably more active, digs at the floor, turns her head as if to snap at her rear, strains as if to pass stool and may cry out. As her uterus contracts she tightens her abdominal muscles and concentrates on bearing down. At this point a novice queen may become extremely anxious, seek out her owner and cry pitifully. Take her back to her kittening box and sit beside her. Speak soothingly and continue to comfort and pet her. Many queens, however, do not need or want the presence of their owner and may hiss and spit if disturbed.

With the onset of labor, one uterine horn contracts and pushes the presenting part of the kitten down into the central cavity. Pressure against the cervix causes it to dilate. At complete dilatation, the kitten slides into the vagina. The water bag around the kitten may rupture before the kitten is born. If so, yellow or straw-colored fluid is passed. A kitten should then be delivered within 30 minutes.

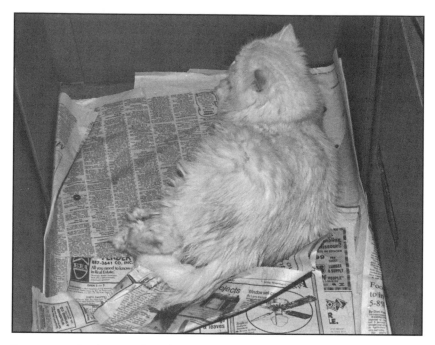

The queen in her kittening box, beginning to strain.

Getting ready to deliver.

The water bag around the kitten can be seen bulging through the vulva.

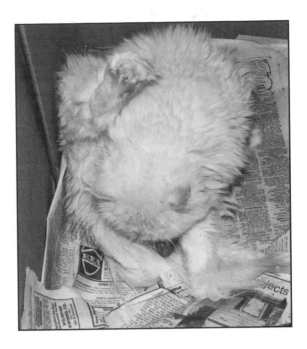

The mother licks and removes the fetal membranes and severs the umbilical cord.

About 70 percent of kittens are born in the "diving" position with feet and nose first. After the head is delivered, the rest of the kitten slides out easily. The mother instinctively licks and removes the fetal membranes with her rough tongue and severs the umbilical cord. The mother now vigorously licks the kitten's face to clear the nose and mouth. As the kitten gasps, the lungs inflate, and the breathing begins.

No attempt should be made to interfere with this normal maternal activity that is an important part of the mother–kitten bond. This is her kitten, and she must learn to take care of it. If she appears rough, it is only because she is trying to stimulate breathing and blood circulation. However, if the queen is occupied with another kitten and fails to remove the amniotic sac, you should step in and strip away the fetal membranes so the kitten can breathe (see *Helping a Kitten to Breathe*).

A placenta follows shortly after the birth of each kitten. The queen may consume some or all of the placentas. This is an instinctual reaction and may stem from the days when it was important to remove the evidence of birthing. However, it is not essential that she do so. The ingestion of several placentas can produce diarrhea. You may wish to remove some or all of the placentas from the nest. They should be counted since a retained placenta can cause a serious postnatal infection (see *Acute Metritis*).

If the cord is severed too cleanly or too close to the kitten's navel, it may continue to bleed. Be prepared to clamp or pinch off the cord and tie a thread around the stump. The stump should be disinfected with iodine or some other suitable antiseptic.

As soon as some or all of her kittens are born, the mother will curl up on her side and draw the kittens to her nipples with her paws. Their sucking action stimulates uterine contractions and helps bring on the colostrum, or first milk of the queen, containing the all-important maternal antibodies.

Most kittens are born 15 to 30 minutes apart, but this is quite variable. Although most deliveries are complete in two to six hours, it occasionally happens that a queen goes out of labor, appears at ease and cares for the kittens, then goes back into labor 12 to 24 hours later and delivers the rest of the litter. It is important to be aware that this can happen, so undue anxiety or unnecessary surgery can be avoided. Abnormal causes of arrested labor are discussed below.

ASSISTING THE NORMAL DELIVERY

When labor is going well, it is best not to interfere. But on occasion, a large kitten may get stuck at the vaginal opening. The head or presenting part appears during a forceful contraction and then slips back when the queen relaxes.

This situation can usually be corrected by lubricating the birth canal liberally with K-Y Jelly. If the queen does not deliver the kitten within 15 minutes, proceed as follows:

As the presenting part appears at the vaginal opening, place your thumb and index finger on each side of the perineum just below the anus and push down gently to keep the kitten from slipping back into the mother. Next, grip the kitten in the birth canal and slide the lips of the vulva over the head. Once this is accomplished the lips will hold the kitten in place, giving you a chance to get another grip.

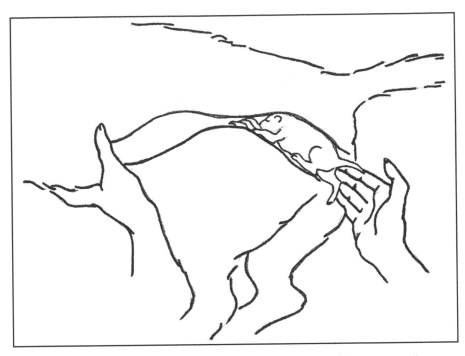

The hind foot or posterior presentation occurs about 20 percent of the time. It seldom causes problems.
—Sydney Wiley

Now grip the skin of the kitten with a clean piece of cloth behind the neck or along the back and draw the kitten out. Apply forceful traction only to the skin, not to the legs or head. It may be helpful to rotate the kitten first one way and then the other, especially when something seems stuck because the birth canal is usually wider in one direction. If these measures are not successful, proceed as described under *Feline Obstetrics.*

PROLONGED LABOR (DYSTOCIA, DIFFICULT LABOR)

Queens can *voluntarily* prolong, delay, and even interrupt the normal birthing process for up to 24 hours. Domestic cats apparently retain this feral attribute—the ability to quickly move a nest if danger threatens. Accordingly, excessive disturbances, interruptions, the arrival and departure of strange people, and other perceived threats can easily induce voluntary cessation of labor.

Nonpsychological causes of prolonged and difficult labor are **mechanical blockage,** that is, the diameter of the kitten is too wide in relation to the birth canal diameter, and **uterine inertia** (the uterus becoming too exhausted to contract). These two are often related—fatigue following unrelieved blockage.

Dystocia is rarely a problem in the healthy, well-conditioned queen. It is more likely to occur with small litters in which individual kittens are relatively large, with older brood queens and with queens allowed to become too fat. When present, it usually involves the first kitten.

MECHANICAL BLOCKAGE

The two common causes of mechanical blockage are an oversized kitten and a malpositioned kitten in the birth canal. Most kittens come down the birth canal *nose and feet first* (the diving position) with their backs along the top of the vagina. When a kitten comes down backward, the hind feet or tail and rump show first. As the hind foot (*posterior*) presentation occurs about 20 percent of the time, it may be accurate to classify this position as a malpresentation, but it seldom causes a problem. However, the tail or rump first position (*breech*) can cause a problem—particularly if it occurs with the first kitten. One other presentation that can complicate labor is a head bent forward or to the side.

A queen with a history of a fractured pelvis is likely to have problems. X rays before pregnancy may disclose a narrowed pelvis. Consideration should be given to having her spayed.

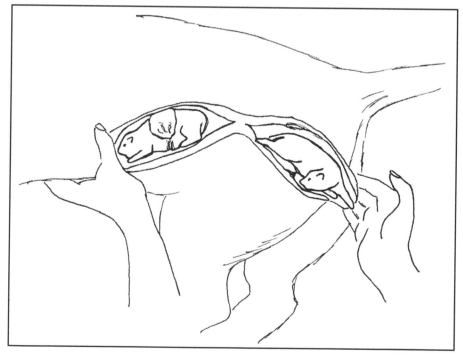

A deviated head is a common cause of mechanical blockage.   —Sydney Wiley

Uterine Inertia

Uterine inertia is an important cause of ineffectual labor. As the uterine muscle fatigues, the uterus becomes incapable of producing forceful and effective contractions. Mechanical factors that can lead to uterine fatigue are a single large kitten in a small uterus, a very large litter, twisting (torsion) of the uterus and *hydrops amnion*, a condition in which there is an excess of amniotic fluid.

Some *primary* inertia is caused by a deficiency of oxytocin (produced by the pituitary gland) or calcium or both. The uterus may respond to injections of oxytocin (*Pitocin*) and calcium gluconate, which stimulate stronger contractions. *Note: If there is a mechanical blockage, oxytocin can lead to rupture of the uterus. The decision to use it should be made by a veterinarian.*

If labor is prolonged and a kitten cannot be seen or felt in the birth canal, it is best to x-ray the queen to determine the kittens' positions and relative sizes.

When to Call the Veterinarian

It is better to call your veterinarian on a "false alarm" if only to gain reassurance than to delay in the hope that in time the problem will be corrected without help. Often the situation can be dealt with rather simply if attended to at once. However, the same problem, when neglected, becomes complicated—often leading to emergency procedures.

> **The signs of birthing problems are**

- 60 minutes of intense straining without birth of a kitten.
- 10 minutes of intense labor with a kitten visible in the birth canal.
- 10 minutes of *fresh bleeding* (several teaspoons) during or after kittening.
- Sudden apathy and weakness with a rectal temperature above 104°F or below 97°F, suggesting maternal infection.
- Labor stops and there are signs of restlessness, anxiety, weakness or fatigue. *Kittens come approximately 15 minutes to two hours apart.* Over three hours between kittens is a sign of trouble. This provision need not apply if the queen is resting happily and nursing kittens without signs of distress.

The passage of yellow fluid means rupture of the water bag (amniotic sac) surrounding the kitten. When this happens, the kitten should be born within 30 minutes. A dark green vaginal discharge indicates that the placenta is separating from the wall of the uterus. When this happens, the first kitten should be born within a few minutes. After the first kitten, however, passage of dark green fluid is not a concern.

Feline Obstetrics

If it is impossible to get prompt veterinary help and labor cannot proceed because of an abnormal presentation, the following should be attempted:

- Clean the outside of the queen's vulva with soap and water. Put on a pair of sterile rubber gloves and lubricate your finger with *Betadine* solution, K-Y Jelly or Vaseline. Before inserting your finger into the vagina, be careful not to contaminate your gloves with stool from the anus.

- Place one hand under the abdomen in front of the pelvis of the queen and feel for the kitten. Raise the kitten into position aligned with the birth canal. With your other hand, slip a finger into the vagina and feel for a head, tail or leg. When the head is turned and will not pass through the outlet of the pelvis, insert a finger into the kitten's mouth and gently turn the head, guiding it into the birth canal. Now apply pressure on the perineum just below the anus (a maneuver called feathering). This induces the queen to strain and holds the kitten in the correct position so its head won't slip back into the original position.

- When the kitten is coming as a breech (rump first), hold the kitten at the pelvic outlet as described. With the vaginal finger, hook first one leg and then the other, slipping them down over the narrow place until the pelvis and legs appear at the vulva.

- If the mother is unable to deliver a large kitten coming normally, the problem is caused by a shoulder locking in the birth canal. You will see the head protruding through the vulva. Insert a gloved finger into the vagina alongside the kitten until you can feel front legs at the elbow. Rotate the kitten first one way and then another so the legs can be brought forward. Hook them and pull them through individually.

- Once in the lower part of the birth canal, a kitten should be delivered without delay. To stimulate a forceful push by the mother, gently stretch the vaginal opening. If you can see the kitten at the mouth of the vagina appearing and disappearing with straining, grip the kitten with a clean piece of cloth and pull out as described under *Assisting the Normal Delivery*. Time is of the essence—particularly when the kitten is breech. It is better to take hold and pull out the kitten even at the risk of injury or death since this kitten and perhaps all the others will die if something is not done.

- Occasionally, the blockage is caused by a retained placenta. Hook it with your fingers and grasp it with a clean piece of cloth. Maintain slow and steady traction until it passes out of the vagina.

When the uterus becomes exhausted and stops contracting, it is difficult to correct an arrested labor. Many veterinarians feel that if after two injections of oxytocin 20 minutes apart effective labor and delivery do not occur, *Cesarean section* is indicated.

Helping a Kitten to Breathe

The amniotic sac that surrounds the newborn kitten should be removed within 30 seconds to allow the kitten to breathe. If the queen fails to do this, you should tear open the sac and remove it, starting at the mouth and working backward over the body. Aspirate the secretions from mouth and nose with an eyedropper or small syringe. Rub the kitten briskly with a soft towel. Another method of clearing the secretions is to hold the kitten in your hands while supporting the head. Then swing the kitten gently in a downward arc. This helps to expel water from the nostrils. Present the kitten to the mother to lick, clean and cuddle.

After a difficult delivery, kittens may be too weak or too flaccid to breathe on their own. Squeeze the kitten's chest gently from side to side and then from front to back. If the kitten still will not breathe, place your mouth over the nose and blow gently until you see the chest expand. *Do not blow forcefully* because *this can rupture the lungs.* Leaving the mouth uncovered helps to prevent this complication. Be sure to remove your mouth to allow the kitten to exhale. Repeat this several times until the kitten breathes easily.

CESAREAN SECTION

Cesarean section is the procedure of choice for any type of birthing problem that cannot be relieved by drugs or obstetrical manipulation. *The decision rests with the veterinarian.* Consideration is given to the condition of the queen; length of labor; results of X rays; size of the kittens in relation to the pelvic outlet; failure to respond to oxytocin; and a dry vaginal canal.

The operation is done under general anesthesia in the veterinary hospital. The risk to a young healthy queen is not great. However, when labor has been unduly prolonged, toxicity is present, the kittens are dead and beginning to decompose or uterine rupture has occurred, the risks are significant.

Usually a queen is awake, stable and able to nurse her kittens at home within three hours of the operation. A queen who has a cesarean section may or may not require a cesarean section with her next litter. This depends on the reasons for the first cesarean section.

POSTPARTUM CARE OF THE QUEEN

Twelve to twenty-four hours after the queen delivers, ask your veterinarian to do a postpartum checkup. Palpation of the uterus rules out a retained kitten or placenta. Many veterinarians prescribe an injection of oxytocin to aid emptying of the uterus. This reduces the likelihood of postpartum infection. He or she will want to check the color, consistency and quality of the queen's milk. Milk that is thick, stringy, yellowish or discolored may be infected. Take the mother's temperature at least once a day for the first week. A temperature of 103°F or higher indicates a problem (retained placenta, uterine or breast infection).

A variable amount of reddish-tinged or dark greenish discharge is normal for the first 7 to 10 days and may persist for up to three weeks. A foul-smelling, brownish, *purulent discharge* is abnormal and suggests a retained placenta or uterine infection (see *Acute Postpartum Metritis*). The cat is often depressed, runs a fever and may appear pale (anemia). Be sure to consult your veterinarian if the vaginal discharge becomes purulent or if it persists for more than three weeks.

A nursing queen should be kept indoors or taken out only when supervised. During this period she could go into heat. If mated, she may conceive another litter. *Breeding should not be allowed at this time.*

FEEDING DURING LACTATION

Depending on the size of the litter, a lactating queen needs two to three times more calories than before pregnancy. If she does not get these needed calories, she will not be able to produce enough milk to nourish her kittens. *Inadequate milk supply is the most common cause of kitten mortality.*

Feed a high quality food designed for growth of kittens. Diets or foods formulated for growth contain all the essential nutrients required to support lactation. The daily caloric requirements of nursing queens and recommended amounts to feed are shown in Table 2 in the chapter FEEDING AND NUTRITION. This chapter should be consulted for general information on quality of cat foods and choice of products.

A nursing queen should be given all the food she can eat. There is no possibility for weight gain in a queen nursing four or more kittens. Dry ration can be fed free choice. Canned food should be fed three or four times a day. By the second or third week, a nursing queen should be eating three times her normal daily maintenance ration or the equivalent of three full meals a day. Vitamin and mineral supplements will not be necessary and could even be dangerous. They should be avoided unless the queen refuses to eat the pregnancy lactation diet or has a preexisting deficiency or chronic illness. In these circumstances, seek veterinary consultation.

POSTPARTUM PROBLEMS

Problems that can affect a queen following delivery are *postpartum hemorrhage, acute metritis, mastitis, caked breasts, inadequate milk supply* and *milk fever*. A few queens have problems accepting their kittens because of emotional upsets and psychological blocks.

POSTPARTUM HEMORRHAGE

Vaginal bleeding after an *easy* delivery is not common and is usually caused by a vaginal tear associated with mechanical blockage and difficult labor. A retained kitten or placenta is another possibility. Occasionally, the uterus does not return to normal condition. Most of these problems will be evident on postpartum examination.

Excessive loss of blood may produce shock and death. If you see bright fresh or clotted blood that persists for 10 minutes or longer (several teaspoons), notify your veterinarian at once. Fresh bleeding should not be confused with the normal passage of a variable amount of reddish to dark greenish vaginal discharge that persists for several days (up to three weeks) following delivery.

ACUTE POSTPARTUM METRITIS

Acute metritis is a bacterial infection of the lining of the uterus that spreads upward through the birth canal during the birthing process or immediately thereafter. Unsanitary kittening quarters can cause it. Placentas provide an ideal medium for bacterial growth. Immediately after delivery, change the bedding of the kittening box and remove all remaining products of delivery.

Acute metritis is likely to occur when part of a placenta has been retained in the uterus. Some cases are caused by a retained fetus that has become mummified. Other cases are caused by contamination of the birth canal by unsterile fingers during a difficult or prolonged labor. Vaginitis is a less common cause. Vaginitis should be treated as soon as it is diagnosed, preferably before heat and certainly before labor and delivery.

Acute endometritis and **Pyometra** are other uterine infections that may be confused with acute postpartum metritis. They are discussed under *Diseases of the Female Genital Tract* in the chapter SEX AND REPRODUCTION.

Most cases of acute metritis can be anticipated and prevented by a postpartum checkup. The veterinarian often will want to clear the uterus with an injection of oxytocin. Preventive antibiotics are indicated if labor was difficult and the birth canal contaminated during delivery. A queen with acute metritis is lethargic, hangs her head, refuses to eat and has a rectal temperature of 103°F to 105°F. She may not keep the nest clean or care for her kittens. The kittens appear unkempt, cry excessively and may die suddenly. This could be the first indication that the queen is ill.

There is a heavy, dark, bloody, greenish or tomato souplike discharge that appears two to seven days after delivery. It should not be confused with the normal greenish discharge present for the first 12 to 24 hours after delivery or the light reddish, serosanguinous discharge that can last up to three weeks but decreases in volume with time. A normal discharge is not accompanied by high fever, excessive thirst or other signs of toxicity such as vomiting and diarrhea.

Treatment: Acute metritis is a life-threatening illness. A veterinarian should be consulted immediately to save the queen's life. The kittens will usually be taken off the mother and raised by hand (see *Raising Kittens by Hand* in the PEDIATRICS chapter). *If the queen is toxic, her milk may also be toxic.*

MASTITIS

The cat normally has four pairs of mammary glands or eight individual breasts.

There are two breast conditions that can affect the nursing queen: caked breasts and acute septic mastitis. A breast swelling resembling acute mastitis but which does not occur during lactation is *Mammary Hypertrophy*. For more information, see *Breast Swellings and Tumors* in the chapter TUMORS AND CANCERS.

Caked Breasts (Galactosis). An accumulation of milk in the mammary glands is normal in late pregnancy and lactation. However, milk accumulation may

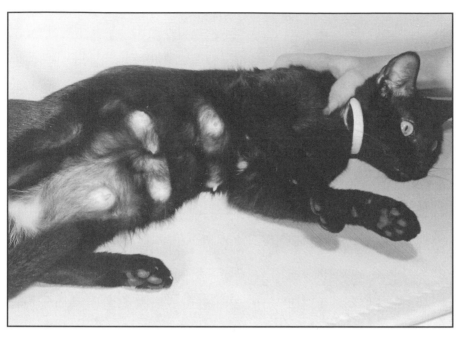

Breast caking is caused by an excessive buildup of thick coagulated milk.

increase to the point that the breasts become painful and warm. Infection is not a factor, and the queen does not appear ill.

Fluid expressed from the breast will look like milk. Litmus paper may be used to test acidity. Normal feline breast milk tests to a pH of 6.0 to 6.5. If the pH is 7.0, see *acute septic mastitis.*

Treatment: Apply warm moist packs twice a day and express the gland to draw out some of the coagulated and caked milk. Your veterinarian may prescribe a diuretic to relieve swelling and have you reduce the queen's food intake. If the queen has no kittens, the breasts are dried up as described under *Weaning* in the PEDIATRICS chapter.

Severely or persistently caked breasts may become infected, thus leading to an acute mastitis. This can be prevented by administering an antibiotic such as amoxicillin.

Breast Infection or Abscess (Acute septic mastitis). Acute mastitis is an infection of one or more of the mammary glands caused by bacteria that get into the nursing breast from a scratch or puncture wound. It can occur from 24 hours to six weeks postpartum. Some cases are bloodborne and associated with *acute metritis.* The milk from an infected breast is toxic and often contains bacteria that can cause kitten septicemia and sudden death. In all such cases, be sure to check the vagina for a purulent discharge and each breast for signs of acute infection.

A mammary gland with acute mastitis is swollen, extremely painful and usually reddish-blue. Milk may be blood tinged, thick, yellow or stringlike. In some cases the milk will look normal, yet test to a pH of 7.0 or greater. Mothers with acute mastitis refuse to eat, appear listless and run a high fever (which suggests abscess formation).

Some cases of acute mastitis can be prevented by trimming the nails of kittens when they are two to three weeks old. The hair around the queen's nipples is protective and should not be clipped unless it is matted.

Treatment: *Remove all kittens immediately and contact your veterinarian.* This disease should be treated by a professional. Routine measures include bacterial culture of the infected milk and the use of appropriate antibiotics selected on the basis of sensitivity tests. Gently massage the glands three or four times a day, and apply moist warm packs. When only one breast is involved, it may be possible to tape the nipple of the infected gland and allow the kittens to nurse the others. If more than one gland is involved or if the queen is quite toxic, the kittens should be raised by hand as described in the PEDIATRICS chapter. If the kittens are three weeks old, they can be weaned. The procedure for drying up the breasts is explained under *Weaning*.

When milk from an infected breast returns to normal appearance and tests to a pH of less than 7.0, the kittens can nurse at that breast.

INADEQUATE MILK SUPPLY (AGALACTIA)

The suckling action of the newborn kittens is an important stimulus to let down the milk. When kittens do not suckle for 24 hours, the milk supply begins to dry up.

Experienced queens will encourage their kittens to suckle soon after delivery. A nervous, upset, insecure or frightened queen may not exhibit this normal maternal behavior. Speak to her in a calm, soothing voice. Lay the queen on her side and put the kittens to the nipples. Continue this process until she learns to accept them.

A deformed nipple may cause difficulty in suckling. Examine all nipples to be sure they are open, fully formed and erect. A recessed nipple can be improved by massaging to stimulate the flow of milk and then putting a vigorous suckler directly on that nipple.

Occasionally, it becomes apparent that a queen is not making enough milk to satisfy all her kittens. This is most likely to occur with novice queens and those with large litters. It is most important that a nursing mother receive adequate nutritional support. The most common cause of inadequate milk production is failure to supply enough dietary calories, especially after the second week, when nursing demands are greatest. This cause is correctable (see *Feeding During Lactation*). When the litter is large or the mother is constitutionally unable to produce enough milk, supplemental feedings using kitten milk replacer may be required (see *Raising Kittens by Hand* in the PEDIATRICS chapter).

MILK FEVER (ECLAMPSIA, PUERPERAL TETANY)

Eclampsia is a muscular spasm associated with a low serum calcium. It is called milk fever because it usually occurs several days to several weeks postpartum, when there is a steady drain on the body's calcium stores because of nursing. It is more likely to occur in queens with large litters. It is much less common in cats than in dogs.

The first signs of eclampsia are restlessness, anxiety, rapid breathing and pale mucous membranes. A queen frequently leaves her kittens and begins to pace up and down. Her gait is stiff-legged, uncoordinated and jerky. Tightening of the face muscles exposes the teeth and gives the face a pinched look. As the condition worsens, she falls on her side, exhibits spasms in which she kicks all four legs and salivates profusely.

The temperature is often elevated to as high as 106°F. This causes more panting, washes out carbon dioxide, raises the pH of the blood and lowers the serum calcium even further. *If there is no treatment within 12 hours, the queen will die.* Certain queens seem predisposed to milk fever. If your queen has had milk fever in the past, ask your veterinarian about supplementing her diet with calcium during the last half of pregnancy.

Treatment: Milk fever is an emergency. Notify your veterinarian at once. Intravenous calcium gluconate is a specific antidote indicated at the first signs of tetany.

If the rectal temperature is over 104°F, treat as you would for *Heat Stroke*.

Take the kittens off the queen for 24 hours and feed them by hand. If they are at least three weeks of age, they can be weaned. Younger kittens may be returned to the queen when she has recovered completely if you limit nursing to no more than 30-minute intervals two or three times a day. If there are no adverse effects, these restrictions can be gradually relaxed over the next 48 hours until a normal routine is established. Mothers who must continue nursing should be supplemented with calcium, phosphorus and Vitamin D.

MOTHERS WHO NEGLECT OR INJURE THEIR KITTENS

The mother–kitten bond begins during and shortly after birth. The mother recognizes each kitten by a distinctive odor. During the process of licking, cleaning and nursing the kitten, she establishes a relationship that will sustain that kitten in her care throughout the first few weeks of life.

This bond may be less secure initially when kittens are born by cesarean section, although it is stronger when at least some of the kittens are born before the surgery or when the kittens are put to her nipples before she wakes.

A novice mother may have difficulty coping with a litter of squirming kittens for the first few hours. With a little help, she can be shown how to nurse her kittens and to keep from stepping on them.

An emotional upset caused by excessive noise or too much handling of her kittens by children or strange people can adversely influence a queen's normal maternal behavior. It is important not to allow visitors for the first few weeks, especially when the queen is high-strung and not well socialized to people.

Spoiled dependent house pets that are excessively people oriented may neglect or abandon their kittens to be with their owners.

Occasionally, a queen's milk does not come down for the first 24 hours. During this time she may reject her kittens. Milk flow can be helped by oxytocin. Once the milk comes in, the kittens are usually accepted.

Postpartum problems that can depress the queen and interfere with mothering behavior are milk fever, breast infection and uterine infection. Depending on the severity of maternal infection, these kittens may need to be removed from the queen and raised by hand.

A fading kitten whose body temperature has dropped below normal due to sickness or constitutional weakness may be pushed out of the nest. This is nature's way of culling.

A queen often attempts to relocate her nest when the kittens are about four days old. This behavior may stem from a natural instinct, when it was necessary to move from a soiled nest to one less likely to attract predators. If the nest she chooses is not a satisfactory substitute for the kittening box, you should return the entire family to the kittening box and stay with the queen, talking softly and stroking her often until she settles in comfortably. Do not allow her to become agitated or frightened while carrying kittens because she could accidentally injure them by biting too hard. Nest seeking can be prevented by introducing the queen to her kittening box two weeks before delivery and requiring her to sleep there.

Cannibalism is a form of abnormal maternal behavior in which the queen consumes her young, particularly the firstborn. It occurs commonly, particularly in catteries.

Queens routinely consume stillborn kittens and the products of delivery. While consuming a placenta, a queen could accidentally consume a kitten. A queen might damage the kitten while attempting to sever an umbilical cord, especially if a large umbilical hernia is present. In some cases cannibalism may actually involve the intentional destruction of a constitutionally inferior or malformed kitten. Other cases of maternal aggression may be activated by fear, anxiety, anger or a perceived threat to the queen's survival.

In summary, most cases of kitten injury or neglect are caused by psychological factors—in particular, those producing emotional insecurity.

Treatment: Provide a quiet kittening location away from all distractions, where the queen will feel least threatened and most secure.

If the cannibalism occurs with the firstborn kitten, remove the kittens as each is born, placing all of them in a warm accessory kitten box. Leave them in the box until the queen has completed the birthing process. If the queen continues to exhibit aggression and you cannot persuade her to accept the kittens, they may need to be raised by hand or placed with another queen. See *Raising Kittens by Hand* in the Pediatrics chapter. If possible, *ensure that the kittens nurse for the first 24 hours to receive the all-important colostrum*.

Newborn kittens nurse vigorously and compete for nipples.

17

PEDIATRICS

NEWBORN KITTENS

During the neonatal period from birth to three weeks of age, a healthy kitten is the picture of contentment, sleeping much of the time and awakening only to eat. Newborns spend long hours nursing—often eight hours a day—with sessions lasting up to 45 minutes. Most neonatal kittens quickly develop a preference for nursing at a particular breast, which they locate by smell. Breasts not suckled will stop producing milk in three days.

A good mother instinctively keeps her nest and kittens clean. By licking the belly and rectum of each kitten, she stimulates the elimination reflex.

Kittens are born with their eyes closed. The eyes begin to open at 8 days and are completely open by 14 days. The eyes of shorthaired cats open sooner than those of longhairs. All kittens are born with blue eyes. Adult colors do not appear before 3 weeks and may take 9 to 12 weeks to reach the coloring required by the breed Standard. The ear canals, which are closed at birth, begin to open at 5 to 8 days. The tiny folded-down ears become erect by 3 weeks.

The sex of kittens can be determined shortly after birth, although it may be easier to do this when they are older. See *Determining the Sex* later in this chapter.

Kittens are sight and sound oriented at 25 days. They usually begin to crawl by 18 days and can stand at 21 days. Soon after, they begin to walk and can feed from a

The eyes begin to open at eight days.

Kittens begin to crawl at 18 days. The folded-down ears become erect at three weeks.

bowl. They can control the urge to eliminate at four weeks. At this time they prefer to use papers instead of soiling the nest.

It is best to disturb newborn kittens as little as possible—at least until they are a few weeks old and moving about freely. Most queens display anxiety when their kittens are constantly handled. There is a theory that such handling interferes with a kitten learning to identify with and relate to the mother and littermates. These species interactions are necessary in establishing the kitten's self-awareness as a cat. When these early social interactions do not take place, a kitten could possibly exhibit aggression, shyness, an eating disorder or some other behavior problem later in life. However, after six weeks, social interaction with human beings and exposure to new and non-threatening situations are important for proper development of a happy, well-adjusted pet.

CARING FOR THE NEWBORN

Newborn kittens are born with a limited capacity for adapting to environmental stress. With proper care and attention to the special needs of these infants, many neonatal deaths can be avoided. The two crucial factors to watch closely are the kitten's *body temperature* and *weight*. Also, the kitten's appearance, breathing rate, crying sound and general behavior can provide useful information about the animal's overall health and vitality. These parameters are discussed below.

GENERAL APPEARANCE AND VITALITY

Healthy kittens feel round and firm. They nurse vigorously. Their mouths and tongues are wet. When disturbed, they burrow down next to their mother or littermates for warmth.

For the first 48 hours, kittens sleep with their heads curled under their chests. While sleeping, they jerk, kick and sometimes whimper. This is called "activated sleep" and is normal. It is the newborn kitten's means of exercise and helps to develop muscle tone. A newborn's skin is warm and pink. When pinched, it springs back in a resilient fashion. A kitten stretches and wiggles energetically in your hand when picked up. When removed from the mother, the kitten crawls back to her.

A sick kitten presents a dramatically different picture. These kittens are limp, cold and hang like a dishcloth. Sick kittens show little interest in nursing and tire easily.

Healthy newborn kittens seldom cry. Crying indicates that a kitten is cold, hungry, sick or in pain. Distressed kittens crawl about looking for help and fall asleep away from the life-sustaining warmth of their mother and littermates. Later, sickly kittens move slowly and with great effort. They sleep with their legs splayed apart and their necks bent to the side. Their mew is plaintive and may continue for 20 minutes or longer. Such a kitten is often rejected by the queen, who senses that the kitten is not going to survive and pushes it out of the nest rather than waste her energies caring for it. This situation can be reversed if the kitten is treated and the body temperature brought back to normal.

Body Temperature

A newly born kitten's body temperature is the same as the mother's. Immediately afterward, the temperature drops several degrees (how much depends on the temperature of the room). Within 30 minutes, if the kittens are dry and snuggled close to the mother, their temperature begins to climb back up. Over the next three weeks, the body temperature remains between 96°F and 100°F.

A healthy kitten in the nest can maintain 10 to 12 degrees above room temperature. But when the mother is away for 30 minutes in a room 70°F (well below the recommended level), the kitten's temperature can fall. The kitten quickly becomes chilled, a condition that gravely reduces metabolism.

Most neonatal kittens have little subcutaneous fat. Nor do they have the capacity to constrict their skin blood vessels to retain body heat. Energy for heat production is supplied through feedings. As there is little margin for reserve, a kitten that does not eat *frequently*, for whatever reason, is likely to become chilled.

Chilling is the single greatest danger to the infant kitten. The temperature of the kittening box and the area in which it is kept must be 85°F to 90°F during the first week. Thereafter, it should be lowered five degrees each week until it reaches 70°F. The construction of a suitable kittening box is described in the chapter PREGNANCY AND KITTENING.

Warming a Chilled Kitten

Any kitten whose body temperature is below normal for its age is a chilled kitten and must be warmed gradually. Rapid warming (for example, by a heating pad) causes dilatation of skin vessels, increased loss of heat, added expenditure of calories and greater need for oxygen. These are detrimental.

The best way to warm is to tuck a kitten down next to your skin beneath a sweater or jacket, letting your own warmth seep into the kitten's system. If body temperature is below 94°F and the kitten is weak, warming will take two to three hours. Afterward, the kitten may have to be placed in a homemade incubator and raised by hand.

Never feed formula or allow a cold kitten to nurse. When chilled, the stomach and small intestines stop working, and formula will not be digested. The kitten will bloat and perhaps vomit. A chilled kitten can utilize a *warmed* 5 percent to 10 percent glucose and water solution or *Pedialyte* solution (both can be bought at drugstores). Give 1cc per ounce body weight every hour and warm slowly until the kitten is warm and wiggling. If one of these solutions is not available, use honey and water, or as a last resort, use household sugar and water: one teaspoonful per ounce.

Importance of Weight Gain

A healthy kitten weighs three to four ounces at birth (110 to 125 grams) and should double this birth weight in seven to nine days. Weight at 5 weeks should be about one pound; at 10 weeks about two. Kittens should be weighed on a gram scale at birth, daily for the first 2 weeks of life and thereafter every three days until they are a month old. A steady weight gain is the best indicator that a kitten is doing well. Failure to gain weight is a cause for concern.

When several kittens in the litter are not gaining weight, you should check maternal factors, especially *inadequate milk supply*. If the mother is not getting enough calories, her milk supply will be inadequate to support a large litter. A nursing queen needs two to three times more food than does a normal adult cat. In addition, the diet must be balanced to meet the needs of lactation. See *Feeding During Lactation* in the chapter PREGNANCY AND KITTENING. Other maternal factors to be considered are *toxic milk* and *acute metritis*.

WHEN TO SUPPLEMENT

Kittens gaining weight steadily during the first seven days are in no danger. Kittens experiencing weight loss not exceeding 10 percent birth weight for the first 48 hours and then beginning to gain should be watched closely. Kittens that lose 10 percent or more of their birth weight in the first 48 hours and do not gain by 72 hours are poor survival prospects. Start supplemental feedings immediately (see *Raising Kittens by Hand*).

If at birth a kitten is 25 percent under the weight of its littermates, you can expect a low survival probability. Place this kitten in an incubator to be raised by hand. Many immature kittens can be saved if their condition is not complicated by diseases or congenital defects.

DEHYDRATION

Kidney function in the newborn is 25 percent of what it will be later. Because immature kidneys are unable to concentrate the urine, kittens must excrete large amounts of dilute urine. When kittens stop nursing, they dehydrate quickly. Therefore, consider dehydration whenever a kitten fails to thrive, loses weight, becomes chilled or is too weak to nurse. This obligatory kidney water loss must be offset by sufficient intake of milk, or in kittens raised by hand, by a formula containing adequate amounts of water. A sudden drop in weight with diarrhea is due to water loss.

Signs of dehydration are lack of moisture in the mouth, a bright pink tongue and mucous membranes of the mouth, loss of muscle tone and weakness. When dehydrated skin is pinched, it stays up in a fold instead of springing back.

Dehydration is treated as described for diarrhea in *Common Feeding Problems*.

FADING KITTEN SYNDROME

The first two weeks of life present the greatest risk to the newborn. During this period, diseases acquired *in utero* and birth injuries acquired during labor and delivery begin to take their toll. Some deaths are undoubtedly due to lack of advanced preparation—especially failure to provide adequate heat in the kittening quarters, failure to vaccinate the prospective queen and failure to get her onto a high-quality feeding program that provides adequate calories and essential nutrients, including *taurine*.

The developmentally immature kitten is at a distinct disadvantage because of *low birth weight* and lack of muscle mass and subcutaneous fat. Such a kitten may be unable to breathe deeply, nurse effectively and maintain body warmth. Birth weight may be 25 percent below that of littermates. Such a kitten is likely to be crowded out by brothers and sisters and forced to nurse at the least productive nipples.

With chilling, failure to nurse and dehydration, the kitten develops a shocklike state due to circulatory failure. This causes a drop in temperature, heart rate and breathing. As the body temperature drops below 94°F, vital functions are further depressed. The crawling and righting ability is gradually lost, and these kittens lie on their sides. Later, poor circulation affects the brain, causing tetanic rigors and coma accompanied by breathless periods lasting up to a minute. At this point the condition is irreversible.

A common cause of subnormal birth weight is inadequate nourishment during growth and development while in the uterus. When all the kittens are undersized, a poorly nourished queen is the prime consideration. When one or two kittens are below par, most likely the fault is one of placental insufficiency, perhaps due to overcrowding or a disadvantageous placement of a placenta in the wall of the uterus. These kittens are immature by development rather than by age. If they are to survive, they must be separated from the queen and raised by hand.

If the queen is infected with *feline leukemia, feline panleukopenia* or *feline infectious peritonitis*, she may transmit the infection to her kittens in utero. These kittens are small and weak at birth. They sicken and die within the first few days.

Mothering attributes are important determinants of kitten survival. Novice queens with first litters and obese queens experience higher kitten mortality than do experienced and well-conditioned queens. The quantity and quality of mother's milk is of utmost importance. *Inadequate milk is the most common cause of death of kittens.* While size of litter and genetic influences may play a role, in most cases a diet low in calories *and* essential nutrients is the principal cause of this problem. Cannibalism and maternal neglect are occasional causes of kitten death.

Congenital defects do occur and can be lethal. Cleft palate, often associated with harelip, prevents effective nursing. Large navel hernias allow prolapse of abdominal organs. Heart defects can be severe enough to produce circulatory failure. Other developmental disorders that may be responsible for the occasional mysterious or unexplained death include esophageal closure (atresia), pyloric stenosis, anal atresia and malformations affecting the eyes and skeletal system (see *Congenital and Inherited Defects*).

Other causes of early kitten mortality, which may present as failure to thrive, are discussed in *Kitten Diseases*.

RAISING KITTENS BY HAND

A queen could be incapable of raising a litter because of uterine or breast infection, toxic milk, eclampsia, inadequate milk supply or emotional disturbance. In such cases the kittens have to be supplemented or hand fed.

The decision to supplement a kitten is based on general appearance and vitality, weight at birth and progress in comparison to littermates. As a rule, it is better to intervene early and start hand feeding in borderline cases and not wait until the kitten is in obvious distress. Depending on the overall condition of the kitten and response to supplemental feeding, it may be possible to feed two or three times a day

Commercial milk formulas are available as liquids and powders. They can be given by kitten nurser or tube and syringe.

and let the kitten remain with the mother. Other kittens must be raised entirely as orphans.

If your kitten needs supplemental feeding, calculate the total daily requirement (the method is given in *Calculating the Right Formula*) and assume that a nursing kitten eats four to six times a day. Smaller and weaker kittens should be fed at least six times a day. Space the feedings as evenly as possible over 24 hours. Accurate record keeping is important at all times but is absolutely essential when kittens are raised by hand. Weigh them on a gram scale at birth, at eight hour intervals for four days, daily for the first two weeks and then every three days until they reach one month of age.

Three areas of critical importance are furnishing the right environment, preparing and feeding the right formula and providing the right management. Feeding equipment should be thoroughly cleaned and boiled. Visitors should not be allowed in the nursery. All personnel should wash their hands before handling the kittens—especially if they have handled older cats. Many diseases, including feline viral respiratory infections, can be transmitted to kittens by someone who has recently treated an infective cat.

If the kittens were not able to receive colostrum, the first milk of the queen, they lack passive immunity and are susceptible to a variety of feline diseases. Vaccinations are then started at three weeks of age.

Since chilling is the single greatest danger to the newborn kitten's survival, you will need an incubator.

THE INCUBATOR

You can make a satisfactory incubator in a few minutes by dividing a cardboard box into separate compartments, so each kitten has one. These pens are especially important if kittens are orphaned because having no nipples to suckle, they suckle each other's ears, tails and genitalia. This suckling damage occurs for the first three weeks, after which they should be put together to establish normal socialization and behavior patterns.

The incubator temperature is of critical importance since the kittens will not have a mother to snuggle against when they are chilled. The incubator temperature will be the same as room temperature, provided there are no drafts. You can insulate the floor beneath the incubator with heavy padding. If the room temperature cannot be maintained with the existing heat system, you can provide additional heat by using *overhead infrared heat lights* with thermostatic controls. These lights should be placed so that kittens can move to a cooler area out of direct heat if necessary.

Heating pads are not as safe as overhead lights. Kittens can become severely dehydrated or burned by continuous exposure to heating pads. If used, they should be heavily padded and should cover only one-half of the bottom of the box.

On the floor of each pen place a cloth *baby diaper* that can be changed as it becomes soiled. This also provides a method for checking the appearance of each kitten's stool, which is an excellent indicator of overfeeding and an early warning sign of infection.

A *thermometer* should be placed in the incubator to monitor the surface temperature. Keep the temperature between 80°F to 90°F for the first week. During the second week, reduce it to 80°F or 85°F. Thereafter, gradually decrease the temperature to 75°F by the end of the fourth week. Maintain constant warmth and avoid chilling drafts.

Maintain the room humidity at about 55 percent. This helps to prevent skin drying and dehydration.

GENERAL CARE

Keep the kittens clean with a damp cloth. Be sure to cleanse the anal area and abdomenal skin. A light application of baby oil should be applied to these areas and to the coat to prevent dry skin. Change the bedding often to prevent urine scalds. When present, they can be helped by applying baby powder. When inflamed, apply a topical antibiotic ointment (*Neosporin*; *Triple Antibiotic Ointment*).

For the first three weeks, gently swab the kitten's anal and genital areas after each feeding to stimulate elimination. (This is something the mother would do.) A wad of cotton or tissue soaked in warm water works well. Dry and massage the kitten gently.

Hand Feeding

Whenever possible, kittens should nurse for the first two days of their lives. During this period, they will receive the all-important passive antibodies in the queen's colostrum that provide temporary immunity to many contagious feline diseases. Commercially available milk formulas such as *KMR*, *Kittylac*, *Nurturall*, *Just Born* and others are the best formulas for infant kittens because they most closely approximate the composition of the queen's milk. These milk replacers are available through veterinarians and many pet supply stores.

The composition of various milk sources is shown in the following table:

Composition of Maternal Milk and Substitutes

	% Solids	Calories per 100cc	% Protein	% Fat	% Carbohydrate
Queen	18	90	42	25	26
Cow	12	70	25	309	38
Bitch	24	150	33	33	16
Milk Replacer	18	100	42	25	26

The composition of cow's milk is not suitable for raising kittens. While commercial milk replacers are the most desirable substitutes for queen's milk, home formulas are sometimes adequate, especially in an *emergency* situation, when used as a temporary expedient. Mix well and warm before using. Refrigerate the unused portions:

Formula #1:

8 ounces homogenized whole milk

2 egg yolks

1 teaspoon salad oil

1 drop liquid pediatric vitamins

(Provides 1.2 Kcal/cc)

Formula #2:

1 part boiled water to 5 parts evaporated milk (reconstituted to 20 percent solids)

1 teaspoon of bone meal per quart

(Provides 1.0 Kcal/cc)

Kitten milk replacers can be purchased as premixed liquids or powders. The powdered forms are reconstituted by the addition of water. Unused formula should be refrigerated but not frozen. Preparation and feeding instructions vary with the product. Follow the directions of the manufacturer.

CALCULATING THE RIGHT FORMULA

The best way to determine how much formula each kitten needs is to weigh the kitten and use a table of caloric requirements. Daily requirements according to weight and age of kitten are given in the following table:

Calculating a Milk Formula for Kittens					
Age in Weeks	Average Weight	Kcal Needed per day (estimated)	cc of Milk Replacer per day*	cc of Emergency Formula per day	Suggested Number of Feedings per day
1	4 oz.	24	32 cc	48	6
2	7 oz.	44	56 cc	77	4
3	10 oz.	77	80 cc	90	3
4	13 oz.	107	104 cc	104	3

*The composition of various milk replacer products is similar. However the exact amount to feed may vary with the specific formulation.

To calculate the amount of formula for each feeding, weigh the kitten to determine how much formula to give *per day* and divide by the number of feedings. *Example*: A four ounce kitten during the first week requires 32 cc of milk replacer per day. Divide by the number of feedings (6), which gives 5 cc to 6 cc per feeding.

Small, weak kittens at birth are often dehydrated and chilled (see *Dehydration*). Before feeding formula, they should be rehydrated by feeding a *warmed* 5 percent to 10 percent glucose in water solution or *Pedialyte* solution at the rate of 4 cc per feeding every one to two hours until they are warm and well hydrated. Then begin using the calculated formula and feed every four hours. Older, larger kittens can manage on three meals a day. However, if a kitten cannot take the required amount at each feeding, then the number of feedings should be increased.

When fed adequately, a kitten's abdomen will feel full—but not tense or distended. Milk may bubble out around the lips, especially when using a nursing bottle. *Avoid overfeeding because this produces diarrhea.*

As long as the kitten does not cry excessively, gains weight, feels firm to the touch and has a light brown stool four to five times a day, you can be almost certain that the diet is meeting nutritional needs. Gradually increase the amount you are feeding, using the above table as a guide.

At three weeks most kittens can learn to lap milk from a dish. At four weeks you can mix the formula with a commercial kitten food. Weaning to solids can begin at this time (see *Weaning*).

HOW TO GIVE THE FORMULA

Kittens may be fed by a baby nursing bottle or stomach tube. With either, it is important to keep the kitten upright so formula won't be aspirated into the lungs. *Always
be sure to feed formulas at room temperature.*

The *baby bottle* has the advantage of satisfying the suckling urge but requires
that the kitten be strong enough to suck. When using a small doll's bottle or a
commercial kitten nurser with a soft nipple, you will usually have to enlarge the
hole in the nipple with a hot needle so the milk will drip slowly when the bottle is
turned over. Otherwise, the kitten will tire after a few minutes and will not get
enough nourishment. However, the hole in the nipple should be small enough to
prevent the milk from coming out too fast because this will cause the kitten to
choke.

The correct position for bottle feeding is to place the kitten in an upright position on the stomach and chest. *Do not cradle* like a human baby because the formula
will run into the kitten's windpipe. Open the kitten's mouth with the tip of your
finger, insert the nipple and hold the bottle at 45 degrees. The angle of the bottle is
such that air does not get into the kitten's stomach. Keep a slight pull on the bottle
to encourage suckling. When a kitten has had enough formula, you will see bubbles
come out around the mouth. With a slow drip, feeding takes five minutes or more.
Afterward, the kitten will need to be burped.

Tube feeding has several advantages. It takes about two minutes to complete
each feeding and little air is swallowed. This ensures that a proper amount of formula is administered to each kitten. *It is the only satisfactory method of feeding immature or sick kittens that are too weak to nurse.* If too much formula is ingested or if it is
ingested too rapidly, it will be regurgitated. This may cause aspiration and can be

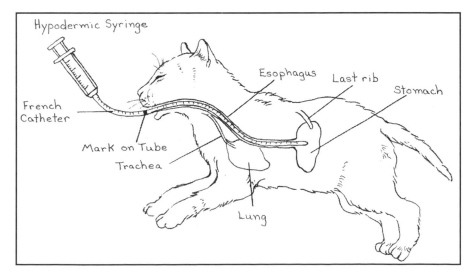

Tube feeding is the best way to feed an immature or sick kitten.   —Rose Floyd

avoided if care is taken to monitor the weight of the kitten, compute the correct amount and administer slowly. Kittens fed by tube must be kept in separate incubator compartments to avoid suckling damage to littermates.

Tube feeding is not difficult and can be mastered in a few minutes. It requires a soft rubber catheter (size 5 French for smaller kittens—size 8 or 10 for larger kittens), a 10 cc or 20 cc plastic or glass syringe and a gram scale to calculate each kitten's weight and monitor progress. These items can be bought at drugstores.

A kitten's stomach is located at the level of the last rib. *Measure the tube* from the mouth to the last rib and mark the tube with a piece of tape. *Connect the tube* to the syringe and *draw the formula* up through the tube into the syringe, taking care to expel all air from the system. *Warm the formula* to body temperature by immersing the syringe in hot water.

Arouse and place the kitten on its chest and stomach in a *horizontal* position. *Moisten the tip of the tube* with formula and allow the kitten to suckle it briefly. Then pass the tube slowly over the kitten's tongue and into the throat. With steady pressure, the kitten will begin to swallow the tube. Pass it to the level of the mark. *Slowly inject* the formula down the tube and into the kitten's stomach. *Remove the tube, raise the kitten* to a vertical position and *allow a burp.* Then swab the anal and genital areas to stimulate voiding and defecation.

At about 14 days old, the windpipe of many kittens will become large enough to accommodate the smaller tube. If the tube goes down the wrong way, the kitten will begin to cough and choke. Change to a larger tube (size 8 or 10 French). By now the kitten may be strong enough to suckle from a bottle.

COMMON FEEDING PROBLEMS

The two most common feeding problems are overfeeding and underfeeding. *Overfeeding* causes diarrhea. *Underfeeding* causes failure to gain weight. A steady weight gain at the rate of 10 grams or $^1/_3$ ounce a day and a normal stool (firm, light brown) are good indications that you are feeding the right amount. Experience indicates that owners are much more likely to overfeed than underfeed. The best way to tell is to monitor the stools. If a kitten is fed four times a day you can expect four to five stools, or about one stool after each feeding.

The first sign of overfeeding is a loose stool. A loose yellow stool indicates a *mild* degree of overfeeding. Reduce the strength of formula by diluting it one-third with water. As the stool returns to normal you can gradually restore the formula to its full strength.

With moderate overfeeding, there is a more rapid movement of food through the intestinal tract, indicated by a greenish stool. The green color is due to unabsorbed bile. Dilute the strength of the formula by one-half (using either *Pedialyte* or water). You can add two or three drops of *Kaopectate* to the formula: administer every four hours until the stools become formed. Gradually return the formula to full strength as the kitten recovers.

Unchecked overfeeding leads to a depletion of digestive enzymes and causes a grayish diarrhea stool. Eventually, when there is little or no digestion of formula due to rapid transit, the stool looks like curdled milk. At this point the kitten is getting no nutrition and is rapidly becoming dehydrated. As a temporary expedient in this urgent situation, discontinue the formula and administer water or *Pedialyte*, 1 cc per 2 ounces body weight per hour by bottle or stomach tube. Balanced pediatric electrolyte solutions, which in this situation are preferable to water, are available at drugstores. Add *Kaopectate* three drops per ounce body weight every three hours while awaiting the arrival of your veterinarian. Other supportive measures such as warming a chilled kitten are indicated. Your veterinarian may choose to administer additional electrolyte solution subcutaneously. Kittens with grayish diarrhea stool may be suffering from neonatal infection.

Kittens who are being *underfed* cry continuously, appear listless and apathetic, frequently attempt to suckle littermates, gain little or no weight from one feeding to the next and begin to chill. Kittens dehydrate quickly when not getting enough formula. Review your feeding procedure. Check the temperature of the incubator.

Constipation. Some kittens have fewer bowel movements than others do. This is not a cause for concern unless the stools are quite firm and there appears to be difficulty passing them. The kitten's abdomen may feel firm and appear bloated. If the kitten is constipated, a warm soap-water enema can be given by eyedropper (two or three full droppers after each feeding). Alternately, you can give up to 5 cc of mineral oil by enema. *Milk of Magnesia* (three drops per ounce body weight) can be given by mouth.

Keep in mind that hand fed kittens need to have their anal and genital areas massaged with a wad of cotton soaked in warm water after each feeding to stimulate the elimination reflex.

KITTEN DISEASES

KITTEN MORTALITY COMPLEX

The kitten mortality complex, once thought to be caused by the virus of feline infectious peritonitis is best viewed as a spectrum of illnesses that can affect young kittens during the first weeks of life. Some kittens are predetermined to fail the test of survival because of low birth weight and influences affecting growth and development in the uterus.

During the first two weeks of life, kittens are at risk for neonatal illnesses, including kitten septicemia, umbilical infection, toxic milk syndrome, isoerythrolysis, feline infectious peritonitis and panleukopenia. While these diseases do cause neonatal kitten mortality, statistically, they cause fewer deaths than low birth weight, birth trauma, and inadequate milk supply. These conditions are discussed elswhere in this chapter.

From five to 12 weeks of age, kittens are most susceptible to infections—in particular, viral pneumonia. This susceptibility is caused by a decline in passive immunity when active immunity (by vaccination) is not yet well established.

NEWBORN ANEMIA

Iron deficiency anemia affects the offspring of queens that are anemic. It is caused by a low iron content in the milk. This is an uncommon cause of kitten anemia. Intestinal parasites also can cause iron deficiency anemia because of chronic blood loss through the gastrointestinal tract. This is more common in older kittens and adults.

Kittens with iron deficiency anemia are undersized, grow slowly, tire easily and have pale mucous membranes. They should be examined by a veterinarian so tests can be made to determine the cause. Early detection of iron deficiency anemia is important because this anemia is easily treatable by giving the queen and her kittens iron supplements and vitamins.

A rare cause of anemia in kittens is a disease called *feline porphyria*. It is due to a defect in the formation of red blood cells and can be recognized by seeing a peculiar brownish discoloration of the teeth, and a reddish brown urine.

Neonatal Isoerythrolysis. The most common cause of kitten anemia is *neonatal isoerythrolysis*, also called hemolytic disease of the newborn. It affects purebred kittens most often and is more common in cats than in dogs. It begins shortly after kittens ingest colostrum containing antibodies that destroy their red blood cells.

These antibodies are manufactured by the queen during pregnancy when fetal cells of a different blood type than hers cross the placenta and sensitize her immune system. The antibodies produced are transmitted to the kittens during the first few hours of nursing. Symptoms appear within hours or days. Affected kittens become weak and jaundiced and pass dark reddish urine containing hemoglobin. Death can occur in twenty-four hours, or the kittens may simply "fade away" in a matter of days. In some cases the only symptom is tissue death of the tip of the tail.

Treatment: On suspicion of hemolytic anemia, stop all nursing. The kittens may require blood transfusions from a compatible donor to restore their red cells. Kittens from subsequent litters should not be allowed to receive colostrum from the queen.

Toxic Milk Syndrome

Queen's milk can be toxic to kittens. The primary cause is *acute septic mastitis*, a breast infection or abscess. *Acute metritis* also can lead to toxic milk. These conditions are discussed in the chapter PREGNANCY AND KITTENING. Kitten formulas that are not properly prepared or stored may become contaminated with bacteria and cause this problem.

Toxic milk syndrome usually affects kittens at one or two weeks of age. Kittens appear distressed and cry continually. Diarrhea and bloating are especially common. The anus often is red and swollen from continuous diarrhea. One complication of this syndrome is *kitten septicemia*.

Treatment: The kittens should be removed from the queen and treated for diarrhea and dehydration as described in *Common Feeding Problems*. Chilled kittens should be warmed, placed in an incubator and hand fed. Obtain veterinary attention for the queen and kittens. Do not allow the kittens to return to the mother until veterinarian approval.

Umbilical Infection

The navel (umbilicus) can be the site of infection. This is most likely to happen whenever a cord is severed too close to the abdominal wall. This leaves no stump to wither up and separate cleanly later. The stump can become infected. Predisposing causes are a queen with dental infection who transmits bacteria to the umbilical cord during severing and an unclean kitten box contaminated by stools.

An infected navel looks red and swollen and may drain pus or form an abscess. There is direct communication to the liver, which makes even a low-grade umbilical infection potentially dangerous. Untreated, signs of kitten septicemia are likely.

Treatment: If the cord has been clipped too close to the naval ring, cleanse the area with a surgical soap and apply warm compresses. Medicate with *Triple Antibiotic Ointment* or *Neosporin*. Watch the queen carefully to be sure she does not repeatedly lick the area because this can aggravate the situation and increase the chance of infection. At the first sign of skin infection or abscess, telephone your veterinarian. Injectable penicillin should be started at once. This disease can be present in other kittens in the litter. Prophylactic iodine applied to the navel stump at birth may reduce the chance of this complication.

KITTEN SEPTICEMIA

Bloodborne infections in infant kittens are caused by bacteria that spread rapidly and cause signs mainly in the respiratory tract and abdomen. They occur in kittens under two weeks old. The usual portal of entry is an abscessed umbilical stump. Other sources of infection are possible. Bacteria from infected milk can penetrate the lining of the intestinal wall and enter the bloodstream.

The initial signs are crying, straining to defecate and bloating. They are like those of toxic milk syndrome. At first they may be mistaken for simple constipation. But as the disease progresses, the abdomen becomes distended and takes on a dark red or bluish tint. These are signs of *peritonitis*. Other signs include refusal to nurse, chilling, weakness, dehydration and loss of weight. Many kittens simply appear to fade away and succumb in the first three to seven days of life.

Treatment: The cause must be discovered at once; otherwise, the whole litter can be affected. Sick kittens should be treated for dehydration, diarrhea and chilling as described elsewhere in this chapter. They should be treated aggressively with an injectable penicillin antibiotic, removed from the kitten box and raised by hand. Septicemia must be managed by a veterinarian.

VIRAL PNEUMONIA

Viral pneumonia is a leading cause of respiratory induced death in kittens older than two weeks. It is caused by the same herpes and calici viruses that produce the *feline viral respiratory disease complex* discussed in the chapter INFECTIOUS DISEASES. The severity of illness varies from kitten to kitten and from outbreak to outbreak, but overall, the mortality rate approaches 50 percent.

In kittens younger than six weeks old, the chance of infection is increased if the mother was not protected by current vaccinations during pregnancy and did not pass protective antibodies to the kittens during the first two days of nursing. Regardless of which viral group is responsible, the signs are similar. The incubation period is one to six days.

Neonatal kittens abruptly stop nursing, cry pitifully and weaken rapidly. At times, kittens may be found dead without apparent cause. Older kittens may experience sneezing, nasal congestion, eye discharge, coughing and fever. Ulcers of the tongue and palate and a conjunctivitis that may become complicated by ulcerations of the cornea can occur.

Treatment: *Veterinary assistance is required.* Weak, dehydrated kittens should be given intravenous fluids. Kittens with nasal congestion or mouth ulcers who may be unable to nurse should be fed by tube. Steam vaporization helps to keep mucous membranes from drying. The eyes should be swabbed gently with a cotton ball moistened in warm water at regular intervals and then medicated as described in the section EYES: *Conjunctivitis in Newborn Kittens.* Idox uridine eyedrops are of assistance for corneal ulcers caused by the herpes virus.

Prevention of viral respiratory disease is discussed in the INFECTIOUS DISEASES chapter.

NEONATAL FELINE INFECTIOUS PERITONITIS (FIP)

The FIP virus has been implicated as a cause of sudden neonatal death and fading kittens. Other related problems believed to be produced by this virus are reduced litter size (one or two kittens); repeated abortions; fetal reabsorptions; stillborns; and deformed kittens.

In newborn kittens signs of FIP include a low birth weight associated with weakness, emaciation and ineffective nursing. In some cases kittens appear healthy but then grow weak, lose weight, stop nursing and die within a few days (fading kittens). Others experience sudden difficulty breathing, turn blue and die within hours from circulatory collapse.

This condition is especially serious in catteries, where entire litters can be lost. Preventive measures are discussed in the chapter INFECTIOUS DISEASES (see *Feline Infectious Peritonitis*). Treatment involves supportive measures as discussed in the section *Caring for the Newborn.*

NEONATAL FELINE PANLEUKOPENIA

The virus of panleukopenia can be transmitted to unborn kittens and to kittens shortly after birth. Like FIP, it may be responsible for fading kittens and some cases of reproductive failure.

Kittens that recover from this infection may develop cerebellar damage. These kittens develop a jerky, uncoordinated gait and tend to overshoot or undershoot when pouncing or reaching for objects.

Panleukopenia is discussed in the chapter INFECTIOUS DISEASES.

SKIN INFECTION OF THE NEWBORN

Scabs, blisters and purulent crusts can develop on the skin of newborn kittens one to two weeks old. They usually appear on the abdomen. These sores sometimes contain pus. They are caused by poor sanitation in the kitten box and secondary bacterial infection.

Treatment: Keep the nest clean of food, stools and dried debris. Cleanse scabs with a dilute solution of hydrogen peroxide and wash with a surgical soap. Then apply an antibiotic ointment such as *Triple Antibiotic Ointment* or *Neomycin.* In severe infections oral or injectable antibiotics may be required.

A kitten with cerebellar hypoplasia following recovery from neonatal panleukopenia. Note lack of coordination and difficulty in moving.

The eyelids have to be opened in neonatal conjunctivits to remove pus and to treat the infection.

CONJUNCTIVITIS OF THE NEWBORN

This condition is due to a bacterial infection beneath the eyelids. Some cases are associated with the herpes virus. It occurs in kittens before their eyes are open. It is discussed in the chapter EYES.

CONGENITAL AND INHERITED DEFECTS

Structural defects are not common in kittens. The ones you might be able to recognize are hernias; cleft palate and harelip; absent (imperforate) anus; extra toes (polydactyly); enlarged head (hydrocephalus); absent tail; kinked tail; undescended testicle(s); cross-eyed look (strabismus); eyelid rolled in (entropion); and developmental eye diseases.

Other defects, which require special studies to diagnose, are malformations in the urogenital tract (kidneys, uterus); pyloric stenosis; sterility in tortoiseshell cats; deafness in white cats with blue eyes; and cerebellar hypoplasia (incomplete development of this part of the brain).

Birth defects can be inherited, in which case they are produced by genes (e.g., deafness in white, blue-eyed cats; sterility in tortoiseshells). Or they can be caused by something that affects the growth and development of the fetus in utero. In either case they are *congenital*—that is, they exist at or date from birth. Malformations

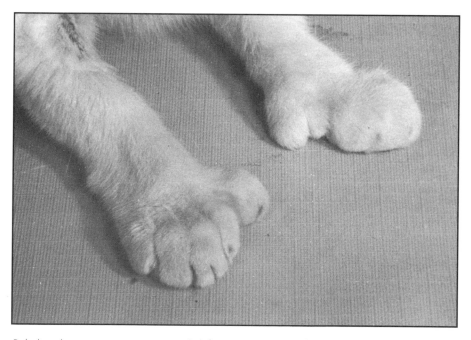

Polydactyly is a common congenital defect. Extra toes are found most often on the front feet.

Navel hernia.

in the growing fetus can be produced by X rays, cat viruses (FIP, panleukopenia), live virus vaccines, some flea and insecticide preparations and certain antibiotics.

An antifungal agent called *Griseofulvin*, used in the treatment of ringworm infection, has been found to be associated with severe congenital defects, including hydrocephalus, spinal cord defects, missing eyes, cleft palate, imperforate anus and fused toes. This drug should not be given to pregnant females. It is important to remember this, especially in a cattery where ringworm has been chronic and where several individuals might be under treatment.

Potentially treatable congenital defects are:

Hernia. A hernia is a protrusion of the abdomen's contents through an abdominal wall opening that would normally close during development. When a bulge can be pushed back into the abdomen, the hernia is said to be *reducible*. When it cannot, the hernia is *incarcerated*. An incarcerated hernia becomes *strangulated* if the blood supply to the tissues in the sac is pinched. Accordingly, a painful hard swelling in a typical location could be an incarcerated hernia—which is an emergency. Seek professional help.

Hernias have a hereditary basis. There is a genetic predisposition for delayed closure of the abdominal ring, in most cases. An occasional navel hernia may be caused by severing the umbilical cord too close to the abdominal wall.

Umbilical Hernia is the most common hernia. It is often seen in kittens at about two weeks of age. It usually gets smaller and disappears before six months. If not, you can have it repaired. The operation is not serious, and the kitten usually goes home the same day. If your kitten is female and you are planning to have her spayed, repair can be postponed until that time.

Inguinal Hernias are not common. The bulge appears in the groin, usually in a female. It may not be seen until she is mature or bred. A pregnant or diseased uterus may be incarcerated in the sac. Inguinal hernias should be repaired.

Cleft Palate. This is a birth defect of the nasal and oral cavities commonly associated with harelip. It is caused by failure of the palate bones to develop and fuse. This results in an opening from the oral to the nasal cavity. It is usually impossible for a kitten to nurse. Survival depends on tube feeding. A similar condition can occur in adult cats from a blow to the face associated with a fracture of the palate.

Harelip can occur by itself. It is due to abnormal development of the upper lip. This problem is primarily cosmetic.

Cleft palate and hairlip can be corrected by plastic surgery.

Pyloric Stenosis. Congenital pyloric stenosis is caused by a thickening of the ring of muscle at the outlet of the stomach. The narrowed pyloric canal prevents food from passing out of the stomach. This deformity tends to occur among related individuals (often in the Siamese breed), suggesting a heritable basis.

The characteristic sign is vomiting of partially digested food without bile, usually several hours after eating. Vomiting may not appear until weaning, when the kitten begins to eat solids. The diagnosis is confirmed by upper gastrointestinal X rays that show the typical deformity. Pyloric stenosis can be treated by an operation that divides the enlarged muscular ring, allowing food to pass through the channel, or by dietary management. Treatment can be determined by your veterinarian.

Achalasia is a condition in which the lower esophageal ring enlarges and blocks the passage of food into the stomach. It is characterized by regurgitation of undigested food. It is discussed in the chapter DIGESTIVE SYSTEM: *Esophagus.*

Imperforate Anus. This uncommon birth defect is caused by failure of development of the anal opening. Examination of the perineum will show that the anus is either absent or sealed by skin, preventing passage of stool. Surgical correction may be applicable in some cases.

WEANING

Weaning time depends on several factors that include the size of the litter, the condition of the queen and the availability of her milk. If a queen with a small litter were left to her own devices, she might continue to nurse for 6 to 10 weeks or even until the birth of her next litter. In general, kittens should be weaned when they are about 25 days old.

Choose a commercial cat food formulated to meet the needs of growing kittens. A number of good products are available at grocery stores. Read the label to be sure the product is suitable for feeding *kittens* three to four weeks of age and older. Many people prefer to use dry kibble, but canned products are also satisfactory. The daily caloric and nutritional requirements for kittens of different ages are shown in Table 2 and Table 3 in the FEEDING AND NUTRITION chapter.

Weaning procedure: To stimulate appetite, remove the queen two hours before each feeding. After the meal, let her return to nurse. To promote socialization and avoid behavior problems, feed kittens together until they are at least six weeks of age.

Feeding dry ration: Mix one part kibble to three parts water or kitten milk replacer. Warm to room temperature. Feed in a somewhat shallow saucer. Dip your fingers into the mixture and let the kittens lick it off. Offer this three to four times a day.

When the kittens are eating this mixture well, reduce the moisture content in successive stages until the kittens are eating the mixture dry. This usually occurs by seven to eight weeks of age. At this time there is less demand on the queen's milk supply. You should decrease her intake of food if you have not already started to do so. This initiates the drying-up process.

Kittens who eat too much food may get diarrhea. This may be due to excessive food or some degree of intolerance to the food. Temporarily reduce the number of ration feedings and continue with breast feedings.

Feeding canned ration: Begin with two parts canned ration to one part water or kitten milk replacer. Follow the same steps as above.

Kittens have high water requirements and will dehydrate quickly if they do not get adequate fluids. (Prior to weaning, these requirements were being supplied by the queen's milk.) Accordingly, *it is of utmost importance to keep a bowl of clean fresh water available at all times.* The procedure for feeding older weaned kittens is discussed in the chapter FEEDING AND NUTRITION (see *Feeding Kittens*).

Vitamin/mineral supplements are not necessary *or desirable* when you are feeding a nutritionally balanced growth ration.

If it becomes necessary to dry up the queen's milk supply, withhold all food and water for 24 hours. The next day, feed one-fourth the normal amount, the third day one-half the normal amount and the fourth day, three-fourths the normal amount. Thereafter, restore her to an adult maintenance ration.

At 10 to 14 weeks of age kittens become susceptible to respiratory and digestive tract infections because they have lost the protective immunity of the mother's milk. Should illness occur, there is a marked reduction in food intake at a time when they should be gaining six or more ounces a week. As a result, they stop growing and become weak and debilitated. This further impairs their resistance to illness. Such kittens should receive special attention. Every effort should be made to ensure adequate nutrition. Appropriate vaccinations during kittenhood will prevent most of these ailments.

THE NEW KITTEN
DETERMINING THE SEX

The sex of kittens can be determined shortly after birth. Kittens' genitalia are more difficult to see than adults'. However, there should be no problem if the following steps are taken:

With the kitten facing away from you lift the tail to expose the anal area. In both sexes, you will see two openings. The first opening just below the base of the tail is the anus.

In the *female* kitten, the vulva is a *vertical slit* seen immediately below the anus. In the adult female the space between the anus and vulva measures about one-half inch—but it is closer than that in the kitten. In the *male*, the opening for the penis

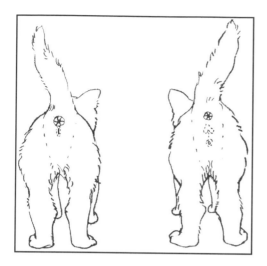

Determining the sex. In the female, the vulva is a vertical slit just below the anus.

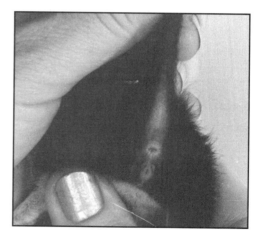

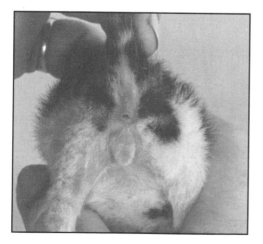

In the male, the opening for the penis is found below the scrotal sacs.

is directed backward. The tip of the penis is hidden in a small round opening located one-half inch below the anus. These two openings are separated by the scrotal sacs, which appear as raised darkish areas. The testicles may not be easily felt until the kitten is six weeks old. In the adult tom or neutered male the anus and opening for the penis are more than one inch apart.

DECLAWING

This operation may be considered for indoor individuals of both sexes who have developed the vice of scratching and tearing upholstery and furnishings—particularly when attempts to train them to use a scratching post have not been successful.

There is controversy about whether a cat should be declawed. One view is that declawing is unnatural and psychologically harmful. Another is that it does not involve a hardship and that cats get along well without their front claws. *Cats that live outdoors should not be declawed.* This affects their ability to climb and defend themselves.

Declawing is best done when a kitten is three months of age or older. Many veterinarians suggest that the operation be deferred until a kitten is four to five months old, at which time it can be done at the same time as neutering. Young cats learn to cope without claws more quickly than do adults. In most cases only the front claws are removed. The hind claws are not used to scratch furniture. Leaving them affords the cat a measure of usefulness.

The operation, done under general anesthesia, involves the removal of the claw to include the nail matrix and part or all of the last bone of the toe. Less complete removal can result in regrowth of the claw or a misshapen nail. The feet are firmly bandaged. Dressings are removed in a day or two and the cat can go home. The feet will be tender for several days, so filler in the litter box should be replaced with shredded *paper to prevent sand from getting into the healing incision.*

Choose a balanced diet—don't leave it up to your cat.

—Sue Giffin

18

FEEDING AND NUTRITION

GENERAL INFORMATION

The commercial importance of cat foods has made the industry a billion dollar business. Accordingly, well-known cat food manufacturers have conducted extensive research and feeding trials to establish nutritious and highly palatable diets that do *not* require supplements.

When choosing a cat food, it is important to determine whether it has been formulated to meet all the daily protein, fat, vitamin and mineral requirements of your cat. Federal law requires that all cat food manufacturers provide a listing of ingredients in their rations. Ingredients are listed according to amount: the greatest amount first, the least amount last. However, the required labels do not contain enough information for you to determine the exact nutrient content of the product with reference to tables of cat nutritional requirements.

An important indicator of quality is a statement on the label that states the diet has been found adequate by the Association of American Feed Control Officials (AAFCO). Also look for a statement on the label that describes the product as "complete, balanced, perfect, or scientific." *If it does not so state, you can assume it is not a complete diet and you should choose another product.* If designed for the growth of kittens (also used for pregnant and nursing queens), the product will be advertised as one that supports growth, is suitable for young kittens or is suitable for the first year of your kitten's life.

Another indication of quality is the reputation of the manufacturer. Well-known manufacturers noted for their research generally produce quality food. These products may be more expensive than generic brands; but this is because the ingredients are derived from higher quality food sources.

You can also gauge the effectiveness of a product by observing its effect on your cat's stool. Poor quality protein passes through a cat's intestinal tract unused, resulting in loose, mushy or diarrhea stools. Very large stools, on the other hand, indicate excessive amounts of fiber and other indigestibles that are not being utilized by your cat's body.

Nutritional Requirements

The nutritional requirements of adult cats and 10-week-old kittens are shown in Table 3. Cats in nature are meat eaters. In fact, cats require considerably more protein than dogs do. They also require a high-calorie diet. Because they metabolize protein and fat well, they get more of their energy from these sources than from carbohydrates.

Certain essential amino acids must be supplied by a cat's diet. **Taurine** is one of the most important, particularly for the growing kitten. *Taurine deficiency is associated with central retinal degeneration and blindness, feline cardiomyopathy and heart failure, reproductive problems* including infertility, death of unborn kittens, and birth of *fading kittens.* Taurine is found in highest concentration in certain seafoods. Cat foods should contain at least 0.02 percent taurine on a dry-weight basis.

Arginine deficiency leads to high levels of ammonia in the blood and death in a matter of hours. It is difficult to produce this deficiency in cats.

Cats cannot convert **tryptophan** to niacin or **beta carotene** to Vitamin A and have a special need for **arachidonic acid** and **Vitamin B$_6$** (pyridoxine). These nutrients are found almost exclusively in animal tissue.

Calcium deficiency is the most frequent nutritional disorder among cats. It should not occur if the cat is eating a nutritionally balanced diet. It may be brought on by exclusively feeding meats or by lactation that puts an extreme drain on a queen's calcium reserve (see Pregnancy and Kittens: *Milk Fever*).

Types of Cat Food

There are three types of cat food: *dry, semimoist* and *canned.* Because their physical forms are different, making direct comparisons of levels of energy, protein and fat among them can be difficult.

For example, the amount of protein per unit of product weight in dry cat food is about 35 percent and in canned food about 10 percent. Canned foods contain more water. When the water content is factored out and the products compared on a dry-weight basis (Table 1), it can be seen that canned foods actually contain *more* protein (41 percent). Another way to compare products is by energy content. Again, factoring out the moisture content, dry food provides 105 Kcal per ounce, while canned food provides only 29 (Table 1). You would have to feed three to four times more canned food than dry food to provide the same amount of energy.

A common misconception is that the protein in dry rations is of cereal origin, while protein in semimoist and canned food is of meat origin. In fact, all varieties contain protein from meats and cereals. While vegetable protein is the least expensive, it is also the least desirable. The cost of the food thus becomes an index of protein quality, with the more expensive cat foods having a greater percentage of their proteins in the form of meat products.

Popular pet food manufacturers often add ingredients to increase palatability—but this may be at the expense of nutritional value. Gourmet foods, in particular, usually contain meat from one specific source such as tuna, shrimp, chicken, liver or kidney. They have excellent palatability and a high protein and fat content but being from a single source, they are not nutritionally balanced and must not be fed as the only food. In addition, cats quickly become addicted to gourmet foods.

The value of a cat food depends not on the form but on the quality of the ingredients used to produce it. Good quality and inferior quality products are available in all three types. Each has advantages and disadvantages.

Dry cat food is a cereal-based food mixed with meat or dairy products. During processing, dry foods are cooked to 150°F, which breaks down the starch in the cereals, increasing digestibility. The temperature flash also sterilizes the product and removes most of the moisture. Complete foods contain added vitamins and minerals. Dry foods are the least expensive. Because they are abrasive, they are best for the teeth and gums. One other advantage of dry food is that it can be left out at all times, allowing the cat to eat at will.

A disadvantage of dry food is that palatability may be less than other types. However, most cats accept it well. Free choice or hand feeding usually does not result in either weight gain or weight loss.

A theoretical disadvantage of dry food is that it may predispose to FUS (feline urological syndrome), a condition that affects about one percent of adult cats. This may be due to its low water and high magnesium content. To prevent recurrences of FUS, the magnesium content of any cat food should be less than 0.1 percent on a dry-weight basis. Keep in mind that this provision applies to cats that have had at least one bout of FUS. Special diets low in magnesium are *not* necessarily recommended for all cats. This subject is discussed in the chapter URINARY SYSTEM (see *Feline Urologic Syndrome*).

Dry rations tend to lose their nutritional value over time and should not be used after six months of storage.

Semimoist cat food has more eye and taste appeal but is more expensive than dry food. It is made up from many protein sources such as fresh fish, beef, liver, chicken, and thus has advantages of both dry and moist foods. The water content is higher than dry ration.

Canned cat food is twice as popular as semimoist food and four times as popular as dry food. It is also the most expensive. There are two types of canned preparation: those sold in 6 ounce or large 12 to 15 ounce cans; and the specialty or gourmet flavors sold in small flat 3-ounce tins.

Foods in the *large cans* contain protein derived from meat, fish and vegetable sources along with vitamins and minerals. Not all products are complete and balanced foods. Canned foods usually contain more fat and therefore more energy. They may be preferred for the energetic cat who will not eat other foods because of taste preference. They are *not* suitable for self-feeding. Like the semimoist varieties, canned rations do not reduce dental tartar. The small specialty *gourmet canned* foods contain high concentrations of protein, usually from a single source. These are the most expensive cat foods. The majority of these products are not nutritionally complete formulas and must not be used as the sole source of food. In fact, most are intended to supplement a more complete diet for variety, flavor and taste appeal.

TABLES OF NUTRITIONAL REQUIREMENTS FOR CATS

Table 1—Average Nutrient Content (dry-weight basis) and Amount to Feed of Various Commercial Cat Foods*

Variety	Water	Protein	Fat	Ca	P	Kcal/oz.	Ounces to Feed 6-10 lb. cat per day
Dry	6–10%	34%	12%	1.6%	1.1%	105	2–3$^1/_2$
Semimoist	30–40%	36%	17%	2.4%	2.2%	75	2$^3/_4$–4$^3/_4$
Canned	75%	41%	14%	2.0%	1.4%	29	7$^1/_2$–12
Canned Gourmet	75%	53%	27%	1.5%	1.5%	35	6–10

*Modified from Lewis, Morris, Hand, *Pet Foods; Small Animal Clinical Nutrition*, vol. 3, 1987.
Note: 3 ounces of dry food consitutes one level cup and equals 4 ounces of semimoist or 7$^1/_2$ ounces of canned food.

Table 2—Daily Caloric Requirements for Cats of Different Ages

Age	Expected Weight	Kcal/Pound	Kcal/day	Ounces of Dry Food/day (105 Kcal/oz)
1 week	4 oz.	190	24	—
5 weeks	1 lb.	132	132	1$^1/_4$
10 weeks	2–2.5 lbs.	112	225–275	2–2$^3/_4$
20 weeks	4–5.5 lbs.	60	250–325	2$^1/_4$–3
6 months	5–6.5 lbs.	50	260–335	2$^1/_2$–3$^1/_4$
Adult maintenance	6–10 lbs.	35	210–350	2–3$^1/_2$
Pregnant queen	7 lbs.	45	315	3
Nursing queen	6 lbs.	65–125	390–750	3$^3/_4$–7

Table 3—Nutritional Requirements (per pound body weight) per Day of Adult Cats and 10-Week-Old Kittens*

Nutrients	Adults	Kittens
Protein (gm)	2.9	8.6
Energy (Kcal)	40	115
Fat (gm)	1.5	3.2
Minerals		
Calcium (mg)	90	290
Phosphorus (mg)	80	230
Magnesium (mg)	5	14
Potassium (mg)	30	90
Sodium Chloride (mg)	50	140
Iron (µg)	10	30
Copper (µg)	0.5	1.4
Manganese (µg)	0.9	2.8
Zinc (µg)	3.2	8.6
Iodine (µg)	0.1	0.3
Vitamins		
Vitamin A (IU)	100	290
Vitamin D (IU)	10	29
Vitamin E (IU)	1	3
Thiamin (mg)	0.05	0.14
Riboflavin (mg)	0.05	0.14
Pantothenic Acid (mg)	0.1	0.28
Niacin (mg)	0.5	1.0
Choline (mg)	20	57
Pyridoxine (µg)	45	140
Folic Acid (µg)	9	30
Biotin (µg)	0.5	1
Vitamin B$_{12}$ (µg)	0.2	0.6

*Adapted from National Research Council's *Nutrient Requirements for Cats*.

FEEDING YOUR CAT

Food Preferences

Many owners assume a cat will eventually eat a nutritionally balanced diet if given a variety of foods from which to choose. *This is incorrect.* Many cats will starve rather than eat a product they find unappetizing. In general, cats prefer meat—especially kidneys—whether cooked or raw makes no difference. They prefer food at body temperature, rather than hot or cold. In the wild, mice are the primary food of cats.

Cats may become addicted to single-ingredient foods (such as liver or tuna) if given exclusively. However, there is no reason a cat should not develop a preference for a particular product as long as it is *nutritionally complete*. The problem arises when a cat develops a preference for a food that is not a complete cat food. Canned specialty or gourmet foods, in particular, are highly addictive.

Another type of food preference occurs when an owner oversupplements an already complete diet with a highly palatable item such as liver, kidneys, milk, eggs or chicken. The cat then develops a preference for that item and refuses to eat the complete diet. More tidbits are then required and a vicious cycle ensues. Many cats develop a liking for liver. Large amounts should not be given because of high concentration of Vitamin A, which could produce *Vitamin A toxicity*. Similarly, raw fish and raw eggs should not be given in excess. Both contain antivitamin factors that could produce a lethal deficiency.

Meat alone is not a complete diet. If you feed it exclusively, your cat will probably develop a preference for meat and stop eating anything else.

Many cats enjoy milk. How much they can consume without experiencing diarrhea varies greatly with the individual. Milk should not sit out for more than two hours—nor should canned food—because of the risk of spoilage.

Feeding the Adult

The average daily caloric requirements for cats of different ages is shown in Table 2. For example, an adult cat (nine lbs.) at maintenance requiring 300 Kcal per day (35 Kcal/lbs.) would thus consume about three ounces of dry, four ounces of semimoist (one cup in each case) or two six-ounce cans of canned food per day. The actual amount of food eaten varies among cats of equal weight because of differences in metabolic rate and activity level.

Cats vary widely in the amount of food required to maintain normal body weight and should be fed whatever is necessary to maintain body condition. This condition is present when the ribs cannot be seen but are easily felt, and the abdomen is trim but not flabby. See *Obesity*. Older, sedentary cats require fewer calories than the amounts indicated in the table, while active cats require more. Considerably more food is required for nonmaintenance activities such as pregnancy and lactation.

Select several nutritionally complete cat foods and offer them one at a time to your cat for several days in succession. Note which ones your cat seems to like best. Having found two or three products acceptable to your cat, use them interchangeably to provide variety and appetite appeal.

Cats may be fed free choice, where food is available at all times. If you keep a number of cats or are unable to feed your cats at regular intervals, a dry or semimoist ration may be more convenient and will be less expensive. The ration can be left out and fed free choice. This also assures that timid cats are not denied access to food. If the cat tends to overeat, however, it is best to feed by hand. Here it becomes important to consult Table 2 to determine caloric requirements—with a view to keeping the cat healthy and trim. Canned products should be fed twice a day, at the same time each day.

Remember to keep a bowl of clean, fresh water available at all times.

Don't box your cat in by letting her get too fat.   —Sue Giffin

FEEDING KITTENS

Most breeders supply diet guidelines with a new kitten. This should be followed, at least for the first few days since an abrupt change in diet can cause indigestion. Ten-week-old kittens require about twice as much protein and 50 percent more calories per pound than do adult cats. Accordingly, it is important to feed a nutritionally complete diet specifically formulated to support the growth of kittens.

Labels on cat food packages provide recommended daily feeding amounts. They are useful guidelines but are not applicable to every kitten. As a rule, young kittens should be fed as much as they will eat. Overeating to the point of obesity is rare. Kittens can be fed free choice—which may be preferable when feeding a litter—or they can be fed by hand. If using canned food, feed three times a day until kittens are seven months old. Then reduce the number of feedings to two per day. When kittens are one year old, switch to a maintenance adult cat food.

Food preferences are generally established before a kitten is six months old. Therefore it is important to accustom your kitten to eating a nutritionally complete diet at an early age. You should choose two or three products that fulfill these requirements and then use them interchangeably as discussed in the section *Feeding the Adult*.

Vitamin and mineral supplements are not necessary if you are feeding a nutritionally balanced diet. In fact, they may even be harmful. If your kitten is a poor eater and you think these supplements may be needed, discuss this with your veterinarian.

SWITCHING DIETS

It may become necessary to adjust a cat's diet and switch to a new food because of a health problem. If the cat refuses to eat the new diet, the procedure for switching is as follows:

To 80 percent of the original food add 20 percent of the new food, mix together thoroughly, and feed the mixture until the cat accepts it. Once this is accomplished, increase the amount of new food to 40 percent while reducing the original ration. Continue in this fashion until the switch is complete.

OBESITY

Overfeeding leads to obesity. This is a big problem in cats. If you think your cat may be overweight, determine the ideal weight in proportion to the cat's height and bones. There should be a layer of subcutaneous fat over the ribs, thick enough to provide some padding and insulation, but *not too thick*. You should be able to feel the ribs as individual structures.

The average cat weighs about eight pounds, but this varies considerably with the breed, age and sex. Food preferences and single-food-source addictions present problems in redirecting the cat's eating habits. Review your feeding practices and take the following steps:

1. Feed a restricted-calorie reducing diet, preferably the dry type in the amount you would feed for ideal weight, not the cat's current weight. Hill's *Feline r/d* is a suitable diet and is available through veterinarians.

2. Do not feed supplements (gourmet cat foods, table scraps, treats).

3. Monitor the cat's activity to be sure food is not being found elsewhere.

4. Chart weight at weekly intervals. The cat should lose about 4 percent of its body weight per week.

5. Provide daily exercise and human companionship.

6. After four to eight weeks or when ideal weight is obtained, feed a dry or semimoist high-quality balanced food, preferably not too palatable, in the proper amount for ideal weight. Alternatively, you can continue to feed the reducing diet in larger amounts.

A very obese cat may require hospitalization for dietary management.

COMMON FEEDING ERRORS

A frequent error is feeding dog food. Cats require twice as much protein and B vitamins as do dogs. Cats, unlike dogs, cannot convert certain dietary precursors into necessary amino acids and water soluble vitamins. A cat given *dog food* over a long period can develop *taurine deficiency; Vitamin A deficiency (night blindness); niacin deficiency; retinal degeneration;* and other serious or fatal illnesses.

Another common error is to overdose a cat with Vitamins A and D or calcium and phosphorus, either by giving the vitamins directly or by supplementing the diet with products high in them (such as raw liver or fish oils). Excess Vitamin A causes

Kittens love to play. Provide suitable toys—*not* a ball of string!   —Sydney Wiley

sterility and loss of hair coat. Excess calcium, phosphorus and Vitamin D cause metabolic bone and kidney disease.

Raw fish should not be fed to cats. Raw fish contains an enzyme that destroys Vitamin B_1. A deficiency of this Vitamin (thiamin) results in brain damage. Fish is also deficient in Vitamin E and has the potential to transmit diseases.

SOME GUIDELINES FOR FEEDING CATS

- Never feed dog food. It is deficient in essential nutrients required by cats.
- Specialty foods and even table scraps can be given as treats once or twice a week—but only after the base diet is eaten. Cooked meats (liver, kidney), cottage cheese, cooked vegetables, cooked fish, milk and yogurt are foods with strong taste appeal that cats seem to enjoy.
- Never feed meats exclusively.
- Treats should never exceed 20 percent of a cat's total daily ration.
- Uncooked meat and raw fish should not be given because of the dangers of vitamin deficiency and transmitting diseases.

- Vitamin/mineral supplements are not necessary or desirable if you are feeding a balanced cat food.
- Cats have highly selective eating habits. The location of the food dish, noise, the presence of other animals and other threats or distractions can adversely affect how much they are willing to eat. A boarded cat may go an entire week without eating.
- Cats prefer to have their food served at room temperature.

19

FELINE BEHAVIOR AND TRAINING

THE SOCIAL NATURE OF CATS

Knowledge of the social structure of cats in the wild is somewhat limited. It was thought that cats were not social animals and avoided direct contact with their own kind except when mating and nursing kittens. Recent studies, however, suggest that competition for food and territory may be more important than antisocial attitudes in keeping cats apart. When adequate food and shelter were made available, free-ranging cats were found to congregate in groups that consisted of several adult females and their female offspring. Kittens remained with their mothers for long periods and often were not fully weaned until three months old. Kittens between 8 and 16 weeks often accompanied their mothers on excursions within her home range to familiarize themselves with the hunting territory. Older kittens hunted alone but continued to rest together and groom each other throughout their first year.

Between 10 and 14 months, male kittens stayed away from the core area for progressively longer periods and eventually migrated to areas away from the social activity of other cats. Even when resources were plentiful, adult toms did not live together. Some females, however, remained within the maternal group for life. Others moved away to establish new female groups of their own.

At three to five years old, fully mature tomcats began to challenge rivals for the right to breed. If successful, they became the dominant breeding males for that

Four-week-old kittens, during the period of primary socialization, learning to interact successfully with members of their own species.

particular group, a position they seldom held for more than two or three years. In one field study, no breeding males were identified over age 6.

Domestic cats raised in the wild do not have natural attachments for people, nor do they seek human companionship. When approached by curious people, wild cats retreat quickly. Proximity to humans initiates fear. When cornered, a wild or untamed cat will growl, hiss and defend itself tenaciously. Note, however, that domestic cats raised by humans from birth to maturity do not exhibit flight and fight behavior.

The young of all species pass through a period of learning from other members of their species in which they acquire the skills to interact successfully and survive. This period is called *socialization*, or the formative period. In kittens, it occurs at three to nine weeks.

Kittens raised as house pets associate humans with suckling, warmth, mother's milk and learning play. If the mother is docile, affectionate and people oriented, it is natural for the kittens to acquire these attributes also. Early weaning and removal from the nest before six weeks old can interfere with this socialization process and can lead to behavior problems such as slowness to learn, shyness and aggression. Such a kitten may identify with people or other animal species and not fully actualize its own identity as a cat. This accounts for many unusual stories such as cats playing with rabbits.

During this formative period from three to nine weeks, a kitten should have varied exposure to many new and different experiences to become more flexible and able to adjust later in life. This is the hallmark of a well-socialized individual. It is extremely important for pet owners to select kittens that are well socialized as they make better companions and pets. Qualities to look for in selecting a kitten are discussed in the Appendix (see *What to Look for in a Healthy Kitten*).

One feline characteristic that is not lost during domestication is territorial attachment. A cat is very strongly bonded to home, yard and neighborhood—places the young cat has come to know and regard as home territory. People are often seen as just an extension of this territory. If forced to make a choice between location and owner, a cat will often choose the location. This can create problems for a family moving to a new house. The cat will often attempt to return to its former residence.

This singular possessiveness of territory is a major reason behind many behavior problems. Adding a new cat or person to the household can trigger jealousy or even a lapse in social behavior. Just how well the cat is able to adjust depends on flexibility and training, inherited disposition, sex and state of mind and physical well-being. How to deal with these and other behavioral problems is discussed below.

TRAINING

Cats learn quickly if we account for certain aspects of cat psychology. Of all the traits we admire in cats, independence and self-sufficiency stand out most. Submission, as we see it in dogs, simply does not exist in cats. A cat may retreat or attack but will never submit. Administer a stern rebuke and many cats will hiss in defiance. Accordingly, training strategies that rely on traditional submissive roles of pet to master will not be successful in gaining the cooperation of cats.

Striking a cat in anger is definitely inadvisable. This teaches cats only to distrust and avoid their owners. Cats are quite likely to associate punishment with the person doing the punishing, rather than the unacceptable act from which the lesson resulted. Corrective punishment should be administered indirectly. It is best to associate the act with some unpleasant yet seemingly impersonal happening such as a startling "No!" or a stream of water from a plastic spray bottle.

Cats generally do not respond to commands unless it is convenient, fun or profitable for them. Devising a system of rewards involving praise and tasty tidbits may suffice if it holds the cat's attention. However, many behavior problems are best managed by removing the cause. For example, if the cat is not using a dirty litter box, frequent cleaning of the box will help.

It is much easier to train a kitten than it is to change the misbehavior of an adult. To break a bad habit, it is nearly always necessary to find a substitute activity for that behavior—and rechannel the cat's behavior from that which is bad to that which is socially acceptable.

Unacceptable behavior often stems from boredom. Cats are fun loving and playful and should be given suitable toys with which to distract and amuse themselves. Choose toys that are sturdy and cannot be torn or chewed apart. They should be large enough so they can't be swallowed.

The best results are achieved with patience, steady praise, love and consistent reward for accomplishments well done.

HOUSEBREAKING

Contrary to popular belief, mother cats do not teach their kittens to use kitty litter. Kittens begin to dig in and use dirt and dry, loose material at about four weeks old without ever having observed their mothers doing so. This natural instinct is utilized in training kittens to use the litter box. Begin as soon as the new kitten arrives.

Satisfactory litter boxes can be bought, or you can use a plastic or enamel-coated tray with disposable plastic liners. A number of different kinds of filler are sold at pet stores. In general, they are much more absorbent than shredded newspapers or sand and dirt. Some fillers contain chlorophyll and deodorizing chemicals. The odor of the chemical may be objectionable to the cat and can be one cause of litter box aversion, discussed elsewhere in this chapter. Odor-free fillers are available and often preferable. If the odor of urine and feces becomes a problem, you can add a drop of liquid deodorant, sold especially for this purpose, to a tray containing plain filler. In any case, do not use household disinfectants that are toxic to cats and can irritate their skin and paws.

If the kitten was trained to the litter box by a previous owner, use the same type of box and filler. Place the kitten in the litter box after a nap, a meal and whenever your kitten appears inclined to urinate or defecate. When mistakes occur, pick up the kitten and set the offender down in the box. Do not discipline *just before* placing the kitten in the box. A reprimand such as a loud "No!" or a squirt of water will be associated with being placed in the litter box—thus causing an aversion to the litter box instead of the act of soiling.

Rubbing a cat's nose in a mess is strongly *discouraged* because few cats will understand the reason for the punishment. However, to avoid another episode, they may begin to eliminate in out-of-the-way places where the urine and stool may go unnoticed.

Once the kitten becomes accustomed to the litter box, it is important to keep the box clean because dirty boxes turn cats away. Scoop out solid material once or twice a day, and stir the filler to keep the surface dry. Change the filler every three or four days, more often if necessary. Wash the pan thoroughly and let it dry completely before adding new filler. Place the box away from heavy traffic and loud distracting noises so the cat can have privacy. Should it be necessary to move the box, make the change gradually, moving it step by step.

Problem elimination is discussed in *Inappropriate Elimination.*

SCRATCHING THE FURNITURE

Destructive scratching is common. Cats sharpen their claws as part of normal grooming. In this process, the claw's worn-down outer sheath is caught and removed, exposing a new inner claw beneath. To prevent damage to upholstery and furnishings, two alternatives are available. One is to have the kitten declawed. This subject is discussed in PEDIATRICS: *Declawing.* The other is to provide a suitable substitute such as a scratching post.

Scratching posts can be bought or made at home. Some commercial posts are too short and inclined to tip over. The post, either horizontal or vertical, should be sturdy and tall enough so the cat can stretch out comfortably and stand on its hind feet while sharpening its front claws. A satisfactory post can be made by mounting a 30-inch long pine board on a two foot square wooden base. Cover it with tightly woven carpet or sisal rope. A 45 degree slant can be constructed by using a second piece of board to form a triangle. Some people use a wooden box covered with carpet or sisal. Others tack the material to the wall or simply use a log with the bark still on.

The scratching post should be ready when the kitten arrives. Take the kitten to it several times a day, after naps, the first thing in the morning and whenever the cat scratches at upholstery. Be firm and consistent and reward the kitten for good behavior.

Locate the scratching post close to the kitten's sleeping area. Cats like to scratch shortly after awakening. Toys and catnip can be placed next to the post to draw the kitten's interest. Reprimanding the cat by a verbal "No" or a squirt of water when caught in the act can be effective but requires constant vigilance and consistent application. It is better to anticipate the behavior and take cats to the post before they begin to scratch. After a reprimand, do not take the cat immediately to the scratching post; otherwise, the cat may associate the punishment with the act of being taken to the post and develop an aversion to the post.

A good way to keep a kitten from scratching at a favorite spot is to place several spring-loaded mousetraps *upside down* around the area. When the kitten steps on the back of the trap, the resulting "pop" provides a scare. Having been frightened two or three times, most kittens will avoid the area. Another trick is to cover furniture the cat favors with double-sided cellophane. Tape the covering in place until the cat consistently uses the scratching post. An older cat can be trained to use a scratching post, but this takes more time and patience. An aversion to furnishings and upholstery also can be established by applying a cat repellent.

A harness is more secure than a collar for walking a cat.

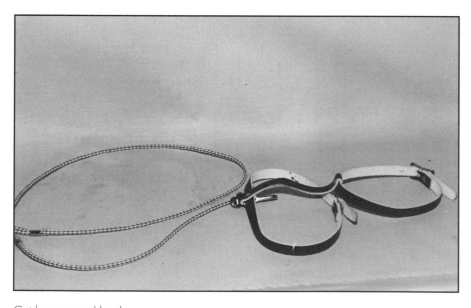

Cat harness and leash.

COLLARS AND LEASHES

Kittens and cats that go outdoors should wear a collar containing an ID tag. Buy a well-designed collar with an elastic insert that stretches over the cat's head in an emergency such as a foot getting caught in the collar or the collar getting caught on a fence. A bell can be added to alert birds.

Walking on a Leash: A harness provides better control than a collar. For the first few days, put the collar or harness on for short periods until the kitten gets used to it. Then, attach a leash that can be dragged behind. Next, pick up the leash and follow the kitten without trying to control the direction. When the kitten has learned to accept the arrangement, begin to lead with occasional firm tugs, interspersed with lots of praise and petting.

COMING WHEN CALLED

It is important to teach your kitten to come when called. Because cats normally respond to commands only when it is to their advantage, get their cooperation by rewarding them with tasty treats and affection. At mealtimes, call your kitten by name and follow it with the word "Come." Repeat this exercise when the cat comes to you for stroking. With repetition, the kitten will learn to associate the word "Come" with a pleasurable experience. The cat that refuses to come when called can often be enticed by throwing a toy nearby.

Do not expect obedience for something your cat does not enjoy—and *never* call the cat for punishment!

BEHAVIOR DISORDERS

Cats are solitary and independent. They resent intrusions and changes in their routines. Frustration often stems from a change in the living pattern or the inability to express normal biological drives such as sex, hunting and aggressive play.

While behavior is strongly influenced by instinct and early socialization, it is also modified by genetic determinants that give each cat an individual disposition and temperament. Behavior also is rooted in the state of health, age and sex of the individual.

Some cases of inappropriate behavior are caused by physical ailments; for example, the cat with FUS that urinates often in the wrong places. The common behavior problems you are likely to encounter are discussed below.

INAPPROPRIATE ELIMINATION

Inappropriate elimination is the most common behavior problem reported by cat owners. Male and female cats are equally at fault. In some cases, there is a urinary tract infection or an illness such as colitis. In most cases, however, there is no medical explanation for the cat's behavior. Some owners may blame themselves for doing something that put the cat off-track.

Male and female cats urinate in the squatting position. The urine is voided downward onto a flat surface. Spraying occurs in the standing position. The tail is held straight up and typically quivers. Urine is sprayed horizontally at ankle height onto walls and furniture. Both male and female cats spray, although males are more likely to do so than females. Females in estrus urine-mark in the squatting position.

Soiling in the house can be looked at as two separate behaviors. One is urine marking (which *includes spraying*). The other is regularly urinating and defecating outside the litter box.

Causes of Urine Marking. Urine marking is an expression of territorial dominance. It is associated with the rubbing of body oils from the chin and tail on favorite objects. It occurs when a cat feels threatened by an intruder. Often, it is an advertisement that sex is available. It increases during the mating season and especially during courtship. It sends a message to other cats to avoid competitive encounters.

A number of stimuli may elicit urine marking or spraying. An indoor cat looking out a window may observe a new neighboorhood cat spraying on or near the house. The indoor cat initiates defensive activity that involves spraying and may include threat behavior such as running to the door, hissing or growling at the windows and intensely watching the rival. The introduction of a new cat to the household may elicit spraying by either the resident cat or the newly arrived cat. In fact, any disturbance in a cat's routine that arouses the cat or is perceived as a threat can elicit spraying.

Urine marking can be distinguished from other elimination problems by noting that the cat usually voids small amounts, the activity generally involves several locations, and the cat continues to use the litter box for defecation and *most* urine elimination.

Treatment of Urine Marking and Spraying: **Intact males and estrous females should be neutered.** This is effective in 80 percent to 90 percent of cases. Neutered cats that continue to spray or urine mark often respond to drugs and modification of the environment or medication. See *Drug Treatment of Behavior Disorders* later in this chapter.

Environment modification techniques are effective if the stimuli that elicit urine marking and spraying can be identified and extinguished. For example, competition between an indoor and outdoor cat can be lessened by driving the outdoor cat away or by preventing the indoor cat from seeing the outdoor cat. (Simply close the door to the viewing room.) You may need to block the view from windows using plastic, blinds, curtains or shades. Indoor cats that go outdoors may improve if allowed to spend more or less time outside, depending on response to trial.

Treat conflict between indoor cats by reducing competition, separating the cats or reducing the number of household cats.

If spraying occurs in one or two locations, it may be possible to create an aversion to these locations by spraying the area with a commercial cat repellent. Other substances that may repel the cat are mothballs in cloth bags, orange peels and rubbing alcohol. Try setting the cat's food dish near the spot. Cats do not like to soil near their feeding areas. Placing upside-down mousetraps around a favorite spraying area may work.

Causes of Litter Box Failure. One or more of the following may explain why some cats fail to use the litter box:

- The cat may develop a dislike for the litter box, the litter in the box or the box's present location.
- The cat may develop a surface or location *preference*.
- The cat may have an emotional problem that is expressed as inappropriate elimination.

A common belief is that cats are attracted to the odors of urine and feces, and mainly because of attraction, they return to the same spot to eliminate. This belief is at odds with the observation that cats avoid dirty litter boxes and do not like to eat or play in areas where they eliminate. Accordingly, there must be other explanations for the cat's consistent return to the same spot.

Cats that regularly use a litter box dig and paw in the litter, often bury the urine and feces but sometimes leave the box with the elimination still in view. A cat may dig in the litter before eliminating and not afterward—or vice versa. Apparently, the pawing and digging is not simply to cover the elimination. The movement of the paws through the litter and the feel of the litter as the paws are drawn through it seem to provide a tactile-kinesthetic sensation that gratifies the cat and eventually becomes associated with elimination. It follows then that cats prefer to dig in litter or on surfaces that give the best sensation of digging and are averse to digging in material that provides the least. In fact, evidence from one study suggests that coarse-grained litter, either sand or clay, is less satisfying to cats and a fine-grained "clumping" litter is much preferred.

It has also been observed that cats acquire a preference for eliminating on specific surfaces. Outdoor cats use a variety of surfaces such as loose dirt, leaves or sand in which to dig and scratch, eliminate and cover their excrement. Indoor cats have fewer options. An indoor cat can dig either in the litter provided or on the carpet or linoleum next to the box. Cats that dig and scratch outside the litter box, either before or after eliminating, may have acquired a preference for the new surface and begin to eliminate on that surface. Adjustments such as covering the surface with plastic, moving the litter box and cleaning the carpet with deodorizers and chemicals can be made; however, the cat proceeds to eliminate on carpets or floors elsewhere in the house.

In another example, a cat may begin to soil a carpet because the litter was dirty or a cover was placed on the box. Because of an acquired preference for the carpet, the cat may continue to use the carpet even after the box is cleaned or the cover removed. A cover can make the litter box unattractive by preventing dissipation of disagreeable odors and interfering with the cat's normal posture or the ability to dig and paw in the litter. A cat frightened by a loud noise or chased or threatened by another cat while using a common litter box may seek and find another location with privacy. Scolding a cat and immediately placing it in the box can lead to future avoidance.

Cats with mild litter box aversion typically do not dig, cover and bury feces and may stand on the edge of the box to avoid physical contact with the filler, run quickly out of the box and show other signs of distaste for the litter box or its contents. They may still continue to use the box part-time. Cats with an intense aversion rarely if ever use the box.

Cats learn to associate specific activities with specific locations. They prefer certain spots for sleeping, sunning, eating, self-grooming and apparently, eliminating. A cat may use a litter box consistently primarily because of that specific location. When the box is moved, the cat may eliminate on the floor where the box had been located.

Emotionally related influences cause a relatively small number of cases of house soiling, one exception being *separation anxiety*. Unlike dogs, cats generally do not exhibit separation anxiety when left alone for short periods but may do so when left alone for eight hours or longer. Typically, the owner returns to find that the cat has deposited a mess on the bed, clothes or favorite furniture. The cat may seem to be "piqued" or "getting even" with the person for being left alone. In fact, it is more likely that the cat was attracted to the objects that carried the owner's scent.

Treatment for Failure to Use the Litter Box: Determine why the cat is not using the box if possible, keeping in mind that one reason may have initiated the problem and yet another is now maintaining it.

Litter box aversion. Clean the box more frequently. Follow the procedure discussed in *Housebreaking*. Use a nondeodorized litter without additives. Switch to a fine-grained, clay-based litter. Do not cover the box. If the cat scatters the litter, try using a bigger box or one with higher sides.

Litter box location aversion. Increase the number of litter boxes, placing a new one where the cat is now soiling. Later, remove an unused litter box. Prevent sneak attacks by another cat while the first is using the box. Avoid stimuli that frighten the cat while it is using the litter.

Location and surface preferences. Ascertain that the litter or litter box is not a turn-off by looking for signs of litter dislike. If none are apparent, move the litter box to the site of soiling. If this is effective, the litter box should not be moved back immediately to its original location. Instead, the box should be moved several inches each day for the first several days, and then progressively greater distances until the box is back to the original site.

Other possible actions include changing the surface by removing a rug, adding a rug or covering the area with a hard surface material—but only if it seems that this would not cause the problem to become generalized and involve other similar surfaces in the house. Create an aversion to the new location by feeding or playing with the cat at the site of soiling.

Separation anxiety. Decrease the time the cat is alone. Provide a cat sitter who will play with and pet the cat during the owner's absence. Consider a companion cat.

ENERGY RELEASE ACTIVITIES

Cats have natural drives that include hunting, bringing home prey, eating grass and engaging in play-fighting. When outlets for energy excess are not provided, the cat may engage in activities unacceptable to the owner.

Compulsive Self-grooming (Neurodermatitis; psychogenic alopecia). This is an energy displacement phenomenon that occurs in cats that are emotionally high-strung. Ninety percent of cases are reported in Siamese, Burmese, Himalayans and

Abyssinians. It occurs in cats that are hospitalized, boarded, stressed, deprived of their freedom or subjected to long periods of boredom. A prominent sign of compulsive self-grooming is thinning of hair in a stripe down the back. The skin does not appear inflamed in most cases, but compulsive self-licking and chewing may progress to involve the abdomen, flanks and legs. Unless you see this behavior, it may not be obvious that the cat is doing this.

Diagnosis is made by excluding other causes of hair loss (see SKIN: *Hormone Skin Diseases*). A modification of the cat's routine to include a more active and varied lifestyle along with a reduction in stress factors is the best approach to treatment. Progesterones and tranquilizers have been used but should be reserved for cats in whom the skin reaction is severe.

Eating Houseplants. Some cats acquire the urge to eat grass. When not available, they turn to houseplants, some of which may be poisonous. See *Poisoning* for a list of indoor plants with toxic effects. Eating grass is not dangerous. You can try to satisfy the cat's needs by allowing access outside or by growing grass in a flower pot. In any case, all poisonous houseplants must be made inaccessible to the cat or eliminated from the house.

Bringing Home Prey. Well-fed cats do not relate killing with the need to eat. However, the hunting instinct is deeply ingrained in cats. They will deposit a variety of dead or near dead things at your door. If you attach a bell to the cat's collar, it will be more difficult for the cat to surprise mice and birds. However, this does not always work. In fact, most cats learn to stalk without ringing the bell. If you do not want the cat to hunt and kill small animals, confine your pet to the house.

Play-fighting. This energy-releasing mechanism includes biting at the ankles or attacking imaginary objects. It is not the same as aggression. You can provide your cat with a toy substitute or more exercise, or allow play with another cat.

EATING DISORDERS

Anorexia Nervosa (Refusal to eat). A cat with a strong food preference will starve itself if the preferred food is not available, or if it is not the right texture, odor or taste. This subject is discussed in FEEDING AND NUTRITION: *Food Preferences*.

Remember, loss of appetite and aversion to food are much more likely to be caused by an acute or chronic illness than by an eating disorder. *Veterinary examination is indicated.* Refusal to eat based strictly on emotional or psychological reasons (*anorexia nervosa*) is much less common and presumably is related to a deep-seated insecurity or nervous stress. Entice your cat by offering treats. Tranquilizers can reduce tension and may be indicated in the treatment of anorexia nervosa.

Cats that do not eat for several days or longer are subject to *Idiopathic Hepatic Lipidosis*.

Obesity is the most common eating disorder in cats. *Overfeeding* is the cause of nearly all cases of feline obesity. Many cats will continue to eat as long as they are fed. Taste gratification explains these cases, but some cases are caused by lack of exercise. Boredom, feeding cats together, (which encourages competition) and hormone diseases may be contributing factors. The number is small when compared with the total number of obese cats.

Little evidence exists that cats exhibit eating compulsions based on emotional stress and psychological influences. Treatment is discussed in FEEDING AND NUTRITION: *Obesity.*

ABNORMAL SUCKING BEHAVIOR

It has been suggested that a kitten's vice of sucking on fabrics, people, clothes and even itself can be traced to an unsatisfied nursing drive. Typically, this behavior involves a kitten that was orphaned, prematurely weaned or nutritionally deprived early in life. *Wool sucking* is a special case in which the preference is for wool clothing. It usually stops by sexual maturity. It occurs most often in the Siamese.

Treatment: This habit often can be stopped early by catching the kitten in the act and rapping it on the nose. This is how a queen would reprimand. You can apply hot sauce, tobacco juice or some other offensive tasting substance to the fabric to create a taste aversion. This works well in some cases.

AGGRESSIVE BEHAVIOR

Aggression in cats is usually defensive and related to self-protection. This is not *offensive* aggression as it occurs in some dogs. During socialization, a kitten learns to relate to and trust humans. This trust must be strong enough to overcome the natural fear and avoidance behavior seen in cats that grow up in the wild.

Cats that miss the period of primary socialization at three to nine weeks of age may never make a good adjustment and will always retain some anxiety when confronted by strange people.

Many cases of unexplained aggression are brought on by environmental stress, leading to heightened fear. The cat allows instincts to overcome trust. A distressed cat may suddenly attack someone nearby, even though that person played no part in causing the upset. A cat that has just been in a fight may accept handling by one person, yet scratch and bite another who approaches too closely. When cornered, a frightened cat will nearly always take aggressive action. Some cats, when they are rubbed vigorously under the belly or along the back near the tail, will turn suddenly and scratch or bite. These cats are saying "no" to petting. Some cats like to be petted; others do not.

Cats that develop a thyroid problem often become aggressive. Hunger and physical stresses may induce irritable behavior.

Cannibalism is a special kind of aggressive behavior. It occurs in the postpartum queen. See *Mothers Who Neglect or Injure Their Kittens* in PREGNANCY AND KITTENING.

To determine the cause of aggressive behavior, consider how and when it started, the circumstances under which it occurred and what the various attacks may have in common. True aggression should be distinguished from play-fighting, discussed above.

Treatment: A poorly socialized cat should be allowed to retreat from threatening situations and not forced to confront the causes of anxiety. These cats are often "one person" cats. They make excellent companions but must be watched carefully around strangers, particularly children.

When cornered in strange surroundings, a frightened cat may exhibit defensive agression.

A frightened cat that resists handling should be left alone until relaxed. Minimize all stimuli that impose stress and elicit fear. One way is to feed the cat. Sit alongside as the cat eats and speak soothingly. Soon, the cat will come to you for petting.

Cats that like to be petted or handled on their own terms should be respected as individuals and treated accordingly.

SEXUAL BEHAVIOR

Cats have strong sex drives. One expression of this is mounting. It is a tension release phenomenon in which the individual seeks gratification by using a queen substitute—such as a furry pillow or perhaps another cat. *Spraying* can be a manifestation of sexual tension. It is discussed in *Inappropriate Elimination*.

Neutering curbs sexual behavior in the majority of cases. However, approximately 10 percent of neutered males retain some overt sexual behavior.

DRUG TREATMENT OF BEHAVIOR DISORDERS

The best approach in treating a cat with a behavior disorder is to identify the underlying cause of the abnormal behavior and remove it. In general, it is best to use drugs only when other methods have failed. The drug should be withdrawn from time to time to see if the problem behavior recurs. Because of the potential for dangerous side effects, *behavior drugs should only be prescribed and monitored by a veterinarian.*

Tranquilizers: *Acepromazine* has a general depressive effect. It acts on the pain center and relieves anxiety. *Valium* is less depressive and much preferred for most behavior problems requiring a tranquilizer.

Tranquilizers are useful for calming an injured or frightened cat and for relieving anxiety attacks caused by moving, shipping, grooming, bathing or mating. A side effect of tranquilizers is that they block cortical inhibitory impulses. A tranquilized cat may stop using the litter box or may bite and scratch at the least provocation.

Progesterones: *Provera, megace* and other progestins have a calming effect and depress the pain center. They are useful in modifying aggressive behavior, particularly sexual. Effects are similar to those of castration.

Progesterones also are effective in treating urine marking and spraying, destructive scratching, compulsive self-grooming and cannibalism. *Side effects include cystic endometrial hyperplasia, mammary hyperplasia, pyometra, adrenal gland disease, weight gain, excessive drinking and urination and the potential for diabetes.*

20

TUMORS AND CANCERS

GENERAL INFORMATION

A *tumor* is any sort of lump, bump, growth or swelling such as an abscess.

Tumors that are true growths are called **neoplasms.** *Benign neoplasms* are growths that grow slowly and are surrounded by a capsule, do not invade and destroy and do not spread to other areas. They are cured by surgical removal, provided that all the tumor is removed. *Malignant neoplasms* are the same as cancers (also called *carcinomas*, *lymphomas* and *sarcomas*, depending on the cell type). Cancers tend to enlarge rapidly. They are not encapsulated. They infiltrate into or invade the surrounding tissue. When on the surface, they often ulcerate and bleed. At some point in their growth, cancers spread via the bloodstream or lymphatic system to remote body parts.

Cancer is graded according to the degree of malignancy. *Low grade* cancers continue to grow locally and reach a large size. They spread to distant organs late in the course of the illness. *High grade* cancers spread early, when the primary focus is still quite small or barely detectable.

Cancers are approached in the following manner: Suppose a female cat has a lump in her breast. Since it is solid, it is probably a neoplasm. It could be benign or malignant. A decision is made to *biopsy* the lump. This is surgery during which the lump or part of the lump is removed and sent to the pathologist. A pathologist, a medical doctor trained to make a diagnosis by inspecting the tissue under a microscope, can tell whether a growth is a cancer and can often provide additional information about the degree of malignancy. The pathologist's report gives the rationale for the best type of treatment.

An ulcerating tumor that may be an *abscess* or a *neoplasm*.

What Causes Cancer?

Cancer is a condition in which rapid cell division and tissue growth occurs at the expense of organ specific function. For example, a cancer from a cat's kidney is biopsied and found to be a mass of tissue that bears only slight resemblance to normal kidney cells under the microscope. The mass on the kidney does not function as kidney tissue nor does it help the kidney to make urine. If the cancer goes untreated, it eventually replaces the kidney while simultaneously metastasizing to other parts of the body. In time, through a number of possible events, it causes the cat's death.

Cancer is genetically influenced. Some genes, if present at certain locations on chromosomes, cause cells to become cancers. Other genes suppress cancer genes at these sites; still other genes inhibit the suppressors. Thus cancer is a multifactor, largely unpredictable phenomenon involving the interaction of many genes and chromosomes—all subject to familial and environmental influences.

Carcinogens are environmental influences known to increase the likelihood of cancer in proportion to the length and intensity of exposure to them. Carcinogens gain access to tissue cells, cause alterations in genes and chromosomes and disrupt the orderly system of checks and balances that controls cellular growth and tissue repair. Examples of carcinogens known to increase the risk of cancer in people are ultraviolet rays (skin cancer); X rays (thyroid cancer); nuclear radiation (leukemia); chemicals (aniline dyes causing bladder cancer); cigarettes and coal tars (causing lung and skin cancer); viruses (causing sarcoma in AIDS patients); and parasites (a cause of bladder cancer).

The feline leukemia virus causes several types of cancer.

A prior injury or blow is sometimes thought to be the cause of cancer. Trauma can be a cause of certain benign swellings. However, it is rarely the cause of a cancer. An injury to a breast, for example, may cause the breast to be carefully examined, resulting in the incidental finding of a preexisting breast cancer.

Some benign tumors such as warts and papillomas are clearly due to a virus. Other benign tumors such as lipomas adenomas of the breast and other organs simply just grow for reasons unknown.

No evidence exists that cancer in pets can spread to people.

TREATMENT OF TUMORS AND CANCERS

The effectiveness of any form of treatment depends on early recognition. Early-stage cancers have a higher cure rate than do late-stage cancers. This holds true for all types of cancer.

Complete *surgical removal* of a cancer that has not spread is the most satisfactory treatment possible. Cancers that have spread only to regional lymph nodes may still be cured if all the involved nodes can be removed. Even when disease is widespread, local excision of a bleeding or infected cancer can provide relief of pain and improve quality of life.

Electrocautery (a heated needle to destroy tissue) and cryosurgery (freezing tissue) are two techniques by which tumors on the body's surface can be controlled or cured by burning or freezing. These treatments provide alternatives to surgical removal, but special equipment is required.

Radiation therapy is useful in the management of some surface tumors and deeply situated tumors that cannot be controlled by surgery. Cures are possible. Radiotherapy must be performed in a medical center because it requires expensive equipment and the services of a trained radiotherapist.

Chemotherapy employs anticancer drugs given at prescribed intervals. These drugs, even when tightly controlled, have *major side affects*. They are useful in the management of some widely spread cancers. *Hormone therapy* and *immunotherapy* also have been successful in the management of some tumors.

CANCER IN THE CAT

Cats have higher rates of cancer than dogs and other domestic animals do. Most feline cancers occur in middle-aged and older individuals 10 to 15 years of age. Lymphosarcoma is an exception, occurring most often in young cats. The majority of feline cancers are not visible by outward inspection except for skin and breast tumors. These neoplasms can be detected by inspection and palpation.

The high cancer rate in cats is related to the feline leukemia virus. Common sites of involvement are lymph nodes (*lymphosarcoma*) and circulating blood cells (*leukemia*), but any organ or tissue in the cat's body can be affected. Taken together, the feline leukemia virus accounts for perhaps half the internal cancers, the majority of which are lymphosarcomas. It is also associated with other serious cat diseases, including anemia, feline infectious peritonitis, glomerulonephritis and toxoplasmosis. The depressed immunity level associated with feline leukemia

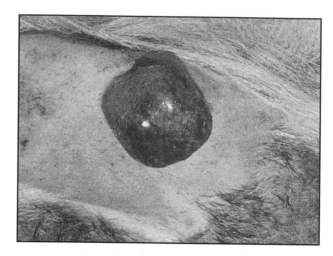

Only a *biopsy* can determine if this skin tumor is benign or malignant.

virus disease complex undoubtedly contributes to the high incidence of such secondary diseases.

Skin tumors are common in cats. Many skin tumors are not malignant; however, the incidence of skin cancer is still high and accounts for 7 percent of feline cancers. Next in frequency is the breast (5 percent).

Growths of the mouth account for 3 percent to 4 percent of feline cancers. Nearly all of them are malignant (squamous cell cancers). Signs are drooling, difficulty eating and the appearance of a lump or ulcerated growth involving the tongue or gums. A mouth cancer should be distinguished from an infected mass produced by imbedded foreign bodies such as needles, wood splinters or string cutting into the underside of the tongue.

A young cat with *lymphosarcoma*. Note the rough coat and emaciated appearance, the only outward sign of cancer.

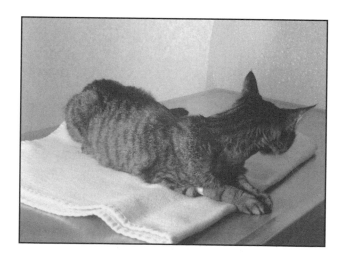

Other cancer sites include the digestive and female reproductive tracts. Such cancers may grow large before they are detected—usually by the presence of a palpable mass or by signs of intestinal blockage. Early detection of these cancers rests on a suspicion that a symptom caused by some internal disorder could be due to a cancer. You should consider the possibility of cancer when your cat has difficulty eating or digesting food or when there is an unexplained bowel disturbance such as constipation or the passage of blood. Cancers of the reproductive tract in females cause few signs, but you should look for vaginal discharge and bleeding.

Primary lung cancer is rare among cats. The lung, however, is often a site for metastases. The same applies to the liver.

Bone cancer also is rare (3 percent of cancers). The first sign may be swelling of the leg or a limp in a mature cat without a history of injury. Pressure over the swelling causes varying degrees of pain. Bone cancer spreads early and to the lungs. The bone marrow may be involved by a group of diseases called *myeloproliferative disorders*. In these diseases, the marrow stops making red or white blood cells. These disorders are rare and difficult to detect. Diagnosis is made by bone marrow biopsy.

Signs and symptoms of common tumors affecting the internal organs are discussed in the chapters dealing with these organs.

COMMON SURFACE TUMORS

CYSTS (WENS, SEBACEOUS CYSTS)

Sebaceous cysts are benign tumors that arise from glands found beneath the skin. They can occur anywhere on the body. Although less common in cats than in dogs, they are still the most common surface tumor in cats.

A sebaceous cyst is made of a thick capsule that surrounds a lump of cheesy material called keratin. It may grow to an inch or more. Eventually, it is likely to become infected and will have to be drained. This sometimes leads to a cure. Most cysts should be removed.

WARTS AND PAPILLOMAS

These growths are not nearly as common in cats as they are in people. They tend to occur on the skin of older cats. Some are on a stalk while others look like a piece of chewing gum stuck to the skin. If they become irritated or start to bleed, they should be removed.

LIPOMAS

A lipoma is a growth made of mature fat cells surrounded by a fibrous capsule that sets it apart from the surrounding body fat. It can be recognized by a round, smooth appearance and soft, fatlike consistency. Lipomas grow slowly and may get to be several inches in diameter. They are not common in the cat and are not painful.

Surgical removal is indicated only for cosmetic reasons or to rule out a malignant growth.

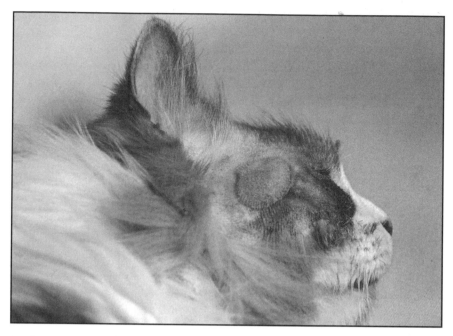

A sebaceous cyst in front of the ear.

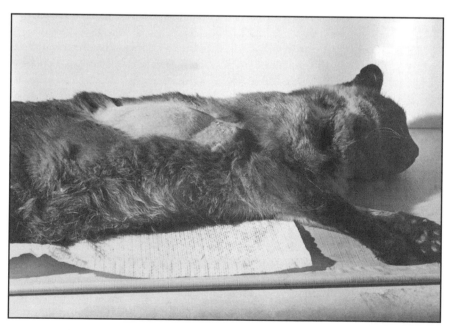

Lipoma on the side of the abdomen.

HEMATOMAS

The hematoma is a collection of blood beneath the skin, caused by a blow or contusion. Small hematomas may resolve spontaneously. Large ones may need to be opened and drained. Ear flap hematomas require special care (see EARS: *Swollen Ear Flap*).

TENDER KNOTS

A small knot may be present at the site of an injection and is often present for a few days in kittens that have been given their vaccinations. It seldom requires treatment.

A painful swelling beneath the skin may be an abscess. Abscesses are discussed in the SKIN chapter.

SKIN CANCERS

Several types of skin cancer can affect cats. It is important to distinguish a cancer from a benign neoplasm. Signs that a growth might be a cancer are visible enlargement, ulceration of the skin with bleeding and a sore that does not heal. Physical appearance alone is not always a reliable indicator. Surgical removal or biopsy is necessary to establish an exact diagnosis. The following are the most common malignant skin tumors in the cat:

Squamous Cell Cancer: This neoplasm, also called an *epidermoid carcinoma*, appears as a cauliflower-like growth or hard flat grayish-looking ulcer that does not heal. Size is variable. These cancers tend to occur around body openings and in areas of chronic skin irritation. Hair may be lost because of constant licking.

A peculiar form of squamous cell cancer involves the upper and lower lips of cats that suffer from a condition called *indolent ulcer* (see *Eosinophilic Granuloma Complex* in the SKIN chapter). Another type involves the ear tips of white cats exposed to ultraviolet sunlight (see EARS).

Early detection and treatment of squamous cell cancer are important. This neoplasm is capable of spreading to other locations.

Basal Cell Cancer: Basal cell carcinomas occur as small nodular growths beneath the skin, often next to each other, producing solid sheets of bumps. They tend to occur on the back and upper chest. Basal cell tumors enlarge locally and spread by direct extension. They do not metastasize. Wide local removal prevents recurrence.

Mast Cell Tumors: Mast cell tumors are single or multinodular growths, usually less than an inch long. The skin overlying the tumor may be ulcerated. Look for these neoplasms on the hind legs, scrotum and lower abdomen. About one out of three is malignant. Malignancy is more likely when growth is rapid and the neoplasm is larger than one inch. Malignant mast cell tumors spread to distant organs. Cortisone may be given to temporarily decrease the size of mast cell tumors. The treatment of choice is wide surgical removal.

Melanomas: A melanoma is a malignant neoplasm that takes its name from the brown or black pigment usually associated with it. Some melanomas develop in preexisting moles. You should suspect melanoma when a pigmented spot starts to enlarge or spread, becomes raised above the surface of the skin or starts to bleed. Melanomas may be found anywhere on the skin and may occur in the mouth. A suspicious pigmented spot on the skin should be removed. Melanoma spreads widely, often at an early stage.

Breast Swellings and Tumors

The cat normally has four pairs of mammary glands. The upper two pairs (1 and 2) have a common lymphatic channel and drain into the axillary (armpit) lymph nodes. The lower pairs (3 and 4) also have a common channel and drain into the inguinal (groin) lymph nodes. Infections and tumors of the breasts may cause enlargement of the corresponding lymph nodes.

Mammary Hyperplasia: Unspayed female cats can experience an enlargement of one or more breast glands that begins one to two weeks after their first heat cycle. This condition, called mammary hyperplasia or *mammary hypertrophy,* is caused by high levels of progesterone (see *Hormonal Influence During Estrous* in the chapter Sex and Reproduction). Pregnant queens also may experience mammary hypertrophy that begins during the first two weeks of pregnancy. The condition has been reported in neutered females and males receiving progesterone therapy.

The breast enlargement may or may not be painful. In severe cases, characterized by rapid increase in breast size, there is reddish blue discoloration, warmth, pain, and ulceration of the skin overlying the swollen breast.

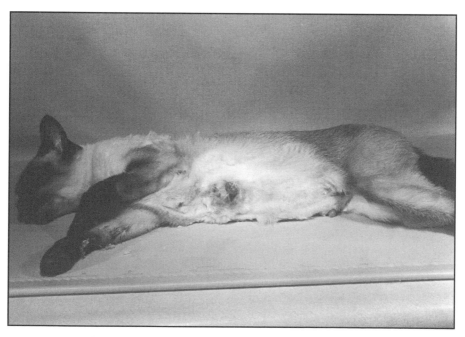

A severe case of *mammary hyperplasia* with skin ulceration. This breast swelling is caused by high levels of progesterone.

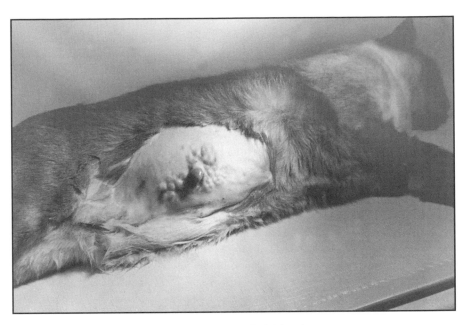

A rapidly growing multinodular neoplasm typical of *feline breast cancer.*

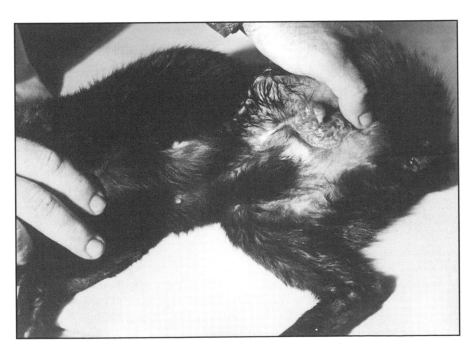

An ulcerating form of breast cancer.

One very severe complication of mammary hyperplasia is clotting of veins in the breast. This occurs in a small number of cases. The clotting process extends centrally. If the clots break free and are carried to the lungs, these cats may die suddenly from *pulmonary thromboembolism*.

Treatment: The best treatment for mammary hyperplasia is spaying. When the condition is related to pregnancy or progesterone therapy, either allowing the queen to deliver or discontinuing the progesterone may be considered. The risks must be balanced against the benefits. Breast biopsy is indicated only when breast swelling or enlargement occurs in a cat that is neither pregnant nor experiencing her first estrous or when the swelling does not disappear after the source of the progesterone has been removed.

The subject of painful swollen breasts in lactating queens is discussed in *Postpartum Problems* (see PREGNANCY AND KITTENING).

Breast Tumors: Breast tumors occur frequently. Eighty percent are malignant (adenocarcinoma). The rest are benign adenomas.

The typical picture is a painless firm nodular mass in one or more breasts, most commonly involving pairs 1 and 2. Ulceration of the skin occurs as the tumor advances. Most cats so affected are intact females over six years old. Breast cancer is rare among spayed females, especially those neutered before their first heat cycle. Progesterone therapy may increase the risk of breast tumors, including cancers. Feline breast cancer is a rapidly progressing neoplasm that has a high rate of local recurrence following treatment. It tends to spread widely, with the lungs being the favored site for metastases. A chest X ray is advisable to rule out lung involvement before embarking on radical surgery.

Surgical removal is the treatment of choice for all breast tumors. The success of the operation depends on the stage of the tumor at the time of surgery. The earlier the lump is discovered and treated, the better the outlook. Close follow-up, to detect local recurrence after surgery, is advisable.

When your female is three or four years old, begin examining her breasts at least once a month. If you detect a suspicious swelling or a firm lump, ask your veterinarian to examine it.

21

GERIATRICS

GENERAL INFORMATION

The average house cat now lives 15 years, and it is not uncommon in veterinary practice to see and care for cats 18 to 20 years of age. A table showing the comparative ages of cats to humans is found in the APPENDIX. However, the examples shown are estimates only. All cats do not age at the same rate. A cat's biological age depends on genetic inheritance, nutrition, state of health and lifetime sum of environmental stresses. *Being a purebred or freebred does not alone influence the aging process.*

The domestic cat in the wild has a short life expectancy—about six years. Accidents, diseases, the trials of securing food and the stresses of multiple and frequent pregnancies all contribute to this shortened life. The city cat fares somewhat better but still contends with infectious diseases and accidents. The indoor pet, being well nourished, vaccinated against infectious diseases and protected from accidents, fares the best.

Of greatest importance is the care the cat has received throughout life. Well-cared-for pets suffer fewer infirmities as they grow older. But when sickness, illness or injury is neglected, the aging process is accelerated. Care of the older cat is directed at preventing premature aging, minimizing physical and emotional stress and meeting the special needs of the elderly. Cats older than seven should have a complete veterinary examination at *least* annually. This exam usually includes a urinalysis, stool exam and complete blood count. For specific indications, liver and kidney function tests, chest X ray and electrocardiogram are indicated.

CARING FOR THE ELDERLY CAT

BEHAVIOR CHANGES

Older cats are more sedentary, less energetic, less curious and more restricted in their scope of activity. They adjust slowly to changes in diet, activity and routine. They are less tolerant to extreme heat and cold. They seek out warm spots and sleep longer. When disturbed, they are cranky and irritable. Most of these behavior changes are because of physical ailments—diminished hearing and smell, arthritic stiffness and muscular weakness—that restrict a cat's activity and ability to participate in family life. A cat so deprived may withdraw, engage in compulsive self-grooming or begin to eliminate in places other than the litter box.

Encourage your cat to participate more actively by finding a warm nesting spot near the center of family activity. Take the cat outside twice a day for a comfortable walk in the yard or neighborhood. Activities providing human companionship will be deeply appreciated and will give the cat a sense of being valued and love.

Boarding and hospitalization are poorly tolerated in old age. Such cats eat poorly or not at all, become over-anxious or withdrawn and sleep poorly. If possible, care for them at home under the guidance of your veterinarian. Instead of boarding the cat, ask a friend to drop by once or twice a day to attend to the cat's needs. Some communities offer cat-sitting services.

Behavior changes caused by physical infirmities may improve with treatment. If they do not, abnormal behavior can sometimes be modified or improved through the use of progesterones or tranquilizers as described in the chapter FELINE BEHAVIOR AND TRAINING.

PHYSICAL CHANGES

The cat's life cycle can be divided into three stages—kittenhood, adulthood and old age. The periods marked by youth and old age are relatively short when compared with the length of adulthood. After puberty, an adult cat's physique changes very little until quite close to the end of life.

A periodic examination may reveal an age-related condition that can be improved by modification of the cat's care or routine. *Although aging is inevitable and irreversible, some infirmities attributed to old age may be in fact due to disease, and thus correctable or at least treatable* by your veterinarian.

Musculoskeletal Exam. Flex the front and rear legs, noting any stiffness or movement limitation. Compare one side with the other. Look for swollen, painful joints.

An early sign of aging is loss of muscle tone and strength, especially in the legs. The muscles may begin to shake. The cat becomes less agile and perhaps incapable of jumping up to a favorite spot. Degenerative changes in the joints and muscles lead to stiffness and intermittent lameness, most apparent when the cat gets up from a nap. Stiffness in the joints is made worse by drafts and by sleeping on cold, damp tile or cement. Make a comfortable bed for the cat indoors on a well-padded surface. The cat may need to be covered at night.

Older cats are sendentary. Being less active, they need fewer calories.

Moderate exercise helps to keep joints supple and should be encouraged. However, older cats should not be forced to exert beyond their comfort level—best judged by themselves. A specific condition (such as heart disease) may require that exercise be restricted.

Coat and Skin Exam. Skin disorders are more frequent in aging cats. A debilitated or depressed cat quickly loses interest in self-grooming. A stiff, old cat may be unable to flex enough to groom. Any chronic illness can be reflected in poor coat quality or even loss of hair.

One skin problem that tends to occur more frequently in the aging cat is maggots. A cat's fur that has become matted and soiled becomes a target for flies. Then, too, the debilitated individual is less capable of keeping flies away.

Hair loss may be associated with compulsive self-grooming, a condition that has an emotional cause. Old cats are subject to this problem, which is discussed in FELINE BEHAVIOR AND TRAINING.

Elderly cats should be combed or brushed every day. Examination of the hair and skin may reveal tumors, parasites or other skin disorders that require prompt veterinary attention. Frequent grooming and cleaning with a damp cloth keep the coat free of parasites and the skin healthy. Cats enjoy the stroking and attention that accompanies these sessions. As self-esteem is restored, the cat may once again begin to take pride in his or her appearance and begin self-grooming again.

Occasionally, it may be necessary to bathe a cat whose coat has become matted or especially dirty. The procedure for giving a bath is described in the SKIN chapter. Old cats chill easily. They should be towel dried and kept in a warm room.

Toenails may need to be trimmed more often. They are less likely to be worn down by activity.

Special Senses. Gradual hearing loss occurs as cats grow older but may not be apparent before 14 years old. A cat with impaired hearing compensates by relying on other senses. Accordingly, it is often difficult to tell if a cat is going deaf. Techniques to test your cat's hearing are described in the EARS chapter (see *Deafness*). Senile deafness has no treatment. A hearing problem could be exacerbated by a wax blockage in the ear canal or some other problem such as ear mites or a tumor, *all of which can be treated.* A hearing problem should not be assumed to be caused by aging alone. *Veterinary evaluation* is suggested.

Loss of eyesight is also difficult to assess in the cat—again, because the other senses become more acute. Old age cataracts are uncommon in cats. In fact, loss of vision in the elderly cat is more likely to be caused by retinal diseases, *uveitis* and *glaucoma.* How to test your cat's vision is discussed in the chapter EYES.

Cats adjust well to loss of eyesight if they retain their hearing. Even when both senses are impaired, cats can still adjust to familiar surroundings and get around nicely by using their whiskers, the carpal hair on the back of their front legs and the pressure receptors in their feet.

Loss of smell is a serious handicap. The cat's odor-sensing mechanism is a powerful stimulant to appetite. If cats cannot smell, they may lose interest in food. You may be able to measure the cat's sense of smell by passing an alcohol swab under its nose. A cat with an impaired sense of smell should be fed highly aromatic and palatable foods. See *Diet and Nutrition* below.

FUNCTIONAL CHANGES

Alterations in eating and drinking patterns, voiding habits and bowel function occur frequently in older cats. If you are not especially alert to such changes, you may overlook an important clue to a developing health problem. Elimination can be difficult to observe. Some cats dislike using their litter boxes in front of their owners. Some effort will be required outdoors to see if the cat is having problems defecating or voiding.

Increased Thirst and Frequency of Urination. Most very old cats develop some degree of kidney failure. The kidneys appear to wear out sooner than do other organs. Early signs of kidney failure are increased frequency of urination and a compensatory increased frequency of drinking. These are also signs of diabetes, a condition more common in older cats.

Older cats that stop using their litter boxes and begin wetting in the house may be suffering from urinary tract disease or some other treatable condition, discussed under *Urinary Incontinence* in the chapter URINARY SYSTEM. Prostate enlargement is *not* a major cause of urinary symptoms in the cat.

Constipation is one of the most common problems in older cats. Contributing factors are lack of exercise, voluntary fecal retention, improper diet, reduced bowel activity and weakness of the abdominal wall muscles. Along with a tendency to drink less water, this produces hard, dry stools that are difficult to pass. Hairballs, which produce constipation in cats of all ages, are particularly troublesome in the older individual.

It is important not to mistake straining to urinate with straining to defecate. The obstructed bladder is an emergency that requires immediate veterinary attention to relieve the cause of the blockage (see *Feline Urologic Syndrome*).

Treatment of constipation and the prevention of hairballs is discussed in the chapter DIGESTIVE SYSTEM.

Diarrhea. Diarrhea may go unnoticed in outdoor cats. Cats with chronic diarrhea exhibit skin irritation around the anus, dehydration and weight loss and a poor coat. Chronic diarrhea in the elderly cat can be a sign of cancer, pancreatic disease or malabsorption syndrome. When due strictly to old age, diarrhea is controlled through diet and medication.

Abnormal Discharges are those containing pus or blood. Often, they are accompanied by an offensive odor. Discharges from the eyes, ears, nose, mouth, penis and vagina suggest infection. In the elderly cat, cancer is a consideration.

Pyometra (abscess of the uterus) typically occurs in older, barren queens. Signs are lethargy and depression, loss of appetite, increased thirst and excessive drinking. These signs may at first suggest kidney failure, but the abdomen of the queen becomes quite markedly distended and firm. Purulent vaginal discharge makes the diagnosis obvious, but in some cases, a discharge is absent. *Pyometra is a true surgical emergency requiring immediate veterinary attention* (see *Uterine Infection* in SEX AND REPRODUCTION).

Mouth, Teeth and Gums. Periodontal disease and tooth decay are much more common in the older cat. Mouth pain is often accompanied by halitosis and drooling. A cat with a painful mouth eats poorly and loses weight rapidly.

Treating a dental infection relieves suffering and improves health and nutrition. Loose teeth should be removed. If the cat is unable to chew dry cat food, switch to semimoist or moist rations or feed canned food formulated for older cats. Cats of all ages should be put on a program of good dental hygiene as described in MOUTH AND THROAT: *Care of Your Cat's Teeth.*

Weight Changes. Weight loss is serious in the aging cat. Many cases are caused by kidney disease; others by cancers, periodontal disease and loss of smell. Weigh your cat once a month. Weight loss is an indication for a veterinary checkup.

Excessive weight gain is an important but largely preventable problem that must be corrected in the elderly cat. Obesity is a complicating factor in kidney disease, arthritis and heart disease. Overweight cats are less likely to exercise and maintain their overall strength and vitality. To prevent and treat this problem, see *Diet and Nutrition* below.

A large "pot belly" may appear to be a fat problem when in reality a heart, liver or kidney disease with *ascites* (fluid buildup in the abdomen) is the cause. Thus, a change in physique with a swollen abdomen is an indication for veterinary examination.

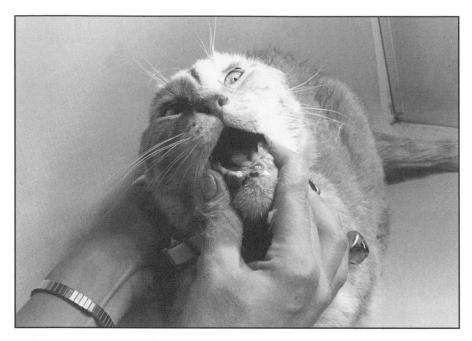

Tooth and gum disease are handicaps in the aging cat.

Note loss of weight associated with hyperthyroidism. This cat underwent thyroidectomy to remove a toxic nodular goiter.

Temperature, Pulse and Respiration. The rectal temperature is an important indicator of health. How to take the temperature is described in the APPENDIX. A temperature over 103°F indicates inflammation. In the older cat, the usual sites are the lungs and urinary tract.

A rapid heart rate is a sign of anemia, infection or heart disease. Anemia is suggested by paleness of mucous membranes, especially the tongue. Possible causes of anemia include liver disease, kidney failure and cancer.

A rapid breathing rate (over 30 breaths per minute at rest) suggests lung disease. Rarely, it is related to heart disease. *Chronic cough* suggests bronchitis or airway disease. A new onset cough suggests cancer.

Danger Signals in the Elderly Cat. In summary, any one of the following abnormal signs indicates further investigation by your veterinarian:

1. Loss of appetite or weight.
2. Cough, labored breathing or shortness of breath.
3. Increased thirst or frequency of urination.
4. Change in bowel function with constipation or diarrhea.
5. Bloody or purulent discharge from a body opening.
6. An increase in temperature, pulse or breathing rate.
7. A growth or lump any place on the body.
8. Weakness or difficulty getting about.
9. Unexplained change in behavior.

FELINE HYPERTHYROIDISM

This disease is caused by excessive amounts of circulating thyroid hormone (*thyroxin*) produced by the thyroid gland. The gland, for unknown reasons, enlarges and produces a swelling in the neck. This is called a *toxic nodular goiter*. Cancer in such a goiter is rare. Although hyperthyroidism is now recognized as the most common hormone disorder in cats, it occurs almost exclusively in geriatric individuals 12 years and older. Signs are related to the increased metabolic rate produced by circulating thyroxin.

Affected cats often appear unusually restless and irritable, pace up and down, exhibit excessive hunger and food consumption. Weight loss, vomiting and increased volume of feces are common. A major problem in the elderly cat relates to the effects of thyroxin on the heart. The work of the heart is increased at a time when the heart is less strong. A form of *cardiomyopathy* occurs that can lead to congestive heart failure (see CIRCULATORY SYSTEM).

The diagnosis of hyperthyroidism may not be suspected in the elderly cat for many months because of other illnesses of aging that may obscure the symptoms. A cat may lose a surprising amount of weight while eating well and appearing bright and alert.

Treatment: Thyroid blood tests establish the diagnosis. Treatment is directed at returning the cat to a normal thyroid status. This can be accomplished by antithyroid drugs, surgery to remove the thyroid gland, or administering radioactive iodine at a referral center equipped to handle radioactive materials. Your veterinarian will advise you about the best treatment for your cat.

Diet and Nutrition

Geriatric cats (over nine years old) are less active and require 30 percent fewer calories than younger cats. If the cat's diet is not adjusted accordingly, overfeeding will result in weight gain. Remember, the prevention of obesity is the single most important consideration in prolonging the life of the cat.

In general, an elderly cat of ideal body weight (not too fat or thin) needs only 20 to 25 Kcal per pound weight daily to meet caloric needs. Dry rations supply about 105 calories per ounce; semimoist, 75 calories per ounce; and canned rations, 29 calories per ounce. Weigh your cat and compute the daily calories required, then determine the ounces of ration to feed each day. Adjust the ration up or down depending on whether the cat is above or below its ideal weight and whether it is active or sedentary. Overweight cats should be placed on a weight-loss diet, described in the chapter FEEDING AND NUTRITION (see *Obesity*).

Since older cats eat less, it is most important that the ration be highly digestible to assure adequate absorption of nutrients. Protein *quality* also is of particular importance. Information on quality and nutritional value of various cat foods is found in the chapter FEEDING AND NUTRITION. Highly digestible foods formulated for older cats are available at most grocery stores. These products are balanced but modified in protein, fat, calcium and salt content to accommodate the needs of the elderly.

Although protein is important, a diet too rich in meat produces an increase in nitrogen that must be eliminated by the liver and kidneys. Old cats have reduced kidney function. When given protein in excess of capacity to excrete it, the blood urea nitrogen level (BUN) rises, and the cat develops *uremia* or kidney failure. This can happen from adding meat products to a balanced diet in excess of 10 percent of the total daily ration.

Phosphorus, too, has been shown to accelerate the progress of kidney failure. Most senior rations contain reduced levels of phosphorus. For cats with kidney failure, a special prescription diet (Hill's *Feline k/d*) is recommended.

Since taste and smell diminish with age, the palatability of food becomes increasingly important in encouraging appetite and acceptance. The maintenance food should be supplemented if the cat will not eat enough to maintain body weight. High-quality supplements suitable for the digestive tract of older cats can be supplied by adding small amounts of white meat chicken, white fish meat, boiled egg, cottage cheese or skimmed milk. If the cat does not maintain weight on this diet, add small amounts of fat to increase palatability and supply extra calories. Wesson oil is a good fat supplement.

Older cats need more vitamins and minerals. The absorption of vitamins through the intestinal tract diminishes as the individual ages. In addition, B vitamins are lost in the urine of cats with reduced kidney function. Calcium and phosphorus in correct balance (1.2:1) help prevent softening of the bones. Most commercial foods for elderly cats contain added B vitamins and balanced minerals. If you are feeding one of these products, you should not need to add vitamin and mineral supplements. If the cat has an eating problem, however, discuss supplements with your veterinarian.

A ration low in magnesium (less than 0.1 percent on a dry-weight basis) is an important consideration for cats suffering from FUS. However, low-magnesium diets are not necessarily recommended for all cats.

If feeding canned cat food, divide the daily ration into two equal parts and feed the first half in the morning and the second half in the evening. Underweight cats may be better off with three or four feedings a day. Cats that eat well can be fed dry or semimoist ration free choice.

Special Diets. Prescription diets from Hill's Pet Products or other manufacturers may be required for cats with heart disease, kidney disease, intestinal disease or obesity. They are available through veterinarians.

PUTTING YOUR CAT TO SLEEP (EUTHANASIA)

The time may come when you are faced with the decision to put your pet to sleep. This is a difficult decision to make—for you and your veterinarian.

Many an old and even infirm cat can be made quite comfortable with just a little more thoughtfulness and tender loving care than the average healthy cat needs and can still enjoy months or years of happiness in the company of loved ones. But when life ceases to be a joy and a pleasure, when the cat suffers from a painful and progressive condition for which there is no hope of betterment, then perhaps at this time we owe our pets the final kindness to die easily and painlessly. This is accomplished by an intravenous injection of an anesthetic agent in sufficient amount to cause immediate loss of consciousness and cardiac arrest.

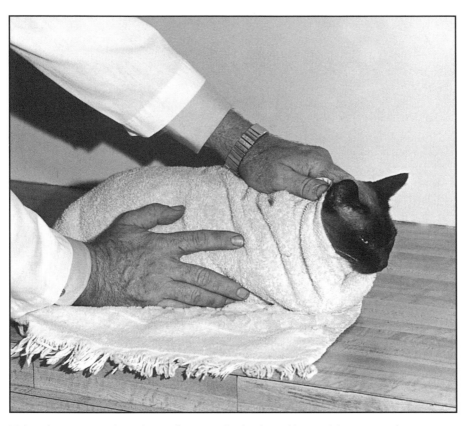

Unless the cat is used to taking pills, wrap the body and legs tightly in a towel.

—J. Clawson

22

DRUGS AND MEDICATIONS

GENERAL INFORMATION

Cats are unusually sensitive to drugs and medications. It has been suggested that the ability of the liver to metabolize drugs is less efficient in cats than in most other animals. Many drugs and medications that are safe in humans when used according to the manufacturer's recommendations are not safe for use in cats.

Drugs are dosed by patient weight. Since the margin of safety is often quite small, the body weight of the cat becomes important. Estimated weights can lead to significant under- or overdosing.

In summary, it is important to adhere strictly to the veterinarian's recommendations about what medications to give and dosage and frequency of administration.

Tranquilizers are discussed in the chapter FELINE BEHAVIOR AND TRAINING.

Antibiotics and Steroids are discussed in the next chapter.

ANESTHETICS AND ANESTHESIA

Anesthetics are drugs used to block the sensation of pain. They are divided into two categories—locals and generals.

Local anesthetics are used for operations on the surface of the body, where they are injected into tissues and around regional nerves. They may be applied topically to mucous membranes. Local anesthetics (such as *xylocaine*) have the fewest risks and side effects but are not suitable for most major operations.

General anesthetics render the cat unconscious. They can be given by injection or inhalation. Light anesthesia sedates or relaxes the cat and may be suitable for short procedures such as removing porcupine quills from the mouth. Inhaled gases (such as *halothane* and *isoflurane*) are administered through a tube placed in the windpipe. Combinations of anesthetics often are used to lessen potential side effects.

The dose of an anesthetic is computed by the cat's weight. Since cats are unusually sensitive to ordinary doses of a drug such as *pentathol*, veterinarians often administer the anesthetic in repeated small doses—until the desired affect is obtained—rather than giving it all at once.

Anesthetics are removed from the cat's sytem by the lungs, liver and kidneys. Impaired function of these organs can cause dose-related complications. If your cat has a history of lung, liver, kidney or heart disease, the risk from anesthesia and surgery is increased.

A major risk of a general anesthetic is having the cat vomit when going to sleep or waking up. The vomitus refluxes into the windpipe and produces asphyxiation. This can be avoided by keeping the stomach empty for 12 hours before scheduled surgery. If you know your cat is going to have an operation, *do not give anything to eat or drink after 6 P.M. the night before*. This means picking up the water dish and keeping the cat away from the toilet bowl and other sources of water as well.

PAIN RELIEVERS

Analgesics are drugs used to relieve pain. There are many classes of pain killers. All must be used with caution in cats. Demerol, morphine, codeine and other **narcotics** are subject to federal regulation and cannot be bought without a prescription. The effect of these drugs on cats is highly unpredictable. Morphine, in a dose appropriate for a small dog, produces apprehension, excitability and drooling in the cat. When this minimum dose is exceeded, the cat may convulse and die.

Aspirin (acetylsalicylic acid) is a safe analgesic for home veterinary use in dogs, *but it must be administered with **extreme care** to cats*. Small doses of aspirin when given to cats can produce loss of appetite, depression and vomiting. One aspirin tablet a day for three or four days is sufficient to cause salivation, dehydration, vomiting and a staggering gait. Severe disturbances in acid/base balance may ensue. The bone marrow and liver may show signs of toxicity. Gastrointestinal bleeding is frequent. Cat owners should be aware of *potential toxicity* and use aspirin only under veterinary direction. The recommended dosage for cats is 5 mg per pound body weight every 48 to 72 hours. One adult aspirin tablet (324 mg) is eight times the recommended dosage for an eight pound cat.

NSAIDs (nonsteroidal anti-inflammatoroy drugs) such as ibuprofen (*Motrin*), *Anaprox* and other aspirin substitutes used for treating muscular aches and pains in humans have the same *implications for toxicity as aspirin in cats*. Furthermore, these drugs are not as well tolerated as aspirin. Their absorption patterns are highly unpredictable in small animals. *All this makes these drugs unsuitable for use in cats.*

Tylenol (acetaminophen) is another analgesic that must *never* be administered *to cats*. A cat given a child's dose of Tylenol can develop hemolytic anemia and liver failure.

Butazolidin (phenylbutazone) is an analgesic prescribed for horses, dogs and other animals. When used as recommended in these animals, it is safe and effective. *When used in cats it produces toxicity* much like that of aspirin and Tylenol. In addition, Butazolidin causes kidney failure. Therefore Butazolidin is not recommended for use in cats.

In summary, *even though analgesics are common household items, they should not be given to cats*. The only exception is aspirin (enteric coated or buffered) which should *not* be given without solid indications and then only under veterinary direction. At the first signs of toxicity, the drug should be withdrawn.

COMMON HOUSEHOLD DRUGS FOR HOME VETERINARY USE
Dose for the Average-Sized Adult Cat

BETADINE SOLUTION (topical antiseptic and wound cleanser): Dilute 1:10.

CHARCOAL (activated): Mix one part to six parts cold water. Give four to eight teaspoons by mouth.

DRAMAMINE (motion sickness): 12.5 mg one hour before traveling.

HYDROGEN PEROXIDE (3 percent): *To induce vomiting*—one teaspoon per five pounds body weight (up to three teaspoons per dose) every 10 minutes, or until the cat vomits. Repeat three times only. For *topical application* to wounds—dilute one part to five parts water.

KAOPECTATE (diarrhea)*: $^1/_2$ to one teaspoon per five pounds body weight every two to six hours.

METAMUCIL POWDER (constipation): one to three teaspoons once or twice a day mixed into wetted or liquid food.

MILK OF MAGNESIA, unflavored (constipation): $^1/_2$ teaspoon per five pounds body weight. Give once daily or as directed.

MINERAL OIL: one teaspoon per five pounds body weight mixed into the cat's food, once or twice a week.

PANOLOG (ear drops and ointment): As directed.

ROBITUSSIN (cough): $^1/_4$ teaspoon per five pounds body weight every six hours.

TRIPLE ANTIBIOTIC OINTMENT (surface skin infection): Apply two or three times a day.

WHITE PETROLEUM JELLY (not carbolated)—see DIGESTIVE SYSTEM: *Intestinal Foreign Bodies*: $^1/_2$ teaspoon, once or twice a week. Apply to cat's nose.

*Note: Do not use Paregoric.

HOW TO GIVE MEDICATIONS

PILLS AND POWDERS

Unless the cat is used to taking pills, wrap the body and legs tightly in a towel. If working alone, you can cradle the cat in one arm. However, it is much more convenient to have an assistant who can hold the cat while you administer the pill.

Place one thumb and forefinger on either side of the cat's face. Apply gentle pressure at the space between the teeth. As the cat's mouth opens, press down on the lower jaw and deposit the pill well to the *back* of the tongue. Close the mouth and massage or rub the throat until the cat swallows. If the cat licks its nose, the pill has been swallowed.

Avoid breaking up pills. Pills broken into powder make an unpleasant taste that is poorly accepted. Many pills have a protective coating that is important for delayed release in the intestinal tract.

Powders can be diluted in water and administered as a liquid. Powders such as *Metamucil* that do not require strict dosing can be added to the cat's food. If the powder has an unpleasant taste, disguise it by adding brewer's yeast, cheese or strong fish oil. Powders should be added to food that is wetted or semiliquid.

LIQUIDS

Liquid medicines are administered into the space between the molars and the cheek. A small medicine bottle, eye dropper or plastic syringe is used to dispense the medication. Cats can be given an amount of liquid up to three teaspoons (one tablespoon) as a single dose. Measure the required amount into the bottle, syringe or dropper. Secure the cat as described above.

Insert the end of the dispenser into the cheek pouch and, while tilting the chin upward, slowly dispense the medication. The cat will swallow automatically.

INJECTIONS

Should it become necessary to give your cat injections, it is highly desirable to have the procedure demonstrated by your veterinarian. Some injections are given under the skin (*subcutaneous; SC*); others into the muscle. Directions accompanying the product will indicate the correct route. The injection itself usually is not painful to cats, although intramuscular injections may hurt somewhat as the medicine is injected. Cats should be secured as described in EMERGENCIES: *Handling and Restraint.* An assistant is helpful.

Begin by drawing the medicine up into the syringe. Point the needle toward the ceiling and press the plunger slightly to expel all air from the syringe and needle.

The back of the cat's neck or shoulder is used for subcutaneous injections because the skin here is loose and readily forms a fold when pinched. Intramuscular injections are given in the back of the thigh, halfway between the knee and hip.

Select the injection site and swab the skin with a piece of cotton soaked in alcohol.

For *subcutaneous injections* (SC), grasp a fold of skin to form a ridge. Firmly push the point of the needle through the skin into the subcutaneous fat in a course

The correct way to give a pill—in the middle at the back of the tongue.

—J. Clawson

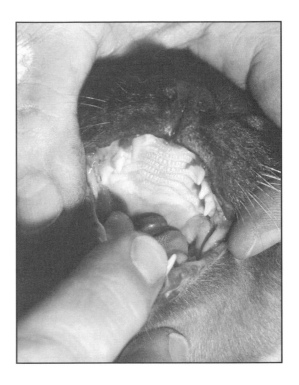

Incorrect pill placement. The pill is too far forward.

—J. Clawson

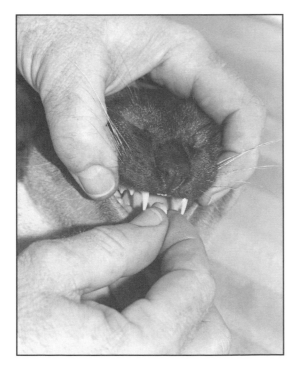

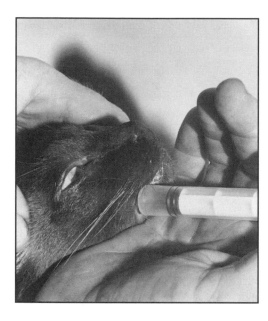

Liquids are administered into the cheek pouch between the molars and the cheek.

—J. Clawson

A medicine dropper can be used in this way.
—J. Clawson

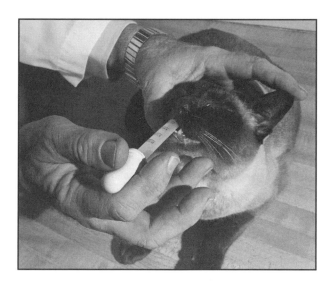

somewhat parallel to the surface of the skin. Before any injection is given, always pull back on the plunger and look for blood. If blood appears, the medicine might be injected into a vein or artery. Withdraw the syringe and start again. Once you see that the injection can be given safely, push in the plunger. Withdraw the needle and rub the skin for a few seconds to disperse the medicine.

For *intramuscular injections*, angle the tip of the needle so as to enter muscle while avoiding the bone. Injections into bones, nerves and joints can be avoided by

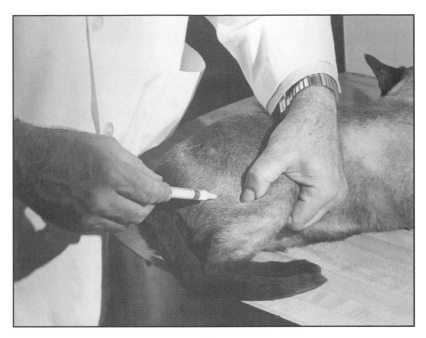

Give intramuscular injections into the back of the thigh as described.

—J. Clawson

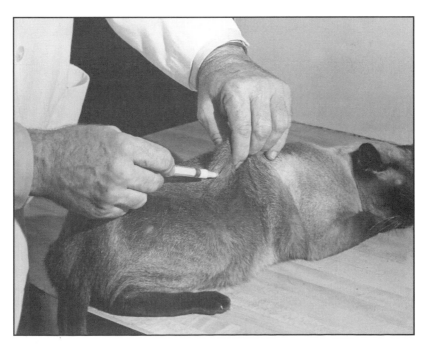

Subcutaneous injections are given beneath the loose skin in back of the shoulder.

—J. Clawson

giving the shot in the described location. Repeat the same procedure as described for subcutaneous injections. Remember to withdraw the plunger and check for blood in the syringe before giving the injection.

Anaphylactic Shock. One danger of giving a foreign substance by injection is that of producing a sudden allergic or *anaphylactic* reaction in which the cat goes into severe or fatal shock through *circulatory collapse*. This is a type of hypersensitivity reaction of the immediate type (see SKIN: *Allergies*). The most common agent producing anaphylactic shock is penicillin. Note that *penicillin is used as a preservative in some vaccines.* Therefore, your pet could be sensitized to penicillin even though to the best of your knowledge the drug was never administered. As a precaution, do not administer a drug by injection to a cat that has any sort of past history of allergic reaction (such as hives) to that drug.

Emergency treatment of anaphylactic shock involves intravenous adrenaline and oxygen, ordinarily not available at home. This is one reason why it is best to have your veterinarian give injections—as he or she has the drugs on hand to treat such reactions in time.

ENEMAS

Enemas are used to treat fecal impaction. The subject is discussed in the chapter DIGESTIVE SYSTEM. Enemas should not be given until a veterinarian has made the diagnosis and prescribed the treatment. Enemas ordinarily are not used to treat *chronic* constipation because there are better ways to manage this problem.

Fleet *phosphate enemas should never be given to cats because of the danger of causing a fatal overdose of phosphate.*

SUPPOSITORIES

When the oral route is not satisfactory (for example, when a cat is vomiting), medications can be given by suppository. Your veterinarian may prescribe a suppository to treat a bout of severe constipation.

The suppository is lubricated with vaseline and slipped all the way into the rectum where it dissolves. Suppositories for constipation contain a mild irritant that draws water into the rectum and stimulates a bowel movement. Dulcolax is good for this purpose. You can buy it at any drugstore. The dose for an adult cat is one-quarter to one-half a suppository. *Do not give suppositories to cats who are dehydrated or who might have an intestinal obstruction.* A *Painful Abdomen* is another contraindication to the use of suppositories. See EMERGENCIES.

EYE MEDICATION

How to medicate the eye is discussed in the chapter EYES.

EAR MEDICATION

How to medicate the ears is discussed in the chapter EARS.

23

ANTIBIOTICS AND INFECTIONS

GENERAL INFORMATION

Antibiotics are extracts of basic plants such as molds and fungi. They are capable of destroying many microorganisms that cause disease.

The age of modern antibiotics began with the discovery of penicillin by Sir Alexander Fleming. In 1928, Fleming made a fortuitous and accidental discovery. He observed that a strain of penicillin mold that had fallen on a culture plate could prevent the growth of a bacteria colony. Although he tried to isolate extracts of the fungus to treat infections, the broths proved too weak.

It remained for a group in Oxford, England, in 1939, under the direction of Sir Howard W. Florey, to isolate potent antibiotic extracts from the mold *penicillium notatum*. The impact of this success on the control of infection sent scientists back to the soil in search of other natural substances having antibiotic activity. This led to the discovery of tetracycline and chloromycetin as well as many other antibiotics in use today. Taking the basic nucleus of an antibiotic grown in deep broth cultures, researchers added side chains by chemical synthesis. This created a whole new spectrum as synthetic drugs.

Antibiotics fall into two general categories: *bacteriostatic* and *fungistatic* drugs inhibit the growth of microorganisms but do not kill them; *bactericidal* and *fungicidal* drugs destroy the microorganisms outright.

Bacteria are classified according to their ability to cause disease. *Pathogenic* bacteria are capable of producing a particular illness or infection. *Nonpathogenic* bacteria live on or within the host but do not cause illness under normal conditions. They are referred to as normal flora. Some actually produce substances necessary to the well-being of the host. For example, bacteria in the bowel synthesize Vitamin K, which many animals cannot do for themselves. Vitamin K is important in blood clotting.

Antibiotics are specific for certain bacteria. The number now available brings with it new possibilities for animal sensitivity and allergy and multiplies the potential hazards of administration.

ANTIBIOTICS YOUR VETERINARIAN MAY PRESCRIBE

Note: Unless otherwise stated, antibiotics should be continued for at least 48 hours after the cat becomes free of signs and symptoms. If the condition does not improve in 48 hours, check with your veterinarian before continuing the antibiotic.

Antibiotic	Dose (by cat weight)	Used in Infections of	Adverse Reactions
Penicillin G, procaine	10,000 u/lb every 6h orally, IM, SC	Skin, Mouth, Tonsils, Uterus, Wounds	Allergic reaction
Penicillin G, potassium	20,000 u/lb every 6h orally	Skin, Mouth, Tonsils, Uterus, Wounds	Allergic reaction
Ampicillin	10 mg/lb every 8h orally	Same as penicillin Genitourinary tract Respiratory tract	Allergic reaction
Cephalosporins	Depends on the specific drug	Urinary tract Respiratory tract	Kidney damage
Aminglycosides:			
Neomycin	10 mg/lb every 8h orally Topically 3 to 4 times daily	Diarrhea (orally) Hepatic encephalopathy, Eye*, Ear, Skin (topically)	Kidney damage Allergic reaction
Amikacin	3.5 mg/lb every 12h IM or SC	Kitten Septicemia	Kidney damage Deafness Brain injury in newborns
Gentamycin	1.1 mg/lb every 12h IM first day, then once a day Topically 3 to 4 times daily	Skin, Respiratory tract Urinary tract Eye*, Ear (topically)	Kidney damage Deafness
Tetracycline	9 mg/lb every 8–12h orally 3 mg/lb every 12h IM	Respiratory tract	Skin, Stained teeth (Unborn kittens) Retarded bone growth (Kittens)

Chloramphenicol	7–9 mg/lb every 8–12h orally, Eye preparations three times a day	Skin, Mouth, Respiratory tract, Urinary tract, Eye* (topically)	Bone marrow depression (Do not use high doses for more than 5 days)
Silvadene Cream 1%	Topically 2 or 3 times daily	Burns	Rare
Erythromycin	5 mg/lb every 8h orally	Penicillin substitute when cat is allergic to penicillin	Rare
Lincomycin	10 mg/lb every 12h orally 5 mg/lb every 12h IM	Skin, Wounds, Penicillin substitute	Diarrhea
Tylosin	5 mg/lb every 8h orally Same as Erythromycin	Same as Erythromycin	Rare
Sulfa Drugs	Depends on the drug	Urinary tract, Gastrointestinal tract, Eye*	Forms crystals in urine, Anemia Allergic reaction
Baytril	1.13 mg/lb every 12h orally	Skin, Urinary tract Respiratory tract	Rare
Griseofulvin	5–25 mg/lb every 12h orally, for 4 to 6 weeks. Take with fat.	Ringworm	Do not use in pregnancy (teratogenic; causes fetal malformation)
Nystatin	100,000 u/lb every 6h orally for 7 to 14 days	Thrush	Diarrhea

*Preparations used in the EYE must be labeled specifically *for ophthalmologic use*.

WHEN ANTIBIOTICS MAY NOT BE EFFECTIVE

MISDIAGNOSIS OF INFECTION

At times, signs of inflammation (such as heat, redness and swelling) can exist without infection; for example, sunburn. When one sees inflammation and purulent discharge (pus), infection can be presumed to exist. Often the discharge has an offensive odor. Other indications of infection are fever and an elevated white cell count.

INAPPROPRIATE SELECTION

An antibiotic must be effective against the specific bacteria in question. A preliminary choice can often be made by the type of illness. The best way to confirm that choice is to recover the organism, culture it and identify it by colony appearance and microscopic characteristics. Antibiotic discs are then applied to the culture plate to see which discs inhibit the growth of colonies. The results are graded according to whether the microorganism is *sensitive*, *indifferent* or *insensitive* to the

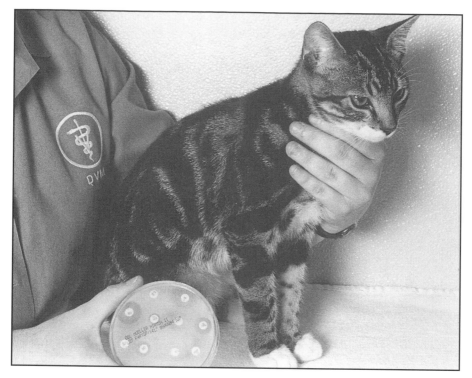

Discs containing various antibiotics on a culture plate show which antibiotics inhibit growth.

effects of the antibiotic discs. Laboratory findings, however, do not always coincide with results in the patient. Nevertheless, antibiotic culture and sensitivity testing is the surest way of selecting the most effective agent.

INADEQUATE WOUND CARE

Antibiotics enter the bloodstream and are carried to the source of the infection. Abscesses, wounds containing devitalized tissue and wounds with foreign bodies (dirt, splinters) are resistant areas. Under such circumstances, antibiotics can't get into the wound. Accordingly, it is important to drain abscesses, clean dirty wounds and remove foreign bodies.

ROUTE OF ADMINISTRATION

An important medical decision rests in selecting the best route for administration. Some antibiotics should be given on an empty stomach and others with a meal. Incomplete absorption from the gastrointestinal tract is one cause of inadequate blood levels. In severe infections antibiotics are given intravenously, or by intramuscular injection to circumvent this problem.